SEMI-DETACHED EMPIRE

SEMI-DETACHED EMPIRE

Suburbia
and the Colonization of Britain,
1880 to the Present

TODD KUCHTA

University of Virginia Press

CHARLOTTESVILLE AND LONDON

University of Virginia Press
© 2010 by the Rector and Visitors of the University of Virginia
All rights reserved
Printed in the United States of America on acid-free paper

First published 2010

1 3 5 7 9 8 6 4 2

Library of Congress Cataloging-in-Publication Data
Kuchta, Todd, 1970–
Semi-detached empire : suburbia and the colonization of Britain,
1880 to the present / Todd Kuchta.
p. cm.
Includes bibliographical references and index.
ISBN 978-0-8139-2925-5 (cloth : alk. paper) — ISBN 978-0-8139-2926-2 (pbk. : alk. paper) —
ISBN 978-0-8139-2958-3 (e-book)
1. English fiction—20th century—History and criticism. 2. English fiction—19th
century—History and criticism. 3. Degeneration in literature. 4. Regression (Civilization)
in literature. 5. Suburbs in literature. 6. Suburban life in literature. 7. Great Britain—In
literature. 8. Great Britain—Civilization—20th century. 9. Literature and society—Great
Britain—History. I. Title.
PR888.D373K83 2010
823'.9109355—dc22   2009039652

CONTENTS

ACKNOWLEDGMENTS

I often thought this book about suburbia might sprawl on forever, so I take great pleasure in thanking those who have helped me, directly and indirectly, to finish. It began under the guidance of Patrick Brantlinger, whose support and friendship have meant a great deal to me. Purnima Bose, Thomas Foster, and James Naremore offered positive and practical feedback, and Joanne Wood provided encouragement just when I needed it. Richard Higgins and Justus Nieland have been my most engaged readers from the start, always at the ready with shrewd advice, moral support, and friendship. Sincere thanks also go to Hamilton Carroll, Sara Maurer, Tobias Menely, Brook Miller, Tyrone Simpson, and Steve Wender, all of whom responded generously to my early ideas. For teaching me how to think and write, I thank my earliest academic mentors at John Carroll University, especially Jeanne Colleran, David LaGuardia, Brian Macaskill, and Maryclaire Moroney.

At Western Michigan University my work on this project has been supported by Arts and Sciences Faculty Teaching and Research awards and Faculty Research Travel grants. I've been honored to work alongside the wonderful faculty, staff, and graduate students at Western, whose presence has helped to shape these pages in various ways, especially Martha Addante, Jeffrey Angles, Patti Bills, Beth Bradburn, Meg Dupuis, Catherine Hart, Michelle Hruska, Yan Jiang, Arnie Johnston, Cynthia Klekar, Donald Martin, Lisa Minnick, Mustafa Mirzeler, Ilana Nash, Nat O'Reilly, Eve Salisbury, Bethlynn Sanders, Richard Utz, Joyce Walker, Nic Witschi, and Yen Li Loh. For their help with this book, heartfelt thanks go to Jon Adams for being right and sticking to his guns, to Jil Larson for her sympathetic support, to Chris Nagle for sense and sensibility, to Jana Schulman for letting me vent, to Gwen Tarbox for making me let go, and to Allen Webb for his unflagging enthusiasm.

For their interest in my work, thanks to Nancy Armstrong, Susan Brook, Peter Kalliney, Anthony King, Robert Markley, and Sheryl Sachs, as well as to Vesna Goldsworthy and Rebecca Preston at the Centre for Suburban Studies,

Kingston University London. At the University of Virginia Press, Cathie Brett-schneider, Morgan Myers, and Ellen Satrom guided my manuscript toward publication with greater speed and care than I thought possible. The anonymous readers gave me a very happy birthday, Carol Sickman-Garner provided excellent copy editing, and Bill Nelson made a wonderful map. Finally, my sincere thanks to Jonathan Partington and the Greenwich Heritage Centre, London, for permission to use the cover photograph.

Chapter 6 originally appeared in *Novel: A Forum on Fiction* 36, no. 3 (Summer 2003), and portions of chapters 1 and 5 appeared in *Nineteenth-Century Prose* 32, no. 2 (Fall 2005), a special issue on cultural studies and British imperialism. I thank the editors of these journals for permission to reprint.

I feel least capable of expressing my gratitude to those who deserve it most. My parents have always supported me, and their example made this book possible in more ways than they will ever know. I hope they see something of themselves in it. For absolutely everything else I do not know how to thank Amy and Laryn. Though meager recompense, this book is for them.

PART ONE
Foundations

1

Semi-Detached Empire

In an 1891 article for the *Contemporary Review*, the journalist and historian Sidney Low revealed a striking trend in the previous decade's census returns. Contrary to popular belief Britain's population was growing "not in the cities themselves, but in the ring of suburbs which spread into the country." The data led Low to what must have been a startling conclusion. "The English-man of the future," he declared, "will be a suburb-dweller. The majority of the people of this island will live in the suburbs; and the suburban type will be the most widespread and characteristic of all" ("Rise" 548). If Low's prognosis showed incredible foresight, it was also a document of its time. Like countless Victorian social ethnographies his article draws its language and its logic from Britain's imperial imagination. In contrast to the disorder, primitivism, and degeneracy of the urban jungle—what he calls "this Brazilian forest of houses, this Sargasso Sea of asphalte and paving"—Low foresees suburbs of hygienic, quasi-militaristic colonies that can safeguard the future of the British race: "The people of London will dwell outside [the city] in 'urban sanitary districts' . . . residential encampments which will spring up all over the south and east of England. . . . Not one, but a dozen Croydons will form a circle of detached forts round the central stronghold" ("Rise" 551). The citizens of such suburbs, Low argues, will be fit for national defense—superior in mind and body to overstimulated urbanites and sluggish rustics. Young men from Wimbledon and Putney "could make up a regiment which would hold its own on a battle-field against a *corps d'élite* selected from any army in the world" ("Rise" 554). While such rhetoric sought to quell pervasive fears of Britain degenerating into a nation of slums, Low's language occasionally undermines his own argument on behalf of regenerative imperial suburbs. If London is the heart of the empire, then its "life-blood is pouring into the long arms of brick and mortar and cheap stucco that are feeling their way out to the Surrey moors, and the Essex flats, and the Hertfordshire copses." Britain's growth is taking place *there,* Low suggests, and "not, as hasty observers have imagined, in the teeming alleys of 'Darkest London'" ("Rise 550).

Fanciful as it may seem, Low's vision of suburbia helps to correct our views of the relationship between imperialism and national identity in Britain. In *The Country and the City,* Raymond Williams famously argues that imperialism represented the global expansion of Britain's urban-rural dynamic. At the height of empire, Williams points out, the colonies replaced the countryside as a source of raw materials for metropolitan consumption, effectively transforming "distant lands" into "the rural areas of industrial Britain" and forcing millions of unemployed laborers into already overcrowded cities (280). Yet around 1880, Williams suggests, this "dramatic extension of landscape and social relations" coincided with "a marked development of the idea of England as 'home.'" This idea manifested itself in images of London, "the powerful, the prestigious and the consuming capital," but it became absolutely central to nostalgic visions of the countryside. No longer a site of labor, "the 'residential' rural England" was romanticized in contrast to "the tropical or arid places of actual work . . . the tensions of colonial rule and the isolated alien settlement" (281–82).

Yet as Sidney Low points out, it was during the 1880s, when Williams claims imperialism forged a distinctly English sense of home in the country and the city, that modern suburbs began to colonize Britain's own landscape.[1] These low-density residential areas—geographically marginal to yet economically and socially dependent on an urban center—first emerged in the eighteenth century and grew most dramatically between the 1920s and 1930s. But the last two decades of the nineteenth century saw their transformation from exclusive enclaves for the wealthy to commonplace communities for the masses. In the 1880s the four places in Britain with the largest population increase were London railway suburbs for the working and lower middle classes. In the 1890s the nation's fastest-growing areas were virtually all suburban in character. By the turn of the century, Britain's ten largest towns included three London suburban boroughs. Nor was the trend limited to London. As early as the 1850s suburbs were cropping up in every English town with a population over fifty thousand. Within a few decades Birmingham, Manchester, and Leeds boasted well-known suburban communities, as did Edinburgh, Glasgow, Belfast, Dublin, and Cork.[2] "On the outskirts of every city" in Britain, Asa Briggs points out, "undeveloped land was turned into suburbia" (28). The country and the city may have been the nation's imaginary home in the age of empire, but more and more citizens were migrating to the suburbs.

Today suburbs dominate Britain both literally and figuratively. They cover much of its land and house most of its citizens. But they also represent a national reversal of fortune, their reputation for petty lives and mortgaged futures belying an era when Britannia ruled the waves. This book examines imperialism as central to suburbia's construction on the ground and in the imagination. More specifically, it treats the rapid rise of suburbia and the slow but steady decline of empire as intimately linked and mutually articulated historical trajectories. In the chapters that follow I show how fiction by H. G. Wells, Arthur Conan Doyle, Joseph Conrad, E. M. Forster, George Orwell, and Hanif Kureishi bears witness to the suburb's emergence from dissolving local and global boundaries—between country and city, but also between metropole and colony. In doing so, I argue that these writers reveal suburbia's long-standing investment in imperialism even as they lament the cost: an increasingly suburban nation that degenerates into an uncanny afterimage of its own colonial territories. The result is a paradoxical situation in which suburbia colonizes Britain while its own inhabitants are relegated to the status of colonized subjects.

Suburbia is both the epitome and the antithesis of the nation's home—on the one hand quintessentially English, on the other hand bristling anxiously over its perceived inferiority. *Semi-Detached Empire* traces this ambivalence to suburbia's emergence from imperial views of the country and the city, whereby the rural represented racial purity and the urban its decadent other. Fusing a countryside considered the essence of Englishness and a city believed to be swamped by racial degenerates, this "crowd of half-bred towns," as a contributor to the *Architect* called suburbs in 1876 (qtd. in Olsen 201), elicited a number of pressing questions. Were suburbs the first line of colonial expansion emanating from the heart of the empire, homegrown settler colonies sending the nation's healthiest citizens to its urban frontiers? If suburbs were the bulwark of British civilization, did that also make them its endangered outposts, threatened by both urban degeneracy and the darkness beyond the nation's borders? Worse yet, could suburbia itself be a degenerate borderland that would overtake the nation? As these questions suggest, some likened suburbs to new colonies, bastions of racial regeneration at home and abroad, while others viewed suburbia as a threatening terra incognita, whose inhabitants made up a barbaric species beyond the pale of authentic Anglo-Saxon culture. Still others criticized suburban sprawl as emblematic of the empire's impending decay, so that suburb and empire alike represented omnivorous, cancerous growths leaving shoddy, mass-produced civilizations in their wake. These views variously shape the work of Wells, Doyle, Conrad, Forster, Orwell, and Kureishi, who show how imperialism contributed to suburbia's material and discursive formation at the same time as suburbia came to signify the empire's inevitable decline and enduring traumas.

The colonial foundation of Britain's domestic sphere has been a focus for much recent criticism, which traces life in the frenetic city and idyllic countryside alike to colonial expansion and exploitation. Alternately, scholars have shown that British notions of home and domesticity were frequently exported to the colonies, playing a substantial role in the imperial mission overseas.[3] Such work has corrected the view that once divided home and empire into separate spheres. Yet like Williams in *The Country and the City*, it reinforces a mythic division between urban and rural Britain. The same can be said for scholarship in a variety of disciplines influenced by imperial and postcolonial studies: while metropole-colony relations constitute a conjoined unit of analysis and guiding conceptual rubric for work in history, anthropology, geography, architecture, and urban studies, most scholars continue to see Britain as a nation sundered between country and city.[4] *Semi-Detached Empire* revises these coordinates, showing how imperialism transformed suburbia into the nation's predominant living space at the same time as suburbia was reconfiguring residential and recreational areas across the globe.

As both a guiding metaphor and an organizing principle, my title invokes the type of home synonymous with British suburbs for over a century. The semi-detached house conceals a mirrored pair of separate dwellings under a single roof, thereby giving two smaller, independent residences the façade of a large free-standing or detached home (fig. 1).[5] This structure provides an architectural correlative for my treatment of suburb and empire as spaces that are geographically distinct but materially and imaginatively linked. As we shall see, colonial wealth financed residential speculation, and institutions for foreign investment and trade swelled the ranks of suburbia's representative specimen, the clerk. Retired officials from the subcontinent domesticated the Asian bungalow into an archetypal suburban home. Elements of suburban layout and design both shaped and were shaped by colonial spaces such as the compound, cantonment, club, and hill station. Following the Boer War, fears of racial decay and a lack of healthy urban spaces inspired the garden city and garden suburb movement, which proliferated throughout Britain and, in turn, led to the redevelopment of cities in Asia, Africa, and Australia. If imperialism contributed to the British suburb's economic and geographic development, suburbia informed colonial praxis and spatial dynamics around the world.[6]

But the metaphor of semi-detachment reveals a more complex relation to empire at the suburb's foundation. Just as the "semi" conjoins two separate residences behind one façade, so too do the ostensible uniformity and

homogeneity of the British suburb conceal a variety of internal oppositions—
between country and city, suburb and slum, metropole and colony, dominator
and dominated, "civilized" and "savage." These oppositions, I argue, are central
to suburban identity in ways I discuss more fully below. For now I want to
emphasize that these oppositions result in the suburban male's degeneration
from an imperial pioneer to a colonized slave. While imperialism inspired fantasies like those of Sidney Low, in which suburbia provides racial regeneration
and spatial security as an antidote to urban degeneracy, the texts I examine
view suburbanization as a botched colonial mission that threatens the health,
welfare, and continued global dominance of Britain and its empire. Indeed, the
separation-in-connection that characterizes the semi-detached home informs
my central argument that imperial decline is at the heart of British suburban
identity. In this sense semi-detachment offers a figure for the embattled relation between suburb and empire, viewing the dissolution of imperial power
as fundamental to Britain's ambivalence toward its suburbs. Semi-detachment
ultimately reflects the nation's inability to disavow its suburbs, whose reputation for middling monotony and stifling conformity has become as widely
acknowledged as it is deplored.

Semi-detachment thus provides a layout or blueprint of the relations between
suburb and empire at the same time as it offers a way of reading those relations
as simultaneously parallel and incongruous. In historical terms, for example,
both suburb and empire began to spread in earnest with the close of the Napoleonic Wars in 1815, and both came to a sort of end with World War II. During the intervening period, especially from the 1880s to the 1920s, suburb and
empire shared an intensified ascendance and consolidation. In the last decades
of the nineteenth century, as the suburb's shift toward mass housing coincided
with the phase of rapacious colonial annexation known as New Imperialism,
the terms *imperialism* and *suburbia* both entered popular parlance.[7] But the
conjunction of imperial expansion and suburban development underwent a
dramatic shift in the 1920s and 1930s. While rising anti-colonial movements in
India, Africa, and Ireland augured the empire's formal dismantling, this same
interwar period saw suburbia's greatest growth. Four million new homes were
built in England and Wales between the wars, and the residential area of London doubled, accounting for a third of the population increase in those countries (Inwood 722; J. H. Johnson 142). Alison Light claims that the interwar
period "saw a move away from formerly heroic and officially masculine public
rhetorics of national destiny . . . in 'Great Britain' to an Englishness at once less
imperial and more inward-looking, more domestic and more private" (8). As
the private sphere took on new public importance, Light suggests, the suburban

home and garden became a privileged national space. Rather than seeing the colonial frontier abandoned for the front garden, however, I argue that Britain brought its anxieties of waning national and imperial stature home to the suburbs. As the empire began to lose its footing, suburbia gained more ground than ever before, dominating the social and political landscape at the same time as it came to represent Britain's decline on the world stage.

World War II brought an official end to both suburban development at home and colonial supremacy abroad. As Britain prepared to lower its flags overseas, the suburb's explosive interwar growth was halted by legislation enforcing green belts and New Towns as antidotes to further sprawl. But by this time suburbia had come to be seen as the nation's predominant—if predominantly disparaged—living space. This disparagement, I claim, has as much to do with Britain's declining imperial and international stature as it does with patrician and

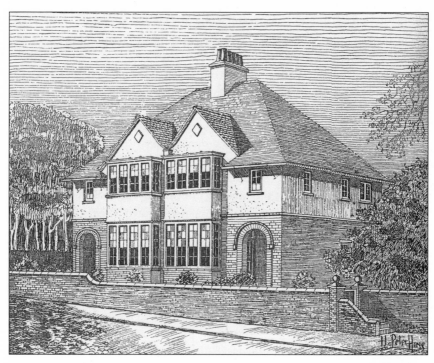

Figure 1. (*spread*) Semi-detached houses conceal a mirrored pair of separate dwellings under one roof. (Hugh B. Philpott, *Modern Cottages and Villas: A Series of Designs for Small Houses Costing from £150 to £1000. Selected from the "Illustrated Carpenter and Builder,"* 2nd ed., London: John Dicks, 1908)

haute bourgeois anxiety about the masses contaminating the countryside. The hope of some in the 1880s and 1890s, that suburbs would provide a new form of racial regeneration at home and a groundswell of further colonization abroad, had declined significantly during the Edwardian era and was all but dashed by the 1920s and 1930s, when the empire suffered serious setbacks. Indeed, it is this conjunction of unprecedented suburban growth and the inevitable decline of empire that made suburbia so disparaged. In the national and imperial imagination, suburbia replaced the empire as a colonizing force, picking up where the

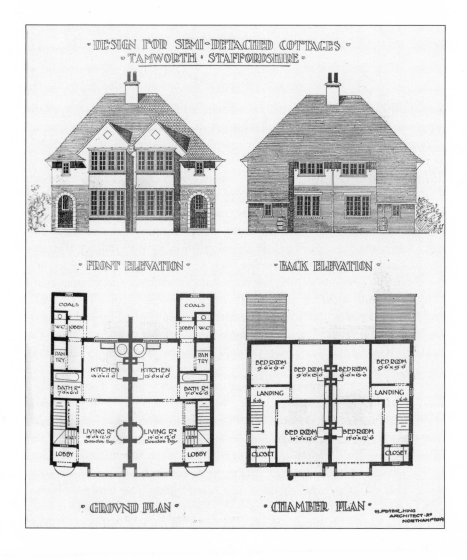

empire left off and succeeding where it failed—but dominating its own citizens in the process. Bringing this dilemma full circle is the historical conjunction of midcentury slum clearance with the first wave of postcolonial immigration. The urban proletariat became middle-class by moving to suburban housing estates just as the formerly colonized arrived to become Britain's new working class. Descendents of these immigrants now represent a new generation of suburbanites themselves, but rather than a postcolonial novelty, today's multiracial British suburbs—epitomized by Hanif Kureishi's *The Buddha of Suburbia*—bring home suburbia's long-standing colonial legacy. They make manifest the racial concerns that have always been at the foundation of the suburbs, though hidden behind a façade of coherent British identity.

Missing Links

Reading the long twentieth century in terms of semi-detachment fundamentally alters our view of modernity. In his history of English housing, John Burnett calls the rise of suburbia "perhaps the greatest single change in the living habits of the English people since the industrial revolution" (187). Yet among cultural historians and literary critics, suburbs have received remarkably little sustained attention and continue to be "curiously invisible in the accounts of modernity" (Silverstone 4).[8] Part of this invisibility is a legacy of literary modernism. Suburbs emerged as a popular fictional setting in the late nineteenth century, inspiring a subgenre of domestic realism that flourished between roughly 1890 and World War I. This "fiction of suburbia," as Kate Flint has called it, drew to varying degrees on elements of urban investigation, melodrama, and social comedy. While its authors included canonical figures like George Gissing, H. G. Wells, and Arnold Bennett, the fiction of suburbia was dominated by highly popular but now forgotten writers including George and Weedon Grossmith, William Pett Ridge, J. H. (Charlotte) Riddell, Jerome K. Jerome, Barry Pain, Shan Bullock, Keble Howard, and Edwin Pugh. Many modernists openly declared their aesthetic agendas against suburban literature and culture. The first manifesto of *BLAST* levels suburban Putney and Clapham, along with the favored middle-class authors Marie Corelli and George Grossmith (Lewis 18–21). Yeats castigated Wells's scientific romances as "the opium of the suburbs" (377), and Eliot launched the *Criterion* to counter what he called "suburban democracy" in aesthetic taste (qtd. in Ackroyd 143). Joyce admired Kipling's artistry but disliked his values, particularly the "crude practicability" that reminded him of a "suburban subaltern" (qtd. in Power 57). Clearly, suburbia's perceived intellectual and aesthetic deficiencies made for poor literature in the eyes of many modernists, who snubbed the suburb as a haven of philistines and lowbrows, consumer kitsch and ersatz culture.[9]

Many critics continue to follow suit, despite long-standing attempts to heal the great divide between modernism and mass culture. To be sure, scholars of modernism have largely abandoned an earlier generation's just-so stories of aesthetic autonomy from the social sphere and transcendence over everyday life. Revealing modernism's deep engagement with the past, with popular culture, and with its own political status, recent critics have broken the once monolithic category of Modernism into a plurality of competing and often radically opposed modernisms, especially in their quotidian, popular, and vernacular modes. Yet modernism remains the default category for discussing early twentieth-century writing, long after Raymond Williams argued that it represents a "misleading ideology," "a highly selected version of the modern which then offers to appropriate the whole of modernity" (*Politics* 31, 33). This situation is especially problematic in England, where, compared to the Celtic fringes and the Continent, modernism took a relatively weakened form, constituting what Jed Esty admits was "a compromise formation, a semimodernized modernism" (5).[10] A number of critics have attempted to challenge modernism's presumed dominance over English literary production and consumption in the late nineteenth and early twentieth centuries.[11] Yet modernist ideology continues to exert its force over the period. As a result suburbia remains little more than a footnote to literary history—one filled with forgotten texts of dubious merit. While this study does not eschew modernism, neither does it assume its dominance. It is no coincidence, for example, that the two figures who bookend my central chapters, H. G. Wells and George Orwell, are perhaps the primary casualties of a twentieth-century British canon shaped by the ideology of modernism.

Driving this study is a conviction that we have yet to appreciate the suburb's relevance to literary and cultural production in the late nineteenth and early twentieth centuries. *Semi-Detached Empire* insists that we take suburbia seriously, not by celebrating it but by broadening our perspective on a place many presumed not worth knowing. While I draw substantially from the fiction of suburbia throughout my study, that genre does not constitute my primary focus. Instead I use it as a reference point for considering how suburban themes and forms can be brought to bear on a broader and—from the perspective of literary history and criticism—more significant range of texts. This study reveals suburbia exerting a cultural influence that is neither subsumed by notions of domesticity nor limited to texts explicitly about the suburbs. To demonstrate this influence, the chapters that follow reveal suburban plots on unexpected ground: the Thames Valley of H. G. Wells's Martian attack and the gaslit London of Arthur Conan Doyle's Sherlock Holmes, but also the tropical backwaters of Joseph Conrad's Malay Archipelago and the stifling Anglo-Indian communities of E. M. Forster and George Orwell. Offering a more capacious view of suburban literature, *Semi-Detached Empire* demonstrates suburbia's vital role in a variety of genres: science fiction and the detective tale, which Franco Moretti calls the "super-niches" of late-Victorian publishing (*Graphs* 8); Condition-of-England novels from both the Edwardian era and the 1930s; modernist narratives of imperial decline; and contemporary fiction of postcolonial London.

In broadening the parameters of suburban fiction and demonstrating its influence on the long twentieth century, *Semi-Detached Empire* also complicates our understanding of suburbia itself. So far I have been describing "suburbia" as if it were a relatively coherent entity, but this belies a more complex reality. In the British context, as F. M. L. Thompson points out, suburban environments run the gamut "from costly and leafy to inexpensive and gimcrack" (17).[12] Indeed, while Britain and the United States share a view of suburbia as uniformly monotonous, the British suburb is often in closer proximity, geographically and imaginatively, to the slum. Consider the topography sketched in an article on London housing problems in the 1901 collection *The Heart of the Empire:* "In the wealthy suburbs we see the spacious houses of the rich and well-to-do; in other suburbs are the detached and semi-detached villas tenanted by the lower middle class; nearer to the heart of the city, or perhaps in a poorer class suburb, are to be seen streets upon streets of monotonous houses" inhabited by the working class. Not far beyond these, "hidden away from sight down a back court here, or a blind alley there, are . . . the slums of our great cities." This sketch is striking not only for the gradual devolution of suburbs into slums, but for the slum's relative confinement compared to the suburbs. "The housing problem," this author writes, "is a problem compounded of the last two, or perhaps three, of these subdivisions" (F. W. Lawrence 62). In other words, the only parts of London excluded from the evils of inferior housing are the most "wealthy suburbs," while a vast nether region of lesser suburbs congeals with the slum.

This topography of London housing problems highlights a recurrent theme in the literature I examine: the threat of the slum invading the suburb is no greater than the threat of suburbs degenerating into new slums. In *The Nether World* (1889) George Gissing implores the reader to "look at a map of greater London, a map on which the town proper shows as a dark, irregularly rounded patch against the whiteness of the suburban districts. . . . Another decade, and the dark patch will have spread greatly further" (364). The urban historians

H. J. Dyos and D. A. Reeder have investigated the breakdown of boundaries between suburb and slum, arguing that these seemingly opposed environments were in fact "mutually determined" (360).[13] Despite the slum's centrality to work by a range of literary critics and cultural historians over the past few decades, however, its relation to the suburb has gone largely ignored. Focusing on portrayals of London's East End—known variously as Outcast London, the city of dreadful delight, the abyss, darkest London, and the urban jungle—scholars have pored over depictions of the poor as racial primitives and colonial others. Such imagery dominates writing in the latter half of the nineteenth century, from Henry Mayhew's *London Labour and the London Poor* (1861–62) to a slew of late-Victorian social tracts including General William Booth's *In Darkest England and the Way Out* (1890).[14] Inspired by Henry Morton Stanley's best seller *In Darkest Africa*, Booth associated the East End with Stanley's African interior, suggesting that urban degeneration at home mirrored the barbarism found in Britain's colonies. The same analogy recurs with disturbing consistency in writing by "urban explorers" like George Sims, James Greenwood, and Charles Booth; diarists like A. J. Munby; forgotten novelists like Margaret Harkness; and canonical figures like Arthur Conan Doyle, Jack London, Joseph Conrad, and T. S. Eliot.[15]

But Gareth Stedman Jones points out that while "propertied London" saw poverty as a source of revolutionary threat in the 1880s, public concern for the "residuum" or "casual poor" actually declined in the 1890s (327, 330). This trend continued into the Edwardian period: for all their anxiety about the urban "abyss," Edwardians tended to view the very poor as statistical units, so that "fictional depiction of the working class and of the unemployed poor largely disappeared" (Stoll 24). Significantly, this is precisely the period when the suburb displaced the slum as a popular literary setting. As Peter Keating points out, the 1890s witnessed a "topographical shift" in focus "from the slum to the suburb." A great deal of fiction "sought to reverse the class bias of the slum novel, and . . . to re-assert the right of the middle classes to more sympathetic consideration" (*Haunted* 320; also see Trotter 128–29). Yet a subtle dialectical relation to the slum continued to inform representations of the suburb. Following Gissing, architectural journals and social commentaries alike typically viewed new suburbs as future slums. In the Edwardian era the *Builder* lamented "the future of the near suburbs . . . now so desolate and almost squalid," while the *Building News* saw new suburbs "provid[ing] the slums for the next generation" (qtd. in Hegglund 409–10). In the same period the social commentator C. F. G. Masterman described suburbs as "the slums of the future" (*Peril* 156). Suburbia thus both eased and exacerbated that pervasive Victorian fear of England one day deteriorating into a nationwide slum. As suburbia overtook the slum as the nation's future home, it also absorbed the discourse that portrayed the slum as an urban jungle of racialized savages. The successor to late-Victorian representations of "darkest London," suburbia—in particular its lower-middle-class residents—was endowed with a racial otherness once reserved for the urban poor and working classes.

The genealogy of "degeneration theory" helps to explain how the rhetoric of primitivism and savagery was projected upon the suburban masses. Daniel Pick argues that "the socio-biological theory of degeneration emerged in and beyond the 1880s most powerfully as a counter-theory to mass-democracy and socialism" (218). But after the Edwardian era "certain images of the degenerate had receded from view and the fear of a working-class population explosion in Britain subsided. . . . Degenerationism did not disappear, however, but refracted through a further range of European social representations," especially "the perception of 'mass society'" (232–33, 234). The discourse of suburbia reflects the shift of "degenerationism" from the poor and working-class to the suburban masses. Exemplary in this regard is the 1938 collection *Britain and the Beast*, a call for rural preservation that featured contributions from J. M. Keynes and E. M. Forster. In his essay Thomas Sharp claims the problem with those who have fled the cities for suburbia "is that their new places are hardly more civilized than those from which they are in headlong flight. Their new romantic villas and bungalows with their pebble-dash, their half-timbered gables, their 'picturesque' leaded-lighted windows, are certainly striking in contrast to the terrace houses of their old congested quarters. But the contrast is merely between one type of barbarism and another" (144–45). Another contributor puts it more pointedly: "The British Isles are at stake. If an invading army were occupying our hill-sides and lanes and shores, we should do something about it; and yet we allow an equally destructive and ruthless enemy to plunder our country treasures virtually without resistance" (Marshall 174).

Replacing the nineteenth-century fear of Britain being swamped by slums, suburbia thus took shape in popular and literary discourse as an instance of reverse colonization, that late-Victorian genre in which racial others or their gothic surrogates wreak havoc on British soil. In such narratives, Stephen Arata points out, "the 'civilized' world is on the point of being overrun by 'primitive' forces," so that "the colonizer finds himself in the position of the colonized, the exploiter is exploited, the victimizer victimized" (108). Inspiring the same anxieties that animated tales of reverse colonization, suburbia spawned fictions haunted by fears of invasion, degeneracy, and national decline. Indeed, in subsequent chapters I argue that Wells's *War of the Worlds* and Doyle's *Sign of*

Four, two classic reverse colonization narratives, figure suburban development in terms of foreign invasion. In this sense suburban narratives domesticate the fantastic elements of reverse colonization even as they push that genre's implications to another level. Where reverse colonization plots typically pit the British against some "marauding, invasive Other" (Arata 108), the narratives I examine represent suburbia as a colonization of Britain by the British themselves. Such narratives thus extend the logic of reverse colonization so that the British— not their exploited others—colonize their homeland. The waning of reverse colonization as a literary motif in the early years of the twentieth century did not therefore spell an end to the anxieties that shaped it. Rather, the anxieties of invasion were projected upon suburbia itself. If Britain no longer feared reverse colonization by foreign forces, this was because suburbia replaced them as a more viable threat to national identity. Initially idealized as imperial pioneers, suburban males degenerate into ineffectual colonizers, threatening savages, and powerless slaves.

As this description of suburban male degeneration suggests, my study takes up a distinctly masculine problematic. Indeed, while the relative absence of female authors in a book about suburbia may surprise readers, it should underscore the fact that suburbia's gender implications are not limited solely to women. Catherine Jurca's claim that U.S. suburban fiction is "a male-authored and frequently male-focused body of literature" (11) is no less true of the British context, whether in the traditional fiction of suburbia or in the more obliquely suburban narratives I examine. As F. M. L. Thompson points out, the nineteenth-century sundering of male identity between work and home was crucial to the suburb's development: "The creation of an environment in which this division of middle-class male lives between a public world of work contacts and a private world of family life was what the rise of suburbia was all about" (9). Yet suburbia also blurred the very boundaries it perpetuated between public and private, male and female, making beset manhood a recurrent preoccupation of suburban literature. Embodied by the hapless clerk Charles Pooter in George and Weedon Grossmith's *Diary of a Nobody* (1892), the suburban male is often mocked for his "pretension, weakness, and diminished masculinity" (Hammerton, "Pooterism" 292). The historian John Tosh suggests that lower-middle-class suburban males at the turn of the century responded to their "acute gender insecurity" by embracing "the quintessentially masculine ethos of empire" as an "easily improvised way of reaffirming their masculinity" (194). By the 1920s and 1930s, however, the diminished masculinity once attributed to the lower-middle-class suburban male had come to define national identity in general, which shifted from heroic imperial rhetorics "to an Englishness at once less imperial and more inward-looking, more domestic and more private" (Light 8). The rise of suburbia and the fall of empire together played a crucial role in making diminished manhood a central facet of British national identity. If my focus on men risks downplaying female subjectivities and experiences as they relate to suburb and empire, it has the virtue of reinforcing the profound male investment in blaming suburbia for national and imperial decline, whether by progressives like Wells and Forster, conservatives like Conan Doyle and Conrad, or a self-proclaimed "Tory anarchist" like Orwell (Crick 126).

My emphasis on British national identity may seem counter to suburbia's common association with England in particular. This choice is less descriptive than strategic.[16] Recent criticism tends to contrast a localized, place-bound Englishness with a more expansive and imperial Britishness. According to Ian Baucom, Britishness brought together "the nation *and* the empire. It was a global system that could incorporate local differences but would not define itself by local difference. 'British' space was thus read as homogeneous, interchangeable, everywhere alike, while 'English' space remained unique, local, differentiated" (10, original emphasis). Following Baucom, I use *British* as a term that conjoins nation and empire but that also distances them from an essentialized England. In this sense suburbia is British because it emerges with empire but also because it remains inadequately Anglicized. *British* designates for me an identity based more on disavowal than inclusion—on an uneasiness with suburbia rather than any claims for it on the nation's behalf. Indeed, Baucom's reference to British space as "homogeneous, interchangeable, everywhere alike" echoes a common complaint lodged against suburbia itself. In any case, I describe suburbs as British neither to indicate my geographical terrain nor to affirm for them some national essence, but precisely to underscore their frequently lamented lack of national essence. Their recurrent depiction by the writers I examine makes suburbs inherently imperial and, at the same time, insufficiently English. In short, suburbia remains a British space because it fails to become an English place.

If a semi-detached perspective clarifies suburbia's role in shaping modern British identity, it also seeks to resist one of the pitfalls of mapping the relationship between metropole and colony. In a recent collection on the "imperial turn" in the discipline of history, Antoinette Burton notes a tendency to assume (1) the coherence of nation and empire as distinct categories and (2) the nation's precedence to empire in terms of causality and force. Burton asks, "Is it possible to challenge the dichotomies of 'home' and 'away' that underwrite national and imperial histories; to merge center and periphery and posit an imaginative and material space where metropole and colony emerge simultaneously, rather than in a teleological, imperialized sequence?" (11). We can answer Burton in the affirmative by considering the origins of the modern suburb. Robert Fishman begins his history of the suburb in eighteenth-century London, a city whose increasing prominence amid "a worldwide network of ocean-going trade routes" made it "the political capital of the British Empire and its center for the production and consumption of luxury goods" (*Bourgeois* 19). Fishman sees London as the birthplace of the modern suburb, whose typical resident was "a merchant engaged in overseas trade and the financial operations that accompanied it," part of a "relatively small circle of entrepreneurs control[ling] the vast revenues that derived ultimately from Britain's naval and colonial supremacies" (*Bourgeois* 27–28). Yet the colonies—the British and Dutch East Indies in particular—provide evidence that challenges London's claim to be suburbia's birthplace. According to John Archer, European merchants and civil servants in the colonies created the first suburbs by establishing residential areas in "contrapositional" (opposed but not subordinate) relation to their respective towns. Europeans in such areas could seclude themselves from racial others as well as from the town's official duties. Such areas, which offered a distinctly colonial setting for constructing modern bourgeois identity, first appeared in Dutch-controlled Batavia (now Jakarta), but they spread more rapidly around cities ruled by the British East India Company. After the British took control of Bengal in 1757, Calcutta became the Company's economic and political capital, and clusters of British homes sprang up on an esplanade outside the city. This district, Chowringhee, became Calcutta's "principal European residential quarter" (Archer, "Colonial" 47). Likewise, in Madras "suburban living had become the rule for the mercantile and official elite" by the end of the eighteenth century (Neild 224). As in Calcutta's Chowringhee, European residents of Madras began to use property to articulate new forms of prestige and power. Between 1760 and 1800 the villages surrounding Madras were transformed from indigenous farmland to white residential property. By this time residential suburbs were also well under way outside Bombay and Patna (Dossal 19; Brown 162–63).[17]

Some historians suggest that these colonial areas inspired suburbs in Britain. Archer claims that suburbs in eighteenth-century Madras emerged "simultaneously, or perhaps even earlier" than those in the Thames Valley ("Colonial" 41). Marc Girouard suggests the prosperous suburbs of nineteenth-century Britain got their inspiration from Calcutta's Chowringhee (242). It may be that suburban growth began in the colonies, given that they made wealth accessible to a wider range of Europeans than at home, and that the rural environs of Indian cities, unlike those outside London, were available to Europeans either via military control (as in Calcutta) or by purchasing land from the local elite (as in Madras). More important than chronological precedence, however, is that we see the suburb emerging from a nexus of metropolitan and colonial interactions. Such evidence also suggests that, despite the importance of empire in reshaping urban and rural life in Britain, imperialism exerted an even greater force over suburbia's very emergence as an architectural and residential space.

Even if suburbs did not originate overseas, it is clear that by the early nineteenth century the colonies were integral to suburban development in Britain. As Greenwich shifted from a riverside town to a London suburb, it had a number of families connected with maritime trade in general and the East India Company in particular. A local housing speculator was the son of an East India Company director, and the member of another local family that made its fortune whaling in the South Pacific—and taking convicts to Australia en route—named his home Ceylon Place (Platts 214–17). The first consciously designed suburbs took shape near what is now Regent's Park. The surveyor John White's improvement scheme featured a "grand sweep of villas [that] was suggestive of the great houses round the Esplanade in Calcutta." While White's plan was not executed, it influenced many of the new villa parks spreading throughout England, including one at Cheltenham, a town popular with East Indian officials (Girouard 278–80). John Nash, White's successor at Regent's Park, became famous for his "orientally influenced" use of "verandahs, balconies, loggias, terraces, pergolas, gazeboes and above all, bay windows" (N. Taylor 105). Surrounded by many people with direct links to India, Nash was crucial to the emergence of suburban landscape and architecture and, at a dire point in designing Regent's Park, was saved by a millionaire gunpowder contractor for the East India Company (Summerson 73).[18]

To the west of Regent's Park was another early suburb with colonial connections, St. John's Wood. Its Eyre Estate, consisting of semi-detached villas instead of more traditional eighteenth-century terraces, was England's first "full-blown suburban neighbourhood," and its likeness to "the garden quarters of Calcutta and other Anglo-Indian quarters" may have attracted the large number of East India Company residents (Girouard 277–78). St. John's Wood represented the northern tip of an "inner colonial perimeter" popular with officials and civil servants (Dennis 127). Its southern tip, Kensington, was still suburban in the early nineteenth century, when it was called "Imperial Kensington," the court suburb (Reeder 255). Between Kensington and St. John's Wood was Bayswater, a suburb famous for its Anglo-Indian residents. Known as "Asia Minor" by the 1860s, it boasted a premiere shopping thoroughfare, Westbourne Grove, called "The Chowringhee of Bayswater" after Calcutta's famous suburb. Many of Westbourne Grove's specialty shops catered to colonial clientele, and London's first department store, Whiteley's, became a center of social life in the mid-1860s, with shoppers flocking to see the exotic flora and fauna on display in its lounge (Buettner, *Empire* 211–18).[19]

Proximity to Bayswater and Westbourne Grove may have attracted one of the most important developers of nearby Notting Hill, a retired Indian civil servant named Charles Henry Blake. Using money sent home from India, Blake purchased land, financed speculation, and built housing around Notting Hill in the 1850s and 1860s. Although he was almost bankrupted by his ambitious plans for the Kensington Park Estate, his speculation in a suburban railway paid off, allowing him to continue building. The dearth of archival materials makes it impossible to know how many developers began, like Blake, with resources from the colonies (Dyos, "Speculative" 646–47). But there are some notable examples of suburban developers with ties to the empire. One East India Company director returned home in the 1850s to chair the railway that would suburbanize rural Bromley; the line was obstructed, ironically, by a landowner who was an ex–Indian colonel (Rawcliffe 43, 52). In West Hampstead a big-game hunter whose family owned much of the area named a cluster of roads after his shooting estates in Kashmir and eastern Africa. Nearby lived an India and dye merchant and the official dyer for Queen Victoria, who named Hampstead's Kidderpore Avenue and Gardens—and his own home, Kidderpore Hall—after a district in Calcutta (Bebbington 71, 269). The land's former owner, Thomas Pell Platt, was a translator of Ethiopic, Syriac, and Amharic biblical manuscripts and an early member of the Royal Asiatic Society (Bebbington 258, 365; Norgate 542).

Admittedly anecdotal, such examples nonetheless sketch a view of suburbs emerging from the interaction between metropole and colonies in the eighteenth and early nineteenth centuries. Our analysis can become more systematic, however, as we near the late nineteenth century, when imperialism's economic importance helped to formalize the bond between suburb and empire. The sources of British suburban development have for too long been seen as contained within the nation's boundaries: migration from rural to urban areas, population growth, slum clearance, the increasing availability of land and capital for building, rising income and consumption rates, and an evolving network of mass transportation. Only recently have scholars begun to suggest that suburban growth "be seen in the context of a world economic system which facilitated the expansion of export markets for manufactured goods on the one hand and the extraction of resources from peripheral to core societies on the other" (Leaf 342). One of the suburb's most neglected aspects, according to the architectural scholar Anthony King, is "the inherently and constitutively international context in which it developed," a context bound to "the processes of imperialism, colonialism and the . . . international division of labor" (*Spaces* 99–100).

In the latter half of the nineteenth century, the shift from a nationally based agricultural economy to one dependent on international trade and finance fundamentally changed the use of British rural land. Increases in free trade and a growing dependence on imported foodstuffs after midcentury led to a series of agricultural depressions that depopulated Britain's rural areas. Land fell from a quarter of the nation's overall wealth in 1878 to less than a twelfth in 1914, and its value dropped even more precipitously (Harris 97–98). As agriculture declined, however, Britain continued to dominate the world economy. The enormous amount of surplus wealth that flowed into its capital was also integral to suburbia's rise during the last decades of Victoria's reign, when an expanding urban bourgeoisie could parcel the depopulated countryside into zones of middle- and upper-middle-class residence and leisure (King, *Urbanism* 117). While King points out that the precise relationship between suburban expansion and the imperial economy requires further research, he cites Kensington, Bayswater, and St. John's Wood as examples that overseas capital contributed to suburban development. Likewise, he suggests, "overseas trade combined with transport developments to fuel the habit of country living in what, in the twentieth century, was to become the 'stockbroker belt' round London in Surrey, Sussex, and Berkshire" (*Global* 79–80).

If colonial trade helped bring about the demise of British agriculture, suburbia offered what the geographer David Harvey calls a "spatial fix." Harvey uses this phrase to describe the way capitalism solves its internal crises by reorganizing geographical space "in its own image" (*Spaces* 54). Harvey has discussed both European imperialism and U.S. suburbanization as spatial fixes for capitalist overaccumulation; he has also recognized that the nineteenth-century British city was inherently "an imperialist city," not only because its growth depended on colonial resources but because its overaccumulation "spawned industrial development in far-off lands" (*Urbanization* 201–2). Yet Harvey does not synthesize these insights into an analysis of British suburban growth as it relates to imperial expansion. Largely silent on the British suburb, Harvey rightly contends that the U.S. suburban boom after World War II transformed particular industries (auto and construction) and resources (oil, rubber, timber) from luxuries to necessities for the average citizen (*Urbanization* 207).[20] But this process began in late nineteenth-century Britain, when, along with the decline of agriculture and the influx of foreign wealth, suburbs benefited from an international division of labor that transformed the nation's colonial possessions "into specialized producers of one or two primary products for export"

(Hobsbawm, *Age of Empire* 64). Colonialism made products such as oil, rubber, and timber "available for the development of suburbanization" (King, *Urbanism* 81). The suburb thus provided a spatial fix for the vicissitudes of Britain's changing economy, absorbing resources made available by colonial possessions and giving new value to the British agricultural land rendered obsolete by imperialism.

One of the primary forms that this new value took was residential construction. In the late nineteenth and early twentieth centuries, an inversely proportionate cycle linked house building at home to investment abroad. Money diverted from risky foreign ventures was often channeled into safer investment in housing (hence the phrase "safe as houses"), while excess housing development would be checked by shifting capital to overseas investment (Fishman, "American" 244). And this investment was largely imperial. Between 1865 and 1914 Asia, Africa, Australasia, and South America together accounted for just over half of Britain's foreign capital, with the rest going to the United States and Europe. But over the course of this period, the investment clearly shifted toward colonial and semicolonial territories. By the outset of World War I, only a quarter of Britain's foreign capital went to the United States and Europe, and by the late 1920s India, the dominions, and Latin America far outpaced Western powers in attracting British investment (Hobsbawm, *Industry* 138; Edelstein 177). When foreign investment peaked in the early 1870s, the late 1880s and early 1890s, and the later half of the Edwardian era, domestic building slumped; likewise, the building booms of 1874–84 and 1898–1901 occurred in periods of low foreign investment. The result was not that too few houses were built when capital went abroad, but that too many were built when it was again available for use at home.[21] The point is that suburban housing in Britain and colonial investment abroad functioned like two sides of the same coin, or two halves of the same semi-detached house. When money was not going overseas, one of its primary uses was suburban building.

Greater London and Greater Britain

As Williams suggests in *The Country and the City*, imperialism reconfigured the British countryside at the same time as it transformed London into the heart of the empire. Much recent work on turn-of-the-century London emphasizes this transformation, which manifested itself in two contrasting ways. On the one hand, a number of urban locales, particularly in the West End, served as the empire's political, economic, scientific, and cultural core. Westminster provided the ceremonial center of imperial London, government offices were located in the Strand, international finance and trade operated out of the City. The museums of South Kensington acted as archives of Britain's historical and scientific knowledge, and a number of imperial markers ran along the Thames—from the shipping nexus of the London docks to projects like the Embankment and the Tower Bridge (Driver and Gilbert, "Heart"; Crinson, *Modern* 5–10). Obviously, such monuments placed London's citizens at the center of British civilization.

But as Joseph Conrad would show, the heart of the empire could also be a heart of darkness. In a study on representations of London as an urban jungle, Joseph McLaughlin argues that "far from being the antithesis of those colonial and imperial places and peoples that comprised the British Empire," London and its inhabitants "were actually their curious doubles" (5). The East End, often referred to as "darkest London," was considered the primary site for pedestrian miscegenations of all kinds—threatening if exhilarating encounters with the foreign, the exotic, the other. The perceived alterity of the East End was not only due to its function as a port of entry and erstwhile community for immigrants to Britain; it was also due to the frequency with which the East End's poor and working classes—British or otherwise—were depicted as a separate race or species. As I have already mentioned, a host of critics have demonstrated how consistently the Victorian bourgeoisie viewed urban space through imperial eyes, conflating London's underclass with Britain's colonized subjects: "Drawing on the imperial progress narrative and the figure of the journey into the interior, journalists, social workers and novelists figured the East End slums in the language of empire and degeneration" (McClintock 120).

Many saw the antidote to urban decay in the countryside, precisely because it offered a substitute for colonial migration. General William Booth's *In Darkest England,* for example, proposed a "farm colony" as a remedy for urban degeneration and a transition to colonial emigration for the poor. His scheme involved "forwarding [the poor] from the City to the Country, and there continuing the process of regeneration, and then pouring them forth on to the virgin soils that await their coming in other lands . . . and so laying the foundations, perchance, of another Empire to swell to vast proportions in later times" (92–93).[22] As the historian Martin Wiener points out, Booth's plan exemplifies the "parallels [that] were often drawn between English country life and the open-air life in overseas possessions," both of which "were contrasted to the decadent life of modern cities" (56). This link between English country life and colonial emigration was nowhere clearer than in the idea of a "Greater Britain" espoused in the latter third of the nineteenth century. The travel writer and politician Charles Wentworth Dilke brought the term *Greater Britain* into vogue with his 1868 book of that name. In his preface Dilke writes, "If two small islands are by courtesy styled 'Great,' America, Australia, [and] India, must form a Greater Britain" (x). The Cambridge history professor J. R. Seeley further popularized the idea in *The Expansion of England* (1883). Believing that colonization would increase the bounds of English political and racial sovereignty, Seeley uses the term *Greater Britain* as a call to make the colonies safe for widespread emigration and settlement and as a signal of the regenerative capacities of imperial expansion. As he writes in *The Expansion of England:* "Our colonial empire so-called may more and more deserve to be called Greater Britain. . . . Then the seas which divide us might be forgotten, and that ancient preconception, which leads us always to think ourselves as belonging to a single island, might be rooted out of our minds" (298).

But emigration overseas was a daunting prospect, and the decline of British agriculture meant many citizens led an increasingly urban life. Hence the growing popularity of the suburbs, which responded both to fears of urban degeneracy and to the increasing inaccessibility of rural life, whether at home or in the colonies. In so far as they approximated a semirural existence, suburbs could be associated with an expansion of English civilization in imperial terms. Indeed, if "darkest Africa" and other colonial spaces inspired the Victorian image of "darkest London," then the expansion of Greater Britain shaped the identity of suburban Greater London. A designation whose official use dates to 1875, Greater London included suburbs beyond municipal borders but within reach of the city by train, tram, and tube (Dyos and Reeder 362). From 1861 the outer ring of Greater London grew about 50 percent each decade until the turn of the century, when the number of residents reached nearly two million (Dyos, *Victorian* 19–20). By 1901 Greater London accounted for a fifth of the population of England and Wales, and though the population of central London steadily declined, that of Greater London continued to grow. In this sense the suburbs of Greater London provided "settler colonies" for the metropolitan core. Just as Greater Britain extended the nation's boundaries beyond its shores while maintaining a common language and culture, the suburbs extended the peripheries of the imperial capital while preserving a shared metropolitan identity.

Reinforcing these parallels between Greater Britain and Greater London was the London County Council (LCC). Formed in 1888, the LCC merged the city's 117 square miles into a single county, bringing about London's first unified government since Roman occupation (Porter 240). Until the late nineteenth century London lacked a cohesive municipal identity, its citizens aligning themselves with their local parishes and vestries (J. Davis 5–6). When Progressives attempted to unify London's government after 1880, their debates with localists took on imperial overtones. Progressives pitted an antiquated London of byzantine vestries against their bold vision of "Imperial London" (Young and Garside 20–21, 31). This was perhaps not surprising, since an imperial culture pervaded the LCC: many of its employees had served in the colonies, and some clerks hoped to export their municipal planning ideas overseas (Pennybacker 20).[23] Moreover, a number of the Progressives who backed London's centralization—including Joseph Chamberlain and *Greater Britain* author Charles Dilke—were also ardent imperialists. Likewise, the LCC's first chair, Lord Rosebery, was one of the key figures shaping colonial policy at the end of the nineteenth century. Rosebery's stints as foreign secretary and prime minister coincided with his tenure as LCC chair, and though he did not desire a centralized London as fervently as many Progressives, there are clear parallels between his municipal and imperial views. For Rosebery the British empire was "not a centralised Empire," but "a vast collection of communities spread all over the world . . . all with their own governments" (2: 196). This federalist view is of a piece with his avowed aim to make London "not a unit, but a unity" (qtd. in R. R. James 199).[24] Despite his zeal for unity, Rosebery wanted neither imperial nor municipal consolidation at the expense of local self-government. In this way Rosebery saw suburban Greater Londoners as akin to white settlers in Australia and other British dominions.

Yet Rosebery's moderate stance did little to alleviate Greater Londoners who resisted an LCC "invasion" and "annexation" (Young and Garside 7, 130). During the Edwardian era in particular, boroughs beyond the LCC mounted a defense against their colonization, and conservatives rallied on their behalf in the name of "Home Rule" (J. Davis 182–83, 195, 203). In the years leading up to World War I, when debates over national governance were divided between "Little England" and "Greater Britain," so too was the debate over municipal governance waged between "Little London" and "Greater London" (Young and Garside 126–27). Regardless of its ruling party, the LCC consistently pursued a policy of suburban population dispersal (Saint, "'Spread'"). Thus, while the LCC forged links between suburban Greater London and imperial Greater Britain, its increasing tendency toward municipalization led many Greater Londoners to see their local identity and self-determination as threatened by the LCC. Whether suburban Greater Londoners sought to expand the borders of the imperial metropolis or escape its encroachment, they articulated their concerns within the frame of colonial discourse.

Like Greater Britain, which promised to reinvigorate the Anglo-Saxon race through imperial expansion, Greater London offered an opportunity to escape the degenerative effects of the urban jungle and to establish middle-class dominions amid suburbia's fresh air and open spaces. The suburban inhabitants of Greater London were often described as pioneers, colonists, and emigrants who were annexing and settling new territories. An unsigned 1884 article in the *Spectator* on the phenomenon of "Suburbanity" described "the numberless middle-class colonies which encircle London" ("Suburbanity" 483). Among the more respectable examples were Hampstead and St. John's Wood, the latter of which Charles Booth described in *Life and Labour of the People in London* as home to "an influential colony of workers in art, science, and literature" (2: 425). Another such example was Jonathan Carr's fashionable development of Bedford Park, begun in the late 1870s. Combining populist imperial rhetoric with a vision of traditional English village life, a writer in the *Bedford Park Gazette* described the community as "a tiny colony" of happy "colonists": "If we claim to be thus a colony of a new and hopeful sort, we also aspire to a sort of modern revival of the very ancient conception of a village community" (qtd. in Bolsterli 78). Bedford Park's residents, like "the first settlers and colonisers" of Walter Besant's suburban South London, were decidedly upper-middle-class (315). Likewise, an 1881 guide to London's suburbs describes Kilburn and Paddington as constituting "a large area of most valuable property colonised by men of wealth and position" in what had only recently been "a hopeless desert" (Clarke 306–7). The themes of migration and settlement also informed suburban developments for the petit bourgeoisie and working class. At the close of the nineteenth century, organizations like "The Home Colonisation Society" and "The English Land Colonisation Society" set out to build healthy suburban housing for the lower middle class (Gaskell 171). In the early years of the twentieth century, the London County Council took up the same mission with its "pioneer schemes" in places like Tooting, Tottenham, Norbury, and Hammersmith (Young and Garside 114). These trends confirm H. G. Wells's claim that, regardless of class, a suburban home satisfied every Briton's desire "for a little private *imperium*" (*Anticipations* 55, original emphasis).

A number of suburbs displayed their imperial identity more prominently. After the Great Exhibition, for example, the Crystal Palace moved from Hyde Park to suburban Sydenham, where the symbol of British industrial and commercial prowess was rebuilt as a hothouse for foreign plants, fish, and birds. With tropical habitats that could not be experienced at the London Zoo or the British Museum, the Crystal Palace popularized exotic gardening among the British public (Hassam 182–83; Preston 201). It was also a site of public ceremonies: Disraeli gave a famous speech there inaugurating a more aggressive phase of imperial expansion (Said 72), and the 1911 Pageant of London emphasized the city's imperial and suburban identity (Ryan 120). A more monumental display of imperial grandeur took place at the British Empire Exhibition held in

Wembley in the summers of 1924 and 1925. Since no area in central London could accommodate the exhibition's proposed scale, the government purchased the 219–acre Wembley Park, building a stadium; an amusement park; palaces of industry, engineering, and arts; and pavilions devoted to each of Britain's colonial possessions (Hewlett et al. 189). It was "the biggest fair Britain had ever known," drawing some twenty-seven million—over half the British population and four times the number of visitors to the Great Exhibition (J. Morris 30). It was also responsible for transforming Wembley from a relatively quiet village into a bustling suburb. Wembley was located in "Metro-land," the promotional name for the northwest suburbs served by the Metropolitan Railway, as well as the title of its popular home-buying guidebook during the 1910s and 1920s. Published in conjunction with the exhibition, the 1924 issue of *Metro-land* gave Wembley pride of place, advertising area homes in the context of a spectacle that "reproduce[s] in miniature the entire resources of the British Empire" (qtd. in O. Green 12). Thanks to *Metro-land,* the British Empire Exhibition, and residential sites like the Wembley Hill Garden Suburb, which was built to coincide with the exhibition (Saint, *London* 182), Wembley's population rose almost 200 percent during the 1920s (Hewlett et al. 189). At a moment when unemployment, the memory of World War I, and rising anticolonial movements were eroding British confidence at home and abroad, the Wembley exhibition encouraged visitors to view suburban Metro-land as the new home of a worldwide empire.[25]

While Sydenham's Crystal Palace and Wembley's British Empire Exhibition forged rather formidable bonds between suburb and empire, other areas manifested less monumental imperial markers. In East Sheen, near Richmond, a number of houses still boast "Indian-inspired domes" (Saint, *London* 224). In Croydon a Victorian residential estate was built on the grounds of the former East India College, whose memory is preserved in the names of nearby roads (Clarke 128–29). Tooting's former resident Daniel Defoe inspired a number of street names—including Robinson, Crusoe, Friday, and Island. Indeed, given that so much suburban development took place at the height of empire, scores of new roads and avenues took their names from colonial possessions, battles, and military leaders. Battersea has four street names linked to the Second Afghan War, three to the Sudan campaign, and one each to the 1857 Indian "Mutiny" and the 1867 Ethiopian invasion. Norwood has six roads named for places in the West Indies. Greenford and Ilford each have the same number for cities in Australia and New Zealand. Easily the most common imperial referent, however, is the Boer War. Eight suburban areas feature clusters of three or more roads named after British leaders (Kitchener and Milner), battle sites

(Colenso, Durban, Natal, Pretoria, Tugela), and sieges (Kimberley, Ladysmith, Mafeking).[26]

Darkest London and the Rise of the Suburbs

"The Rise of the Suburbs," Sidney Low's 1891 article in the *Contemporary Review,* provides one of the most sustained imaginary links between suburban Greater London and imperial Greater Britain. As I suggest in my opening pages, Low's analysis of census data from the 1880s led him to frame an optimistic prognosis of Britain's expanding suburbs within the logic of imperial discourse. Indeed, Low bolsters this prognosis by asking readers to look beyond their shores. "The suburban type is just as pronounced" in Britain as it is "in some of our colonies," he suggests, singling out Australia for special mention. Rather than a "dashing pastoralist, who shears sheep [and] rides buck-jumping horses," the typical Australian "lives in his own house, provided with a verandah and a piano . . . and reads his morning paper as he comes down to his daily work by the train or tramcar" ("Rise" 551–52).[27]

In later writing Low would continue to imagine Britain's colonies in suburban terms. He visited India to cover the Prince of Wales's 1905 tour, and, like his description of Australia in "The Rise of the Suburbs," his published account makes the subcontinent out to be a sprawling colonial suburb. Minor officials in Madras boast estates with lavish gardens, recalling "a sort of Hampstead Heath or Putney Common." The civil station outside Aligarh features "bungalows set back in suburban-looking gardens and avenues of fine trees." Even the tidy British campsite, "when pitched on the dusty maidan, a mile or so from a small native town . . . look[s] like a canvas suburb itself" (*Vision* 236, 283, 328). Likewise, Low's prime specimens of British society in India are explicitly suburban. His archetypal official, "Tompkyns Sahib," recalls his earlier image of a domesticated Australian: "If he were at home he would . . . probably live in a middle-class suburb and go down to his work every morning by the omnibus" (*Vision* 301). Reinforcing this claim is a lengthy hypothetical sketch of Tompkyns *frère* as a lower-middle-class London clerk. Meanwhile, Mrs. Tompkyns, now a memsahib who commands her own wagon about the civil station, hails from Streatham, where she once traveled "by omnibus or in the London County Council's inexpensive tramcars" (*Vision* 315).

Many came to share Low's vision of suburbs colonizing Britain and the globe—his belief that, whether in Putney or Patna, "suburbs are to be the homes and living places of the bulk of Englishmen, if not the bulk of all the Anglo-Saxon and Anglo-Celtic peoples, in the time to come" ("Rise" 558). Indeed, his account of India throws into sharper relief the imperial subtext of "The Rise of the Suburbs," confirming a recent claim that representations of suburbia in the 1890s tend to feature "echoes of colonial discourse—of migration, of new worlds, of setting up a new community in a better environment and of maintaining traditional values away from the dangers and the corruption of the city" (Hapgood, *Margins* 56).[28] Though accurate, this description deserves to be extended and qualified in a number of ways. As we have already seen, echoes of colonial discourse predate the 1890s, and as I show in subsequent chapters, the links between suburb and empire would remain at the forefront of popular and literary discourse throughout the twentieth century.

More than widening our historical frame, however, we should recognize that suburbia took on a number of varied and contradictory meanings within Britain's imperial imagination. For instance, the intrepid pioneers carving middle-class colonies out of the wilderness could sometimes make their new society too tame and refined, engendering a life of perpetual boredom, convention, and restraint. When it epitomized a sheltered and homely life, suburbia could become the very antithesis of masculine heroism and adventure represented by emigration to the colonies. Such is the case with George Gissing's *In the Year of Jubilee* (1894). Set in the south London suburb of Camberwell, the novel deals with the deferred marriage between Nancy Lord and Lionel Tarrant, the latter of whom avoids wedded domesticity by pursuing a money-making scheme in the Bahamas. The contrast between emasculating suburban routine and rugged colonial adventure is thrown into greater relief by Shan Bullock's 1907 novel *Robert Thorne: The Story of a London Clerk,* a central text in the traditional fiction of suburbia. Early on we learn that Thorne's namesake was a sixteenth-century explorer who attempted the North-West passage and that his father praised "what he called natural men," especially "pioneers and colonials" (3). Among them is Thorne's own brother, an émigré to New Zealand who figures as a shadowy though constant reminder of a more vital life. Though Thorne believes he was never meant for such a life, the psychological degradation and financial insecurity of clerical work and suburban domesticity ultimately lead him to emigrate. The novel ends with Thorne exiting the swinging doors of his office for the last time, having decided to "be more of a man" in New Zealand (290). As Lynne Hapgood notes, suburban fiction by Edward Thomas and William Pett Ridge also proffers colonial emigration as a solution to suburban drudgery and gendered constraint (*Margins* 83, 181).

Yet perhaps because suburbia could be overly effeminate and constraining, it also came to be seen as a breeding ground for bullheaded nationalism and downright jingoism. Following Britain's early victories in the Boer War, "all the

London suburbs had their patriotic processions complete with bunting, floats, bright lights and flags" (Price 91). Suburbia's conservatism was also espoused in the pages of its favorite newspaper, the *Daily Mail:* "The newspaper's jingoism was renowned; its jingo rhetoric quintessential: of the potential re-conquest of the Sudan, it remarked 'a little blood letting is good for a nation that tends to excess luxury'" (Price 96). Paula Krebs traces the emergence of tabloid journalism to the *Daily Mail's* coverage of the Boer War, arguing that the newspaper played a conscious role in constructing its audience's jingoism: "After the establishment of the *Daily Mail* in 1896, as tabloid journalism emerged coincident with the New Imperialism, public opinion about the Boer War became quite directly dependent on newspapers" (4). Around the same time the Liberal journalist C. F. G. Masterman groused that Lord Salisbury, then the prime minister, could be "confident in the devotion of villadom to the New Imperialism" ("Realities" 14). From that moment on, Harold Perkin points out, conservative influence in suburban villadom, a phenomenon known as "villa Toryism," became a defining feature of Britain's political landscape (45–46), one that the Liberal politician L. T. Hobhouse condemned as "a greater burden on the nation than the slum" (68).

Such representations—which depict suburbia as either tame and effeminate or masculinist and jingoist—complicate the notion that suburban residents were consistently imagined as benign adventurer-emigrants. Indeed, popular and literary discourse of the late nineteenth and early twentieth centuries more commonly presents suburbia as territory that is foreign, primitive, and unredeemed by civilization—eerily familiar to the "darkest London" that was the suburb's ostensible other. In *Basil* (1852) Wilkie Collins refers to a suburban square as "a colony of half-finished streets, and half-inhabited houses," hardly an inviting prospect for would-be settlers (158). In *Our Mutual Friend* (1864–65) Dickens describes Holloway as "a tract of suburban Sahara," indicating a wasteland "where tiles and bricks were burnt, bones were boiled, carpets were beat, rubbish was shot, dogs were fought, and dust was heaped by contractors" (33).[29] Such images were not limited to fiction. In 1883 a contributor to the *Architect* draws on common parlance for the slum to describe suburbia itself as "a *terra incognita.*" Characterizing "househunting" as "an adventure of despair," the *Architect* writer associates suburbs with a barbaric wilderness better left unexplored (qtd. in Olsen 211). Similar language appears in domestic manuals and house-buying guides that otherwise endorse suburban living. Two of the most famous from the 1890s, Mrs. C. S. Peel's *The New Home* and Mrs. J. E. Panton's *Suburban Residences and How to Circumvent Them,* advise prospective suburban housewives to prepare for a perilous colonial mission. Peel emphasizes the many inconveniences facing a woman "who exiles herself in the suburbs" (15). Panton sees suburbia as "the antipodes of Paradise" for the angel of the house (18), making clear that housekeeping will require nothing short of "a complete conquest of the . . . suburban residence," a "siege . . . that will carry dread even to the stoutest heart" (31, 64). That such perils were not restricted to women is the moral of a 1906 retelling of *Robinson Crusoe* by Barry Pain, a comic author better known for his *Eliza* series. In *Robinson Crusoe's Return* Pain has the castaway wash ashore in Edwardian London—only to find suburbia a less hospitable terrain than his former island. Pain's Crusoe takes lodging with a confidence man in a semi-detached house waiting to be let, fires his musket at reckless automobiles in the Fulham Road, and ends up on Hampstead Heath as a sideshow spectacle during Bank Holiday. "This is indeed a sorry pass to which a man should be brought that was once an Emperor," Crusoe laments (523).

If suburbia was a terra incognita that could not be tamed by even an "Emperor" like Crusoe, then its inhabitants—or so it was feared—may not be imperial pioneers, but rather degenerate savages. Indeed, more often than overlords of a new civilization, the residents of suburbia were seen as a race of invading foreigners and barbarians—a threatening antithesis to English national character. Suburbia's early proponents, like the landscape gardener John Claudius Loudon, may have sought to legitimize middle-class citizens as national subjects, and enthusiastic Anglophiles like the young Henry James may have championed London's suburbs as the essence of Englishness.[30] Nevertheless, the national lineage of the suburb would recurrently be fraught with anxiety. Thus, even as England was becoming increasingly suburban, many commentators expressed doubt that the suburb was truly English. In *The Seven Lamps of Architecture* (1849), Ruskin offered an early instance of a discourse that would become common in later decades, suggesting that newly erected and rapidly decaying suburban homes poison the soil that cultivates English character. Suburbs inspired in Ruskin "a painful foreboding that the roots of our national greatness must be deeply cankered when they are thus loosely struck in their native ground" (8: 226). Ruskin reinforced this national disavowal of suburbia by claiming that "the crowded tenements of [its] struggling and restless population differ only from the tents of the Arab or the Gipsy by their less healthy openness to the air of heaven, and less happy choice of their spot of earth" (8: 226–27). Just as Victorian urban ethnographers conflated slum residents with primitive savages, so too do Ruskin's suburbanites come to be seen as barbaric foreign invaders. Indeed, the "restless population" of Ruskin's suburbs, whose "crowded tenements" fare worse than makeshift Arab or Gipsy shelters, recalls Henry Mayhew's impoverished hordes of wandering tribes and nomads in *London Labour and the London Poor*. Ruskin goes even further in one of the letters of *Fors Clavigera* (1871–84), describing the two halves of the semi-detached home as "fastened in a Siamese-twin manner" and contrasting its inhabitants with the baboons of London's zoo, who "with Mr. Darwin's pardon—*are* of another species; a less passive, and infinitely wittier one" (27: 529, 531, original emphasis).[31]

Given their tenuous position between a countryside considered the essence of Englishness and a capital city that represented both the heart of British civilization and the source of its decay, the suburbs thus occupied a highly ambiguous position within the empire. Even Sidney Low's "The Rise of the Suburbs" is more ambivalent than it may seem, its eventual optimism belying its subject's popular associations with mystery and danger. Indeed, the early section of Low's essay suggests an uneasy relationship between suburb and empire—one that would nonetheless have been more evident to his original audience. Arguing against the prevailing perception that the exodus from rural villages had augmented London's East End, Low claims that "the population is not shifting from the fields to the slums; and the slums themselves are not becoming fuller, but the reverse." Drawing on a poetics of the imperial social body, Low suggests that rather than "the heart of the city being congested with the blood driven from the extremities . . . the larger centres of population are stationary or thinning down," while "the districts all around them . . . are filling up" (548). Such circulation may seem a proper means of ensuring a healthy system, but Low implies that the suburbs are a diseased growth on England: as the blood courses away from a heart grown "stationary" and sclerotic, he imagines it "thinning down," losing its vitality and strength as it spreads out toward suburban appendages: "The centre of population is shifting from the heart to the limbs. The life-blood is pouring into the long arms of brick and mortar and cheap stucco that are feeling their way out to the Surrey moors, and the Essex flats, and the Hertfordshire copses" (550).[32]

So while Low ostensibly attempts to quell popular fears about slum growth, his essay initially figures the suburb as a kind of surrogate slum. As he points out, for example, the population that had in fact moved beyond the city was still thought by most to be crowding, in ever-increasing numbers, into London's East End. Of the suburbs Low writes: "Here is where the increase of 'Greater London,' with its five and a half millions of inhabitants, is found. It is not, as hasty observers have imagined, in the teeming alleys of 'Darkest London'" (550). Although he chides the rhetoric of late-Victorian urban ethnography,

Low simultaneously transfers the symbolic significance of darkest London to the city's outlying suburbs, which become the new home of London's nameless, faceless, masses. In doing so, Low implicitly associates suburban inhabitants with qualities usually reserved for England's urban underclass and colonial others. While Low's suburbs are perhaps less threatening than the urban abyss, they are figured as anonymous and alien spaces—all the more so for their quiet proliferation.

As the suburbs of Greater London failed to achieve Greater Britain's idyll of re-created rural life abroad, they became agents of the degeneracy once thought limited to the inner city or urban abyss. In this sense suburban discourse was a successor to representations of "darkest London." Yet whereas the slum and its inhabitants were seen as clearly separated from the bourgeoisie, to whom the discourse of "darkest London" was addressed, the suburb was uncomfortably close to home. Indeed, for more and more Britons it *was* home. In the 1840s Friedrich Engels could write that the condition of the working class in England "is the condition of the vast majority of the English people" (17). But within half a century Sidney Low had shown that this was no longer the case. By 1909 C. F. G. Masterman would proclaim that "the middle class . . . stands for England in most modern analyses" (*Condition* 14), giving them a central place as "the Suburbans" in his most famous work, *The Condition of England.* Moreover, suburbanization showed no signs of abating. Henry James may have exaggerated in the late 1880s when he wrote that "all England is in a suburban relation to" London (*English Hours* 23). But by the turn of the century, such poetic license had become a stark reality. In a 1904 lead article on suburban growth, the *Times* proclaimed it "no longer possible to escape from the dull suburb into unspoiled country" ("Formation" 8). In 1927 the *Edinburgh Review* looked back on a century of suburban growth, lamenting that "Greater London is now almost identical with the Home Counties" (Tilby 95). It is a sentiment shared by the poet John Betjeman: "Surrey is all one suburb, so is most of Bucks" (qtd. in V. Cunningham 258). By the 1930s suburbia had spread well beyond London. Traversing English coal country, George Orwell witnessed "between all the towns of the Midlands . . . a villa-civilisation indistinguishable from that of the South" (*Road* 105). The same spectacle led D. H. Lawrence to a wholesale condemnation of homes throughout England as "suburban, pseudo-cottagey," and not "truly urban" (293). E. M. Forster echoed these claims, noting that the English middle class "has never been able to build itself an appropriate home." As he flatly declared on the verge of World War II, "the class to which . . . most of us belong" now "live[s] in semi-detached villas" (*Two* 292–93).

Foundations, Façades, Semi-Detachment

While the chapters that follow proceed in roughly chronological order, they are also organized according to the architectural keywords *foundations, façades,* and *semi-detachment.* Having begun in this chapter to plot the material and discursive ground on which popular and literary discourse constructed suburbia as both an extension of the empire and a savage threat to it, I continue to excavate these foundations in chapter 2. Or perhaps *unearth* is the better term, as I focus on the Martian attack in H. G. Wells's *War of the Worlds* as exemplifying suburbia's ambivalent relation to empire. I argue that Wells's oft-cited critique of imperialism in this novel is bound to his long-ignored view of suburbia. Invading the Surrey countryside, his slimy, tentacled aliens spread poisonous fumes and red vegetation—and in doing so invoke Victorian tropes of suburban development, seen by many as a funguslike growth littering the landscape with red villas and train smoke. Wells's depiction of these invaders—as both brutal colonizers and brutish savages—reflects the colonial paradox at the very foundation of the British suburb.

Part Two, "Façades," focuses on suburban homes whose owners seek to repress or conceal the colonial paradox at their foundations. Each chapter of this section features male home owners or home builders who fashion themselves as imperial pioneers, only to be revealed as degenerate colonizers. Like Wells, Arthur Conan Doyle portrays suburbia via the gothic elements of reverse colonization. But Doyle also dilutes these traits in a series of Sherlock Holmes tales where suburbs—rather than any phantasm—mystify the master sleuth himself. Chapter 3 examines a number of these tales, principal among them *The Sign of Four,* which finds a colonial officer murdered in his suburban lodge. Holmes tracks the suspects—primitive savage and urban poor alike—to the slums of darkest London. But there he discovers the murdered officer was avenged for building his home with loot stolen from India. Addressing the colonial origins of suburban wealth, my reading ultimately focuses on the cultural status of the retired colonial officer, whom popular discourse constructed as both a suburban type and an agent of degeneracy.

Chapter 4 takes us to the Malay Archipelago of Joseph Conrad's first novel, *Almayer's Folly.* I argue that Almayer's grandiose home mirrors the poor construction and rapid decay that often characterized suburban dwellings and that the protomodernist Almayer is an amalgam of two suburban types—the speculative builder and the lower-middle-class clerk. Since the folly owes its existence to Almayer's misguided speculations about British interests, Conrad connects the expansionist mandate of modern imperialism to the poor planning and waste of suburban sprawl. Unlike critics who read colonial fiction as exporting England's rural heritage abroad, I situate outposts like Almayer's folly amid the global expansion of urban modernity, arguing that suburbanization offered Conrad a domestic analogue for critiquing imperial progress. Such critiques return home to Britain in the Edwardian era, particularly in the aftermath of the Boer War, when suburbia overtook the urban "abyss" as a defining social problem. Chapter 5 examines Edwardian social commentary and Condition-of-England novels that depict imperialism as exacerbating racial degeneracy at home and reducing England to a suburban cemetery. Augured by the decay of Almayer's folly and Holmes's inquiries into suburban wealth, Forster's *Howards End* and Wells's *Tono-Bungay* feature tycoons whose colonial ventures lead to the degenerate suburbanization of their country homes. It is a process that transforms the countryside itself into a sprawling suburban cemetery.

If Part Two uses the heading "Façades" to expose the myth of suburbia's regenerative imperial fantasies from the 1890s through the Edwardian era, Part Three uses the heading "Semi-Detachment" to join two distinct historical phenomena of the 1920s and 1930s: the impending end of empire and the suburb's colonization of Britain. Chapter 6 argues that late-imperial fiction—notably Forster's *A Passage to India*—attempts to detach Britain from its imperial possessions by disparaging white colonial communities as unforgivably suburban. Planning principles derived from the Edwardian era not only reshaped colonial cities like New Delhi and reinforced racial divisions but also exerted themselves on the content and form of late-imperial fiction. Obsessed with replicating middle-class spaces in their civil stations and clubs, late-imperial communities are incapacitated by nostalgia. Rather than ecstatic reminiscence or elegiac melancholy, however, this nostalgia manifests itself in the impotent outrage of *ressentiment,* under whose shadow the urban planning designed to prolong imperial rule became instrumental to British detachment from its colonies.

My discussion of George Orwell in chapter 7 shows why this detachment was impossible and why Britain's relation to its colonies would remain, at best, semi-detached. Orwell's suburban males in *Keep the Aspidistra Flying* and *Coming Up for Air* are neither the degenerate colonizers nor the primitive savages that populate this study. Subjected to feelings of dispossession and enslavement, and fearing the invasion of their homeland by Nazis, Orwell's suburban men are English avatars of the colonized. Orwell attempts to inspire middle-class socialism by equating capitalist exploitation at home with colonization abroad. Like the previous chapter this one engages the moment when the most intense suburban growth coincides with the onset of imperial decline. But rather than disavowing British colonies, suburbia here colonizes English men.

I conclude with an epilogue on Hanif Kureishi's *The Buddha of Suburbia*, a postcolonial bildungsroman whose mixed-race protagonist embodies the suburb's national and imperial hybridity. The seeming novelty of Kureishi's premise—an Indian immigrant's English-born son, raised in suburbia—reflects the long-standing and intimate history between suburb and empire that I trace throughout the study. Though *Buddha* seems to subvert essentialisms of all stripes, its protagonist's suburban origins continue to structure his behavior and disposition with unequaled power and persistence. If Karim eludes racial essentialism by fleeing the suburbs, his suburban background remains the unbreakable core of his identity, offering a striking commentary on the suburb's continued colonization of Britain in the postcolonial era.

2

Reverse Colonization in *The War of the Worlds*

In the spring of 1895 H. G. Wells moved from London some twenty-five miles southwest, to the Surrey village of Woking. At the age of twenty-nine the former draper's apprentice and schoolteacher had already published two science textbooks as well as a host of literary reviews and scientific articles, mostly unsigned. With the impending release of *The Time Machine* and the prospect of future contracts, Wells felt, as he later put it, "fairly launched as an author" (*Experiment* 447). For the next year and a half, he "lived very happily and industriously" in Woking (*Experiment* 458), where he composed two of his most famous works: *The Invisible Man* (1897) and *The War of the Worlds* (1898). Woking and its environs figure significantly in the latter novel, not merely as the setting for the initial alien invasion but as the reputed inspiration for the Martian attack. According to Wells, it was while strolling through Woking with his brother Frank—they were supposedly discussing the European extermination of the Tasmanians—that Frank entertained a similar fate befalling the British: "Suppose some beings from another planet were to drop out of the sky suddenly . . . and begin laying about [us] here!" (qtd. in Bergonzi 124). The idea of aliens in Woking immediately took hold of Wells, whose latest hobby—bicycling—allowed him to plot their attack in minute topographical detail: "Later on I wheeled about the district marking down suitable places and people for destruction by my Martians" (*Experiment* 458).

Anecdotes of literary inspiration are often suspect, and this one is no exception. For one thing *The War of the Worlds* drew on ideas about human evolution and extraterrestrial life that had occupied Wells from at least 1885 (Hughes and Geduld 1). Moreover, his early science journalism provided drafts for some of the novel's most famous set pieces. Even the sibling discussion about Tasmanians, now de rigueur in accounts of the novel's origin, was a source of subsequent uncertainty for Wells.[1] Nevertheless, with its image of the author scouting attack sites around Woking, the anecdote foregrounds a hallmark of Wellsian realism: its specific attention to geographical locale. While *The War of the Worlds* has long been read as a critique of Britain's global supremacy, however, little has been said about its preoccupation with English place. The anecdote above usefully reasserts the role of the local in Wells's global musings, then, reminding us that while his novel may have been motivated by British exploits overseas, Wells imagined their consequences being revisited on a carefully plotted terrain between Woking and London. But this terrain did more than "inspire" *The War of the Worlds* or provide a realistic backdrop for the novel's fantastic plot. In this chapter I read Woking's rapid transformation from sleepy rural village to burgeoning London suburb as the material foundation for Wells's imaginary Martian attack. *The War of the Worlds* would have been unthinkable to Wells, I suggest, if not for the rise of suburbia. In turn we cannot fully appreciate the novel's most characteristic images and formal qualities without considering either the impact of suburban development on turn-of-the-century British consciousness or the prevalence of suburbia's discursive motifs within the popular imaginary.[2] Moreover, as I will suggest in concluding, the Martian invasion provided Wells a point of departure for his more overt analyses of urban growth and social organization in the fiction and social criticism that follows *The War of the Worlds*.

The suburban landscape between Woking and London thus offers a point of critical reentry into the novel, particularly by clarifying its significance as a narrative of reverse colonization. Illuminating as they are, readings of reverse colonization in *The War of the Worlds* fail to resolve the novel's vacillations between anti-imperialism and racism. While most critics tend to champion Wells's novel as a critique of imperial hubris, some also note that "a thinly concealed racialism underlies . . . the depiction of the Martians" (Arata 109).[3] On the one hand, then, the Martians' superior intelligence, efficient physiology, and technological advancements challenge the global supremacy of Wells's late-nineteenth-century readers, disabusing them of what the novel's narrator calls their apparent "empire over matter" and their naive presumption that beings from Mars would be "inferior to themselves and ready to welcome a missionary enterprise" (3). Yet this position is undermined by the aliens' absolute otherness, which the narrator and his fellow Britons articulate in the commonplaces of colonial discourse. Hence the Martians' landed cylinders are compared with poison darts in human flesh (36, 181), the otherworldly red weed that flourishes in their wake is a "tropical exuberance" (146), and the grotesque alien body with its "oily brown skin" leads one onlooker to describe the Martians as "ugly *brutes!*" (20, 23, original emphasis). From the former perspective Wells challenges the hegemonic assumptions of his audience; from the latter he blunts this anti-imperialism and reverts into an alarmist xenophobe, implicitly depicting Britain's colonized as inherently primitive, threatening, and vengeful.

But we can resolve this tension if we see it not as a reflection of Wells's ambivalence regarding imperialism, but as Wells's rendering of the contradictions inherent in suburban identity itself. As I argue in the previous chapter, suburb dwellers were imagined simultaneously as pioneers whose settlement of new worlds could regenerate a race in decline and as degenerate savages colonizing Britain. My claim in this chapter is that Wells's Martians embody this fundamental split in suburban identity. Wells thus uses the motif of reverse colonization to articulate suburbia's ambivalent position in the British imaginary. Indeed, Woking's rapid development makes the novel's reverse colonization scenario more plausible than it might seem. If we see Wells's long-acknowledged treatment of imperialism in *The War of the Worlds* as ultimately bound to his long-ignored critique of the suburbs, the novel is less a caveat against the British colonizing the globe—and what horrors *might* be revisited on them for it— than it is a reflection of what many Britons believed *was* happening to them: that suburbia was threatening to overtake the nation with a race that fused brutal colonizers and brutish savages. Stephan Arata claims that "in Wells's invader, the late-Victorian reader could discover, distorted but recognizable, both his own face and that of the colonized Other" (109). I would restate this by suggesting that in Wells's invader the late-Victorian suburbanite could discover his own face as that of a colonizing other. Before examining the representational overlaps between suburb and empire in *The War of the Words,* however, I want to consider the novel's formal traits in relation to Woking's suburban development.

Woking and Wellsian Realism

Like most places within orbit of the largest city on earth, Woking underwent a dramatic transformation during the nineteenth century. In large part this transformation was heralded by the arrival of the train. In 1838, when the London and Southampton Railway made Woking its first terminus in Surrey, the village had fewer than six hundred residents. By 1891 almost ten thousand people lived there—the advanced rail service proving a boon to commuters—and before the turn of the century another six thousand arrived. Indeed, the 1890s were explosive years for Woking. In this decade alone the number of houses almost doubled, to over three thousand, and the drainage and sanitation problems caused by construction earned the village the nickname of Woking-in-the-Mud. With the exception of a water and gas company and a few schools, most of its public infrastructure—electric and postal service, local government, fire brigade, and cottage hospital—also emerged during the 1890s (Whiteman and Whiteman 28–40).

As part of this decade's influx, Wells took up "a small resolute semi-detached villa . . . in the Maybury Road facing the railway line, where all night long the goods trains shunted and bumped and clattered." Despite Woking's intense development and traffic, however, Wells attests that just beyond him "in all directions stretched open and undeveloped heath land" (*Experiment* 457–58). That such an experience of Woking persisted into the next decade is evident from a 1908 travelogue titled *Highways and Byways in Surrey,* part of a highly popular series on rural England published by Macmillan (Sillars 58). Like Wells its author has disparaging things to say about "the Woking of the train station, which for many years I imagined to be the only Woking in Surrey." But he goes on to claim that "there is another Woking, and it is as pretty and quiet as the railway Woking is noisy and tiresome." Venturing past "the grinding machinery of the station," he discovers that "the whole plough land was alive with gossamer; and Old Woking lay beyond the gossamer as if that magic veil were meant to shield it from the engines and smoke" (Parker 218).

As the purple prose of this passage suggests, turn-of-the-century Woking must have offered an odd juxtaposition of rural tranquility and unprecedented development. Wells virtually organizes *The War of the Worlds* around this juxtaposition, as the alien emissaries of the future invade the rural environs of London's Home Counties. Consider the narrator's description as he flees the first Martian attack in a horse cart, attempting to speed his wife to relatives in a nearby village:

> In another moment we were clear of the smoke and noise and spanking down the opposite slope of Maybury Hill toward Old Woking.
> In front was a quiet sunny landscape, a wheatfield ahead on either side of the road. . . . At the bottom of the hill I turned my head to look at the hillside I was leaving. Thick streamers of black smoke shot with threads of red fire were driving up into the still air, and throwing dark shadows upon the green tree tops eastward. The smoke already extended . . . to the Byfleet pine woods eastward, and to Woking on the west. (42)

Like *Highways and Byways in Surrey,* with its fragile veil separating agricultural and industrial Woking, this passage emphasizes the horrific proximity of two opposed orders—peace and chaos, silence and uproar, life and death. Moreover, phrases such as "in another moment" and "already," along with the recurrent gerunds ("spanking," "leaving," "driving," "throwing"), add a sense of temporal immediacy. Such rhetoric echoes throughout the novel, in a rapid unfolding of events that are quite literally earthshaking. The first cylinder crashes near Woking's Horsell Common on a Friday morning, flinging sand and gravel in piles visible over a mile away. That evening the Martians begin to unleash their heat ray on a crowd of curious onlookers. Saturday, the aliens spread their radius of destruction twenty miles from the cylinder, as the narrator views "the little world in which I had been living securely for years" as a "fiery chaos" (50): "charred and ruined villages among the green trees, [and] blackened and smoking arcades that had been but a day ago pine spinneys" (67). On Sunday, with the aid of their poisonous black smoke, the Martians advance through the Thames Valley, and although Londoners go to bed "oblivious and inert" that night, they wake Monday "to a vivid sense of danger" (81). With its institutions in chaos London undergoes a complete exodus, and by Tuesday the Martians are in full possession of the Home Counties.

Such minute attention to time and place alongside otherwise implausible circumstances remains one of Wells's primary literary legacies—the other being the "prophetic" content of his work (*The War of the Worlds* famously anticipates lasers, chemical warfare, and cybernetics). Indeed, with his reputation as a serious writer all but demolished by Henry James and Virginia Woolf, Wells now garners scant attention in matters of form and style and is remembered chiefly for grounding his fantastic scenarios in the prose of verisimilitude.[4] But rather than continue to read Wells as some inspired hack divining future worlds in realist prose, I want to underscore his departure from realism in *The War of the Worlds* and the effects of this departure on his rendering of suburban Woking's historical present.

Fredric Jameson's speculations on the role of temporality in science fiction are especially helpful in this regard, for they uncouple the genre's ostensibly future-oriented content from its formal effects. What distinguishes science fiction from other kinds of writing, Jameson argues, is that it "enacts and enables a structurally unique 'method' for apprehending the present as history" (*Archaeologies* 288). According to Jameson, science fiction took up the project of the historical novel as the latter gave way to Flaubertian modernism. As he points out, "the moment of Flaubert . . . in which the historical novel as a genre ceases to be functional, is also the moment of the emergence of [science fiction], with the first novels of Jules Verne" (*Archaeologies* 285). In this sense the genre "registers some nascent sense of the future, and does so in the space on which a sense of the past had once been inscribed." In doing so, however, science fiction for Jameson ultimately serves "not to give us 'images' of the future . . . but rather to defamiliarize and restructure our experience of our own *present,* and to do so in specific ways distinct from all other forms of defamiliarization" (*Archaeologies* 286, original emphasis). In contrast to the conventional formula whereby science fiction = realist form + futuristic content, Jameson emphasizes the genre's role in mediating an otherwise inaccessible present through "elaborate strategies of indirection." Such indirection provides readerly gratification via "distraction and displacement, repression and lateral perceptual renewal" (*Archaeologies* 287).

Before examining such defamiliarization in *The War of the Worlds,* it is worth noting the relatively straightforward way in which the novel's realist armature belies what Roland Barthes refers to as *l'effet de réel.* This is signaled by the repeated failure of journalism, science, and individual perception to understand the Martians or describe them accurately. Time and again the narrator remarks instances of faulty information in newspaper reports, telegrams, and illustrations of the Martians and acknowledges that science has yet to account for their heat rays, poisonous smoke, and even their death. And while the narrator often accuses his fellow humans of ignorance as the Martian attack unfolds, he also acknowledges his own repeated failure to perceive, describe, and remember events properly.[5]

While this resistance to realism registers itself in realist prose, another kind of straining against the premises of realism is evident in the novel's temporal structure and representation of history, which I would include among those "elaborate strategies of indirection" that defamiliarize the historical present in *The War of the Worlds.* As I've already noted, the novel is organized around a rapidly unfolding sequence of events: scene upon scene points to the nearly instantaneous destruction of the landscape, recurrently emphasizing that so much terrain has never undergone such upheaval in such a short time. "Never before in the history of warfare had destruction been so indiscriminate and so universal" (54), the narrator remarks after the first day of the attack. Such refrains are heightened by the novel's catalog of natural and man-made catastrophes: the recent extermination of the Tasmanians (5), "the earthquake that destroyed Lisbon" in 1755 (66), the torching of Moscow to defeat Napoleon (86), and the eruption of Mount Vesuvius (117). Rather than deferrals to realist convention, however, these historical events are invoked less for their similarity to the alien invasion than for a destructiveness that pales by comparison. "Never before in the history of the world had such a mass of human beings moved and suffered together," the narrator notes after the exodus of London, adding: "The

legendary hosts of Goths and Huns . . . would have been but a drop in that current" (103). Together with the novel's ubiquitous biblical allusions (to the flood,
the exodus, and the apocalypse), as well as its suggestion that humans have
reverted to animalistic and prehistoric conditions under the Martians, such references reduce all of recorded time to a period of just over a fortnight.

Recalling Jameson's remarks on the emergence of science fiction, I want
to suggest that in *The War of the Worlds* Wells recalibrates the historical novel's
epochal scale of decades and years to one of hours and moments—or col-
lapses the former within the latter. Rather than deploying the historical novel's
generational sagas and *longue durée,* Wells compresses the prosaic passage of
Time into a breathless exclamation point. It is a variation on the technique
that he made famous—and that made him famous—in *The Time Machine.*
As the Time Traveller journeys to the year 802,701, he experiences a sensation
now commonplace to us through time-lapse photography: "The palpitation of
night and day merged into one continuous greyness. . . . I saw trees growing
and changing like puffs of vapour. . . . I saw huge buildings rise up faint and
fair, and pass like dreams. The whole surface of the earth seemed changed—
melting and flowing under my eyes" (*Complete* 24). Admittedly, *The War of the
Worlds* neither invokes history nor represents time's passing with the persistent
intensity of *The Time Machine.* However, like Walter Benjamin's *Angelus Novus,*
which sees progress not as "a chain of events" but as "one single catastrophe
which keeps piling wreckage upon wreckage" (*Illuminations* 257), the Martian
attack condenses history's diachronic flow into a synchronic, apocalyptic now.

This detour on temporality in *The War of the Worlds* can return us to suburban Woking if we consider the novel's spatial representation. Jameson is again
helpful, for in a companion piece to his essay on temporality and sci-fi, he
theorizes the genre's raison d'être as an imaginative rendering of space—not
galactic, but geographic. Despite the historical insight science fiction affords,
Jameson suggests that the genre is ultimately and inherently spatial. What distinguishes it from other forms of writing and what mobilizes its unique grati-
fications is "the mediation of space itself": "a planet, a climate, a weather, and
a system of landscapes—in short, a map" (*Archaeologies* 312–13). If *The War of
the Worlds* offers a map of Victorian Woking, then Wells's nearly instantaneous
decimation of this area—unparalleled in history but made accessible (indeed,
exhilarating) through the novel's accelerated rhythms and crazy quilt of historical allusions—can be said to mediate Woking's suburban expansion over
the course of the nineteenth century. In this sense the novel's images of overturned and scattered earth, razed wilderness, mass human exodus, and monstrous forms overtaking the Thames Valley indirectly historicize the present

moment of Woking's suburban development. More than this, such images provide examples of what Jameson calls "distraction and displacement, repression and lateral perceptual renewal," transforming unprecedented rural destruction into an object of readerly pleasure. It is the same kind of pleasure I've already noted Wells experiencing when he first conceived the alien attack, as he playfully bicycled "about the district marking down suitable places and people for destruction" (*Experiment* 458). If science fiction mediates one's immediate time and place, historicizing what is not yet past—or, in spatial terms, mapping what has not completely *taken place*—then perhaps no text contemporaneous with suburban development registers that development in its very form as does *The War of the Worlds*.[6]

Wells's later writing bolsters the hypothesis that his alien attack has its formal preconditions in suburban development. In *Experiment in Autobiography*, for example, Wells writes, "It is only because the thing was spread over a hundred years and not concentrated into a few weeks that history fails to realize what sustained disaster, how much massacre, degeneration and disablement of lives, was due to the housing of London in the nineteenth century" (225). Invoking the apocalyptic rhetoric and temporal abbreviations that characterize his Martian invasion, Wells is in fact here recalling his first close encounter with London housing in late-Victorian inner suburbs like Bayswater, Notting Hill, and Kilburn. The memory launches him into a brief history of suburban development that is surprisingly in accord with recent scholarly accounts: from the "regime of unrestricted private enterprise" that emerged with the "economic expansion after the Napoleonic war," to the devising of ninety-nine-year building leases, to the construction of "rows of jerry-built unalterable homes" in which everyone "who ranked between the prosperous householder and the slum denizen . . . had to fit their lives" (*Experiment* 223–25). Likewise, in his 1911 novel *The New Machiavelli*, Wells uses the transparently autobiographical details of his narrator's youth as an entrée to discussing the rapidity of suburban development in the narrator's fictional hometown of Bromstead. Wells himself was born in Bromley, Kent, which he dubbed "a suburb of the damnedest" (qtd. in Bergonzi 23), and the narrator of *The New Machiavelli* situates his childhood at "the beginning of [Bromstead's] real suburban quality" (33): "The roads came,—horribly; the houses followed. They seemed to arise in the night. People moved into them as soon as the roofs were on . . . and already in a year some of these raw houses stood empty again from defaulting tenants." Like the accounts of Woking mentioned earlier, *The New Machiavelli* invokes the rapidity of an "invading and growing disorder" that destroyed "the serene rhythms of the old-established agriculture" (36). Wells drafted a similar elegy for the real Bromley a year before starting *The War of the Worlds*. In an 1894 piece for the *Pall Mall Gazette*, he cataloged elements of suburban blight he had just seen from the window of a passing train, trying in vain to reconcile Bromley's "degeneration" and pollution with his boyhood memories of rolling meadows and pristine watering holes. Like the narrator of *The War of the Worlds*, he was shocked by the immediacy of the destruction, asking himself, "Can it be only twenty years ago?" ("Degeneration" 3).

The British Invasion

With my initial hypothesis in place—that Woking's suburban present is formally mediated in *The War of the Worlds* through the novel's rapidly shifting rhythms and conflation of epochal time—we can now turn to the ways in which suburban development manifests itself more overtly, in terms of representation. Consider the novel's premise. As Wells's narrator points out in the opening pages, Mars's shrinking water supply and thinning atmosphere have made the planet increasingly uninhabitable—much more so than its larger "neighbor," Earth (4). Mars has also experienced a slow cooling, not only because it receives less sunlight than earth, but because it is "more distant from life's beginning [and] nearer its end." Facing extinction, the Martians thus look toward "our own warmer planet, green with vegetation and gray with water" (4). Their predicament certainly recalls those Greater Britons who emigrated to the empire's wider horizons. But it also reflects the plight of late-Victorian city dwellers who fled urban overcrowding and pollution for the open space, greenery, and fresh air of the suburbs. Like the Martians suburbanites were also imagined as the future race—one that appeared homogenous, beastly, and virtually invincible. And the advanced systems of transport that allowed both to travel long distances with unprecedented speed wrought havoc on the countryside—leveling its landscape, displacing its population, and throwing up a new civilization in its wake. The Martians spread themselves through London's suburbs, replacing the humans who reside there, and the displaced humans become increasingly urban: as Wells's narrator learns from an artilleryman, the aliens establish their main "camp" in Hampstead (153), the healthy and fashionable suburb famed as the lungs of London. Humans, on the other hand, will be forced to survive underground in urban sewers and subway tunnels. As the artilleryman says of the human survivors, "Our district will be London" (158).

The novel's reverse colonization narrative further complicates the parallels between suburb dwellers and Martians, who take on the traits of both colonizer and colonized. On the one hand, the Martians' technological and intellectual advances over humans suggest the civilized British at the pinnacle of their imperial power; on the other, the Martians' absolute inscrutability, insect- or animal-like appearance, and apparent savagery render them analogous to colonial others. As Peter Fitting points out, one of the novelties of *The War of the Worlds* is its "interest in the physical appearance and being of the alien": while fictional journeys to other worlds existed long before Wells, such texts represented extraterrestrials as humanoid (127, 131). Wells's Martians are something altogether different in appearance: oversized brains with long tentacles. Yet for all their originality the Martians still combine what imperial ideology would have seen as a mix of civilized and savage: Western intellectual prowess and non-Western bodily abjection. The tentacles serve as the most common synecdoche for the alien body, leading the narrator and others to describe Martians as "sluggish" (32, 50, 74, 92, 130) or to compare them with octopi, fungus, and blight. These primitive appendages are racially coded, as the tentacles are often described in relation to the Martians' skin color. When the narrator sees his first alien, he describes "something fungoid in the oily brown skin" (20), and when he later witnesses a Martian corpse from a distance, it is "a small brown figure" (84). The "gray-brown, shiny, leathery integument" of the aliens thus associates them with racial difference (124).

Despite Wells's originality in depicting aliens as nonhuman, then, his Martians did not drop from the sky. Indeed, while their amorphous, squid-like bodies and slimy tentacles partake of an obvious racial coding, the Martians also give animate form to long-standing representations of the suburbs that combine characteristics of monstrosity and disease. Of course, such representations were first applied to London's *urban* sprawl more than a century before Wells. Perhaps most famously, William Cobbett's "Great Wen" equated the city with a cancerous stain or swelling; similarly, Hugh Walpole described London as "shoot[ing] out every way like a polypus" (qtd. in A. Briggs 12)—this last term referring to both an octopus and a tumor. By the late nineteenth century, however, the monstrous and the diseased parts of London were increasingly its suburban "tentacles." In Arthur Conan Doyle's *The Sign of Four* (1890), which I discuss in the next chapter, Sherlock Holmes and Dr. Watson travel to the south London suburbs, where "interminable lines of new, staring brick buildings" are described as "the monster tentacles which the giant city was throwing out into the country" (*Complete* 99). A year later Sidney Low would reinforce this image in "The Rise of the Suburbs," suggesting that with London's population "shifting from the heart to the limbs," the suburbs might become "the long arms of brick and mortar and cheap stucco" that strangle the Home Counties (550). By the turn of the century, the Liberal politician C. F. G. Masterman imagined

suburbia as "some gigantic plasmodium: spreading slimy arms over the surrounding fields" (*Peril* 165). The *Building News* dubbed London's suburban
sprawl a "fungus-like growth" (qtd. in Olsen 201), while in *Life and Labour of
the People in London,* Charles Booth declared the "huge Metropolitan suburb"
of south London as "invertebrate in character" (2: 391). Wells perpetuated this
discourse himself. The protagonist of his 1911 New Woman novel *Ann Veronica*
lives in "a suburb that had not altogether . . . come off," and among the dispiriting images that drive her toward London are her neighborhood's villas, which
look "like a bright fungoid growth" (4). Descriptions of this kind were ubiquitous in years to come, as suggested by the very titles of Clough Williams-Ellis's
screeds against sprawl—his 1928 book *England and the Octopus* and the 1938
collection *Britain and the Beast.* The latter contains a number of descriptions
that uncannily recall Wells's Martian attack. One writer indicts developers for
"defac[ing] the river valleys" of rural England and "destroy[ing] the pillars of
the trees" to build homes for "aliens incursive into the Home Counties" (W. B.
Thomas 211). Another contributor seems to take his image of suburbia directly
from *The War of the Worlds:* "The electric grid strides across the hill-sides. A
gimcrack civilization crawls like a gigantic slug over the country, leaving a foul
train of slime behind it" (Marshall 164).

As this last image reminds us, Wells's portrayal of the suburban Martians
does not merely link their primordial bodies with Britain's racial others. For
these bodies are housed within the metallic, mechanical tripods that serve as
Martian vehicles and prostheses. Confounding any easy distinction between
primitive and modern, these tripods suggest the futuristic technology of a
superior military power at the same time as their frequent comparison with
spiders and crabs recalls the Martians' octopus-like anatomy (123–24). More
importantly, however, Wells uses the imperial connotations of these tripods to
figure suburban expansion. Note the narrator's first sighting of a tripod upon
returning in a hailstorm to the battle scene, after shuttling his wife to relatives.
His initial impression of the "walking engine" is significant: "At first I took it
for the wet roof of a house," he claims, but flashes of lightning reveal the "swift
rolling movement" of a metallic monster, "higher than many houses, striding
over the young pine trees and smashing them aside in its career. . . . Then suddenly the trees in the pine wood ahead of me were parted, as brittle reeds are
parted by a man thrusting through them; they were snapped off and driven
headlong; and a second huge tripod appeared" (45–46). With the first tripod
taking shape in the form of a house, and joining the second to level the surrounding landscape, these structures body forth the kind of "distraction and
displacement, repression and lateral perceptual renewal," that characterize sci-fi

London going out of Town — or — The March of Bricks & Mortar! —

Figure 2. Suburban development as military invasion. (George Cruikshank, "London Going Out of Town—Or—The March of Bricks and Mortar!" *Scraps and Sketches,* 1829)

for Jameson (*Archaeologies* 287). Fusing the novel's instantaneous rural decimation and reverse colonization tropes with an optical illusion of residential growth, the tripods serve as otherworldly surrogates for the suburban development invading Britain.

In doing so, these tripods—"boilers on stilts," as one horrified onlooker describes them (78)—go some way toward domesticating the seemingly primitive aliens by recalling a number of earlier personifications of suburban development. For example, George Cruikshank's 1829 etching "London Going Out of Town—Or—The March of Bricks and Mortar!" often taken for a caricature of industrialization, focuses more directly on the residential development of London's then-inner suburbs (fig. 2). Cruikshank depicts an army of machine-like figures advancing on the fields of Islington from the direction of St. Paul's Cathedral. Brandishing pipes, ladders, and planks, these figures sport boilers for torsos, spades and pickaxes for limbs, trowels for hands, and hods of mortar for heads. Rows of identical terraces labeled "To Let" rise alongside the army as smoke billows overhead, an advanced detachment digs foundations and uproots trees, and a kiln spews a sinister rainbow of hot bricks toward fleeing animals and haystacks.[7] The battalion leader plants a sign, parallel with two Union Jacks flying in the center, that declares, "This ground to be let on a building lease." The placement of this sign near the flags is telling, for while the Union Jacks seem to provide the countryside with a last line of defense against the suburban invasion, they also figure this onslaught as the new form British civilization will take.

By the mid-nineteenth century such images of suburban invasion would become commonplace. In *Household Words* George Sala describes suburban development as "The Great Invasion"; its leaders are "Brigadier Bricks and Field-Marshal Mortar," and its "weapons of offense" are "scaffold poles and bricklayers' hods" (69). More famously, Charles Dickens and Wilkie Collins would integrate such images into their fiction. In *Dombey and Son* (1846–48) Dickens describes one suburb as "neither of the town nor country. The former, like the giant in his traveling boots, has made a stride and passed it, and has set his brick-and-mortar heel a long way in advance" (555). This imagery reemerges in Wilkie Collins's *Hide and Seek* (1854), a novel dedicated to Dickens, which depicts suburban building as a military invasion of mythic proportion:

> Alexander's armies were great makers of conquests . . . but the modern Guerrilla regiments of the hod, the trowel, and the brick-kiln are the greatest conquerors of all; for they hold the longest the soil that they have once possessed. How mighty the devastation which follows in the wake of these tremendous aggressors, as they march through the kingdom of nature, triumphantly bricklaying beauty wherever they go! What dismantled castle, with the enemy's flag flying over its crumbling walls, ever looked so utterly forlorn as a poor field-fortress of nature, imprisoned on all sides by the walled camp of the enemy, and degraded by a hostile banner of pole and board, with the conqueror's device inscribed on it—"THIS GROUND TO BE LET ON BUILDING LEASES?" (15–16, original emphasis)

Like *Hide and Seek*, which clearly echoes Cruikshank, the *Westminster Review*'s 1866 article "Commons Round London" depicts speculative builders as a vanguard of invasion into the countryside. Their "main army is preceded by an advance of villas, thrown out like skirmishers." Though only "seizing a few picked positions" at first, they are soon reinforced by "the more solid ranks of the semi-detached, forming in continuous lines along the high roads and in the neighbourhood of railway stations" (217). Wells's originality in *The War of the Worlds* involves not only synthesizing such anthropomorphized icons of suburban development into a new form of extraterrestrial, but organizing an entire narrative around them—one that uses the genre of scientific romance to imagine suburban development in terms of reverse colonization.

Breaking Ground

Given the discursive foundations on which Wells constructed *The War of the Worlds,* it is no surprise to see him depicting the colonizing aliens as gargantuan house builders. This link is suggested quite early, when the narrator notes the "hammering" that lasts "all night long" after the first capsule crashes (36; also see 39); as we soon learn, the Martians are working on one of the tripods that the narrator misapprehends for a house. This hammering resumes later in the novel—significantly, after the fifth cylinder falls upon "a small semi-detached villa" in which the narrator and a curate first sought shelter as they approached London. Though they had just left this villa for a larger and more secure residence nearby ("a white house within a walled garden"), the cylinder's impact is enough to bury them (119). The men remain holed up beneath the rubble until they notice "a metallic hammering" and a sound "like the hissing of an engine" (121). As he makes his way to the edge of a large pit, the narrator discovers that "the fifth cylinder must have fallen right into the midst of the house we first visited." Completely obliterated, the semi-detached house is replaced by the Martian cylinder, which "lay now far beneath the original foundations" (123). Such images will be echoed in Wells's subsequent accounts of suburban development, as in *The New Machiavelli* and its narrator's "childish memories . . . of digging and wheeling, of woods invaded by building, roads gashed open and littered with iron pipes amidst a fearful smell of gas, of men peeped at and seen toiling away deep down in excavations" (34).

As if privy to a defamiliarized image of suburban development itself, the narrator and curate view an alien construction site emerging below the foundation of the semi-detached home in which they hide. Of particular interest to them are the "handling machines" with which the Martians excavate earth, maneuver large objects, and construct other mechanisms. Anticipating heavy machinery like bulldozers and cranes, Wells describes "a busy little digging mechanism," whose "excavating and embarking" causes "the rhythmic shocks that had kept our ruinous refuge quivering" (130). When he emerges from the house's wreckage after fifteen days of hiding, the narrator punctuates the correlation between the Martians' building and suburban development by linking them to the novel's reverse colonization motif. Taking in the destruction of the scene around him, he claims: "For that moment I touched an emotion beyond the common range of men, yet one that the poor brutes we dominate know only too well. I felt as a rabbit might feel returning to his burrow and suddenly confronted by the work of a dozen busy navvies digging the foundation of a house." Anticipating the overt descriptions of residential construction in *The New Machiavelli,* the scene casts suburban development as a form of invasion that overturns British imperial hubris. Indeed, the narrator not only sympathizes with "the poor brutes we dominate." He also feels "oppressed" by "a sense of dethronement, a persuasion that I was no longer a master," and a feeling that the "empire of man had passed away" (145).

At the same time as the mammoth Martian construction site transforms the narrator from master to slave, oppressor to oppressed, it also figures him and the curate as temporary home owners fascinated by their disruptive if intriguing new neighbors. Wells implies as much by casting the narrator and curate as a squabbling family unit in miniature—the narrator calls his cowardly companion both "a silly woman" and a "spoiled child" (132)—and their interest in the Martians suggests a form of neighborly snooping.[8] Despite their fear of being seen at the kitchen lookout, the narrator admits that "the attraction of peeping was for both of us irresistible. . . . We would race across the kitchen in a grotesque way between eagerness and the dread of making a noise, and strike each other and thrust and kick within a few inches of exposure" (131). Like the comparison between Martians and house builders, the analogy between Martians and next-door neighbors is established early on, after the landing of the first cylinder: as the narrator's own neighbor offers him a handful of strawberries over his garden fence, he complains of the new settlers that "it's a pity they make themselves so unapproachable" (37). If those first Martians seem no more than eccentric outsiders to the rest of the street, however, their fellow invaders eventually displace the residents of the former community. While the whole first book of *The War of the Worlds* depicts this displacement on a larger scale, we also see it in condensed form when the narrator returns to his peephole after a long absence, discovering that the Martian "newcomers" who crashed near his temporary dwelling have been "reinforced by the occupants of no fewer than three of the fighting machines" (132). Recalling the imagery of Cruikshank and Wilkie Collins, the narrator describes the recent domestic construction for these neighbors ("newcomers" and "occupants") as a form of military invasion ("reinforced" with "fighting machines").

Spying one of the "appliances" that their figurative neighbors are engaged in building, the narrator describes what looks like "a milk can" with "a pear-shaped receptacle," into which the Martians pour a "white powder" (132–33). From this machine they extrude aluminum bars, apparently material for further construction; but the narrator's gastronomic language also sets up the scene that immediately follows, of aliens feeding on "a stout ruddy middle-aged man" (134). The narrator has already explained to us that the aliens "took the fresh living blood of other creatures and *injected* it into their own veins" (125, original emphasis), so their consumption of the man is not our first exposure to their vampirism. But by juxtaposing this account of the Martian mode of feeding with the preceding depictions of aliens as house builders and neighbors, Wells here casts suburban expansion as a monstrous form of parasitism.

This association is captured in one of the novel's central images: the red vegetation that sprouts in the Martians' wake and transforms the suburban landscape into a veritable jungle. As we have already seen, both suburbia in general and Wells's Martians in particular were depicted as mixing the organic (monstrosity, disease, fungus) and the industrial (bricks and mortar, as well as glittering metal and black smoke). This combination also underlies the red vegetation, for when the narrator "gnaw[s] some fronds" of it in desperation late in the novel, he is disgusted by its "sickly, metallic taste" (147). Informed no doubt by Mars's status as the red planet, the red weed and its metallic flavor not only combine the organic and industrial but also recall the vampiric tendencies of the Martians themselves. Significantly, however, red is also the color most often associated with suburban housing. C. F. G. Masterman, whose 1909 book *The Condition of England* provided the most sustained analysis of the suburbs to that point, refers to them as "red tentacles, the slums of the future—little red terraces" (*Peril* 156). The image persists well into twentieth-century fiction: the "red rust" that creeps toward the country house of Forster's *Howards End* (240); "the red suburban stain which fouls the fields" near the rural estate in Rebecca West's *Return of the Soldier* (9); the "straggling red suburb" one character views from an airplane before vomiting in Evelyn Waugh's *Vile Bodies* (284); and "the little red roofs where the bombs are going to drop" in Orwell's *Coming Up for Air* (22). So when Wells's narrator emerges from the house in which he has hidden from the Martians for fifteen days, the ubiquity of red weeds suggests that suburban colonization has taken root in British soil. As so often throughout the novel, the narrator notes the abrupt change of the surroundings: the "straggling street of comfortable white and red houses, interspersed with abundant shady trees," has now become "a mound of smashed brickwork, clay and gravel over which spread a multitude of red cactus-shaped plants, knee-high, without a solitary terrestrial growth to dispute their footing." Like the parasitic suburbs that transformed English fields into a landscape of red rust, an otherworldly jungle, the Martian weed continues to feed on the remains of the host it replaces. Thus, the narrator sees the weed "gr[owing] tumultuously in [the] roofless rooms" of abandoned homes and "cover[ing] every scrap of unoccupied ground" (144). But it is also worth recalling here that the color red, signifier of suburbia, was likewise the color used to designate Britain's colonial possessions on late nineteenth- and early twentieth-century maps. Given the consistent linking of suburban expansion and reverse colonization in *The War of the Worlds,* the red weeds suggest suburbia results not in the healthy spread of British civilization, but in the transformation of Britain itself into colonized territory. An instance of the "elaborate strategies of indirection" that Jameson considers unique to sci-fi, the Martian red weed provides the "lateral perceptual renewal" required to see the suburban present from the vantage of future imperial decline and the colonization of Britain itself (*Archaeologies* 287).

As I have done with much of *The War of the Worlds,* I am reading the red weeds and their suggestions of vampirism in light of Wells's later work, where suburbia emerges as an overtly parasitic form of community. Following the virtual destruction of modern civilization in *The War in the Air* (1908), for example, the protagonist's semirural community returns from its "habits of suburban parasitism to what no doubt had been the normal life of humanity for nearly immemorial years, a life of homely economies in the most intimate contact with cows and hens and patches of ground" (244). It is precisely such "homely economies" that the suburbs obviated. But unlike most commentators who lodged similar complaints, Wells did not seek to return to the communities of the past. In the appendix to his 1903 social tract *Mankind in the Making,* originally presented as a paper to the Fabian society, Wells argues that London needs to be reconceived as a single regional unit encompassing virtually all of southeast England. What necessitated this larger scale was the development of new modes of "locomotion," especially the railroad. Before the railroad, villages, boroughs, and even whole counties "were practically complete minor economic systems" in themselves (376). But rail brought about a "steadily increasing proportion of people—more especially in our suburban areas—who are, so far as our old divisions go, *delocalized*" (380, original emphasis). The question for Wells was not whether the process of delocalization would continue: as if invoking *The War of the Worlds,* he claims "the stars in their courses" assured it (383). Since "the available means of locomotion" almost completely determined "the distribution of population," it followed that any "improvement in locomotion forces the suburban ring of houses outward" (378–79). The question was whether societies and governments would adapt themselves to the forces of delocalization. They could do so, Wells argued, by developing larger regional units, so that expanding suburbs would not continue to feed on "the dwindling, little, highly localized communities of the past" (380). I discuss Wells's arguments about administrative areas more fully in chapter 5. Here it is simply worth noting that for Wells England's suburban classes were, like the Martians, not only "delocalized," having migrated from somewhere else; they also exhibited vampiric tendencies by feeding on the carcass of England's older local communities: "Every tramway, every new twopenny tube, every light railway, every improvement in your omnibus services . . . increases the proportion of your delocalized class, and sucks the ebbing life from your old communities into the veins of the new" (*Mankind* 383). Just as Wells had imagined his Martians feeding on the remains of England's green and pleasant land, so too would he see suburbia as a parasite on the rural societies at the foundation of British culture.

"A Sort of Outlanders"

In the same address to his Fabian colleagues, Wells described the vampiric suburb dwellers who were his subject as "a sort of Outlanders" (*Mankind* 381). The English equivalent of *Uitlanders,* an Afrikaans term for British settlers in South Africa, Wells's Boer War–era designation offers a fitting description of suburb dwellers, one that registers their dual status as both British and foreign colonizers. While Wells articulates Martian otherness via racialized colonial discourse, I have been arguing that the Martians ultimately represent a form of suburban parasitism that is, in the end, British. Note, for instance, that the scenes of Martians injecting themselves with human blood are framed by the equally parasitic behavior of the narrator and curate. Raiding various houses for whatever scraps the fleeing owners left behind, the narrator and curate watch the Martians from the kitchen and scullery of a neighboring home—the only rooms to survive the crash of the Martian cylinder. In doing so, the narrator and curate serve as a more domesticated version of the Martians, whose crash landing on the site of a semi-detached home suggests that the Martians represent a defamiliarized version of suburbia itself.

One moment in *The War of the Worlds* reinforces these claims and synthesizes the concerns I have been discussing in this chapter, combining the novel's formal mediations of a suburban present with its less oblique links between imperial and suburban discourse. In a scene reminiscent of the juxtapositions of rural peace and urban tumult that I addressed earlier, the narrator attempts to return home after fleeing the chaos of the first Martian heat-ray attack. Having blacked out, he now finds himself in a secluded wayside—unable to recollect how he arrived there or to reconcile the horrific attack he just witnessed with the serenity of his current surroundings: "Now it was as if something turned over, and the point of view altered abruptly. There was no sensible transition from one state of mind to the other" (30–31). In this confused condition the narrator witnesses a curious site: "Over the Maybury Arch a train, a billowing tumult of white firelit smoke and a long caterpillar of lighted windows, went flying south—clatter, clatter, clap, rap, and it was gone. A dim group of people talked in the gate of one of the houses in the pretty little row of gables that was called Oriental Terrace. It was all so real and so familiar. And that behind me! It was fantastic! Such things, I told myself, could not be" (31).

The passage wavers between comparison and contrast, similarity and difference, and in so doing embodies the paradox at the heart of semi-detachment. While the passing railway and the congregation of neighbors together suggest quotidian normality, the description also juxtaposes the speeding, clattering train with the quiet street. At the same time the description conjures a visual parallel: "the pretty little row of gables" is an echo of the train's horizontal form, and the train's "long caterpillar of lighted windows" fuses the imagery of primitive tentacles and modern mechanization characteristic of Wells's Martians and suburban discourse more generally. Indeed, the train's presence here recalls the historical importance of the railway to the suburbanization of Woking, as well as to the process of suburban delocalization Wells describes in *Mankind in the Making*. Since the narrator associates the train's noise and tumult, its fire and smoke, with the Martian heat-ray attack he has just fled, the train's visual similarity to the row of houses casts these seemingly benign neighbors as an unsettling analogue to the alien invaders.

Central to the scene above, of course, is that "pretty little row of gables that was called Oriental Terrace." While this exact locale is fictional, there was both an Oriental Place and an Oriental Parade along Woking's Maybury Hill, close to where Wells lived, in the 1890s (Hughes and Geduld 231–32). The names are derived from Woking's Oriental Institute, established in 1884 by the linguist Gottlieb Wilhelm Leitner. Seeking to make the institute Britain's center for Eastern cultures and languages, Leitner had a mosque built there in 1889 in the hopes of attracting Hindu and Muslim students to reside on its grounds. Funded by Her Highness the Begum Shah Jehan of Bhopal, this became known as the Shah Jehan Mosque, and its dome caused something of a local uproar: the *Building News* reported that many in Woking felt "domes are only admissible over tombs and commemorative monuments" (qtd. in Naylor and Ryan 45).[9] In a gesture that seems to echo these concerns, Wells has the Martians destroy the buildings: "The pinnacle of the mosque had vanished, and the roof line of the [Oriental] college itself looked as if a hundred-ton gun had been at work upon it" (40). At the same time the destruction of the college and mosque suggests that it is no longer the presence of real colonial others that threatens the sanctity of semirural Woking, but the residents of Oriental Terrace.

By collapsing the alien, the imperial, and the suburban, the passage above suggests that even pleasant residential suburbs threaten to become destructive and alien and that the suburban attempt to mimic imperial expansion can itself threaten England with a degenerate colonization. The rant by the artilleryman with whom the narrator lodges near the novel's end seems to confirm this claim. Preparing for a future rebellion against the Martians, the artilleryman compares the complacent suburban residents who will be fodder for alien enslavement with the Martians themselves. Fuming at "the sort of people that lived in these houses, and all those damn little clerks" who "haven't any spirit in them . . . running wild and shining to catch their little season-ticket train," the artilleryman implicitly parallels them with the Martians he has seen "hurrying, hurrying— puffing and blowing and hooting to their other mechanical affairs" (156, 159).

These parallels between Martians and suburbanites have striking implications for Wells's reverse colonization narrative when considered alongside Jameson's argument that science fiction "transform[s] our own present into the determinate past of something yet to come" (*Archaeologies* 288). In the novel's opening pages Wells views the present from a future that has seen British imperial hegemony turned inside out. Looking back on "the last years of the nineteenth century" from some as yet undetermined vantage point, the narrator can chide the "infinite complacency" with which "men went to and fro over this globe . . . serene in their assurance of their empire over matter" (3) and indict the "ruthless and utter destruction our own species has wrought . . . upon its own inferior races" (5). He can do so in part because he looks back on the present from a future that has seen Britain colonized by Martians—a future virtually unthinkable for Wells's readers.

What does this perspective teach the narrator? Near the end of *The War of the Worlds*, as he returns to his abandoned home, he enters the small study where he worked busily on the day that the first Martian cylinder landed. A speculative philosopher, he had been drafting a paper "on the probable development of Moral Ideas with the development of the civilizing process," and his last written line was an uncompleted prophecy: "'In about two hundred years . . . we may expect—' The sentence ended abruptly" (177). The narrator finds his unfinished prediction a fitting tribute to the Martian invasion, about which he claims so little has been adequately explained. Despite the questions that remain unanswered about the Martians, however, the narrator suggests that they have taught humanity one important lesson: "that we cannot regard this planet as being fenced in" and that we must therefore "promote a conception of the commonweal of mankind" (181). The scene anticipates the role that Wells himself would soon take up as a professional prognosticator after the turn of the century in books like *Anticipations* and *Mankind in the Making*, and the lesson described by his narrator sounds something like Wells's own later call to unify formerly divisive nations and empires into a single World State. But Wells's warning against planetary parochialism—"that we cannot regard this planet as being fenced in"—is also indicative of his emerging sense that, rather than trying simply to contain unchecked and wasteful suburban sprawl, future communities must be organized on a larger scale. Since the countryside, like Earth itself, was no longer cordoned off, Wells suggested that an entirely new organizational scheme was necessary. It would not be until the Edwardian era, however, that this form of community would take clearer shape in his writing.

PART TWO
Façades

3

Sherlock Holmes and the Case
of the Anglo-Indian

Arthur Conan Doyle's *The Sign of Four* offers a fitting approach to the sub-urban façade. In this, their second adventure together, Holmes and Watson aid Miss Mary Morstan, a client seeking information on the whereabouts of her disappeared father. Whisked via carriage through the "torturous by-streets" south of the Thames, an enamored Watson babbles to Miss Morstan while Holmes calls out the names of each road they pass, fearing aloud that "our quest does not appear to take us to very fashionable regions." Yet Watson is soon awed by their surroundings: "We had indeed reached a questionable and forbidding neighborhood. Long lines of dull brick houses were only relieved by the coarse glare and tawdry brilliance of public-houses at the corner. Then came rows of two-storied villas, each with a fronting of miniature garden, and then again interminable lines of new, staring brick buildings—the monster tentacles which the giant city was throwing out into the country." The mysterious carriage ride ends as they arrive at "the third house in a new terrace." Before they can knock, the door is "instantly thrown open by a Hindoo servant, clad in a yellow turban, white loose-fitting clothes, and a yellow sash." As Watson puts it, "There was something strangely incongruous in this Oriental figure framed in the commonplace doorway of a third-rate suburban dwelling-house" (99–100).[1]

It is an exemplary Holmesian set piece, which one critic claims "might serve as a visual analogue for the entire Holmes canon in which the exotic is repeatedly framed or contained by the familiar and homely" (McLaughlin 58). But this façade does not quite exemplify familiarity and homeliness. Situated at the indiscernible nexus of country, city, and slum, it seems as strangely incongruous to its environs as the Hindu servant within. Thus, the smug indifference with which Holmes begins his foray into the Surrey-side suburbs ("our quest does not appear to take us to very fashionable regions") belies what he discovers there. Directed past the "sordid and common passage, ill-lit and worse furnished," Holmes, Watson, and Miss Morstan enter a chamber decked luxuriously in Eastern exotica: "The richest and glossiest of curtains and tapestries draped the walls, looped back here and there to expose some richly mounted painting or Oriental vase. The carpet was of amber and black, so soft and so thick that the foot sank pleasantly into it, as into a bed of moss. Two great tiger-skins thrown athwart it increased the suggestion of Eastern luxury, as did a huge hookah which stood upon a mat in the corner. A lamp in the fashion of a silver dove was hung from an almost invisible golden wire in the centre of the room. As it burned it filled the air with a subtle and aromatic odour" (100). This is the "little sanctum" of Thaddeus Sholto, a sickly aesthete who knows the fate of Miss Morstan's father. According to Thaddeus, his room is "an oasis of art in the howling desert of South London" (100).[2] "I am a man of somewhat retiring, and I might even say refined, tastes," he confides, offering his guests Chianti and Tokay and displaying original works by Corot and Bouguereau (101). Not only are Holmes's expectations of this seemingly unfashionable suburb shattered, but Sholto rivals Holmes himself in connoisseurship and taste.[3]

If the orientalist decor behind this third-rate façade reflects suburbia's strange incongruity in Victorian epistemologies of place, then Sholto's poor health troubles the belief that suburbs could spur the racial regeneration associated with the empire. In chapter 1 I argued that emigration to Greater Britain, which offered a healthy alternative to degenerate metropolitan existence, in turn shaped the identity of Greater London, the suburban belt beyond the city's municipal boundaries. Doyle himself made much of these parallels in *Beyond the City: The Idyll of a Suburb* (1892). An uncharacteristic comedy of manners, the novel is set in a Greater London neighborhood whose inhabitants—a retired admiral, his stockbroker son, their suffragette neighbor, and her orphaned nephew—all claim respectable ties to the empire.[4] Seeming as close as possible to colonial emigration while still remaining in Britain, *Beyond the City* echoes Sidney Low's "The Rise of the Suburbs" as a virtual encomium to the regenerative potential of suburban Greater London.

Yet as in *The Sign of Four*, where Doyle suggests a darker side to this idyll of suburban and imperial expansion, Low too implied that suburbia might be a locus of mystery and fear. Though he would ultimately champion suburbia as a site for regenerating an imperial race in decline, I have shown hints of a more ambivalent relationship between suburb and empire in Low's account, in which suburban residents take on the qualities usually reserved for England's urban underclass and colonial others—in particular criminality and primitivism.

Low's inquiry into the relation between suburbs and imperial health found a contemporaneous fictional analogue in Doyle's detective tales, particularly *The Sign of Four*. Like Low's article the novel considers whether suburban expansion reflects an invigorated Greater Britain or the degeneracy of darkest London. Doyle initially suggests that the suburb is besieged by the combined threat of the urban poor and colonial other. Most critics conclude that Holmes successfully eradicates this threat, "purging . . . the novel's 'wild, dark' Indian elements from its national and narrative borders" (Mehta 635) and "vanquish[ing] the exotic but violent element of the Orient within Victorian England" (J. Thompson 72).[5] In what follows I suggest that Doyle offers a less reassuring picture of Holmes's powers. Holmes traces a suburban crime to the slums of darkest London, only to reveal its ultimate source in the figure of the retired Anglo-Indian, whom popular discourse constructed as both a typical denizen of suburbia and a cause of physical, moral, and national degeneration.[6]

The Suburban Façade

Even for readers as divergent as T. S. Eliot and Raymond Williams, Sherlock Holmes is virtually synonymous with the "pleasant externals" of late-Victorian London (Eliot, "Books" 553). We all know the nostalgic clichés: "the fog, the gaslight, the hansom cabs, the street urchins," and the solitary figure "who can penetrate the intricacies of the streets" (Williams, *Country* 227). Looking beyond the city, we may recall Holmes wending his way over rugged gothic landscapes like the Devonshire moors in *The Hound of the Baskervilles* (1902). Hardly recognized is suburbia's role in the fifty-six stories and four novels that constitute the Holmes canon. Suburban settings are central to the first three texts—*A Study in Scarlet, The Sign of Four,* and "A Scandal in Bohemia"—and figure as crime scenes or investigation sites in at least a third of the sixty Holmes narratives, far outnumbering the handful of cases limited to central London.[7] In his fascinating *Atlas of the European Novel,* Franco Moretti speculates that "Holmes may well owe his success" to Doyle's shift from the south London suburbs of the early novels to the more urban settings of the *Strand* stories (135). My own map challenges this claim, demonstrating Holmes's frequent forays to the Greater London suburbs (fig. 3).

Yet suburbia's place in the Holmes canon has eluded thorough investigation. Michael Harrison rightly estimates that at least a dozen cases take Holmes and Watson to London's southeast suburbs alone (112). But it is misleading to suggest, as does Peter Keating, that the characters are "perfectly familiar with [suburbia's] tree-lined streets and semi-detached villas" (*Haunted* 323)—misleading because

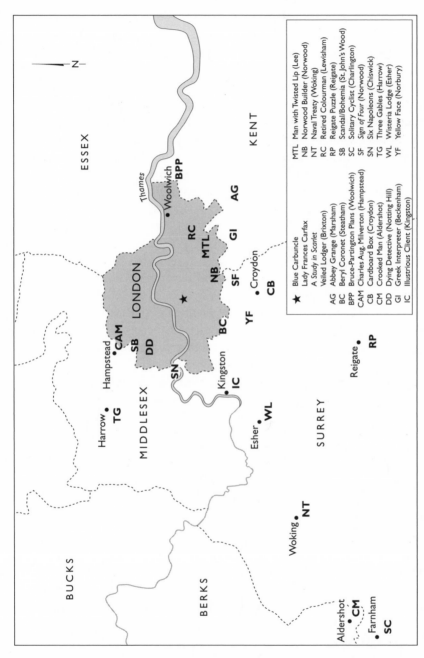

Figure 3. Sherlock Holmes in the suburbs. Suburban settings figure as crime scenes or investigation sites in at least a third of the sixty Holmes narratives.

Doyle depicts the suburbs as being neither so pleasant nor so transparent. In his first investigation with Holmes, a slaying in Brixton in *A Study in Scarlet,* Watson—just returned from military catastrophe in Afghanistan—admits that "never has [death] appeared to me in a more fearsome aspect than in that dark, grimy apartment, which looked out upon one of the main arteries of suburban London" (29). For Doyle suburbs are not merely a backdrop of cozy domesticity that throws into relief more exciting opportunities for urban adventure and mystery. Their privacy and isolation, their traditional associations with crime, and their reputation for dubious morality disrupt any neat distinctions between city and countryside, often pushing Holmes's powers to the limit.

Holmes's investigative approach draws a clear if counterintuitive distinction between city and countryside. While urban space epitomizes mystery itself throughout the stories, the city appears surprisingly transparent to the redoubtable detective, who "loved to lie in the very centre of five millions of people, with his filaments stretching out and running through them, responsive to every little rumour or suspicion of unsolved crime" (423). In fact, Holmes takes greater solace in the darkest examples of urban squalor than he does in the open country: "It is my belief . . . founded upon my experience, that the lowest and vilest alleys in London do not present a more dreadful record of sin than does the smiling and beautiful countryside" (323). Balking at the reputation of the country as a knowable community, Holmes finds the city a site of benevolent connectedness rather than of estranged anonymity. He attributes this connectedness to a proximity among people, networks of information, and institutions of power: "There is no lane so vile that the scream of a tortured child, or the thud of a drunkard's blow, does not beget sympathy and indignation among the neighbours, and then the whole machinery of justice is ever so close that a word of complaint can set it going, and there is but a step between the crime and the dock." In contrast, Holmes views the countryside's scattered dwellings with "a feeling of their isolation and of the impunity with which crime may be committed there. . . . Look at these lonely houses, each in its own fields. . . . Think of the deeds of hellish cruelty, the hidden wickedness which may go on, year in, year out, in such places, and none the wiser" (323).[8]

No less than the countryside, the suburbs throw a wrench into the urban "machinery of justice." Like Holmes's imagined countryside, suburban identity was rooted in isolation and privacy. But unlike the country, where isolation was a necessary function of agricultural life, suburban isolation was an ideal, a choice of lifestyle to be got for a price. Advertising for one of the first consciously planned suburban neighborhoods, near Regent's Park, boasted that the area was designed so "no villa should see any other" and "the streets of houses which overlook the park should not see the villas, nor one street of houses overlook those of another street" (qtd. in Olsen 215). Not surprisingly, such an ideal transformed social relations, limiting the chances—and perhaps the desire—for contact with one's neighbors. As a writer in *The Spectator* put it in 1884, "A neighbourhood . . . cannot be to suburban residents what a neighbour-hood meant in the old times,—namely, a district in which almost every one is more or less known to almost every one else, and in which the strong ties of habitual association and mutual dependence are felt in all their old force. . . . The very essence of the suburban life is that it is one of less knowledge and less intimacy" ("Suburbanity" 483). This view is perhaps best captured by Lewis Mumford's description of the suburb as "a collective attempt to live a private life" (*Culture* 215).

Architecture adapted itself to this collective desire for privacy. In addition to isolating inhabitants from the city and from neighbors, the typical suburban home featured "an interior plan that enabled the different members of the household to isolate themselves from one another" (Olsen 236). Such privacy found its ideal form in the villa. Instrumental to what John Archer calls "the suburbanization of selfhood," the villa was not merely a prototype for the suburban home; it was also key to cultivating a bourgeois subjectivity premised on the isolation of the individual and the separation of public and private life (*Architecture* 91). The villa distinguished itself from Renaissance and eighteenth-century homes, in which interior spaces were hierarchical yet interconnected, with each space open to a variety of public and private uses. Before the eighteenth century, for example, a private room like the bedchamber could have more public uses, including business transactions, entertaining, and conversation. Dining rooms as such did not exist; tables would be temporarily set up in various rooms for each meal (Archer, *Architecture* 125–26). The villa introduced a range of architectural features that reserved particular spaces for particular individuals or uses: it relocated bedrooms from the ground floor to the upstairs; assigned distinct functions to specific rooms; and increased the number of staircases, corridors, and private wings that separated parts of the home. These changes made private activities "incompatible with the public activities on the principal floor," fortifying boundaries between members of a family and between the family and servants (Archer, *Architecture* 98).

Villa architecture sought to make such isolation desirable, but the same isolation could be unsettling when it resulted from poor construction. A demand for ostentatious villas on relatively small plots sometimes yielded homes with bizarre internal dimensions: "Odd spaces and awkward corners appeared, and if they occurred on a landing or in a passage, they were fitted with a door and turned into inconvenient cupboards." Some larger suburban homes were "so ill-planned" that large amounts of space were "wasted by dark, rambling passages" (Gloag 30). Parts of the suburban home could thus be unknowable not only to outsiders but also to its very inhabitants.

Not surprisingly, suburbs were considered especially susceptible to crime. This reputation long preceded their Victorian reincarnation as havens of respectable domesticity. Medieval and early modern suburbs were "the undesirable habitat of [London's] criminal population" (Flint 67), "associated with lawlessness . . . riot and disorder" (Olsen 187). But once suburbs became desirable locales, alarm bells rang when their sanctity was threatened. Throughout the second half of the nineteenth century, the *Times* is rife with reports of suburban "depredators"—thieves, beggars, tramps, vagrants, confidence men, hawkers, and miscreants of all kinds—who regularly invaded neighborhoods and endangered their residents' tranquility. A letter from "A Villa Occupant" in Lewisham is typical: after most male neighbors have departed for work, he claims, his street is invaded by rogues who "enter your front garden as though it was their own. If the street door is open to them they insert one foot" ("Suburban Quiet" 9). "And how many of these roving bands do we see," exclaims a contributor to *All the Year Round,* "and how few policemen!" ("Suburban Miseries" 131). Another letter in the *Times* appeals to the thieves "who for three years past have almost nightly broken into gentlemen's houses, inns, and shops" around Surrey, to "choose some other locality . . . and let us go to bed without fear of having our rest broken and our property stolen" ("Suburban Depredators" 7). As usual, *Punch* both lampooned and legitimized such complaints. On the one hand, it chided suburban home owners with a list of rules to ensure their safety: cut down all foliage, nail doors and windows shut, attach trip wires to a gong, install trick chairs and spring-loaded cabinets, and avoid sleeping at night ("Suburban Safety" 16). On the other hand, *Punch* suggested that suburban homes were easy prey for dubious characters, like the reforming ex-burglars who solicit for the Salvation Army in Charles Keene's cartoon entitled "Retrospection": "Pooty 'ouses they builds in these subu'bs," remarks one, to which the other replies, "Ah! And how 'andy them little balconies would 'a' been in former—" before sheepishly dropping the subject. As members of General Booth's Salvation Army, these figures also represent the threat of darkest London invading suburban civilization.

These texts and images depict suburban residents as besieged innocents, and many of Doyle's suburban tales begin with cases of burglary or murder that play on popular anxieties about threatened sanctity and security. *The Sign of Four,* "The Six Napoleons," "The Norwood Builder," and "The Wisteria Lodge" include dramatic newspaper reports mimicking those in the *Times,* while suburban gangs are the suspected or actual culprits in "The Reigate Puzzle," "The Abbey Grange," and "The Three Gables."[9]

Yet Doyle does not merely associate suburban crime with external threats. The seclusion and lack of social cohesion that made suburbs vulnerable to crime also worked in favor of criminals who were suburb dwellers themselves. Such representations suggest that the real threats to the suburb were those living within its very neighborhoods and homes. In "The Reigate Puzzle" Holmes reveals that a suburban crime wave provided a local judge and his son a smokescreen for robbing their neighbor. In "The Beryl Coronet" Holmes discovers that a banker entrusted with a priceless jewel had it stolen from his Streatham residence by the beloved niece living under his roof. A similar duplicity within suburban households is central to "The Bruce-Partington Plans," "The Naval Treaty," and "The Norwood Builder." Many of Doyle's master criminals also reside in the suburbs. Culverton Smith, an expert on tropical diseases who nearly murders Holmes in "The Dying Detective," lives "in the vague borderland between Notting Hill and Kensington" (936). Baron Adelbert Gruner, the Austrian lothario in "The Illustrious Client," makes his home in respectable Kingston. Charles Augustus Milverton, "the king of all the blackmailers" and "the worst man in London," lives in the healthy surrounds of Hampstead (572). And though not a criminal, Irene Adler of "A Scandal in Bohemia" earns Holmes's undying respect for outwitting him from her unassuming "*bijou* villa" in St. John's Wood (168).

Like its residents suburbia's landscape could also prove deceptive and misleading. In "The Greek Interpreter" the titular protagonist is forced to translate for a fellow countryman held hostage in Beckenham. His captors drive him in circles for hours in a carriage with covered windows, so that the interpreter loses all sense of direction and arrives at the estate "with a vague impression of a lawn and trees on each side of me. . . . Whether these were private grounds, however, or *bona-fide* country was more than I could possibly venture to say" (439). The kidnappers' ruse depends upon the estate's indistinct location between country and city, and to further disorient the interpreter, his captors dump him "on some sort of heathy common" (441). When he finds a railway station, he discovers that he is in suburban Wandsworth, a mere mile from the mammoth Clapham Junction.

Even more misleading than its landscape is suburban architecture. The villa's privacy and isolation make it central to many of Doyle's suburban tales, in contrast to the manors, halls, and ancestral homes that dominate in more remote settings.[10] The villa's potential villainy is best utilized in "The Norwood

Builder." Here the unknowable elements of suburban life structure the very plan of the title character's home, "a big modern villa" where the builder feigns his own murder to frame the son of a woman who once jilted him (503). When Holmes sets a small fire within the house and gets his assistants to scream for help, a door opens "out of what appeared to be a solid wall at the end of the corridor," and the builder emerges (508): "A lath-and-plaster partition had been run across the passage six feet from the end, with a door cunningly concealed in it" (509). While Walter Benjamin links the emergence of detective fiction to the profusion of cases, coverlets, and antimacassars in the nineteenth-century interior—objects upon which individuals left their traces (*Arcades* 9, 19–20)— Doyle offers a suburban interior that conceals any sign of its inhabitants. The Norwood builder's secret chamber serves as an architectural analogue for the suburban unknown, a residential disguise into which he can be virtually absorbed without leaving a trace. As in "The Norwood Builder" homes in "The Retired Colourman" and *The Sign of Four* feature secret rooms and internal chambers where the suburban desire for privacy and isolation turns out to be nothing short of criminal.

Even when Doyle's suburban tales divorce secrecy from criminality, there remains something strangely incongruous about the suburbs. In "The Man with the Twisted Lip," Holmes investigates the disappearance of Neville St. Clair, who, unbeknownst to his wife and children, leaves his Kent villa each morning for an East End opium den. There he disguises himself as a beggar and proceeds to make his livelihood by panhandling. While no actual crime takes place in the story, his family's ignorance is facilitated by the geographic extremes of slum and suburb that constitute his daily route and by the lack of interpersonal contact within his own home and neighborhood. St. Clair claims he panhandled "without anyone having a suspicion as to my real occupation. My dear wife knew that I had business in the City. She little knew what" (243). Though suburb and slum ostensibly constitute the opposite poles of St. Clair's world, Audrey Jaffe suggests that his change of costume in the opium den "has its correlative, in Victorian life, in the imagined transformation of the husband and father who disappears mysteriously into the City each morning, returning at night to a family that has no first-hand knowledge of what he does there" (103). Rather than separate spheres, suburb and slum appear to share a more intimate bond than St. Clair and his wife. She believes herself capable of reading her husband's mind yet knows nothing of his panhandling. In fact, his true confidant is the "lascar," or Indian sailor, who runs the opium den and preserves St. Clair's secret—and whom St. Clair even entrusts with his wedding ring. In turn, the suburban security of St. Clair's wife seems like the story's most potent opiate.

Initially opposed to St. Clair's home, the East End opium den stands in a semi-detached—separate but conjoined—relation to the suburban residence.

If "The Man with the Twisted Lip" blurs the boundaries between the English suburban home and the racial alterity of the East End opium den, then "The Yellow Face" places such racial alterity squarely within the suburban home. In this tale Holmes and Watson come to the aid of Grant Munro, a hop merchant who resides in "a nice eighty-pound-a-year villa at Norbury" (353). Munro is increasingly vexed by his wife, Effie, a widow who was previously married in the United States. Effie has taken a guarded interest in the new inhabitants of a nearby cottage, giving them money and visiting in secret yet refusing to tell Munro why. Rebuffed by a servant when he tries to introduce himself to the neighbors, Munro spies "something unnatural and inhuman" staring at him through an upper window—a figure with a "livid chalky white" face (354–55). Holmes believes this to be a case of marital infidelity aided by the secluded proximity of neighboring homes, and he storms the house with Watson and Munro. Rushing upstairs, they discover that the figure with the yellow face is a small girl. Holmes peels away a mask, revealing "a little coal-black negress" (361), Effie's daughter from her previous marriage to an African American man. Although Munro happily accepts his wife's biracial daughter as his own, "The Yellow Face" replaces marital betrayal with an unsettling image of racial hybridity. Critics have seen this tale as indicating Holmes's failure to detect racial difference and colonial exploitation.[11] I want to suggest that, as with Effie's daughter, Doyle here projects "something unnatural and inhuman" on all of suburbia's inhabitants, racializing the strange incongruity and inherent mystery that seem to reside behind any suburban façade.

Perhaps because suburbs are so disorienting to Holmes, they recur in two types of exceptional tales: those in which Holmes acts as a burglar and those in which he nearly or completely fails to solve the mystery. Among the handful of stories in which Holmes stoops to burglary, all but one of his "crimes" occur in the suburbs, suggesting that these locales confound his sense of right and wrong as well as his investigative skills.[12]

Meanwhile, the suburb's opacity to the gaze and ratiocination of even Holmes is apparent in "The Yellow Face," "A Scandal in Bohemia," "The Greek Interpreter," "The Norwood Builder," and "The Disappearance of Lady Frances Carfax." Discovering the scene of the crime in "The Greek Interpreter" requires the aid of Holmes's more intelligent brother, Mycroft. In "The Norwood Builder" Holmes fears the case "will not figure in that chronicle of our successes" (504), and he ultimately confides in Watson that were it not for a last-minute discovery, the builder would have escaped detection. "The Yellow Face," along with "A

Scandal in Bohemia," also constitutes one of Holmes's only erroneous solutions, concluding as he admits to Watson that "we shall be of more use in London than in Norbury." Indeed, the area's name becomes for Holmes a reminder of his analytic limits: "If it should ever strike you that I am getting a little over-confident in my powers, or giving less pains to a case than it deserves," he tells Watson, "kindly whisper 'Norbury' in my ear, and I shall be infinitely obliged to you" (362).[13]

Darkest London or Greater London?

"The Man with the Twisted Lip" and "The Yellow Face" bring us closer to *The Sign of Four* and its treatment of suburb and empire. Generally, the Holmes stories address these topics in one of three ways. In the first a suburban home safe-guards some valuable object integral to British geopolitical or financial security, be it a secret document ("The Bruce-Partington Plans" and "The Naval Treaty") or a jewel ("The Beryl Coronet"). Such tales depict the respectable home as a microcosm of nation and empire, even though the initial threat of international intrigue is displaced by domestic duplicity. In the second type of story, a for-eign or racial other endangers (or appears to endanger) suburban residents: the Malay opium den in "The Man with the Twisted Lip" (232), the "simian man" who burgles homes in "The Six Napoleons" (586), the "huge negro" who prowls Harrow in "The Three Gables" (1023).

In the third and by far most common type of story—of which "The Yellow Face" is the most benign example—the suburban home and its inhabitants are themselves exoticized as foreign or savage threats to Britain from within. Some of these figures are British ex-colonials, while others are outright foreigners.[14] In "The Dying Detective" a Sumatran planter who lives near Notting Hill tries to poison Holmes with a tropical disease. In "Charles Augustus Milverton" the title character's Hampstead home exudes a "rich, choking fragrance of exotic plants" (578). And in "The Illustrious Client" the Kingston resident Adelbert Gruner lives in a house "built by a South African gold king"; owns a vast collec-tion of Chinese pottery; and has a face that is itself "swarthy, almost Oriental" (996). Holmes discovers in "Wisteria Lodge" that the "lewd and bloodthirsty" former leader of a Central American republic has settled near Esher (884), while "The Mazarin Stone" features a villain, Negretto Sylvius, whose first name is as suggestive of Africa as is his vaguely suburban address, Moorside Gardens, N.W. (1014). Even the "savage" hound of the Baskervilles comes from a pet shop in Fulham (762).[15]

The Sign of Four introduces each of these three themes into the Holmes canon, but where the tales above tend to treat the themes individually, *The Sign of Four* weaves them into a single narrative. As in the first type of story, Thaddeus Sholto learns that his late father, a major in the Indian army, long protected a valuable treasure in his suburban home, putting his safety at great risk. When Thaddeus enlists Holmes and Watson to help him retrieve it, they discover—as in the second type of story—a theft, a murder, and clues pointing to foreign culprits in darkest London. But Holmes's investigation reveals a more complex and unsettling narrative: the crime was an act of vengeance against the real culprit—Major Sholto, the suburban resident himself.

Major Sholto and his home seem to epitomize Sidney Low's correlation of suburban expansion and imperial regeneration. As Thaddeus tells it, somewhat naively we learn, his father "prospered in India and brought back with him a considerable sum of money, a large collection of valuable curiosities, and a staff of native servants. With these advantages he bought himself a house, and lived in great luxury" (102). Called Pondicherry Lodge after a town on India's southeastern coast, Major Sholto's home has a colonial inspiration and military appearance that evoke those suburban "residential encampments" that Low imagined springing up in "a circle of detached forts round the central stronghold" of Greater London. ("Rise" 551). Set in the picturesque and salubrious environs of Upper Norwood, Pondicherry Lodge is located just beyond the London County Council's municipal borders. A guidebook to London from the 1870s notes that Norwood boasted a number of natural springs and wells that were thought to have medicinal qualities, making the district a prime site for convalescent homes, health resorts, spas, and other "hydropathic and homeopathic establishments" (Thorne 453). The author of *London City Suburbs as They Are To-day* (1893) calls the vicinity of Norwood "about the fairest and most 'winsome' of all the suburban dependencies of London" (Fitzgerald 204).

Besides evoking the aura of health and leisure that made Norwood popular, Pondicherry Lodge reflects the prevalence of colonial motifs in late nineteenth-century country houses and suburban homes. The bungalow best exemplifies these motifs. Imported from India by colonial officials, the bungalow became increasingly popular in Britain during the late nineteenth century—first as a seaside house and vacation home, then as a primary residence in rural and suburban areas (King, *Bungalow*). Although *bungalow* technically denotes a detached single-story home, the term came to designate a wide variety of dwellings. When R. A. Briggs published the first book of bungalow designs in Britain in 1891, he emphasized the home's colonial derivation as well as its adaptive form. Briggs notes that in India "bungalows" are "low, squat, rambling, one-storied houses with wide verandahs," while in other colonies the term designates "some rude settlement . . . built of logs" that gives an impression "of 'roughing it.' But this is not the kind of Bungalow suitable for our climate," he claims, "neither is it necessary that it should be a one-storied building or a country cottage." Briggs defines the English bungalow more broadly as "a little country house" (n.p.). But his book includes plans for existing models in Wembley and Hampstead, and according to Anthony King, Briggs was instrumental in "transport[ing] the bungalow from a country to a suburban setting" (*Bungalow* 97). Though Major Sholto's Pondicherry Lodge is not technically a bungalow, it partakes of that dwelling's associations with exoticism, leisure, health, and hygiene—qualities that would make the bungalow one of the most popular types of suburban homes in the coming decades.[16]

But Sholto's home is hardly the kind of carefree residence lauded by Briggs: "Pondicherry Lodge stood in its own grounds and was girt round with a very high stone wall topped with broken glass. A single narrow iron-clamped door formed the only means of entrance" (106). At first this military insularity might recall the most unique suburban home in literature, Wemmick's Castle in *Great Expectations* (1860–61), a miniature cottage designed like a fortress, with mounted guns, a flagstaff, and a retractable bridge. But the imposing exterior of Sholto's home has none of the castle's quaint charm. Even the name Pondicherry, with its exotic allure, has disturbing connotations. The capital of France's holdings in India, Pondicherry was a "small, scattered, and undefended" territory, "militarily emasculated and geographically inconsequential" (Miles 5). According to the 1887 *Whitaker's Almanack,* which Doyle likely used as a source for *The Sign of Four* (Redmond 271), Pondicherry's "fortifications were once strong," but treaties prohibited the reinforcement of its defensive garrisons (386).[17] Pondicherry's status as a French holding may lend Sholto's home a certain "cosmopolitan or transnational quality" (McLaughlin 63). In its grandiosity the lodge may even invoke Pondicherry's famous eighteenth-century governor-general Dupleix, who was known for his ostentatious public ceremonies and displays of power (Chopra 122). But the Pondicherry reference ultimately indicates Major Sholto's sense of entrapment and powerlessness, which Thaddeus reinforces when he explains how his father died. One day Major Sholto received a letter from India that sent him into shock and, not long after, to his deathbed, where he confessed to his sons that he had withheld money owed to his friend Captain Morstan, Miss Morstan's father. Just as he began to disclose the location of the treasure he had hoarded, Major Sholto witnessed a horrific face at his window and died. Doyle's use of Pondicherry may reflect a desire for geographical plausibility (in the novel Sholto served as a prison guard in the Andaman Islands, which are due east of coastal Pondicherry in the Bay of Bengal), or it may simply have been the result of coincidence (the entry for India in the 1887 *Whitaker's Almanack* includes a heading on Pondicherry just above information on the Andamans). But more than reasons of verisimilitude or happenstance, Pondicherry reinforces Sholto's anxiety at being besieged by dangerous forces.

The fears "that there were secret agencies at work all round" Major Sholto are confirmed when Thaddeus takes Holmes and Watson to retrieve the treasure at Pondicherry Lodge (104). There they find Thaddeus's brother slain and the treasure missing. In keeping with Sidney Low's vision of darkest London as the degenerate other of the suburban home, the crime scene at Pondicherry Lodge yields signs of invasion from both the urban underclass and the colonial savage. On a table near Bartholomew's body sits a crude stone hammer; in the flesh above the victim's ear, Holmes discovers a "long, sharp, and black" thorn, which Watson claims "certainly is not" English (113). With these clues Holmes suggests that the murderer "breaks fresh ground in the annals of crime in this country— though parallel cases suggest themselves from India and, if my memory serves me, from Senegambia" (111). Reinforcing his hypothesis, Holmes also finds prints from "a naked foot . . . scarce half the size of those of an ordinary man" (112). Although Watson proposes that they must belong to a child or woman (112, 118), Holmes itemizes the clues—"diminutive foot-marks, toes never fettered by boots, naked feet, stone-headed wooden mace, great agility, small poisoned darts"—until Watson predictably exclaims, "A savage!" (127). The latest encyclopedia confirms Holmes's hypothesis upon their return to Baker Street. In its entry for the Andaman Islands, the volume describes "the smallest race upon this earth," with "remarkably small" hands and feet, that frequently uses "stone-headed clubs" and "poisoned arrows" against their enemies (127–28).[18]

Amid the clues linking the Sholto crime to a "savage" from the colonies, Holmes also discovers traces of the urban underclass. A different set of footprints around a windowsill reveals "the impression of a wooden stump" and "a heavy boot with a broad metal heel" (110). The prints recall an obscure event from Major Sholto's past: Thaddeus noted that his father "had a most marked aversion to men with wooden legs" and once "fired his revolver at a wooden-legged man, who proved to be a harmless tradesman canvassing for orders" (102). The anecdote lends the wooden leg a particular class valence: though "harmless," the tradesman suggests working-class impoverishment. Thaddeus remembers that just before his father died, he saw a "bearded, hairy face, with wild cruel eyes and an expression of concentrated malevolence" at his window (103). Like the prints of the wooden leg and heavy boot, the memory of this "wild, fierce face"

(104) conjures the specter of urban poverty. It is important too that Holmes discovers the boot prints around the windowsill. As Anne McClintock suggests, windowsills—like doorknobs, steps, and banisters—functioned as prominent threshold objects in the Victorian home: because they "maintained the boundaries between private and public," such objects gained "exhibition value as class markers" (170). Boots upset these boundaries by "carrying traces of streets, fields and markets into polished interiors, confusing public with private, work with leisure, cleanliness with dirtiness" (171). The boot prints around the windowsill of Pondicherry Lodge reflect the breakdown of class boundaries and the intrusion of urban dirt and crime upon Sholto's suburban threshold. Thus, Holmes offers the police inspector a description of the second suspect that unmistakably marks him as a member of the urban underclass: "a poorly educated man, small, active, with his right leg off, and wearing a wooden stump which is worn away upon the inner side. His left boot has a coarse, square-toed sole, with an iron band round the heel" (114). Emphasizing the suspect's mental inferiority and physical deformity, Holmes here sketches a member of the urban poor as clearly as his earlier description led Watson to envision "a savage."

Bearing out Sidney Low's view of darkest London as the suburb's degenerate other, these clues lead Holmes and Watson from "the half-rural villa-lined roads" around Norwood into London's "continuous streets, where labourers and dockmen were already astir, and slatternly women were taking down shutters and brushing door-steps" (121). Such images reinforce Holmes's assumption that the crime must have originated in the slums. In his search for the culprits, he accordingly recruits those with intimate knowledge of darkest London: Toby, a scent-tracking mongrel whose owner resides in "a row of shabby, two-storied brick houses in the lower quarter of Lambeth" (116); and the Baker Street Irregulars, "a dozen dirty and ragged little street Arabs" whose movements can go unnoticed (126). To get information on the boat in which the suspects fled, Holmes even disguises himself as a cantankerous "master mariner who had fallen into years and poverty" (133). Such avatars of darkest London mark the novel's trajectory from suburb to slum, from Norwood in the south to the eastern reaches of the Thames, as a police steamer carries Holmes and Watson beyond the West India Docks, Deptford Reach, and the Isle of Dogs.

It comes as no surprise that when Holmes and Watson catch up with the suspects in a boat chase on the Thames, they personify the urban poverty and colonial primitivism that together signify darkest London. Jonathan Small is a wounded ex-convict who has served time in the colonies and returned to England utterly destitute. His sidekick Tonga is a tiny native of the Andaman

Islands whom Small exhibits as a cannibal at fairs and exhibitions, earning them "a hatful of pennies" for a day's work (156). In capturing Small (Tonga is shot and killed in the pursuit), Holmes appears to rectify the threat that darkest London poses to the suburbs of Greater London. However, Small provides a motive for his crime that, for the first time in the novel, challenges the implicit assumption of Major Sholto's innocence. During the so-called Indian Mutiny of 1857, Small got cornered into a native conspiracy to steal treasure from the Red Fort at Agra. Given a choice—be killed or earn an equal share of the treasure—Small aided his captors. But after the Mutiny he was arrested and sent to prison in the Andaman Islands. Major Sholto, one of the prison's commanding officers and a drunken gambler, learned of the treasure's whereabouts and absconded with it to England. Small escaped jail and sought revenge, tracing the treasure back to Pondicherry Lodge.

In the final chapter of the novel, the criminality initially linked to Small and Tonga shifts to Sholto. Small questions the system of justice that will imprison him but has left Sholto's crime unpunished. "A pretty justice!" Small exclaims, asking, "Whose loot is this, if it is not ours?" (144). Indeed, Small is no more—and in some ways much less—a criminal than Major Sholto, proving himself faithful to his Indian confederates and honoring the pact made under "the sign of four." In contrast, Sholto does not even recognize honor among thieves: he steals the treasure "without carrying out one of the conditions on which [Small] had sold him the secret" (155) and cheats his best friend, Morstan, out of his share. Small's arrest thus "turns out to be oddly irrelevant to the larger pattern of criminality revealed in the narrative," a pattern that Holmes "proves surprisingly powerless to address" (Arata 143). Charging Small is "subsequent, and in many ways subordinate, to the original transgression," and though Sholto and Morstan "are guilty of all manner of treachery on the subcontinent, the onus for their offenses seems to melt into air once they have managed to get to English soil" (Childers 208).[19]

Major Sholto's role in instigating Small's revenge challenges the façade of a noble if besieged suburban imperium that the novel initially constructs. Indeed, Pondicherry Lodge proves itself a poor defense against the combined threat of urban poverty and colonial savagery. But what seems more troublesome than the suburban home's inability to protect itself from the dangers of darkest London is that it is the source of those dangers and a more threatening symptom of national and imperial degeneracy than the slum. By emphasizing suburban degeneracy, *The Sign of Four* accentuates what Sidney Low seeks to repress and recontain. Rather than tracing the source of suburban danger to darkest London, *The Sign of Four* directs us back to the home of the returned Anglo-Indian.

By locating the corrupt Pondicherry Lodge on the outskirts of Greater London, Doyle not only challenges suburbia's place in the imperial community of Greater Britain. He also draws upon a common perception that suburbs served as a sort of communal resting home for returned Anglo-Indians.

Suburban Sahibs

Judging from a variety of Victorian sources, the Anglo-Indian sahib was a well-known presence in the suburbs. One guide to London neighborhoods lists "retired officers from India and the Colonies" as prominent inhabitants of St. John's Wood (qtd. in Olsen 239). Another claims that Roehampton has never "been without its East India residents" (Clarke 413). Likewise, "repatriated nabobs" figured among the growing populace of North Kensington (Dyos, "Castle" 127). In *Life and Labour of the People in London,* Charles Booth interviews a Dulwich vicar who reports that in his parish "everyone had something to do with India" (qtd. in Nurse 62). Bayswater gained the nickname "Asia Minor" for the number of residents connected to India: "By the 1860s Bayswater was . . . becoming a symbol of Imperial London" (Porter 212), "attracting the families of colonial administrators to whom the storied boarding houses on the banks of the Hugli were as familiar as those to be found in Paddington" (Reeder 263).[20] Curiously, just over a year after writing about Upper Norwood in *The Sign of Four,* Doyle moved to neighboring South Norwood, and his street nearly intersected with Bungalow Road, named after the home of a retired Anglo-Indian captain. Though this coincidence could not likely have inspired Major Sholto or Pondicherry Lodge, it attests to the suburban Anglo-Indian as a known cultural entity, a recognizable type.[21] And as we shall see in later chapters, this view persists in Forster's *A Passage to India* and the work of George Orwell.

We can begin to understand the connection between sahibs and the suburbs by recognizing the status of the Anglo-Indian community abroad. Francis Hutchins has described Anglo-Indians as a "middle-class aristocracy": because India generally promised Britons a higher standard of living than they experienced at home, they arrived in the subcontinent as "instant aristocrats" (107–8). Like many Anglo-Indians Jonathan Small in *The Sign of Four* attempts to re-create in the colonies a version of rural life lost at home. Born into a respected Worcestershire family, Small is a country idler, "a bit of a rover" who gets "into a mess over a girl and could only get out of it again by taking the Queen's shilling" (144). Joining the Indian Army to escape his domestic troubles, Small numbers among the "superfluous" Englishmen seeking to reinvent themselves in Greater

Britain. Though Small has his leg chewed off by a crocodile while swimming in the Ganges, he is soon hired to oversee coolies on an indigo plantation, improving dramatically on the life of aimlessness and familial disaffection he left behind. In India, he claims, "white folk . . . feel their hearts warm to each other as they never do here at home" (145). Had it not been for the Mutiny and his subsequent arrest, Small claims, he would have been "content to spend the remainder of my life in indigo-planting," in an India that "lay as still and peaceful, to all appearance, as Surrey or Kent" (145).

If Small's re-created rural idyll begins to offer the kind of life that made Anglo-Indians instant aristocrats abroad, Major Sholto personifies the more common view of Anglo-Indians as a demoralized lot—cruel, drunken, and lazy. Sholto loses a considerable amount of money at cards, takes "to drinking a deal more than was good for him," and considers himself "ruined" (153). Sholto fits the profile of those Anglo-Indians who troubled even Charles Dilke, champion of exporting English values across the globe. In *Greater Britain* Dilke shuddered at the typical Anglo-Indian, "uproariously drunk, kicking every native against whom he stumbled. . . . It is impossible to over-estimate the harm done to the English name in India by the conduct of drunken soldiers" (517; also see 415, 427). Such an image was also made famous—unwittingly— by Kipling, especially in *Plain Tales from the Hills* (1888). Oscar Wilde described the book's Anglo-Indians as "jaded [and] second-rate . . . in exquisite incongruity with their surroundings." T. S. Eliot thought Kipling provided a "perfect picture" of Anglo-Indians as "narrow, snobbish, spiteful, ignorant and vulgar" (qtd. in R. L. Green 104, 326). Instant aristocrats abroad, Anglo-Indians were considered an ignoble nobility at home: "Indian service of any sort, including the highest echelon positions filled by noncivilians, was widely regarded as an enterprise solely for second-rate minds and middle-class citizens" (Spangenberg 354). Such a reputation made retirement to London's suburbs a fitting end to colonial service.

Anglo-Indians returned to England distinctly out of place—with esoteric knowledge, an exotic vocabulary, and a dubious past that made them anomalous figures at home.[22] G. O. Trevelyan's epistolary novel about an initiate of the Indian Civil Service, *The Competition Wallah* (1866), captures the Anglo-Indian's melancholy bitterness. His narrator laments that metropolitan society "attaches to the retired Indian the fatal title of 'bore'" without recognizing his substantial drop in status on returning home (124–25): "It is a severe trial for a leader of Calcutta society to become one of the rank and file in the pump-room at the watering place; to sink from the Council-board to the Vestry, and from the High Court to the Petty Sessions" (130). *Punch* poked fun at the Anglo-Indian's social downfall, associating it specifically with his retirement to the suburbs: "The Song of the Six Suburbs" parodies Kipling's poem "The Song of the Cities" (1893), in which colonial metropolitan centers turgidly proclaim their place in the imperial union. (Calcutta, for example, declares: "Me the Sea-captain loved, the river built, / Wealth sought and Kings adventured life to hold. / Hail England! I am Asia—Power on silt, / Death in my hands, but Gold!" [174].) In turn the *Punch* poem chides the false grandeur of London's suburbs by juxtaposing their banal and petty aspirations to the glories of the British empire. Ealing West speaks the closing quartet: "'Last, loveliest, exquisite,' I give to those / Civilian warriors from India rest; / What suburb boasts the dignified repose / That clings to Ealing W.?" (Carrick 54). The lines invoke Auckland's entry in "The Song of the Cities," yet whereas Kipling lauds the men who leave England to populate the colonies, *Punch* envisions their wistful and pathetic retirement to the suburbs.[23]

The Anglo-Indian's status as a social anomaly—if not a potentially sinister threat—received more serious attention in the *Times*. In 1891 "An Indian Civilian" on furlough after almost a decade's service in the subcontinent described the English perception of Anglo-Indians: "We are not free from the imputation of being, as officials, underworked and overpaid; as private individuals, immoral; and as members of a ruling class, overbearing, insolent, and unsympathetic" ("Anglo-Indian's Complaint" 6). The *Times* replied with an editorial that declares the complaint an exaggeration and describes the typical Anglo-Indian as "a strange sort of animal," "a stranger who is not a stranger." Noting that the typical Anglo-Indian "is without a distinct vocation" on his return to England, the editorial claims that he "comes back to discover that he has to create another career amidst unknown circumstances" ("Anglo-Indian's and English Opinions" 7). As Lisa Fluet argues, this exchange confirmed the Anglo-Indian's reputation as a failed professional and even a potential criminal, who exerted a particularly negative influence on English life ("'Distinct'"). The same perception informed J. A. Hobson's 1902 study of imperialism. Abroad, Hobson claims, the Anglo-Indian is "removed from all the healthy restraints of ordinary European society," enjoying the "plunders of the slave trade and the gains of corrupt and extortionate officialism." Upon his return to England he "bring[s] back the characters, sentiments, and ideas imposed by" his life in the subcontinent, namely a "vulgar ostentation, domineering demeanor and corrupting largesse [that] degrade the life of our people" (150–51). Hobson goes on to locate such figures in the areas undergoing the greatest suburban growth: "The South of England is full of men . . . whose character has been formed in our despotic Empire. . . . Could the incomes expended in the Home Counties and other large districts of Southern Britain be traced to their sources, it would be found that they were in large measure wrung from the enforced toil of vast multitudes of black, brown, or yellow natives" (151).

Hobson's critique returns us to Major Sholto and Pondicherry Lodge. As I've indicated, Sholto and his "corrupting largesse" mediate the degenerative effect of Anglo-India on suburban London. Recognizing Sholto as the instigator of reverse colonization allows for a retrospective reading of the novel in which Sholto himself emerges as the agent of decay. Admittedly, as far as detective fiction goes, there is nothing unconventional in Doyle revealing the apparent victim of a crime as its perpetrator. But by using this device with the novel's insistently suburban settings, and involving not one but two generations of Sholtos—each with his own distinct suburban home dependent on colonial loot—Doyle suggests that suburban expansion has its origins in ill-gotten wealth from beyond. By setting *The Sign of Four* where he does, Doyle foregrounds suburban homes as a new form of reverse colonization to be spread by future generations of Britons.

This fear is manifested most notably in Thaddeus and his home. Thaddeus's attempt to ensconce himself among his reliquaries and original works of art suggests a defense against degeneration—hence his disdain for "rough materialism" and "the rough crowd" (101). Moreover, Thaddeus's museum-like decor epitomizes Walter Benjamin's dictum that "the collector is the true resident of the interior," seeking through possession to divest objects of their commodity value and make them part of his own ostensible order (*Arcades* 9). But the gesture is inherently doomed. From Max Nordau and Benjamin to Donna Haraway and Laurie Langbauer, collecting is viewed as an impossible struggle against decay.[24] Thaddeus tellingly refers to his own colonial objets-d'art, inherited from or influenced by his father, as "my weakness" (101)—an appropriate choice of words, since the exotic furnishings are undoubtedly meant to link Thaddeus's decadent lifestyle with the enervating symptoms of his poor health. His relative youth—he's thirty—is belied by his scrawny stature, bald forehead, brooding lip, crooked yellow teeth, perpetual twitching, and weak heart. As the inheritor of his father's financial and historical legacy, Thaddeus has acquired the symptoms of physical decay that go along with it. His bodily condition reflects the popular belief, noted in an 1885 pamphlet titled *Degeneration amongst Londoners,* that "a third generation of Anglo-Indians attaining adult years is impossible." But, the author adds, we may "have the same non-continuance near home without our ever having given it a thought" (Cantlie 45).

Hearth Disease

Thaddeus provides a crucial clue to understanding suburban degeneracy in *The Sign of Four,* linking physical degeneracy to bodily, architectural, and economic problems of *circulation.* When he first meets Dr. Watson, Thaddeus asks for an opinion on his heartbeat, expressing "grave doubts as to my mitral valve" (100), a passageway for oxygenated blood moving through the heart. Watson finds nothing irregular, but as usual his diagnosis could be more adept, for the Sholto case is plagued by characters with poor circulation. Besides his own concerns Thaddeus explains that Captain Morstan "suffered for years from a weak heart" and died "from throwing a strain upon" it in an argument over the Agra treasure (103, 101). Thaddeus's father suffered from "an enlarged spleen" (102), the seat of melancholy as well as the organ that filters blood cells, and his "pulse had ceased to beat" after seeing Jonathan Small's face at his window (103). And thanks to Tonga's poison darts, Thaddeus's brother dies from a condition Watson likens to tetanus, his muscles "in a state of extreme contraction, far exceeding the usual rigor mortis" (112). Though Watson and Holmes fail to recognize it, impeded bodily circulation emerges as a recurrent symptom of suburban degeneracy in *The Sign of Four.*

We have already seen how the suburb's architectural and geographic isolation facilitate criminality throughout the Holmes canon by limiting flows of information and access to clues. In *The Sign of Four* the recurrence of blocked entries, multiple corridors, and private chambers provides a spatial analogue for the poor circulation that afflicts its characters. While Thaddeus welcomes Holmes, Watson, and Miss Morstan into his "little sanctum" (100), their journey is hardly without obstruction—from the carriage driver who refuses to disclose their destination, to the "labyrinth of streets" in south London (99), to the series of passageways through which the Indian servant leads them to Thaddeus. Access to Pondicherry Lodge is even more difficult: initially rebuffed by a guard at the outer gate, Holmes and Watson gain entry to the grounds only to be barred from the house. Once inside they learn that Thaddeus's brother is locked within his laboratory, requiring Holmes to break down the door and search for clues in the recesses of Pondicherry Lodge, including "the secret room" where the treasure was kept (111). Compare these barriers and impediments to the ease with which Holmes and Watson maneuver through darkest London. When Watson makes a midnight run to retrieve a bloodhound from "a row of shabby, two-storied brick houses" in Lambeth, Holmes's name is enough to grant him access (116). Near a rickety Thames-side wharf, Holmes tricks a steamer captain's wife, "a stoutish, red-faced woman with a large sponge in her hand" (123), into describing Small's getaway vessel in minute detail (the way to get "people of that sort" to talk, he tells Watson, "is never to let them think that their information can be of the slightest importance to you" [124]). Unlike suburbia, with its reticence and defensiveness, darkest London willingly surrenders its secrets to Holmes and Watson.

The Sign of Four thus provides a stark contrast to conventional oppositions between slums and suburbs. In "The Rise of the Suburbs," Sidney Low describes slums—that "succession of Stepneys" and "conglomerate of Bethnal Greens"— as "the hard heart of London" ("Rise" 550). Their narrow courts and dark alleys make them places of constraint and immobility: "bad drainage and insufficient light and water and ventilation." Low argues that suburban residents benefit from wide spaces and fresh air, structuring their lives around a "perpetual coming and going, the daily journeys by rail or tram or steamer" ("Rise" 554). In contrast to those penned in by the slums, suburban residents move with "the stream of natural progress" ("Rise" 558). Likewise, Charles Booth's maps of London poverty are color coded according to what Pamela Gilbert calls "a corporeal model of circulation." For Booth, Gilbert argues, "the middle classes represent the healthy tissue . . . the vibrant red following the major thoroughfares of the metropolis," while pockets of poverty appear "in the colors of death" (189). The latter areas "are not connected to the circulatory vessels of the city," Gilbert continues, much less to the suburbs beyond (191). For this reason Booth's final volume of Life and Labour looks ahead to suburbs "spreading" throughout the Home Counties, "not as an escape from evil left behind," but to help disseminate the city's "energy . . . even in its blackest and most squalid centres" (17: 204–5). But unlike Low and Booth, Doyle sees circulation stagnating in the suburbs. If London is the heart of the empire, the center of Greater Britain's vast circulatory system, Doyle suggests that the suburbs are its clogged arteries.

Indeed, suburban constriction takes on medical implications for Doyle, who trained as a physician in the late 1870s and was still practicing when he wrote A Study in Scarlet and The Sign of Four. As both a medical student and a doctor, Doyle was especially interested in circulation and its use for fighting illness. In 1883 he published an article called "Life and Death in the Blood," which offered lay readers a vivid introduction to the circulatory system and showed "remarkable insight . . . into the bacterial causation of disease and prevention through immunization" (Rodin and Key xxi).[25] Doyle's 1885 M.D. thesis on tabes dorsalis, a degeneration of nerve cells in the spinal cord, argued that the resulting skin lesions could be treated with a drug that relaxed blood vessels and increased circulation (Rodin and Key 92–94). And in 1890, the same year he published The Sign of Four, Doyle visited the Hygiene Institute of Berlin, where Robert

Koch proposed a vaccine for preventing tuberculosis. Though Doyle disagreed with Koch's findings, he remained a firm believer in the controversial practice of vaccination, supporting its compulsory use to fight smallpox and typhoid in later years (Rodin and Key 102–11).[26]

Doyle certainly endows Holmes with a great deal of up-to-date medical expertise, but when it comes to "the pathology of bourgeois life" (Arata 143), his healing powers are limited. For Lawrence Rothfield, Holmes reflects the decline of clinical medicine and the rise of more exact sciences like "bacteriology, chemistry, and microscopic anatomy" (141), while for Carlo Ginzburg the detective makes use of "symptomatology—the discipline which permits diagnosis, though the disease cannot be directly observed, on the basis of superficial symptoms or signs, often irrelevant to the eye of the layman" (87). Holmes applies these sophisticated techniques to diagnosing "the etiology of a crime," but as with the arrest of Jonathan Small, he often "treat[s] the symptoms rather than the disease itself" (Childers 208). As a medical and scientific authority, Holmes "exerts a purely negative power: he identifies in order to exclude" (Rothfield 141). This is especially true of the "alien contagions" that appear to threaten British society with "infection" throughout the Holmes canon (Jann 76). The sources of such infection include foreign animals, plants, dirt, poison, addictive drugs, and alluring commodities,[27] and critics often see Holmes battling these pathogens through containment and elimination. "Like a bacteriologist" Holmes works to "identify [foreign threats] and render them innocuous" (Otis 6).

But in a society as dependent on the foreign as Victorian Britain, identification and exclusion offered at best a limited antidote. For all his medical expertise Holmes does not appear to recognize the role of circulation in fighting disease. If Holmes sometimes fails in his attempts at exclusion, however, Doyle himself offers an alternative form of protection in the emerging and controversial practice of vaccination. Doyle views the exotic like a vaccine. Rather than seeking to eradicate or completely remove alien contagions from the social body, Doyle suggests in *The Sign of Four* that small doses of foreign pathogens can actually strengthen British citizens. To work properly, however, these doses must circulate freely throughout the social body. Such circulation is often what the suburban home prevents. By restricting the flow of foreign materials, both Sholto homes inundate their inhabitants with too many foreign contagions. The result is overexposure to the exotic—and consequently, physical and moral degeneration.[28]

Such overexposure is best exemplified by Major Sholto, whose poor circulation is symptomatic of "the cursed greed" that he claims "has been my besetting sin through life" (102). On his deathbed he confesses to his sons a secret he has kept "hidden in his own breast": "The mere feeling of possession has been so dear to me that I could not bear to share [the treasure] with another" (102), namely Morstan, who dies in a dispute over the treasure: "My fault lies in the fact that [I] concealed not only [Morstan's] body but also the treasure and that I have clung to Morstan's share as well as to my own" (103). And as Thaddeus points out, his brother Bartholomew seems to have inherited their father's traits: Bartholomew was "a little inclined to my father's fault" and unwilling to share the treasure with Morstan's daughter (104).

Unlike his father and brother Thaddeus wants to release the secrets of the Agra treasure and provide a shot in the arm to Holmes's investigation. By opening his doors to Holmes, Thaddeus reveals his desire to generate new flows of wealth and information—precisely the qualities that seem so antithetical to suburbs in the Holmes canon. Yet as a recipient of his father's ill-gotten wealth, Thaddeus is already contaminated by the degenerative traits he seeks to remedy. Though Thaddeus imagines his home as a sanctuary from "the rough crowd" (101), it does not provide him the same circulation he offers others. Like his father, a former jail guard, Thaddeus remains a prisoner—albeit a willing one—ensconced in a claustrophobic array of glossy curtains, thick carpets, plush tiger skins, and rich hookah smoke.

If Major Sholto restricts circulation, and Thaddeus suffers the consequences he seeks to remedy in others, then Miss Morstan receives the proper treatment: vaccination from a small dose of the Agra treasure. The "detached pearl" she receives from Thaddeus "at fixed intervals" (104) is enough to protect her from both the grip of poverty and the excesses of wealth. Though Miss Morstan must support herself as a governess, her home with Mrs. Cecil Forrester in Lower Camberwell is an idealized contrast to the congestion of both Pondicherry Lodge and Thaddeus's home. Returning Miss Morstan to her residence, Watson notes that its openness does not undermine its protective coziness. Mrs. Forrester immediately invites Watson in, and on departing, he looks back to see "the half-opened door, [and] the hall-light shining through stained glass." It is not only Watson's infatuation with Morstan that gets his blood flowing; it is also "that passing glimpse of a tranquil English home in the midst of the wild, dark business which had absorbed us" (116). Like Watson's, Miss Morstan's exposure to the "dark business" of both Sholto homes left her "faint," "weak and helpless, shaken in mind and nerve" (116). Though she stands to gain a fortune if the Agra treasure is found, the prospect leaves her uneasy. One pearl each year may have protected her, but half the Agra treasure might constitute an overdose—and it will certainly poison her budding relationship with Watson. It is not surprising, then, that when Watson breaks open the recovered chest, both he and Miss Morstan are relieved to find it empty, and Watson thanks God "from [his] very heart" that he can finally express his true feelings for Miss Morstan (143). The scene reveals Miss Morstan's role in *The Sign of Four* as not only embodying a healthy form of suburban domesticity but revealing its vaccination from small doses of the same foreign contaminants that threaten others. The excess tainted treasure out of circulation, Miss Morstan is protected from the colonial toxins that poisoned her father and the Sholtos.

With her impending marriage to Watson at the novel's close, Miss Morstan also appears set to protect her new husband from such dangers. By now fans of the Holmes tales may have noted that like Major Sholto and Captain Morstan, Watson is also an Anglo-Indian, having served as a surgeon in the second Afghan War. In the canon's opening pages Watson recalls his role in the battle of Maiwand, one of Britain's worst military defeats in the nineteenth century. Separated from his regiment, struck by an enemy bullet, laid low with enteric fever, and emaciated to the point that he is sent home with his health "irretrievably ruined," Watson "naturally gravitated to London, that great cesspool into which all the loungers and idlers of the Empire are irresistibly drained" (15). Watson's account undermines the popular notion of London as the beating heart of the empire, so that rather than spreading the nation's life blood, the city is debilitated by congestion, contamination, and above all, poor circulation. Though Dr. Doyle alters his diagnosis of national degeneracy in *The Sign of Four*—from urban heart failure to suburbia's hardened arteries—his belief in vaccination gives Watson some hope that suburban domesticity with Miss Morstan will keep him on the path to recovery.

4

Outposts of Progress
Joseph Conrad's Suburban Speculation

In *The Soul of London* (1905), an impressionistic foray through the English capital, Ford Madox Ford recalls a sight that "always piques my curiosity." An "odd terrace" thrown together by some speculative builder sits in abandoned decay on a road beyond the city. The structure "contains four immense, thin-walled, pretentious stucco houses . . . break[ing] off in uncompleted doors, uncompleted foundations, and a plot of grimy wasteland." In this deserted edifice Ford imagines "a bold speculation's falling to pieces, getting the nickname 'Blank's Folly,' growing begrimed, being forgotten" (38). The sight is one that had become common in London's late-Victorian suburbs—a speculative housing scheme gone to pot before residents even arrived. But Blank's Folly also recalls the title and central image of the first novel by Ford's friend and collaborator, Joseph Conrad. Though set in eastern Borneo, *Almayer's Folly* (1895) presents a scenario not unlike Ford's: the trader Kaspar Almayer builds a "new but already decaying house" to accommodate British colonists rumored to be annexing part of the Malay Archipelago (4). Like Blank's Folly, Almayer's not only fails to attract residents but quickly molders on its "uneven ground," with "stones, decaying planks, and half-sawn beams . . . piled up in inextricable confusion" (12). As I argue in this chapter, the premature domestic decay central to Conrad's first novel parallels portrayals of suburban housing schemes like Blank's Folly.

Of all the authors in this study, perhaps none seems further removed from suburbia than Conrad. This is especially so with *Almayer's Folly*. Its setting has inspired a great deal of speculation into Conrad's travels in the Malay Archipelago, even though Conrad spent a relatively short time there.[1] By contrast, we know little of Conrad's early years in London. Soon after his first visit in 1878, the city became his shore-leave home until he abandoned sailing in 1894.

During this peripatetic period dominated by sea travel, Conrad's total time in London still adds up to roughly four years. We might imagine this time spent lodging near the East End docks or along the lower Thames, but surprisingly, Conrad lived for about twenty-seven months altogether in the city's northern suburbs—Tollington Park and later Stoke Newington.[2] The period was personally significant: Conrad passed exams for second mate, first mate, and master mariner and became a naturalized British citizen. It was also a watershed moment in suburban history, a period of speculative development run rampant, and Conrad arrived on the crest of a building wave that brought an influx of lower-middle-class residents to the suburbs, thanks to falling costs, rising incomes, and cheaper means of mass transport. Indeed, Britain's top four areas of population growth in the 1880s were London railway suburbs dominated by the lower middle class. The term *suburbia* was coined to describe this social terrain, and by the end of the decade, a distinct genre of suburban fiction had emerged.[3] The speculative building that fueled this monumental growth also brought with it a striking phenomenon: London's "suburbs were glutted with new but tenantless houses" (Dyos, *Victorian* 82).

Conceived and written amid this sea change in metropolitan daily life, *Almayer's Folly* engages many of the concerns that underwrite late-Victorian suburbia. The prematurely decaying house that gives the novel its title typifies the poor construction and rapid ruin thought to characterize the legion of new homes cropping up in London's outskirts. And like many of those dwellings, Almayer's folly is built speculatively, anticipating residents who never arrive. Almayer himself, the first of Conrad's many hollow imperialists, embodies two social types often associated with suburbia—the speculative builder and the lower-middle-class clerk. *Almayer's Folly* thus invokes the central motifs of the suburban fiction that emerged in the 1880s and 1890s. In what follows I argue that these motifs—of speculative building, of new but rapidly decaying residences, and of a rising petit-bourgeois culture—gave Conrad a popular vocabulary for indicting imperial expansion. Transplanted to the jungles of Borneo, the suburban home becomes in Conrad's hands a means of exposing the folly of modern imperialism.

Despite the titular status of Almayer's house, critics tend to downplay its significance in light of its occupant's foolish dreams and Conrad's own domestic anxieties.[4] By contrast this chapter considers the folly an important literary text in its own right. Informed by both popular and elite portrayals of the suburban home, the folly provides Conrad with an architectural correlative for the existential exile and transcendental homelessness that characterize literary modernism.[5] Often considered the first modernist, Conrad straddles the "strategic fault line" where nineteenth-century realism splits into the "distinct cultural spaces" of high literature and mass culture (Jameson, *Political* 206–7). *Almayer's Folly* sits on this fault line. While it deploys elements of the adventure tale—piracy and smuggling, political intrigue and hidden treasure—these are all but drained of their exotic allure by the novel's nascent modernism: its somber tone, slight action, emphasis on subjectivity, and digressions from chronology.[6] Whereas other critics have examined Conrad's emergent modernism in relation to the adventure tale or imperial romance, this chapter considers suburban fiction and its speculative houses as part of his first novel's mass culture foundation. As I suggest, Almayer's speculative housing scheme not only parallels imperial expansion with suburban sprawl. It also allows Conrad to compensate for his own misguided financial speculations during his early years in the London suburbs by succeeding in a rather different speculative venture: writing fiction.

In this sense Almayer's folly—both the book and the building—reflects modernism's grounding in the popular materials it disavowed. While such an account of modernist aesthetic production has become common, suburbia remains beyond the pale of such discussions. The speculations that follow attempt to rectify this situation. Having made a case in the preceding chapters for suburbia's role in mass culture genres like science fiction and the detective tale, I turn to Conrad to suggest that a suburban façade—albeit one imaginatively exported to the colonies—also stands at the foundation of British modernism. Reading *Almayer's Folly* in these terms, however, first requires that we map Conrad's colonial outposts in relation to British urban and rural space.

Greater Britain and Global Urban Culture

In this study we have seen how imperial expansion created a countercurrent of reverse colonization, one that brought fears of invasion and racial degeneracy home to Britain. Like Wells and Conan Doyle, Conrad looked on the turning of the tide with fascinated horror. Most notable in this regard is *Heart of Darkness* (1899), whose very title undercuts London's status as heart of the British empire. Though Conrad exposes the city as the rotten core of Western civilization, Marlow's journey from colonial outpost to metropolitan center also seems to bring darkness and degeneracy in its wake. In subsequent works like *The Mirror of the Sea* (1906) and *The Secret Agent* (1907), Conrad similarly imagines London as infiltrated from beyond or regressing into a forest primeval.[7] As he would later write of his first visit to London, Conrad "walked into the great city" feeling like "a traveller penetrating into a vast and unexplored wilderness" (*Notes* 150).

More often, of course, Conrad looks beyond the capital of his adopted homeland to consider the territories colonized by Britain and the West. In *The Country and the City,* Raymond Williams cites Conrad in arguing that the colonies served as symbolic surrogates for the English countryside in the late nineteenth century, and he includes Conrad's "trading worlds" among those "new rural societies [that] entered the English imagination" via imperialism (281).[8] While organic, premodern traditions inform Conrad's fiction—from the quasi-noble status conferred on Kurtz and Lord Jim to the archaic ideal of fidelity that serves as Conrad's moral compass—his writing consistently depicts the waning of such traditions. Rather than Williams's description of the colonies as "an idyllic retreat, an escape from debt or shame, or an opportunity for making a fortune" (*Country* 281), Conrad's outposts repeatedly fail to revive a rural heritage in decline at home. This is in part because they are palimpsests of varying racial and political formations, which reveal struggles between competing empires and the populations they colonized. The Borneo of Conrad's first two novels, for example, reflects centuries of settlement, migration, and colonialism involving Sulus and Dyaks, Bugis and Balinese, Arabs and Chinese, Dutch and British. Much as Conrad lauded the British empire, then, his colonial settings reveal a racial, cultural, and political hybridity that confounds the unifying pastoral mythos of an imagined imperial community like Greater Britain.

At the same time Conrad feared the relentless drive toward "global connectedness" and "total administration" that marked late nineteenth-century New Imperialism (White, "Conrad" 187). Inaugurated by the 1884–85 Berlin Congo Conference and the subsequent "Scramble for Africa," this intense phase of annexation saw a handful of Western states unify the globe's most far-flung regions into a single economy. New Imperialist expansion served as Conrad's "point of departure as a writer" and remained a prominent concern throughout his career (Bongie, "Exotic Nostalgia" 270). In his late essay "Travel" Conrad laments "this earth girt about with cables," since, "the latitudes and longitudes having been recorded once for all . . . they can no longer appeal to the spirit of adventure, inflame no imagination, lead no one up to the very gates of mortal danger" (*Last* 88, 90). The passage offers a fitting epitaph to Conrad's oeuvre, recalling the atmosphere that dominates his fiction: of adventurers clearing a path for administrators and bureaucrats, of sail ships making way for steamers and submarine cables, of wilderness lined with telegraph wires and train tracks.

Rather than reviving Britain's mythic rural past, then, Conrad's colonies reflect the global ascendance of a distinctly urban modernity. His writing repeatedly underscores how New Imperialism linked colonies and metropole within "a single, interacting and interdependent urban system," a "global urban culture" (King, *Urbanism* 2, 42). In doing so, Conrad emphasizes not only the modernization of cities within the colonies but the absorption of more remote territories into an increasingly urbanized world.[9] In "Travel" Conrad complains that central Africa soon "will be bristling with police posts, colleges, tramway poles, and all those improving things" (*Last* 89). In "An Outpost of Progress" (1897) one of the foolish traders excitedly anticipates his African river station becoming a town with "quays, and warehouses, and barracks, and—and—billiard rooms" (44). In "The End of the Tether" (1902) modern steamers are pejoratively associated with cable trams (176, 182). But such modernization often fails to take. At the Outer Station in *Heart of Darkness,* Marlow witnesses "a boiler wallowing in the grass," a "railway truck lying there on its back," "a stack of rusty rails," and a hole filled with broken pipes (19–20). Like the dilapidated remains of Heyst's Tropical Belt Coal Company in *Victory* (1915), such remnants of progress litter Conrad's empire in a state of premature deterioration and perpetual disrepair. Almayer's "new but already decaying house" is merely the first sign that modern things fall apart in Conrad's colonial outposts (4), which occupy a nether region between encroaching urbanization and a wilderness resistant to the transplanted rural idylls of Greater Britain.

But unlike Almayer, whose folly fails to bring British colonization to Borneo, Conrad built his early reputation on what critics called his "annexation" of the Malay Archipelago. Within a few years of the publication of *Almayer's Folly,* one reviewer praised Conrad as a "notable literary colonist[ ]" who "has annexed the Malay Peninsula for us" (qtd. in Sherry, *Critical* 110). Yet while that region occupies a substantial portion of Conrad's work—from *Almayer* to *The Rescue* (1920)—Conrad spent relatively little time there and admitted to supplementing his spotty knowledge of Malay culture with what he called "dull, wise books" like Alfred Russel Wallace's *The Malay Archipelago* (*Collected* 2: 130). Given Conrad's limited knowledge of the archipelago, there is a general consensus that the region provided him a space on which to project his concerns regarding his original and adopted homelands. Usually this is taken to indicate that Conrad was "wedded to the chivalric codes of his ancestral tradition and disdainful of middle-class materialism" (Parry, *Conrad* 13). Class in Conrad's fiction thus tends to be read in two related ways—as a nostalgic coda to Britain's waning feudal order and as a pessimistic prologue to the bourgeoisie's administrative ascendance.[10] Yet some of the central players in Conrad's colonial fiction are neither gentleman-explorers nor aspiring professionals. They belong instead to an expanding if degenerate underclass of clerks, minor traders, and lesser officials: Almayer and Willems in the Malay fiction; Kayerts and Carlier in

"An Outpost of Progress"; the Station Manager, pilgrims, and members of the Eldorado Exploration Expedition in *Heart of Darkness*. Displaying neither aristocratic virtue nor proletarian gusto, these figures also lack the organizational acumen of the professional-managerial class, embodying Conrad's anxieties about both the masculinity and the skills of those administering the modern empire. Narrow-minded, spiteful, and undeservedly pompous, this rogue's gallery aligns some of the elements of modern imperialism that Conrad most despised with the metropolitan lower middle class. Conrad's colonial agents are often not simply hollow men, but the little men of the petite bourgeoisie.[11]

Conrad's "annexation" of the Malay Archipelago as a primary locale for his early fiction thus serves not to reinvent British aristocracy in the colonies, à la H. Rider Haggard and other practitioners of the imperial romance. Nor is it merely that, as a region largely ruled by the Dutch, the Malay Archipelago gave Conrad "a safe ground, a concrete basis . . . to write with a certain amount of authority yet without the risk of discussing matters with which his English readers were too familiar" (Najder, *Chronicle* 100–101). Rather, Conrad projects upon the unknown archipelago the eradication of Britain's traditional rural life by urban modernity—a process in which the burgeoning suburb played a fundamental role. Indeed, if Conrad links British rural topoi with colonial spaces abroad, it is to suggest that both locales were being threatened by unchecked urban expansion and a rising lower middle class—a premise that parallels New Imperialism with suburban sprawl.

Suburban Sambir

We can see how little Conrad imagined the colonies as a revived English countryside—much less a Greater Britain—if we compare Almayer's domestic arrangements with those depicted by H. Rider Haggard in *Allan Quatermain* (1887), an immediate best seller published two years before Conrad began *Almayer's Folly*. While journeying up a treacherous African river, Quatermain and his crew come upon an unexpected sight: "a substantial-looking European house with a verandah round it, splendidly situated upon a hill, and surrounded by a high stone wall." Soon there appear "three figures, dressed in ordinary English-looking clothes": "a gentleman, a lady, and a little girl . . . walking in a civilised fashion, through a civilised garden" (39–40). The Mackenzies, a family of Scottish missionaries, show the explorers around their enormous garden, where "English vegetables, trees, and flowers flourished luxuriantly," and Mackenzie himself declares his home's protective moat "my *magnum opus*." Upon approaching the house, the explorers see that it is "a massively built single-storied building" with "a handsome verandah in front" and "roofed with slabs of stone" (41–42). Inside the exhausted explorers rest in "tidy rooms" on "clean white sheets" (56).

A veritable showplace for the regenerative potential of Greater Britain, Mackenzie's transplanted rural estate stands in stark contrast to Almayer's folly. Set in the fictional riverside outpost of Sambir, the folly features "great empty rooms" of "sashless windows" and "dust[y]" floors, as well as a verandah of "loose planks" (35, 12). The frame of the house sits on "uneven ground," with "stones, decaying planks and half-sawn beams . . . piled up in inextricable confusion" (12). Further beyond are some "overgrown paths," "ruined godowns" (warehouses), and a "little rotten wharf" (28).[12] Worse yet, the folly that Almayer inhabits by day is a virtual replica of the "old house" to which he retires each night (12). Indeed, Conrad underscores the folly's decay by making it practically indiscernible from Almayer's first home. Set on "rough supports," the old house has a ceiling of "torn rattan screens" and an "uneven" floor with "withered plants and dried earth scattered about" (15–16). There is a sitting room where "nobody ever sat"—for "there was nothing there to sit upon"—surrounded by walls of "dirty whitewash" and windows with "tattered blinds" (90, 158, 16). Outside "the verandah creak[s] loudly" underfoot, and a ladder of "shaky planks" descends to a "heap of rubbish," a "neglected courtyard," and "a narrow ditch, full of stagnant water" (16, 51, 56, 103, 119). Almayer's increasing frustration with his unruly wife and daughter leads to scenes of "smashed crockery," an "overturned table," "broken bottles," and a "chaos of demoralized furniture," and Almayer sleeps as bats fly overhead (144, 157). In the end Almayer torches his old house and moves into the folly for good, where he spends his last days languishing on opium in an attempt to forget his past.

An apparent study in racial degeneracy, Almayer's living conditions also invoke some of the central tropes of Victorian writing on the suburb. Paramount among them is a concern with premature decay. This concern is evident in a number of texts that appeared as Conrad began working on his novel and that are set near his north London lodgings, in lower-middle-class suburbs like Crouch End, Islington, and Holloway (A. Jackson 22). When the Hewetts move to Crouch End in *The Nether World* (1887), for example, Gissing presents the area with a view toward its impending obsolescence: "The streets have a smell of newness, of dampness; the bricks retain their complexion, the stucco has not rotted more than one expects in a year or two; poverty tries to hide itself with venetian blinds, until the time when an advance guard of houses shall justify the existence of the slum" (364). In "The Woes of Mrs. Caractacus Brown," a story published anonymously in an 1892 issue of *Cassell's Family Magazine*, the wife of a gullible bank clerk struggles with ramshackle dwellings in dreary Islington: "There was a black little kitchen, well-stocked with beetles, earwigs, crickets, mice, white ants, and rats. There was a study for Mr. Brown at the back of the house, smelling very mouldy, and with the paper peeling off the walls; and a little conservatory adjoining for Mrs. Brown, which had the single merit of promptly killing every plant that was ever put into it" ("Woes" 12). But perhaps the most famous example of the new decaying home occurs in George and Weedon Grossmith's *Diary of a Nobody* (1892). Widely considered the ur-text of suburban fiction, *Diary* first appeared in *Punch* between 1888 and 1889, just as Conrad was starting *Almayer's Folly*. It charts a year in the life of Charles Pooter, a hapless clerk who moves with his wife into new digs in Holloway. Their home, The Laurels at Brickfield Terrace, plays on the discrepancy between the suburban dream of a rural idyll and its reality as urban sprawl, and Pooter's earnest praise for the virtues of "Home Sweet Home" in the opening pages collides with a catalog of chores required by the new residence (27). Although he lives in slightly better surroundings than the Hewetts or Browns, and is quite pleased with his home, Pooter acknowledges its many faults—including a cracked garden wall and broken doorbell—and is constantly tacking down the carpet or touching up his walls and furniture with red paint.

The fiction of suburbia may seem unlikely source material for Conrad, whom we think of as prizing French masters like Balzac, Flaubert, and Maupassant. But he was a wide and voracious reader, enthralled by a broad range of literary genres: obscure memoirs, naval histories, travel narratives, and Victorian sensation novels. As a boy he read Dickens in Polish, and upon his arrival in England he was consuming anything that could teach him the language, including popular periodical fiction. His apparent submission of a story to *Tit-Bits* in 1886 implies that his reading of *Punch* may have preceded the late 1880s, when *The Diary of a Nobody* appeared.[13] Conrad's reading of Twain in the late 1880s, especially *Life on the Mississippi* (Higdon), may have led him to another prominent text in the fiction of suburbia, Jerome K. Jerome's *Three Men in a Boat*. Wildly popular when it was serialized in 1889, Jerome's tale of clerkly adventuring on the Thames perhaps inspired Conrad's decidedly darker "Story of an Eastern River," the subtitle of *Almayer's Folly*. In any case, regardless of whether he read suburban fiction, Conrad would likely have been attuned to its increasing prominence when he began writing.[14] And once his own literary career took off, Conrad became friends with a number of authors whose work addressed suburbia—Wells, John Galsworthy, Arnold Bennett, J. M. Barrie, and Edwin

Pugh, whose first book, *A Street in Suburbia,* appeared with *Almayer's Folly* in 1895. Conrad also proclaimed his admiration for Gissing, with whom he corresponded (see *Collected* 2: 464–65).

The prematurely decaying home central to much suburban fiction made up part of a broader "discourse of domestic complaint" during the Victorian era. According to Sharon Marcus, this discourse "showed how legal conventions, building conditions, and dwelling practices" all kept London's suburban houses from upholding the first rule of English domestic lore: that every man's home is his castle (108). The discourse of domestic complaint called attention to what seemed an inherent corruption in new middle-class homes. Charles Booth highlights the phenomenon in *Life and Labour of the People in London,* glossing the kind of comments found in the press: "Of one whole district it is said that it has been 'ruined by bad building, having everything else in its favour'; of other parts, and frequently, that 'much iniquitous building has been allowed'; and shoddy houses are pointed to as the probable 'slums of the future.' In one district . . . 'new houses subject to speedy deterioration because badly built' are continually mentioned. Thus, in more detail, we have such statements as: 'houses only up a year, already cracking from roof to front door'" (8: 161–62). As always, *Punch* vividly captures the dilemma (fig. 4). "The New House," an 1871 illustration by George du Maurier, features a male figure ("Paterfamilias") at "his new home in the Suburbs." Just returned from a long trip, he throws himself into his garden chair and begins to "forget the misery" of his journey, enjoying his garden and a "faint fragrance" that "reminds him vaguely of days gone by." He even starts "to warble '*Home! sweet Home!*' when—O horror! . . . He suddenly descries a series of ominous cracks running up the back of his '*newly-built substantial semi-detached suburban residence.*'" His wife then "rushes out to tell him that 'that subtle aroma, so poetically suggestive of the past, proceeds from—*THE DRAINS!*'" Not thirty years before *Heart of Darkness,* it seems a cracked wall and backed-up drains were enough to elicit Conradian cries of horror in the suburbs.

In addition to transporting the prematurely decaying suburban home to Borneo, Conrad also depicts Almayer as a colonial analogue to the suburban type par excellence: the lower-middle-class clerk. Ostensibly a trader, Almayer is in fact little more than an underling to his patron, Captain Lingard, who hires him away from a Celebes warehouse to become a "kind of captain's clerk" and do Lingard's "quill-driving" (9). In Britain such quill drivers were among the largest and most rapidly growing occupational groups at the end of the nineteenth century. Indeed, the number of clerical positions grew fourfold between the 1870s and 1880s alone (Hobsbawm, *Industry* 156; G. L. Anderson 113). Despite

THE NEW HOUSE.

PATERFAMILIAS (with his belongings) returned last night from the Sea-side to his new home in the Suburbs. He has slept on his own spring-bed and breakfasted comfortably, and is beginning to forget the misery of the last four weeks. The children are out. The October sun is shining brightly. A faint fragrance pervades the house, which (he says) reminds him vaguely of days gone by. He strolls into his garden. The young Virginia creeper is turning a lovely red ; the kitten has grown into a cat, and a lily has actually burst into blossom from a bulb of his own planting. In the fulness of his heart, he throws himself into a garden chair, takes out his pipe, and begins to warble "*Home ! sweet Home !*" when—O horror ! . . . He suddenly descries a series of ominous cracks running up the back of his "*newly-built substantial semi-detached suburban residence*"—and the partner of his joys rushes out to tell him that "that subtle aroma, so poetically suggestive of the past, proceeds from—THE DRAINS !"

Figure 4. Semi-detached horror. (George du Maurier, "The New House," *Punch* 21 October 1871)

their growing numbers, G. L. Anderson points out that after 1870 clerks experienced a notable decline in social prestige, economic independence, job security, and advancement opportunities. As such, they were seen as a pathetic lot—engaged, according one commentator, in "adding up other men's accounts, writing other men's letters" (C. F. G. Masterman, *Condition* 70). "We aren't real men," complains the title character in Shan Bullock's *Robert Thorne: The Story of a London Clerk* (1907). "We don't do men's work. Pen drivers—miserable little pen drivers—fellows in black coats, with inky fingers and shiny seats on their trousers" (276). Under Lingard, Almayer occupies a position of servility and dependence similar to that of the typical Victorian clerk. Relations between these "blackcoated workers" and their employers were ruled by "unwritten, tacit expectations of conduct" (Lockwood 29), which recalls the way Lingard's hiring of Almayer depends implicitly on Almayer marrying Lingard's adopted daughter. As with Lingard's empty promises to Almayer about endless wealth, moreover, the Victorian clerk "was often exploited by the employer and great expectations frequently came to nothing" (29).[15] Such exploitation, in turn, fueled deep-seated resentment. The "conflict between such aspirations and the actual conditions of the clerk's servitude, dependence and low income . . . gave rise to frustration" and "considerable dissatisfaction" (Lockwood 30). This was all the more so given the clerk's fumbling attempts at social distinction and extravagant sense of self-importance, epitomized by that most famous clerical nobody, Charles Pooter.

Besides his occupational standing, Almayer's haughty superiority amid increasing squalor reflects a comical arrogance similar to Pooter's. Like Pooter, moreover, Almayer suffers from questionable taste in fashion and an inability to hold his drink, and both men fall victim to bad speculating, defiant servants, and unwanted guests.[16] Almayer's dreams of unlimited wealth and power—wholly incongruous with his ramshackle compound—recall Pooter's "harmlessly snobbish unavailing attempts to keep up appearances in shabby-genteel surroundings" (Porter 282). Indeed, Almayer struggles to save face against local rivals like Lakamba, whose affinity for Western commodities amplifies his cultural superiority. In contrast to Almayer's decaying dwellings, Lakamba's house is not only "a strong structure of solid planks, raised on high piles . . . covered in by an immensely high-pitched roof" (75); it is also filled with the "heavy stuff of European manufacture," including "a big arm-chair," a "European lamp" (75–76), and a music box that plays Verdi (88–89). In contrast to such formidable refinement, Almayer's crassly grandiose taste smacks of low-culture pretentiousness. When Almayer lords it over his compound, proclaiming himself the solitary white settler in eastern Borneo (122, 184, 208) and boasting eccentricities

like a flock of geese—"'the only geese on the east coast'" (122, 203)—his pos-
turing is ridiculously transparent. So much is evident when he shows off the
folly to a Dutch naval contingent that arrives in Sambir after British claims
to annexation dissolve. Dressed in a "white jacket and flowered sarong" (35),
Almayer fashions himself as a combination of European sophisticate and native
rajah, a shallow attempt to mimic both European and indigenous aristocratic
style. As Almayer drunkenly boasts of his new home, the "lighthearted seamen"
are "amazed by [his] wonderful simplicity and . . . foolish hopefulness," making
"salt-water jests at the poor man's expense" (36–37).

Yet unlike Pooter, Almayer is not so easily laughed off. In *A Personal Record*
Conrad recalls meeting Almayer's real-life prototype, the trader William Charles
Olmeijer, "whose name . . . could not be uttered anywhere in the Malay Archipelago without a smile," even though "there was nothing amusing whatever" about
him (138). Conrad plays Olmeijer for comic effect: the trader greets Conrad's
ship clad in flapping cretonne pajamas and awaiting the arrival of a pony that
flees into the forest when Olmeijer fails to control it. But Conrad also endows
this figure, in *A Personal Record* and *Almayer's Folly*, with an undercurrent of
anguish that makes him darker and more self-conscious than Pooter could ever
be. In doing so, Conrad transforms the comical suburban clerk into a subject of
modernist contemplation, if not a modernist subject in his own right. Ian Watt
has famously described Almayer as "a Borneo Bovary" who embodies both "the
petty-bourgeois and the Decadent stages in the history of *Bovarysme*" (51, 52).
Melding the comically lower-middle-class and the disturbingly decadent in this
way, Conrad considers the delusions of a Pooter figure in terms of an emerging
modernist sensibility that takes his interior life seriously. In doing so, Conrad
anticipates later appropriations of lower-middle-class little men—from Wells's
Mr. Polly and Kipps to Forster's Leonard Bast, Eliot's "young man carbuncular," and Woolf's Septimus Smith.[17] Moreover, Conrad universalizes the clerk's
blinkered subjectivity. The epigraph of the novel, taken from Henri-Frédéric
Amiel, asks, "Qui de nous n'a eu sa terre promise, son jour d'extase et sa fin en
exil[?]" (Who among us has not had his promised land, his day of ecstasy, and
his end in exile?). Despite the obvious humor Conrad finds in his protagonist,
this epigraph casts Almayer's plight as emblematic of a transcendental homelessness that bespeaks the modern, if not the human, condition.[18] In *The Soul of
London* Ford Madox Ford applies the same sentiment to an explicitly suburban
context, taking issue with authors who "sniff at the 'Suburbs' as a place of small
houses and dreary lives." Echoing the syntax, rhythms, and moral of Conrad's
epigraph, Ford claims that in every suburban home "dwells a strongly individu-
alised human being with romantic hopes, romantic fears, and at the end, an

always tragic death" (5). For Ford Conrad's ability to depict "an immense number of men in all ages and in all climes" also led to his broad appeal. "So that
just as Bunyan's *Pilgrim's Progress* finds innumerable readers" across the globe,
"so Mr. Conrad's books penetrate into the suburbs of London" (*Thus* 94).

Homelessness and *Ressentiment*

As the epigraph for *Almayer's Folly* suggests, exile is one of Conrad's foremost
preoccupations, and his fiction tends to dramatize feelings of national or existential displacement by means of his characters' inability to feel—or quite literally to be—at home. His second novel, *An Outcast of the Islands* (1896), begins
when the Dutch trader and titular outcast Peter Willems is sent packing by his
wife. Likewise, the opening of *Almayer's Folly* displaces the protagonist's sense of
belonging before it has even been established. As Almayer's wife calls him home
to dinner, her "shrill" and "unpleasant" voice sends him retreating into reverie,
where "his dream of wealth and power" clashes with his memories of "twenty-
five years of heart-breaking struggle on this coast where he felt like a prisoner"
(3–4). Born in Java to parents dissatisfied with colonial life, Almayer recalls leaving his boyhood home like the hero of an adventure story, "ready to conquer
the world, never doubting that he would" (5). He soon becomes protégé to the
famed Captain Lingard, who promises him endless wealth to marry Lingard's
"adopted" daughter, the offspring of slain Sulu warriors. But Lingard's promises
come to naught when he inexplicably disappears, leaving Almayer to fend for
himself amid cunning rivals and a spiteful wife. We learn all this as Almayer
travels from "the verandah of his new but already decaying house" to "the house
where he lived—'my old house' he called it" (4, 12).

Like Almayer's decaying homes his feelings of domestic displacement and
existential exile can be understood in light of the suburban discourse of domestic complaint. According to Marcus, the discourse was at its foundation a critique of English land ownership. Though every Englishman's home should have
been his castle, most of the nation's land belonged to a small number of aristocrats and institutions, known as freeholders, who leased their property to speculators or other developers. Legal reformers believed that because the leasehold
system forced most middle-class citizens to rent homes, it deprived the English
of the freedoms inherent in home ownership (Marcus 109). A freeholder's lease,
often granted in ninety-nine-year increments, also discouraged construction
of more substantial dwellings, since any property reverted to the freeholder at
lease's end. Moreover, speculators often sold parts of the leases to others: "Not
untypically, then, a row of terraces set in a parcel of land that had recently been

sold comprised houses in various states of construction, some fully furnished and occupied, some standing for years as unfinished 'carcasses' because their individual developer had temporarily run out of funds" (Marcus 109). Gissing sets his short story "The House of Cobwebs" in such an area in suburban Surrey: "a little row once tenanted by middle-class folk, but now for some time unoccupied and unrepaired" (3). In this tale an aspiring novelist finds shelter with a former chemist's apprentice who inherited three empty houses from his uncle. The heir is disappointed, however, by the property's condition and the fact that only a year remains before the houses revert to the freeholder. Nevertheless, he relishes the property and intends to stay on until his lease is up: "Property's property, even when it's leasehold and in ruins" (20). "The House of Cobwebs" is to some extent an exception to the discourse of domestic complaint, in that inhospitable lodgings produce genuine feelings of belonging in the occupants. At the same time the story decries the leasehold system that keeps commoners from enjoying home ownership. As the heir asks his lodger, "could anything be more cruelly unjust than this leasehold system?" (19). It is unclear to what extent Gissing is praising residents who feel at home in the most unpropitious surroundings or lamenting the waste of so many uninhabited dwellings. Regardless, by emphasizing the way the leasehold system left many homes incomplete, uninhabited, or in disrepair, Gissing echoes the discourse of domestic complaint in excoriating the suburbs for creating a surplus of English houses but a deficit of English homes.

In a parodic microcosm of that peculiar metaphorical homelessness created by the English leasehold system and its subsequent speculative development, Almayer's multiple houses render him figuratively homeless, since both dwellings cast doubt on his proprietary rights. Almayer was bequeathed his old house when he married Lingard's adopted daughter—an act of questionable generosity that only reinforces Almayer's dependence. Lingard built the house for the newlyweds, and years after his mysterious disappearance the "half-obliterated words—'Office: Lingard and Co.'—were still legible" on one of the doors (15), a sign that he continues to assert his ownership in absentia. Indeed, Conrad figures Lingard as the freeholder who leases his property to Almayer for the price of marriage and Almayer as a tenant who grows disconsolate at his lack of ownership. Almayer's wife also wrests control of the old house from him, turning the curtains into clothing, burning the furniture for firewood, and inviting the Malay statesman Babalatchi into plots against Almayer (26, 90–91, 59). Meanwhile, his new house, the folly, remains an unfinished shell intended for English settlers who never arrive. Almayer's control over his new home is made all the more tenuous when a Dutch naval contingent holds a court of inquiry there to investigate reports that Almayer sold gunpowder to anti-Dutch insurgents. It is on this occasion that, "for the first time in its history," the lights can be seen shining from the folly at night, and the house accommodates someone other than Almayer (144).

The impermanence of Almayer's homes is reinforced by his daily journeying between dwellings, which emphasizes his transience and failure to feel secure in either house. Indeed, his constant movement between homes makes him a parodic colonial double of the male suburban commuter. Almayer recalls two Dickensian clerk-commuters: John Wemmick in *Great Expectations* (1860–61) and Reginald Wilfer in *Our Mutual Friend* (1864–65). Wilfer, a "poor clerk" who lives in Holloway like Pooter, must journey home through "a tract of suburban Sahara, where tiles and bricks were burnt, bones were boiled, carpets were beat . . . and dust was heaped by contractors" (32–33). Wilfer's commute recalls Almayer "wandering sadly in the overgrown paths" between his homes (28), and Wilfer's regret that "what might have been is not what is!" (33) anticipates the opening lines of Conrad's novel, as Almayer slips "from his dream of [a] splendid future into the unpleasant realities of the present hour" (3). Rather than merely echoing Dickens, however, Conrad transforms the daily commute into a vertiginous, never-ending journey that underscores Almayer's sense of exile. His contrasts with Wemmick make this all the more apparent. A male personification of the separate spheres, Wemmick rigidly divides his public and private selves. This division is symbolized by his suburban home, "the Castle," a miniature fortification with cannon, drawbridge, and moat. As Wemmick tells Pip, "The office is one thing, and private life is another. When I go into the office, I leave the Castle behind me, and when I come into the Castle, I leave the office behind me" (231).

Almayer does not enjoy this luxury. While his return to his old house at the novel's outset mirrors the commutes made by Wilfer and Wemmick each evening, Almayer in a sense never really leaves home. This doubling of domestic displacement is reinforced by the fact that Lingard's office occupies the old house. Rather than providing a sanctuary from work, Almayer's old house reminds him of his doomed enterprise, so that even when he comes home, he is returning to a failed business. By the same token Almayer's new house, which he has built himself, represents the culmination of his labor in the archipelago and the final undertaking of his career. Yet this product of Almayer's labor ultimately devolves into a space of retreat and escape. Though Almayer heads there each day as if departing for work, his activities are relegated to aimless wandering and solipsistic fantasizing. Through this intertwining of labor and leisure, of work-space and home-space, Conrad confounds the myth of domestic autonomy from the site of business. The abandoned office of Lingard and Company and the unfinished edifice of the folly represent Almayer's failure to divorce domesticity from work.

Thus, Almayer's feelings of homelessness stem not from an absence of dwelling space, but from an excess of inadequate or unruly domesticity. Catherine Jurca has identified a similar sense of homelessness in depictions of the American suburb—a homelessness based, as in Victorian Britain, on the discrepancy between the ideals of home making and the realities of house building. According to Jurca, the American suburb is riven by the notion that middle-class residences lack requisite emotional depth. Consequently, suburban identity in the United States is structured around a perceived sense of victimization that Jurca calls "sentimental dispossession": "the affective dislocation by which white middle-class suburbanites begin to see themselves as spiritually and culturally impoverished by prosperity" (7). However, rather than Almayer's homelessness anticipating Jurca's diagnosis of an "irresolvable psychic split between the material delights of affluence and its corresponding spiritual horrors" (47), Conrad's allusions to British suburbia demonstrate something altogether different. Whatever horrors Almayer faces, they result not from an abundance of dispiriting wealth, but from its complete and dispiriting absence. Almayer's homelessness thus underscores a distinction between the twentieth-century American suburb, in which material wealth breeds existential poverty, and the late-Victorian British suburb, in which the nebulous distinction between material wealth and poverty—the often indiscernible boundary between suburb and slum—simultaneously provokes feelings of unearned superiority alongside a nagging sense of failure and inadequacy. Such affective confusion is a hallmark of British portrayals of the suburb. Like characters from Charles Pooter to Robert Thorne, Almayer wavers between delusions of grandeur and an inferiority complex, a duality commonly ascribed to members of the suburban lower middle class.[19]

Rather than the sentimental dispossession of American suburbanites, then, Almayer is beleaguered by something closer to *ressentiment*—that mixture of outrage, envy, and consuming ill-will that Nietzsche diagnoses in *On the Genealogy of Morals* (1887). Precipitated by a tension between feelings of superiority and a powerlessness to act upon them, *ressentiment* is for Nietzsche a form of surrogate or repressed vengeance against one's real or imagined enemies. This is familiar affective terrain for Conrad, whom Jameson considers "the epic poet" of *ressentiment* (*Political* 268).[20] While I examine *ressentiment* and its colonial context more fully in chapter 6, I want to emphasize here that the affect manifests itself in a form of envy often associated with the lower middle class. In his 1915 study of *ressentiment,* Max Scheler found the affect "most active . . . in the petty borgeoisie and among small officials" (66), and Jameson sees it as "an adaptation to the constricting situation of the petty bourgeoisie and the objective contraction of possibilities" (*Political* 205). Likewise, Almayer's *ressentiment* regarding his homelessness emerges from his déclassé status in Sambir, where his self-importance is undercut by the eroding condition of his homes. Recall, for example, Almayer's bitterness toward his more wealthy local rivals Lakamba and Abdullah. Indeed, the very sight of Abdullah's home elicits one of the gestures Scheler associates with *ressentiment:* Almayer "shook his fist toward the buildings that in their evident prosperity looked to him cold and insolent, and contemptuous of his own fallen fortunes" (15).

Jerry-Built Empire

The suburban discourse of domestic complaint typically reserved its greatest horrors for speculative housing—residences built before buyers were secured. Speculative development required managing a complex set of variables: anticipating residential demand, acquiring land and capital, and keeping funds from drying up amid inevitable complications (Dyos, "Speculative" 644). The man credited with transforming the housing industry into a speculative enterprise was Thomas Cubitt, London's most prolific nineteenth-century builder. Before him builders typically subcontracted much of their work to specialists—masons, carpenters, bricklayers, plasterers. Cubitt brought together his own cadre of craftsmen and laborers, uniting their disparate trades in a single firm. Without the kind of large-scale operation perfected by Cubitt, the phenomenon of speculative housing and the rise of suburbia would not have been possible (Dyos, "Speculative" 649). Having launched his business with savings earned as a carpenter on an India-bound ship (H. Hobhouse 4), Cubitt experienced the kind of success that eluded the young Conrad, frustrated as he was in searching for sail berths. Cubitt almost single-handedly developed Stoke Newington, where Conrad lived between 1880 and 1886, as well as Bessborough Gardens, where Conrad moved in 1889. Located between the increasingly urban Belgravia and Pimlico, Bessborough Gardens was part of an area built in the mid-nineteenth century as a transition "between the older Georgian model of suburban expansion and the railway-driven, outer London model" (Saint, *London* 235). It was in Bessborough Gardens that Conrad began writing *Almayer's Folly.*

Though Cubitt's own developments were highly regarded, speculative houses gained a reputation for falling to rack and ruin, sometimes before inhabitants were secured. According to Marcus, architectural journalists often "criticized the poor construction of speculatively built London housing and frequently related stories of decaying, 'falling houses' whose lack of permanence also threatened the longevity of their occupants. . . . The very walls and floors that were supposed to provide a secure framework for private space were perceived as liable to gape, sag, and cave in, as though 'prepared expressly for premature decay and ruin'" (111). The poor reputation of speculative building was cemented by the popular epithet *jerry building*. It was a term Conrad would have known, as it derived from nautical slang—the jerry-mast and jerry-rig being shipboard quick fixes (Burnett 21). Moreover, as Conrad recalls in *A Personal Record,* a variant of the term came up during his master mariner's exam, when he was asked how he would construct a "jury-rudder" (188).[21] In any case, although jerry building and speculative building were not equivalent, the terms became synonymous with rapidly constructed homes of inferior quality.

Not surprisingly, the most reviled figure in the discourse of domestic complaint, and the nemesis of naive suburbanites like Pooter, is the speculative or "jerry" builder. Often drawn from a variety of professions by the lure of quick cash, the speculative builder earned a dubious reputation as an architectural scam artist—the used car salesman of the Victorian era, or as one urban historian puts it, "the artful dodger of the suburbs": "the builder of walls without footings, the bricklayer who knew how to mix mortar without cement, the carpenter who could lay floors over green joists, the plumber who knew just how to lay drains without traps or how to install cold water systems which had a positive, intimate, and lethal acquaintance with the sewage arrangements" (Dyos, "Speculative" 674). If the suburb dweller could not find a worthy home, it was thought to be because the speculative builder could not—or would not—construct one. In a typical article on "Suburban Dwellings" during the 1880s, the *Times* reported on two speculative builders summoned before a local board of health for erecting houses with inadequate foundations: "The ground . . . was but little firmer than turf, and the so-called concrete consisted of brick rubbish, spent lime, and other materials from old buildings, and had been put in dry. . . . Samples were placed before the magistrates, who crumbled the material between their fingers with the greatest ease" (4). Their apparent carelessness and irresponsibility notwithstanding, speculative builders were convenient scapegoats for wide-ranging changes in the construction industry and radical shifts in the housing of England's populace (Dyos, "Speculative" 676–77). Indeed, many speculative builders might be excused, if only for not having been professional builders at all. Encompassing practically anyone in a tight financial spot, their ranks included "labourers and mechanics, servants and publicans, shopkeepers and merchants, lawyers and clergymen" (Dyos, *Victorian* 123). After making extensive repairs on his own home, the down-and-out clerk-protagonist of *Robert Thorne* considers building as an occupational last resort, consoling himself that "if the worst comes to the worst I can set up as a jerry-botcher" (Bullock 251).

Almayer makes the very transition Thorne contemplates, transforming himself from a subordinate clerk into a colonial incarnation of the speculative builder. When he begins "building his new house for the use of the future engineers, agents, or settlers" of the British Borneo Company, he spends "every available guilder on it with a confiding heart" (33). But when the rumors of British annexation fail to materialize, "the half-finished house built for the reception of the Englishmen receive[s] . . . the name of 'Almayer's Folly'" (36–37). As one critic suggests, Almayer "is merely a naïve and reckless speculator who, on the basis of guesswork and rumor, has put at risk all of his available cash" (Willy 9). We never see Almayer engaged in any construction, but he apparently builds the folly himself in the hopes of a future payoff. Almayer inhabits the role of jerry builder most notably when a Dutch naval contingent arrives on his shores. As the officers inspect his new home, Almayer "stamp[s] his foot to show the solidity of the neatly fitting floors and expatiat[es] upon the beauties and conveniences of the building" (36). The officers treat Almayer's handiwork with the same humored skepticism that we do.

As an imperial jerry builder, Almayer also represents a form of imperialism that is inherently speculative. Indeed, given that the folly owes its existence to Almayer's misguided speculations about housing British colonists, Conrad connects the expansionist mandate of New Imperialism with the vagaries of metropolitan suburban development. This link would provide later critics of imperialism an apt metaphor for rapacious colonization. In a passage that makes Conrad's depiction of Almayer seem prophetic, a contributor to C. F. G. Masterman's *The Heart of the Empire* (1901) describes the exploits of Cecil Rhodes in terms of speculative building. Citing Rhodes's dictum that expansion is everything, the author describes Rhodes as an "imperial jerry-builder" who "obtain[ed] as much territory as possible, without waiting to see whether it was of any value, or whether he was in a position to deal with it when he got it" (qtd. in C. F. G. Masterman, *Heart* 360).[22]

But Almayer is no Cecil Rhodes, and his single new development hardly compares with the prodigious output of London's speculative builders. Rather than anticipating the onset of New Imperialism, as Chris Bongie argues, Alamyer's plan "proves no more than a folly in an (Old Imperialist) world where colonialism has its limits" (*Exotic Memories* 155). For Bongie Almayer's house is "more an emblem of his own decadence than a sign of the imminent, and eminently reprehensible, colonial ascendancy his murky vision anticipates" (*Exotic Memories* 156). Yet Almayer prepares the ground for further incursions into the archipelago, particularly in his relationship with Lingard. Though Lingard is a trader, Conrad places his motives beyond the realm of pure profit, making him a reservoir of indigenous knowledge and a protector of the archipelago's secrets. In *An Outcast of the Islands,* Conrad describes him as "always visiting out-of-the-way places of that part of the world, always in search of new markets for his cargoes—not so much for profit as for the pleasure of finding them" (14). Dubious as this description may seem, Conrad emphasizes in *Almayer's Folly* that rather than simply opening unknown territories to international trade, Lingard hopes to protect his own interests from further exploitation by imperial governments. He discovered a river whose whereabouts he has kept secret— a fact that places him "above the common crowd of sea-going adventurers" (7) and beyond the reach of encroaching European powers. Thus, Lingard saw that "for many years the green and peaceful-looking islands guarding the entrances to the promised land kept their secret with all the merciless serenity of tropical nature" (8). As "Rajah Laut," or king of the sea, Lingard is ordained with an aristocratic, quasi-divine mission to protect the "promised land" of the archipelago, whose "green and peaceful-looking islands" recall the "green and pleasant land" of William Blake's "Jerusalem."

Whereas Lingard seeks to preserve his peaceable kingdom, however, Almayer has no qualms about bringing greater commercial expansion to the islands, hoping to welcome the British as his new tenants since they "knew how to develop a rich country" (36). Despite Almayer's failed attempt to woo British colonization, he still endangers Sambir's relative independence, attracting Dutch attention to his smuggling of powder and intensifying local trade rivalries. In a discussion with the English Captain Ford near the end of the novel, the Malay statesman Babalatchi recalls an era when fighting in the region was limited to skirmishes between pirates on "silent ships with white sails." For Babalatchi those "old times were best. . . . That was before an English Rajah ruled in Kuching. Then we fought amongst ourselves and were happy. Now when we fight with you we can only die!" (206). Babalatchi implicitly contrasts sail with steam technology and alludes to Sir James Brooke, the "English Rajah." Though the Sambir of *Almayer's Folly* has not yet been invaded by the "police posts, colleges, tramway poles, and all those improving things" that Conrad condemns in his essay "Travel" (*Last* 89), these markers of modernity do not seem far behind.

Speculative Accounts and Personal Records

About a decade after publishing *Almayer's Folly,* Conrad claimed that writing a book "is an enterprise as much as the conquest of a colony" (*Last* 132). The statement seems to acknowledge what reviewers called his annexation of the

Malay Archipelago. But according to his 1912 memoir, *A Personal Record,* Conrad began his first novel without intending to write a book—much less to colonize foreign lands: "The conception of a planned book was entirely outside my mental range," as was "the ambition of being an author" (115). Conrad's speculative foray into fiction suggests a parallel between his own writing and Almayer's enterprise. Critics have noted that Conrad saw Almayer's bitterness, excess pride, lack of perseverance, and overindulgent imagination in himself.[23] Overlooked is that Conrad also shared some of Almayer's occupational experiences before abandoning the sea. Much as he liked to suggest otherwise, Conrad's transition from merchant marine to writer was anything but smooth sailing. He contemplated a surprising variety of economic ventures that included trading in Australia and the East Indies, investing in a Canadian railroad, and whaling (Karl 190–91, 214). His maternal uncle and guardian, Tadeusz Bobrowski, encouraged Conrad to be "a sailor combined with a salesman," advising him to import Ukrainian flour and sugar to England and eventually helping him buy into a London shipping firm (qtd. in Najder, *Polish* 59, 101). Conrad actually managed one of the firm's warehouses for four months in 1891 and later claimed he "introduced a new system altogether both as to book keeping and storage" (*Collected* 4: 21). By that time he had also been working on *Almayer's Folly* for two years, and he describes his memories of writing one chapter as "inextricably mixed up with the details of the proper management of a waterside warehouse" (*Personal* 34).

If Conrad's warehouse work and bookkeeping recall Almayer's early employment in a Celebes warehouse and his position as a "quill driver," Conrad's incompetence managing his finances also parallels Almayer's prodigality and poor economic planning. Bobrowski's letters provide an intriguing window into this side of Conrad—especially since they scold his nephew in terms uncannily similar to Conrad's own descriptions of Almayer and the real-life Olmeijer. In one letter Bobrowski castigates his nephew as being without "endurance and perseverance in decisions," caused by "your instability in your aims and desires." This he attributes to Conrad's father and paternal uncle, who "were always involved in various projects . . . hatched . . . in their imagination." Though they were "offended when anyone criticized them," such criticism usually "gave the lie to their dreams, hence [their] bitterness towards those who saw more clearly." Bobrowski felt the young Conrad risked the same end: "In your projects you let your imagination run away with you—you become an optimist; but when you encounter disappointments you fall easily into pessimism—and as you have a lot of pride, you suffer more as the result" (qtd. in Najder, *Polish* 147–48). Such judgments are echoed in Conrad's account of Olmeijer, whom he describes in

A Personal Record as a "person of weak character," always "aiming at the grandiose" with both "foolish optimism" and "deep-seated mistrust." Conrad claims Olmeijer "governed his conduct by considerations removed from the obvious, by incredible assumptions, which rendered his logic impenetrable to any reasonable person" (26, 126–27, 134).

But Conrad seems most like Almayer in his financial speculations. In an 1880 letter Bobrowski tells Conrad he does not have enough money "to make good all your follies," in this case "speculating on credit." Bobrowski invokes a favorite refrain—the irresponsibility of Conrad's paternal lineage—warning him to "beware of risky speculations based only on hope; for your grandfather squandered all his property speculating, and your Uncle, speculating always with other people's money and on credit, got into debt." Though not against speculation per se, Bobrowski demands that his nephew engage in it only after saving enough of his own money; "otherwise you will always make nothing or, worse still, less than nothing, which is the situation you are in now. . . . That's what you have gained by speculation" (qtd. in Najder, *Polish* 73). Significantly, Conrad contemplates another speculative scheme just after beginning *Almayer's Folly*. In November 1886 Bobrowski implores his nephew "to realize that it was not in order to speculate that I parted with some of my 'precious metal' and sent it to London—not for speculation but to help my nephew who chose to live there" (Najder, *Polish* 112). Bobrowski's wonderfully bad pun on "precious metal" suggests Conrad had an interest in mining that his uncle refused to support. Indeed, when Bobrowski died just months before *Almayer's Folly* was accepted for publication, Conrad speculated away his inheritance—about sixteen hundred pounds—on shares in a South African mine (Knowles and Moore 114).

Given Bobrowksi's impatience with speculation, financial or otherwise, it is not surprising that Conrad never told him he was writing a novel. But in *A Personal Record* Conrad retroactively fashions his writing career as a speculative venture—one taken up without intent of writing a novel, much less publishing it—the better to transform his failed financial gambles into a narrative of successful speculation in writing. Though *A Personal Record* is silent about the failed economic ventures Conrad contemplated in his early London years, its narrative clearly provides a form of financial and emotional compensation. As if challenging Bobrowski's mandates against speculation, Conrad fashions his writing career as an unintended gamble that pays off. This becomes apparent in *A Personal Record* when Conrad imagines an exchange—both conversational and economic—with Olmeijer in the afterlife. Though Conrad admits to a "small larceny" in using Olmeijer's name, he claims it "was the common property

of the winds" (144). Denying theft, Conrad then reverses the charge, suggesting that Olmeijer owes *him*. "Since you were always complaining about being
lost to the world," Conrad points out to Olmeijer, "you should remember that
if I had not believed enough in your existence . . . you would have been much
more lost" (145). The exchange clearly echoes Bobrowski's correspondences with
Conrad. Just as Bobrowski attempted to salvage his nephew's career, so too does
Conrad imagine his writing as saving Olmeijer from greater misfortune. Yet
where Bobrowksi advises against speculation in the hopes of making his aimless
nephew a responsible young man, Conrad shifts the medium of speculation
from finances to fiction, reasoning that without his novel Olmeijer's losses in
life would have been even greater. Rather than improving Olmeijer's character,
as Bobrowski would do for his nephew, Conrad uses Olmeijer's character as
an opportunity for a novel enterprise. Admitting that he may have capitalized
on Olmeijer, Conrad nonetheless credits himself with saving the man—if not
financially, then through fiction.

In cancelling his debt to Olmeijer, Conrad yields an even greater return for
himself. In his condescending comments on Olmeijer's extravagance and lack of
resolve, Conrad makes himself an equivalent to the knowing and occasionally
overbearing Bobrowski. In doing so, Conrad uses *A Personal Record* to expunge
his own personal record of aimlessness, impracticality, and bovarysme. At the
same time Conrad bests Bobrowski by invalidating his uncle's warnings against
speculation. *A Personal Record* suggests that by risking it all on Almayer, the
itinerant Polish sailor took up a new career as one of Britain' foremost novelists, making a speculative development of the territory that Almayer failed to
colonize for Britain.

That Conrad figures his speculations as succeeding where Almayer's failed
is evident when comparing the author's personal record of paid debts with his
protagonist's unbalanced account book. Near the end of the novel, Almayer's
daughter, Nina, abandons him for Dain Maroola, the Balinese prince who was
Almayer's last hope in discovering Lingard's hidden treasure. As Nina and Dain
depart forever, Almayer immediately makes it "his business . . . to forget . . . systematically and in order" (195). The word choice is telling, as if Almayer thinks
a determined blotting of his memories will somehow compensate for both his
lethargic work ethic and the wealth Dain would have brought him. Almayer's
first step in his amnesiac enterprise is to return to his old house and force open
the long-abandoned office of Lingard and Company. The scene, worth quoting at length, mixes financial speculation and writing in a rich counterpoint to
Conrad's own speculations about Almayer in *A Personal Record*. Having com-
piled a "detailed programme of things to do" (198), Almayer

went towards the office door and with some difficulty managed to open it. He entered in a cloud of dust that rose under his feet. Books open with torn pages bestrewed the floor; other books lay about grimy and black, looking as if they had never been opened. Account books. In those books he had intended to keep day by day a record of his rising fortunes. Long time ago. A very long time. For many years there had been no record to keep on the blue and red ruled pages! In the middle of the room the big office desk, with one of its legs broken, careened over like the hull of a stranded ship; most of the drawers had fallen out, disclosing heaps of paper yellow with age and dirt. . . . All those things had cost a lot of money at the time. The desk, the paper, the torn books, and the broken shelves, all under a thick coat of dust. (199)

The passage offers an early example of what Watt calls delayed decoding: Conrad's initial reference to "books" suggests that the office may have been a kind of study or library, but the more specific reference to "account books" corrects that impression. Yet just as the visual impression often "lies closer to the origin of meaning than the operation of subsequent thought" in Conrad's work (B. Johnson 348), so too does a telling ambiguity linger in the initial generic reference to books, linking clerical record keeping with reading and writing more broadly. One effect of this impressionistic trace is to recall the literary ambitions of many fictional clerks. Suburban texts often depict clerks as aspiring litterateurs, perhaps because their jobs involved transcribing documents without leaving any personal imprimatur. But their attempts at art usually lead to further *ressentiment,* which Jameson describes as the domain of "unsuccessful writers and poets, bad philosophers, [and] bilious journalists" (*Political* 202). The most famous clerkly litterateur manqué may be Forster's Leonard Bast, who struggles over Ruskin, peppers his conversation with passé allusions, and is aptly crushed to death by a bookcase. Other clerical nobodies—Pooter, Caractacus Brown, Robert Thorne, Septimus Smith, and the clerks in Gissing's "House of Cobwebs" and Kipling's "Finest Story in the World"—also attempt to transform their workaday musings into art.

Of course, Almayer is neither an intellectual nor a writer, but insofar as he shares the bovarysme of his clerical colleagues, his intention "to keep day by day a record of his rising fortune" reinforces the link between record keeping and writing in the passage above. Almayer's empty account book is thus analogous to an incomplete manuscript or unfulfilled diary.[24] Michael Fried bolsters this analogy in arguing that Conrad's impressionism stems from a "fantasmatic relation to the blank page," a relation "at the heart not just of *Almayer's Folly* but of Conrad's fiction generally" (199). Fried aligns Conrad with Crane and other literary impressionists in their "encounter with the materiality of writing" (199), the physical act of inscribing words on a blank page. What distinguishes Conrad from a more general "'impressionist' problematic grounded in the writer's relation to the act of writing" is that his texts proceed by means of "erasure" (211). At its core, according to Fried, *Almayer's Folly* involves a palimpsestic form of erasure, "a visible marking over a preexisting writing." This Derridean erasure emerges as "a mode of writing that renders irretrievable a prior writing . . . but whose own legibility *as* erasure depends upon a certain material survival of the original 'text'" (212, original emphasis). Fried's notion of erasure operates much like the trace of the original impression that remains after delayed decoding, and his reading pivots on the novel's climactic scene, in which Almayer responds to Nina and Dain's departure by covering over their footprints on the beach. The act reflects a broader "project of erasure, as if not only the imprint of Nina's footsteps in the sand but Almayer's entire store of memories of her . . . were so much writing that now had to be undone" (212).

For all his interest in blankness and inscription, erasure and the process of writing, Fried says nothing of Almayer's empty account books. But Conrad confirms their importance by returning to them in *An Outcast of the Islands*, his second novel and the prequel to *Almayer's Folly*. When Lingard furnishes Almayer's office "with reckless prodigality," Conrad notes a new desk, revolving chair, and bookshelves—items bought "to humour the weakness of Almayer, who thought all those paraphernalia necessary to successful trading" (299). But Conrad places particular emphasis on "a pile of books" that draws great interest from the locals. These "books of magic" inspire rumors of a power "that guides the white men's ship's over the seas, that gives them their wicked wisdom and their strength"; a power that makes white men "irresistible while they live" but "the slaves of Jehannum when they die" (299–300). Were Almayer only so lucky. Though the "empty-headed quill-driver" believes Lingard's furniture puts him "at the head of a serious business," and that "great wealth" will simply "follow upon conscientious book-keeping," Almayer discovers "no successful magic in the blank pages of his ledgers" and soon abandons the office (300). Conrad adds further irony by filtering this flashback through a present in which Almayer enters the office surrounded by "the senseless and vain decay of all these emblems of civilized commerce," most notably "a glass inkstand, solid with dried ink," and a heap of "yellow papers" (301–2).

By depicting these blank pages in both *Almayer's Folly* and *Outcast*, Conrad not only attests to Almayer's failed business enterprise with Lingard. He also figures the blank pages as a forerunner, if not a blueprint, of the folly itself. In building the folly, Almayer seeks to blot out his prior failings and start over with a clean slate. But as the unfinished product of his imaginative and financial speculation, the folly remains as incomplete and empty as his ledgers. Indeed, the dusty blank pages of Almayer's account books have their architectural equivalent in the "great empty [and] dusty rooms" of the folly (35, 41). Recalling Fried's sense of erasure as "a visible marking over a preexisting writing" (212), we see that Almayer's old house is both erased and reinscribed by the folly. For what is the folly if not Almayer's attempt to replace his old house, and the business it represented, by figuratively building over it and its associations with Lingard? But such erasure also emphasizes the folly of Almayer's venture. While his new home seeks to erase the one that Lingard built and furnished, the old house remains, and remains virtually indistinguishable from the new. The folly of Almayer's folly is that it can't eliminate the old home and business—only replicate it in another form. Almayer seeks to bring a newer form of imperialism to Sambir and thereby to replace Lingard's legacy. At the same time the folly also represents Almayer's surrogate attempt to fill in the empty pages of his old account books, thus giving substance to Lingard's empty promises. Together with the folly, Almayer's account books confirm the novel's obsession with erasure. Like the clerks whose diaries offer a record of cultural vacuity, then, Almayer's architectural folly can only reinscribe a blankness that incessantly re-covers (covers over and retains) what it set out to erase.

This dynamic is characteristic of *ressentiment,* insofar as what produces the affect is an inability to forget what gave rise to one's frustration and anger in the first place. As Nietzsche suggests, the man of *ressentiment* is akin to a dyspeptic: "he is never 'through' with anything" (39), continually reexperiencing former slights in a process Michael André Bernstein pithily dubs "reminiscence-as-suffering" (204). Almayer endures such remembered pain throughout the novel, particularly when he tries to erase Nina's and Dain's footprints in the sand. But a more acute form of this inability to forget can be witnessed in Almayer's grandiose gesture of burning down his old house and taking up permanent residence in the folly—an act of attempted erasure that only resumes his suffering. Almayer's systematic attempt to rid himself of Nina's memory in the folly, which Fried rightly calls a project "hyperbolic forgetting" (209), is completely undermined by his recurrent resentment. As Conrad suggests of Almayer, "only one idea remained clear and definite—not to forgive her; only one vivid desire—to forget her" (192). By inverting the proverbial dictate to forgive and forget, Conrad reveals the impossible logic of Almayer's thinking.

Attempting to erase the old house by burning it down, Almayer makes the folly an architectural emblem of the palimpsestic erasure that reinscribes what it set out to expunge.

Conrad's speculations build *A Personal Record* from much the same material. His autobiographical account is an exercise in remembering rather than forgetting, but the incomplete and continually interrupted manuscript of *Almayer's Folly*—which he nearly loses twice as it journeys with him from London to France to Africa to Switzerland to Poland and back to London—haunts the pages of *A Personal Record* just as the unfinished folly haunts Almayer as he travels back and forth between his two homes. Indeed, a recurrent image in *A Personal Record* has Conrad bent over the manuscript of *Almayer's Folly*, whether "tracing on the gray paper of a pad" in his sailor's bunk (18), writing on the same desk where he attends to his "ship's log-book" (38), or placing the pages "on the writing-table" in his boyhood room upon returning to the Ukraine (46). The recurrent image mythologizes Conrad's writing as a natural extension of his maritime work, transforming his desk into a surrogate sailing vessel. In *A Personal Record* he claims that he carried his belief in solidarity and fellowship "from the decks of ships to the more circumscribed space of my desk" (10) and that he preserves the recommendation letters "signed by various masters" from his days as a sailor "in my writing-table's left-hand drawer" (177).

Conrad's ship-turned-desk in *A Personal Record* salvages the desk in Almayer's office, which was "careened over like the hull of a stranded ship" (199). Likewise, Conrad makes it clear that, unlike Almayer, he fills his own blank pages with text. "There was no vision of a printed book before me as I sat writing at that table, situated in a decayed part of Belgravia," Conrad claims, recalling his thoughts before starting *Almayer's Folly*. But the years have left their "evidence of slowly blackened pages" (*Personal* 27). Unlike Almayer, who fails to make good on his own speculative venture, Conrad fashions himself in *A Personal Record* as a protagonist who can fill the empty pages of his account book, transforming his own speculations into a successful writing career. Despite the speculative beginnings of his first novel, Conrad claims he found his new calling "the moment I had done blackening over the first manuscript pages of *Almayer's Folly*" (115). These blackened pages not only contrast with the empty leaves of Almayer's account books. They also become Conrad's new home as he delivers himself from the world of sail to the world of fiction. As he puts it in the preface to *A Personal Record*, "a novelist lives in his work," where he "remains, to a certain extent, a figure behind the veil . . . a movement and a voice behind the draperies of fiction" (4). Perhaps evoking Almayer's dying days in the folly,

Conrad claims he "buried a part of myself in the pages" of the completed manuscript (*Collected* 1: 153).

Almayer's Sans Souci

This chapter has argued that suburban fiction and the discourse of domestic
complaint gave Conrad a foundation for critiquing New Imperialist expansion and at the same time nurturing a modernist sensibility anguished by exile.
In turn Conrad crafted his own writing career as a speculative enterprise that
succeeded where Almayer's failed. I want to conclude by speculating on what
Almayer imagined his new home might have been. Early in the novel we learn
that Almayer's father was "a subordinate official employed in the Botanical Gardens of Buitenzorg" (5). The reference not only hints at Almayer's eventual
plans for the folly but links those plans to the suburban development already
taking place in the colonies where Conrad sets his early fiction. As I suggested in
chapter 1, suburban development occurred around a number of colonial cities
in the eighteenth and nineteenth centuries. Among the earliest of these was the
Dutch East Indies capital of Batavia (now Jakarta). Buitenzorg, which lies some
thirty miles south of Batavia in the temperate highlands of Java, offered relief
from the lowland capital's humid, swampy conditions. Buitenzorg (meaning
"sans souci" or "carefree") originated as a private retreat for the Dutch governor-
general in the mid-eighteenth century. Its proximity to the capital and its cooler
climate helped make Buitenzorg the official summer residence for subsequent
governors-general. In fact, Buitenzorg became the first colonial hill station,
famous "nearly a decade before the British even discovered the Himalayan village of Simla" (Reed 557), the summer capital of the British Raj, immortalized
in Kipling's *Plain Tales from the Hills*.

More than a seasonal retreat for the government, however, Buitenzorg also
marked the southern limit of Batavia's rapidly expanding suburban development. Wealthy Batavians had been constructing country houses in the *buiten-
plaatsen,* or "sites outside" the city, as early as the 1620s (Archer, "Colonial" 35).
By the mid-eighteenth century such houses extended as far south as Buitenzorg.
The "new country elite" who built these houses were not landed gentry, but
landowners tied to Batavia's political and economic power (J. G. Taylor 52, 76).
John Archer describes this class as suburban, since their residences "were not
country 'seats' in the English sense of the term—landed estates that served as a
base of economic and political security *apart from* the metropolis. Rather, their
existence and utility were wholly dependent on their owners' engagement in the

administration and trade of the city" (Archer, "Colonial" 35, original emphasis). But as Dutch officials transferred more of their governmental duties to Buitenzorg, the area became powerful in its own right, "a center of administrative decision second only to Batavia" (Reed 557). During the nineteenth century most of the capital's European residents had migrated in and around a stretch of southern suburbs known as "New Batavia," where they resided in the airy rooms of uniform, single-story white homes (Abeyasekere 54). As the southern extreme of the capital's administrative and residential orbit, Buitenzorg increasingly drew both officials and private citizens away of the city. In doing so, it contributed to the "wholesale suburbanization of Batavia" in the early nineteenth century (Archer, "Colonial" 40).

Buitenzorg's famous botanical garden strengthened the area's political and popular cachet further still, reinforcing its status as a burgeoning tourist destination and health resort. Begun in 1817 as an extension of the governor-general's estate, the garden opened to the public in the second half of the nineteenth century. By this time Buitenzorg had eclipsed Batavia as the official executive residence of the Dutch East Indies, becoming "the foremost locus of political authority in colonial Indonesia" (Reed 558). Thanks to the botanical gardens, Buitenzorg also gained international renown as a center of rest and recreation. An 1854 article in *Fraser's Magazine* describes Buitenzorg as "the pleasure-retreat of the good people of Batavia" and calls the botanical grounds "the paradise of all gardens, both as regards beauty of site, and the extreme order and cleanliness with which they are kept" ("Excursion" 112–13, 115). The 1911 *Encyclopedia Britannica* propounds this view: noting Buitenzorg's political significance, it praises the area as "remarkable on account of its splendid botanical garden," which is "among the finest in the world" ("Buitenzorg" 770). With governmental support the garden developed into a full-blown research institute in the second half of the nineteenth century, boasting its own museum, library, agricultural school, herbarium, and scientific laboratories. Around the same time improved roads increased traffic with the capital, and a new railway cut travel time via carriage by more than half (Abeyasekere 53).[25] According to an American travel writer in the 1890s, all of these elements made Buitenzorg "the pride and show-place of Java, the great center of its social life, leisure interests, and attractions." Besides those living in reach of Batavia, "residents from other parts of the island make it their place of recreation and goal of holiday trips" (Scidmore 49). Indeed, Buitenzorg's suburban thoroughfares merged with the botanical garden itself: "All the suburban roads are so many botanical exhibitions approaching that in the great garden" (Scidmore 72).

Originating as a private estate and semiofficial government retreat, Buitenzorg virtually absorbed Batavia's administrative role as the Dutch colonial capital. Along the way it helped pull Batavia's population into the city's southern
suburbs and transformed itself into a vibrant tourist spot and resort. In doing
so, Buitenzorg epitomized what Cooper and Stoler call "the 'embourgeoise-
ment' of imperialism in the late nineteenth century" (31). Whether Conrad
ever visited Buitenzorg, he no doubt looked askance on its fusion of colonial
bureaucracy and bourgeois leisure. In choosing it as Almayer's boyhood home,
Conrad implicitly endows his first protagonist with the elements of modern
imperialism that Conrad himself despised. Although Conrad tells us the young
Almayer was "nothing loth to leave . . . the parental bungalow" in Buitenzorg,
"where the father grumbled all day at the stupidity of native gardeners" (5),
the setting would have provided Almayer with a prototype for his grandiose
plans. When Almayer begins his new house for the British Borneo Company,
he believes himself to be laying the foundations for a British Buitenzorg, the
"Sans Souci" of Sambir.

Improbable as such a modern spectacle might seem in the jungles of Conrad's Sambir, subsequent writers would discover elements of suburbia in the
"real" Malay Archipelago. Just over a decade after the publication of *Almayer's
Folly*, the colonial official Frank Swettenham described Britain's Malay States as
"the Clapham Junction of the Eastern seas" (342), referring to the busy South
London train station and commercial entrepôt, which one commentator at the
time called "the capital of Suburbia" (Crosland 79). By the 1930s a female writer
who traversed the island of Java by car described "the surface of [its] main
roads" as being "perfect as that of any 'arterial' horror" in Britain; another travel
writer that decade claimed Batavia had "as little interest, character, or beauty
as Zenith," the American suburb where Sinclair Lewis's Babbitt sells real estate
(qtd. in Rush 158, 165). In the 1940s an Englishman who grew up on Java in
the 1890s lamented the "crude elements of the machine-made world" that had
"shoved back the trees, brushed aside the tiny habitations, and straightened the
winding roads" on the island (qtd. in Rush 102).

In many ways Conrad anticipated such changes.[26] Consider Kayerts and Carlier, the protagonists of "An Outpost of Progress," who begin their fated administration of a small African river station in a fit of domestic do-it-yourselfery
that recalls the household tinkering of stock suburban males like Pooter: "The
first day they were very active, pottering about with hammers and nails and red
calico, to put up curtains, make their house habitable and pretty; resolved to
settle down comfortably to their new life" (41). Woefully unprepared for their

impending isolation, they imagine themselves taming the wilderness with ease: "We shall let life run easily here! Just sit still and gather in the ivory those savages will bring" (41). Inspecting their station arm in arm, jocularly issuing each other orders to stay out of the sun, Kayerts and Carlier are "two perfectly insignificant and incapable individuals" (40). Jacques Darras, invoking Flaubert's oblivious copy-clerks, aptly describes Kayerts and Carlier as the Bouvard and Pécuchet of the jungle (53), caricatures of bourgeois myopia attempting to administer a colonial outpost.

Or consider *The Shadow-Line* (1917), in which Conrad's unnamed narrator chucks his berth as first mate of an Eastern ship amid an intense bout of boredom with the globe's shrinking room for adventure. His first stop is the Officer's Home in Singapore, "a large bungalow with a wide verandah and a curiously suburban-looking little garden of bushes and a few trees between it and the street. That institution partook somewhat of the character of a residential club, but with a slightly Governmental flavour about it" (8). In its appearance, standard of conduct, and clientele, the home reflects the narrator's problems with modern imperialism itself, and the home's prosaic façade is symptomatic of the narrator's disenchantment with a world where all mystery is gone: "There was nothing original, nothing new, startling, informing to expect from the world: no opportunities to find out something about oneself, no wisdom to acquire, no fun to enjoy. Everything was stupid and overrated" (23).

Finally, consider "The End of the Tether," in which an aging captain meets the white trader at an Eastern post based, like Sambir, on Conrad's visit to Berau (Visser 37). Sounding both melancholy and exasperated with the future of imperialism, Conrad proleptically claims that Batu Beru was not then "what it has become since: the centre of a prosperous tobacco-growing district, a tropically suburban-looking little settlement of bungalows in one long street shaded with two rows of trees, embowered by the flowering and trim luxuriance of the gardens, with a three-mile-long carriage-road for the afternoon drives and a first-class Resident with a fat, cheery wife to lead the society of married estate-managers and unmarried young fellows in the service of the big companies" (277). Unlike Sambir the future Batu Beru is hardly a study in degeneracy. Yet with its shady streets and carriages, its company men and society wives, it would have struck Conrad with as much horror as anything in the heart of darkness.

5

Beyond the Abyss

Degeneracy and Death in the Edwardian Suburb

The folly of modern imperialism would not come home to many Britons until the Anglo-Boer War (1899–1902). Thanks to its incursions in South Africa, Britain entered the twentieth century victorious—though far from triumphant. In exchange for the Transvaal and the Orange Free State, the British suffered a host of devastating blows. These included unexpected military defeats during "Black Week" late in 1899, reports of physically unfit volunteers by the inspector general of recruiting in 1900, the Prince of Wales's desperate plea— "Wake Up, England!"—in 1901, and a stubborn Boer guerrilla campaign that held out until 1902. By war's end the greatest empire on earth had expended over two hundred million pounds and twenty-two thousand lives on an enemy whose entire population numbered less than a fifth of all British forces in South Africa. Following the war, a series of inquiries into government preparedness and military conduct revealed "official ineptitude and administrative chaos" at all levels (Searle 44). Meanwhile, publicized accounts of sickly recruits led to an Interdepartmental Committee on Physical Deterioration, which rejected fears of widespread degeneracy but called for serious improvements in working-class conditions.[1] A cult of national efficiency ensued, as Britain's poor showing in the war provoked a "demand for fundamental reforms in all branches of public life" (Searle 44). Liberals triumphed at the polls in 1906 on a platform of much-needed reform in the war's aftermath, but voices across the political spectrum clamored for vital changes—in hygiene and medical standards, in education and public administration, in working and living conditions—at the heart of the empire.

While a major target of reform was the urban slum, "the abyss," as Edwardians called it, suburbia became increasingly central to debates about national health following the Boer War. On the one hand, the suburb's low population and proximity to nature were touted as obvious remedies for urban blight, over-crowding, and physical deterioration. On the other hand, unchecked sprawl in the preceding decades led to rural despoliation—and, as many believed, na-tional degeneration—on a massive scale. Seeking an orderly alternative to the ad hoc incongruity of suburban speculative building that had run rampant in the 1880s and 1890s, the London County Council, empowered by the 1900 Housing of the Working Classes Act, purchased land beyond its boundaries for a series of planned cottage estates. Though well-intentioned, the LCC only served to replicate the high density and perpendicular uniformity of that dreary inner-suburban grid, the bye-law street (Tarn 87). To some extent these estates even replaced the East End as a primary locus of national degeneracy. "Who and Where are the Unemployed?" asked the author of *Blackwood's* lead article in April 1905. He answered by pointing to those "workmen's colonies erected dur-ing the past few years" in the north and east of London, which he dubbed "the new suburban slums" ("Who" 453–54). "Any one who has a lingering doubt as to the physical degeneration of the British workman," he suggested, "may have it dispelled by a brief visit to a labour-yard in a London suburb. Men of all trades, all ages, and all sizes are to be seen there. Not one in ten is fit for heavy work. Very few of them take kindly to labour of any kind" ("Who" 455).

Such working-class suburbs were not the only sign of the nation's waning health. Even the more respectable suburbs seemed to have a debilitating effect on an already sedentary middle class. "The conditions of life among clerks and business men generally are most unwholesome," wrote one journalist at the turn of the century, who claimed that "a large mass of them, instead of even getting such exercise as would be gained by walking to and from their homes, take considerable daily journeys in trains, or avail themselves of tramcars" (Almond 668). Likewise, a contributor to C. F. G. Masterman's collection *The Heart of the Empire* (1901) wrote of clerks that "the portion of daylight not allotted to the far from healthy occupations of their calling is consumed in the inevitable journeys to and from the suburbs in which their houses are situated" (F. W. Lawrence 63). Even so, the same author concluded by defending the suburb as a last bastion of racial renewal: "The Housing Problem is not to be solved in the slums. . . . What is essential that the public conscience should realise is that it must protect its suburbs" (F. W. Lawrence 80–81).

Whether viewed as a symptom of national degeneracy or its cure, the sub-urb thus played an increasingly prominent role in Edwardian debates that took questions of national and imperial health beyond the abyss. Indeed, if the suburb emerged as the dominant residential space in Britain with the climax of late-Victorian imperialism, anxieties inspired by the Anglo-Boer War only strengthened the suburb's place in Edwardian debates over urban life, national health, and the future of the empire. In terms of legislation these debates culminated in the 1909 Housing and Town Planning Act, Britain's first major piece of planning legislation, which established regulations for the layout, sanitation, provision of amenities, and use of land for development.[2] Influential as it was, the Town Planning Act was only part of a much wider response to the suburb's role in the social crisis at the turn of the century—a response that engaged architects and social planners, philanthropists and industrialists, as well as journalists, playwrights, and novelists. This chapter surveys suburbia's shifting role in a variety of progressive responses to the Boer War crisis—from Fabian debates over the centralization of London in the scientific prophecies of H. G. Wells, who sought to channel the suburb's misguided energies into a predecessor of his modern World State, to the Little Englander nostalgia of E. M. Forster and the social critic C. F. G. Masterman. In addition to examining these Edwardian writings, particularly Wells's *Tono-Bungay* and Forster's *Howards End,* this chapter also examines the imperial subtext of nonliterary suburban discourses, particularly those addressing Ebenezer Howard's garden city and its more adaptable spin-off, the garden suburb.

What fuses these otherwise disparate accounts of empire and suburbia is a recurring obsession with death—appropriate for an era still grieving Victoria's passing and contemplating its own national and imperial mortality. If imperial exploits abroad, as many felt, led to degeneration at home, then suburban expansion was among the most alarming symptoms. Making Britain a nation of suburbs thus seemed to some a fitting if not very comforting tribute to a race in decline. The writing of the journalist and Liberal politician C. F. G. Masterman offers an especially vivid case study of how, in the crisis following the Boer War, the suburb overtook the slum as a defining social problem of the Edwardian era. For Masterman imperial expansion not only exacerbated degeneracy at home but threatened to reduce all of England to a sprawling suburban cemetery, a sepulcher of the nation's social body.

Masterman's Bitter Harvest

As a Fellow of Christ's College, Cambridge, Masterman came down to London in 1900 but soon left his rooms near Parliament for a tenement in the southern suburb of Camberwell. Within a decade Masterman would establish himself not only as a lecturer, editor, and journalist with four books of his own, but as a Liberal M.P. and a junior minister in Asquith's government. A friend of the Chestertons, Trevelyans, and Webbs, Masterman also moved in circles that included Wells, Shaw, and Winston Churchill.[3] In 1901 Masterman edited his first major work, an essay collection titled *The Heart of the Empire*, whose contributors promoted a new Liberal agenda that defied the Boer War and supported state intervention in social welfare. Underlying each contribution was the conviction that imperialism and domestic social reform were irreconcilable political alternatives (B. B. Gilbert xv). As Masterman puts it in his keynote essay, he and his colleagues agreed that "no amount of hectic, feverish activity on the confines of the Empire will be able to arrest the inevitable decline" of conditions in the metropolis ("Realities" 25). In suggesting that Britain pursued empire building at the expense of its own citizenry, Masterman pointed to the emergence of "a new race," the Town type. Spawned amid the "turbulent rioting over military successes" that gripped London in 1900—known as mafficking (after Mafeking, a South African town taken by British troops)—the Town type represented to Masterman "the problem of the coming years": "Upon their development and action depend the future progress of the Anglo-Saxon Race" ("Realities" 7). Over the next decade Masterman continued to make proclamations of this kind about the future race of England. Yet his work underwent a subtle but significant shift in focus. From the Town type, who would reappear in other texts under slightly different guises, emerged the Suburban, a central player in Masterman's most famous book, *The Condition of England* (1909).[4]

Despite his sometimes overwrought prose Masterman's chapter on "The Suburbans" in *The Condition of England* stands as the most sustained early discussion of this new national contingent. Private, materialistic, and disengaged from social, religious, or intellectual concerns, the Suburbans, according to Masterman, are "easily forgotten." Prizing above all "a life of Security . . . Sedentary occupation . . . [and] Respectability," they are "detached" and "self-centered," if "unostentatious" (*Condition* 68, 69–70). Indeed, the Suburbans are not without worthy attributes, such as "the good nature and ready generosity, the cleanliness of life, the still unbroken family tradition; all animated by that resolution . . . to 'make the best of it'" (*Condition* 82). In the end, however, Masterman finds their lives "laborious and often disappointing": dulled by routine and overtaxed by petty responsibilities, their "cheerless occupations" and expectation to keep up appearances "leave little surplusage of mental energy to be devoted to larger issues" (*Condition* 90). Hence their "communal poverty of interest and ideal," their "noticeable absence of vision," and their "limited outlook beyond a personal ambition" (*Condition* 76, 80). Masterman concludes that even "the most hostile critics" will grant the Suburbans lead "a clean and virile life." But he sounds ambivalent at best in deeming them "the healthiest and most hopeful promise for the future of modern England" (*Condition* 95).

Masterman was a Little Englander, so part of his misgivings about the Suburbans involved their inherently expansive and imperialist aspirations. Throughout *The Condition of England* it is the middle-class male rather than the aristocrat or laborer who has "become the 'frontiersm[a]n of all the world,'" "pursuing his own business, conquering great empires" (*Condition* 14, 18).[5] Masterman saw in Suburbans a reactionary strain that left them susceptible to "an outlook upon Imperial affairs which is less a conception of politics than the acceptance of a social tradition: which leaves suburban seats securely Conservative" (*Condition* 81). As a result of its unthinking jingoism, suburbia had become the home of "that dense and complacent 'Imperial citizen' who despises 'the foreigner,' and could set right or improve upon generals in the field or admirals on the ocean, and is satisfied with its universe and its limitations because it has resolutely closed all doors and windows through which there might appear the vision of larger other worlds" (*Condition* 82).

Perhaps the most surprising aspect of Masterman's Suburban is his emergence from a type that seems his complete opposite: the degenerate city dweller. Although he appears in *The Condition of England* as if fully formed and autonomous, the Suburban slowly takes shape in Masterman's earlier writing. The first manifestation is, in fact, the new Town type in *The Heart of the Empire*. Physically "stunted, narrow-chested, easily wearied; yet voluble, excitable" ("Realities" 8), the latter seems discernibly different from the healthy and subdued Suburban. Yet clear similarities are apparent. The Town type, for example, displays "patience under misfortune, a persistent cheerfulness, family affection, and neighbourly helpfulness" ("Realities" 8), qualities that will be echoed practically word for word in Masterman's description of the Suburban's "family affection . . . cheerfulness, and . . . almost unlimited patience" (*Condition* 74). Likewise, the full-blown philistinism and myopic practicality of the Suburban are foreshadowed by the Town type's "increasing craving for material satisfaction . . . and a concentration on the purely earthly outlook of a commercial Imperialism, heedless of abstract spiritual ideas" ("Realities" 9). This lack of religious conviction, moreover, confronts the Town type with a dilemma that becomes central to the Suburban's identity. Of the Town type Masterman claims, "With the older faiths largely inoperative, and no new enthusiasm to occupy their places, life becomes more and more approximated *either to a dull persistence in routine,* with no attempt to look before and after and to estimate the worth of action, *or else to a fierce and uncontrolled individualism,* concentrated only on the pleasures and advancement of the family, tearing the social fabric into its component threads" ("Realities" 32, emphasis added). While monotony and social fragmentation are fused together in the Suburban, the qualities appear here as alternate consequences of the Town type's loss of spiritual values. Moreover, the unplanned reactiveness of the Town type suggested above will find itself repeated in the Suburban tendency to "act without preparation . . . without preliminary negotiation" (*Condition* 69). Indeed, if the Suburban epitomizes "that dense and complacent 'Imperial citizen' who despises 'the foreigner'" (*Condition* 82), such a quality first appears to Masterman in the Boer War jingoism of the mafficking Town type.

From the Abyss (1902), Masterman's next major work after *The Heart of the Empire,* offers another moment in the evolution from Town type to Suburban as the representative figure of modern England. Written from the perspective of those caught in the hazy region between destitution and lower-middle-class subsistence, *From the Abyss* offers a wide array of urban types. These include the Hooligan (a reprise of the mafficking Town type) and a figure called John Smith. Though clearly of working-class origins, John Smith is, not unlike the Suburban, a "cheery, respectable, ineffective figure" (*From* 62), and the "unconquered human aspiration" Masterman discovers in his home reasserts itself in the "unconquered human aspiration" of the Suburban's pleasant if dreary domicile (*From* 31; *Condition* 70). Indeed, Masterman's ironic description of John Smith—"a British householder and ruler of an Empire upon which the sun never sets" (*From* 62)—anticipates the Suburban's conflation of domestic and imperial interests. Yet another figure in *From the Abyss* is Economic Man, who inhabits a slightly higher rung on the social ladder than John Smith: a "polished, whitewashed variety," Economic Man "drift[s] out to daily work, to write other men's letters" (*From* 35), much like the Suburban male who "is sucked into the City at daybreak," engaged in "adding up other men's accounts, writing other men's letters" (*Condition* 70). For Masterman Economic Man exhibits a leveling of "the highest and lowest elements of human nature" (*From* 35). Though his mechanical existence depletes his vital energy, that energy will one day come back to haunt him: "The seeds of tangled weeds sown long ago will spring up to sudden disfigurement of the well-ordered garden; in some mysterious manner the tides of the great sea will pulsate through the little trim, clean, ordered pond, and trouble the serenity of its surface" (*From* 37).

This description of Economic Man marks a significant shift from Masterman's early Town type to his later Suburban. Here we witness the Town type's inner turmoil and excitability sublimated into Economic Man's repressed primal ancestry. This repression, in turn, finds its most mature form in the Suburban's perennial frustration and *ressentiment.* As I suggested in the previous chapter, *ressentiment* constituted a characteristic affective response to the simultaneous sense of superiority and inferiority harbored by the lower-middle-class suburbanite. In *The Condition of England ressentiment* debilitates Masterman's Suburban for much the same reason: "There enters into his soul a resentment which becomes at times almost an obsession. . . . He wants a little more than he can afford . . . and the demands of rent and the rate-collector excite in him a kind of impotent fury" (*Condition* 73–74). More than the landlord or the tax man, however, it is the working classes that fuel the Suburban's *ressentiment:* "He is becoming every day more impatient with the complaining of the poor. . . . He believes that the 'unemployed' consist exclusively of those who are determined to go softly all their days at the public expense—the expense of himself and his class" (*Condition* 73).

With the Suburban Masterman noticeably externalizes the potentially disruptive if suppressed forces that threaten to well up from within the ostensibly urban Economic Man. That is, Masterman transforms these forces from a sort of ancestral élan vital that haunts Economic Man to the Suburban's outward—and decidedly class-distinct—enemy: the proletariat. The "devitalised life" of the Suburban "is concentrated into revolt against the truculent demands of 'the British working man,'" whom he imagines "surging up his little pleasant pathways, tearing down the railings, trampling the little garden" (*Condition* 73, 72). The primitive forces that threaten to deface Economic Man's "well-ordered garden" from within (*From* 37) have become, for the Suburban, an exterior but no less primitive danger: "the 'letting in of the jungle' upon the patch of fertile ground which has been redeemed from the wilderness" (*Condition* 72).

In emphasizing "the 'letting in of the jungle,'" Masterman's critique of suburban resentment not only deploys a common trope equating the poor and working classes with colonized savages. It also invokes the title of a story by the laureate of imperial fiction, Rudyard Kipling. A chapter from *The Second Jungle Book* (1895), "Letting in the Jungle" recounts Mowgli's revenge on the Indian village that forced him into exile.[6] Under Mowgli's direction his animal friends wreak havoc on the village—chasing off its inhabitants, eating its crops, razing its houses, and allowing the wilderness to overtake any remnants of settled life. Masterman's reference taps into the rich if ambiguous discursive link between suburb and empire. His Suburban believes himself to be standing his ground against invasion by the forces of primitivism and degeneracy. Yet just as Kipling suggests throughout *The Jungle Books* that the animals behave more rationally than humans, Masterman implies that the defensive mindset of the seemingly civilized Suburban is faulty. For, as Masterman goes on to suggest, the Suburban is less a defender of his own enclosed garden than a trespasser colonizing whatever patches of rural land remain unclaimed. This is perhaps nowhere more apparent than when Masterman implies that, rather than shouldering the white man's burden, Suburbans are themselves agents of a dubious civilizing mission. "Civilise the poor," Masterman challenges, "expand their tiny rubbish yards into green gardens, introduce bow-windows before and verandahs behind . . . convert all England into a suburban city—will the completed product be pronounced to be 'very good'?" (*Condition* 77). In such passages Masterman not only challenges the Suburban's self-perception as an innocent defender of peace and tranquility but also imagines him as a degenerate invader. Like the Town type who is "every day pushing great arms forward over the surrounding fields" ("Realities" 11)—or John Smith, who will "continue in his progress to devour the fields and the villas surrounding his present abodes" (*From* 61)— the Suburbans are "covering the hills along the northern and southern boundaries of the city, and spreading their conquests over the quiet fields beyond" (*Condition* 70).

During the course of Masterman's writing, then, we witness a transformation of the mafficking urban Jingo hooligan into the imperial Suburban—a transformation that challenges the myth of suburb dwellers as pastoral pioneers rejuvenating civilization on the fringes of Greater London. Masterman's Suburban is himself an invader, surly and resentful, who undermines England's past and overshadows its future.

Indeed, *The Condition of England* attributes to Suburbans the same voracious expansion that seemed inevitable in the urban poor. In *From the Abyss* the poor "have descended [upon suburban terraces] with the irresistible impulse of our number, and the original inhabitants have fled panic-stricken away" (*From* 11).[7] But Masterman would soon reconsider the inevitable advance of slum over suburb; indeed, he would suggest that the very direction of the tide had reversed. In "The Burden of London," part of his 1905 book *In Peril of Change*, Masterman focuses on urban (especially slum or "ghetto") growth; yet we see a telling hesitation on his part to mark this growth as merely an urban phenomenon. "London is an aggregation," Masterman writes—and as he will later declare of the Suburbs, the aggregation is made of a "homogeneous substance: the City Dweller." However, more than his earlier Town type or Economic Man, this figure is both *of* the city and *beyond* it: "He is coagulated into a broad smudgy ring round the city which lives and moves. He dwells apart from the city which desires and is satisfied" (*Peril* 160). More than a foreshadowing of psychological and affective qualities, we see here a clear geographic shift in the evolution from Town type to Suburban, as the latter assumes a momentum once exercised only by the slum dweller. With his full-blown diagnosis of the Suburban, Masterman suggests that the most dangerous threat to the "Condition of England" no longer comes from the slum, but from the masses who managed to settle in the suburbs beyond the abyss.

In Masterman's Edwardian writing suburbanization replaces what was once the urban slum's degenerate flowering and irresistible flood. As such, Masterman endows the spreading of suburbia with an inevitability matched only by death. "Is this to be the type of all civilisations," he asks in *The Condition of England,* "when . . . progress finds its grave in a universal suburb?" (74). Masterman was not the first to make what Andrew Burke calls the "suburban-necropolitan con-nection"; since the mid-nineteenth century "the spectre of death haunt[ed] the promised vitality and life of suburbia" (148–49). The association between ceme-teries and suburbs emerged when public health reformers like Edwin Chadwick, fearing that dead bodies were intensifying the cholera epidemic, campaigned to move urban graveyards to the outskirts of cities.[8] Formerly integral to the shared spaces of everyday life, cemeteries came to exemplify what Michel Fou-cault calls heterotopias: real spaces that also offer "counter-sites" in which a culture's values are "simultaneously represented, contested, and inverted" (24). With their shift to the suburbs, Foucault suggests, cemeteries "came to consti-tute, no longer the sacred and immortal heart of the city, but 'the other city,' where each family possesses its dark resting place" (25). Like Foucault, Master-man recognized the effect of removing the dead from the space of the living; he lamented that beyond the city "are all the gigantic graveyards, where now lie so quietly under the long grasses the armies of the forgotten dead; mourned for a moment, and then huddled very speedily away from the active life of the living" ("English" 59). In the pastoral topos for which Masterman longed, a proximity to mortality and history renewed the life of the community: "The tombs and gravestones travelled backwards to a near past," and though "the shadowy fig-ures of the dead [were] resting through all the centuries," their "blood still beat" in the veins of the living (*Peril* 151).

When he asks in *The Condition of England* whether suburbia is to become "the type of all civilisations," and whether progress will "find its grave in a universal suburb," Masterman also connects the fated setting to questions of imperial mor-tality. It is not surprising to find Masterman linking suburbs, death, and empire in this way. In *From the Abyss* he suggests that money derived from the colonies led directly to deathly suburbs: "The speculative builder purchases, borrowed money is advanced, perhaps from South African millionaires," and "weird skel-etons of houses" arise (*From* 42). And in an essay on Tooting, Masterman dubs that lower-middle-class suburb "the place of all forgotten things" (*Peril* 155), pri-marily because it serves as the site of a large cemetery.[9] For Masterman Tooting's graveyard is of a kind with its other notable feature: a proliferation of hospitals, workhouses, asylums, barrack schools, and prisons, whose goal is an "ordered and regular existence" where everything would be "smooth, polished, spotlessly clean" (*Peril* 157). As in *From the Abyss,* where the impoverished narrator suggests that "Tooting may wildly seek to terrify our advance by converting its territory into cemeteries and lunatic asylums" (48), these institutions make the area a center of pathology and imprisonment, relegating all its inhabitants—young orphans and elderly derelicts alike—to a form of death in life. Significantly, Masterman's visit to Tooting offers an object lesson in imperialism:

> From the turnip fields of Tooting I apprehended the British Empire and something of its meaning; why we always conquered and never assimilated our conquests; why we were so just and so unloved. Amidst alien races we have brought rest and security, order out of chaos, equality of justice. . . . Yet there is not one amongst these alien peoples who would lift a finger to ensure the perpetuation of our rule, or shed a tear over its destruction. For the spirit of that Empire—clean, efficient, austere, intolerably just—is the spirit which has banished to these forgotten barrack-prisons and behind high walls the helpless young and the helpless old, the maimed, the restless, and the dead. (*Peril* 157–58)

Masterman here posits Tooting's imperative of hygienic efficiency as the Achilles heel of the British empire. Despite their continual annexation of territories around the globe, the British, Masterman suggests, rule not by assimilation, but through exclusion and expulsion, an obsessive maintenance of boundaries that privileges division and segregation. In other words, the British empire survives by a process akin to removing the dead from the space of the living, like the Victorian drive to relocate urban cemeteries to the suburban outskirts.

The turnip fields of Tooting are thus the site of Britain's bitter harvest, and their association with harvesting and inheritance yields another motif through which Masterman links imperialism, suburbia, and death. References to the end of the agricultural cycle recur throughout Masterman's writing, as in the essay "June in England," from *In Peril of Change.* The essay's biblical epigraph—"They made me a keeper of the vineyards: but mine own vineyard have I not kept" (*Peril* 146)—indicts England for failing to tend its own garden and thereby defaulting on its legacy. But it also blames this problem on imperialism, on looking after other fields to the detriment of England's own. As throughout his Edwardian texts, Masterman's equation of imperialist expansion with domestic degeneration was predicated on a belief that with cheaper imports forcing farmers from their land—and thus transforming the countryside into tracts of suburban development—the British were reaping what they had sown. It is a motif that is also central to *Howards End.*

Forster's End

Critics like Brian May and Stuart Sillars have noted ideological and stylistic affinities between Masterman and Forster, but their readings proceed cautiously, as if to justify making the comparison at all.[10] Yet these Edwardian Liberals were more than familiar with each other's work—if not with each other. Forster admired Masterman's writing for the *Independent Review,* a journal Masterman helped found with Forster's mentors Nathaniel Wedd and Goldsworthy Lowes Dickinson (Beauman 218–19). Forster was not only an enthusiastic supporter of the *Review,* which was initiated to oppose Joseph Chamberlain's aggressive imperial policies, but also a regular contributor of essays and short stories. In turn, as the literary editor of the *Daily News,* Masterman lauded *Where Angels Fear to Tread* (1905) and *The Longest Journey* (1907) and gave extensive praise to *A Room with a View* (1908) in the pages of the *Nation*—in each case noting Forster's peculiar insights into suburban life (Gardner 52, 73, 111). If nothing else, Masterman's influence on Forster is apparent from one of Forster's 1909 diary entries. Still at work on *Howards End,* Forster credited Masterman with "ma[king] me see how wide an abyss opens under our upper class merriment & culture" (qtd. in Colmer 104). Forster's reference to the abyss, a recurrent keyword in *Howards End,* not only confirms Masterman's influence on the novel but also suggests the extent to which Forster views socioeconomic status as a matter of life or death. For while the abyss represents urban poverty (a geographical place and a position on the class hierarchy), it is also a figurative grave, marking poverty as a state of social nonexistence. However, Forster's recognition of just "how wide" this abyss had become suggests that, like Masterman's, his focus will fall on those who are—in some cases only slightly—beyond the abyss, in the ever-expanding terrain of suburbia. Forster's representations of suburbia in *Howards End,* like those of Masterman in *The Condition of England* and elsewhere, draw attention to the cycle of life and death, using the motifs of inheritance and harvesting to figure the suburb as a national and imperial cemetery.

Howards End is conventionally read as a meditation on the war between country and city, but readers have begun to recognize the novel's concern with the middling spaces of suburbia. Critical discussions of suburbs in *Howards*

End often focus on the hapless clerk Leonard Bast: once considered a figure from the abyss—and the embodiment of Masterman's Town type—Bast has come to be seen as part of a suburban "infection of Howards End that threatens the house's, and the novel's sacred 'sense of space'" (Hegglund 413).[11] But suburbia casts a still wider net in *Howards End,* and Leonard is hardly its sole representative. Henry Wilcox's son Charles has "his own little house . . . in one of the Surrey suburbs" (70), which we later learn is Epsom (99, 123). Swanage, the southern coastal town that is home to the Schlegels' Aunt Juley, includes a "bourgeois little bay" (136). And even Forster's swelling homage to English landscape, the description of the Purbeck Hills at the beginning of chapter 19, acknowledges the expansion of London's semi-detachment: "Nor is Suburbia absent. Bournemouth's ignoble coast . . . herald[s] pine-trees that mean, for all their beauty, red houses, and the Stock Exchange, and extend to the gates of London itself" (121). If Masterman emphasizes the Suburban's emergence from the abyss, Forster focuses on the suburban colonization of the countryside that results from the imperial exploits of Henry Wilcox, a resident of Howards End and the owner of the Imperial and West African Rubber Company.

Early in the novel the Schlegels' Aunt Juley is sped via train from London to the Hertfordshire village of Hilton and the novel's eponymous country home, where her niece Helen has prematurely declared her love for Paul Wilcox. Before arriving at her destination, Aunt Juley must pass through a netherworld whose vaguely defined boundaries paradoxically suggest both the emergence and the ubiquity of suburbia. The passage recalls a motif common to suburban discourse—the relentless encroachment of a culturally foreign and degenerate modernity into once pristine English countryside. What merits close attention, however, is the scene's subtlety and figurative richness, which I would argue are singular among representations of suburbia:

> At times the Great North Road accompanied [Aunt Juley], more suggestive of infinity than any railway, awakening, after a nap of a hundred years, to such life as is conferred by the stench of motor-cars, and to such culture as is implied by the advertisements of antibilious pills. . . . The station for Howards End was at Hilton, one of the large villages that are strung so frequently along the North Road, and that owe their size to the traffic of coaching and pre-coaching days. Being near London, it had not shared in the rural decay, and its long High Street had budded out right and left into residential estates. For about a mile a series of tiled and slated houses passed before Mrs. Munt's inattentive eyes, a series broken at one point by six Danish tumuli that stood shoulder to shoulder along the

highroad, tombs of soldiers. Beyond these tumuli habitations thickened, and the train came to a standstill in a tangle that was almost a town. . . . Into which country will it lead, England or Suburbia? (13)

Fredric Jameson's provocative essay "Modernism and Imperialism" makes much of this passage, using it to theorize empire as the political unconscious of modernist aesthetics. Because a significant portion of Europe's economic base lay far from its own shores, Jameson argues, the imperial nation-state experienced a "spatial disjunction." This disjunction was the constitutive lack that produced modernism's emphatic will-to-style—whose intimations of autonomy attempt to correct the fragmentary effects of empire on the national psyche ("Modernism" 51). The image of the Great North Road is pivotal to Jameson's reading: it epitomizes the modernist inability to link "colonial suffering" to "daily life and existential experience in the metropolis" ("Modernism" 51), while at the same time it demonstrates how modernist style compensates for a blinkered view of the imperial world-system.

Jameson's essay, though ingenious, raises as many questions as it answers, bracketing from discussion not only the pervasive signs of empire in the modern metropolis but also those literary texts—modernist or otherwise—that directly address imperialism.[12] *Howards End* is a curious choice in this regard, since empire is one of the novel's overt concerns, and Forster is sensitive to its characters' limited cognition of the colonies. If Margaret Schlegel's visit to Henry Wilcox's Imperial and West African Rubber Company does little to link his wealth to "the formlessness and vagueness that one associates with Africa," then Forster's narrator clears up any confusion. He notes an office map that depicts "a *helping* of West Africa" and another that shows the whole continent "looking like a whale marked out for a blubber" (141, emphasis added). Likewise, Forster's Great North Road may not give direct access to colonial reality, but a close examination of Forster's language suggests that it is hardly the circuitous or politically unconscious route to empire that Jameson makes out. Rather than designating the outer limits of the imperial unknown, Forster's Great North Road leads us to the heart of suburban degeneracy.

Jameson rightly claims that Forster's depiction of the Great North Road "is characteristic of [his] duplicities, and offers an amiable simplicity filled with traps and false leads" ("Modernism" 52). Among these I would include the scene's suggestions of renewed life: Aunt Juley's trip coincides with the reincarnation of the Great North Road, which wakes like Rip van Winkle after a century's sleep. Likewise, Hilton boasts "residential estates" that have "budded out" along its main thoroughfare. And yet these signs of rebirth are haunted by more sinister harbingers—ads to remedy the effects of an unhealthy diet, cars with polluting fumes, and developments whose growth recalls the cankered blossoms of Masterman's suburbs. Punctuating these images are the "six Danish tumuli" that interrupt the flat landscape. Monuments to England's Viking invasion between the eighth and eleventh centuries, the tombs serve as a Conradian caveat, reminding us that modern England was once a dark wilderness occupied by barbarians and that Britain's present empire must one day face a fate similar to that of its predecessors. Forster invokes the analogy between Roman and British empires later in *Howards End* by referring to these tombs as the Six Hills; like the Great North Road itself, which dates back to Roman occupation (Weinreb and Hibbert 326), the reference associates this suburban plot with the fallen empire of Rome and its emergence from that city's famous Seven Hills. The tumuli and the suburban habitations beyond not only recall the decline of Viking and Roman empires but portend the fall of their modern suburban successors.[13]

Just as these graves along the Great North Road allude to the inevitable end of empire, the word *tumuli* evokes a series of verbal cues and visual rhymes that link suburbia and death. As permanent resting places for Danish soldiers, the tumuli contrast with the "tumult" of London's expansion—the commotion caused by speeding trains, stinking cars, and burgeoning estates. The constant spreading of this tumult is thus of a piece with its "tumorous" quality; recalling the popular descriptions of suburbia as a cancer or fungus-like growth, suburbia's tumorous swelling is further seen in the "habitations [that] thickened" beyond the Viking graves. Since *tumor* connotes something hollow or swelled, the word seems especially relevant in this context—not only to the pretensions of suburbia in general, but in particular to Henry Wilcox and his children. Nouveaux riches whose affected grandeur contrasts with what Forster figures as the authentic nobility of Mrs. Wilcox, Henry and his children, as we shall see momentarily, are themselves responsible for lessening the distance between Howards End and suburbia. Finally, the word *tumuli* evokes the railway "termini" that begin and end Aunt Juley's trip. Only a few paragraphs before Juley sets off, Margaret Schlegel meditates on the significance of railway termini, thinking of them as "gates to the glorious and the unknown" (11). Margaret's duplicitous sense of a terminus as both the beginning and the end of a journey relates to the question that concludes the Great North Road passage: "Into which country will it lead, England or Suburbia?" This is not only a spatial question, with its implication of suburban terrain as antithetical and wholly foreign to the real England. It also has a temporal component, as if contemplating what comes next—what follows for those who travel beyond this particular moment in English history. Asking "into which country" the Great North Road leads, "England or Suburbia," is akin to asking whether its terminus is the country of the living or the dead.

Significantly, the Great North Road and its nearby suburbs do not appear again until the funeral of Ruth Wilcox, the matriarch of Howards End and a dying rural England. Forster presents much of her funeral through the eyes of the rural laborers on hand, like the wood cutter "pollarding" the branches of a tree as the funeral party arrives: "From where he sat he could see the village of Hilton, strung upon the North Road, with its accreting suburbs" (65). Forster here echoes his description of Hilton in the previous passage—as a village "strung" along the road like electrical wire and as "a tangle that was almost a town." These images of proliferating confusion contrast with the wood cutter's pollarding and pruning, handiwork that paradoxically yields a fuller blossom by trimming and cutting away. The wood cutter's pollarding thus suggests a more redemptive fate than the Danish tombs, and Forster has his own ax to grind with those "accreting suburbs." As an intransitive verb *accreting* refers to growth or to separate objects joining together; in its transitive form it means causing something to grow *toward* or be attracted *to* something else. While the term has connotations of natural and organic growth, and is used in relation to plants, particles, and bodily organs, Forster's reference to "accreting suburbs" seems in contrast to the pollarding that intentionally cuts away to nurture fuller growth. Suburban accretion leads for Forster toward hypertrophy and exhaustion, suggesting a mindless expansiveness as well as a conscious capacity to coalesce with and subsume country and city alike.

The term *accretion* also has a legal and economic meaning that is especially relevant to *Howards End*. Related to both *accrual* and *accession,* the term can denote any addition to one's property or land. This meaning gains in significance when considered in relation to the only other passage in which a form of the word appears in the novel—a passage that emphasizes Margaret's difficulties finding a new home: "The feudal ownership of land did bring dignity, whereas the modern ownership of movables is reducing us again to a nomadic horde. We are reverting to the civilization of luggage, and historians of the future will note how the middle classes accreted possessions without taking root in the earth, and may find in this the secret of their imaginative poverty" (109). While there is no explicit reference here to suburbia, the passage echoes *The Condition of England*—particularly Masterman's discussion of the Suburbans' "communal poverty of interest and ideal" (76). As Forster suggests, the "imaginative poverty" of the middle classes accounts for their imperative to increase property by "accret[ing] possessions." And as in the earlier passages, degeneracy and death haunt the scene. By claiming that modern society "revert[s]" to an earlier stage of evolution and is "reduce[ed] . . . to a nomadic horde," Forster not only emphasizes the atavism of the bourgeoisie but suggests that Edwardian suburbanites have replaced the Victorian poor, whom urban ethnographers like Henry Mayhew described as civilization's "nomadic" tribes and "wandering hordes" (1–2). Moreover, Forster associates the bourgeois propensity toward accretion with the tombs of the Vikings. Yet the peace of burial is not granted to the middle class, whose ceaseless wanderings are a form of living death. Indeed, in contrast to the more natural forms of life that "tak[e] root in the earth" and return to it in death, Forster also uses *accrete* here to suggest the unnatural and inferior character of the bourgeois desire for constant movement and material possessions: as an adjective the term is synonymous with *factitious*—that is, man-made, conventional, artificial, a sham.

This unnatural desire for "accreting possessions" sheds light on Forster's earlier reference to "accreting suburbs" in the scene of Ruth Wilcox's funeral, illuminating a final meaning of accretion: namely, the process of gaining or increasing an inheritance due to the absence of a preceding heir. Of course, Forster is obsessed with inheritance in *Howards End:* as Lionel Trilling famously put it, the question at the novel's center is "Who shall inherit England?" (118), and its narrative arc follows Margaret Schlegel as she unknowingly assumes her legal and—more important to Forster—spiritual ownership of Howards End, which Ruth Wilcox has willed Margaret from her deathbed. Appropriately, Ruth's funeral, and its view of the "accreting suburbs," leads to a conference of surviving Wilcoxes, in which they learn that Ruth has left her home to Margaret: "To them Howards End was a house: they could not know that to [Ruth] it had been a spirit, for which she sought a spiritual heir" (73). Deeming her change of the will a senile blunder, and throwing her penciled request into the fire, the Wilcoxes take back material possession of Howards End by surreptitiously accreting it from its spiritual heir.

If the surviving Wilcoxes retain proprietorship over Ruth's home via an act of subversive accretion, they are also responsible for Howards End's accretion in its coalescence with suburbia. This becomes apparent when Henry Wilcox runs into the Schlegel sisters on the Chelsea Embankment after the women's discussion club, whose topic has been "how one ought to leave one's money" (96). The sisters learn that although Howards End has not grown bigger—indeed, Henry complains that it's "impossibly small"—Henry has modernized it in ways that threaten its rustic character and align it with the encroachment of suburbia. As "one of those converted farms," which "don't really do, spend what you will on them," Howards End has suffered Henry's addition of "a garage all among the wych-elm roots" and a rockery where there was once "a bit of the meadow" (99). Like his other conversions—Henry later explains that he "sold off the two and a half animals, and the mangy pony, and the superannuated tools . . . [and] thinned out I don't know how many guelder-roses and elder-trees" (148)—these changes reflect Henry's accretion (enlargement) of the farm into a suburban residence. His beliefs that "the days for small farms are over," that maintaining "small holdings" is "philanthropic bunkum," bespeak Henry's privileging of accretion as the enlargement of material possession: "Take it as a rule that nothing pays on a small scale," he confides to Margaret regarding his frustration with Howards End (147). But Henry's conversions also reveal the unnatural and even morbid quality of such accretion. Henry's unearthing of the elm roots to make space for his auto not only recalls the middle class's constant mobility and failure to take root in the earth. Given Henry's business—harvesting African rubber—it also seems fitting that he uproots the fields to make room for a garage. Meanwhile, his transformation of the meadow to a rock garden replaces the fertility of organic life with a sterile form of artifice. Though decorative, the stones marking the former meadow make the rockery less a garden than a grave.

While Henry complains that "the neighbourhood's getting suburban," he fails to recognize his own hand in the process (99). The rubber he extracts from Africa no doubt contributes to the traffic that pushes suburbia farther up the Great North Road.[14] Like his father Charles Wilcox also contributes to the suburbanization near Howards End. As Henry points out to the Schlegel sisters, Charles "took a house at the other end of Hilton, down by the Six Hills" (99). Referring to the Danish tombs from Forster's first description of Suburbia, and implicitly calling to mind the Seven Hills of Rome, Henry's mention of the Six Hills aligns Charles's new suburban home with Britain's long-dead empires. Although it is the other Wilcox son, Paul, who currently lives in Nigeria, Charles himself has served in the Boer War (118). And like the rest of his family, Charles "had the colonial spirit, and w[as] always making for some spot where the white man might carry his burden unobserved" (146). Forster's narrator affords us a brief glimpse of Charles and his wife as they consider Henry's impending marriage to Margaret. We see them in their garden at Hilton, brooding over what no doubt amounts to their own reduced inheritance: "He and Dolly are sitting in deck-chairs, and their motor is regarding them placidly from its garage across the lawn. A short-frocked edition of Charles also regards them placidly; a perambulator edition is squeaking; a third edition is expected shortly. Nature is turning out Wilcoxes in this peaceful abode, so that they may inherit the earth" (134). Once again Forster's imagery and word choice are both evocative and duplicitous. Though reclined in their garden, the deck chairs give Charles and Dolly the appearance of river boat captains, surveying from their stationary lookout a world they are simply passing through. This ambiguous sense of movement-at-rest is reinforced by their parked car, which "regard[s]" them as if awaiting its next journey. Juxtaposed with the garden and lawn, Charles's auto recalls Henry's installation of the garage over the elm roots at Howards End; and just as the car seems like a member of the family, so too are the Wilcox sons referred to as "editions," the latest models whom "nature is turning out" on a kind of organic assembly line. As the passage implies, then, this "peaceful abode" is not a long-term home. The Wilcoxes are incapable of the abiding needed to inherit the earth. Rather than read *abode* as a noun, the verb form (meaning to presage in an ominous way) seems more fitting here: it suggests that the peaceful abode is Nature's own, as it awaits the inevitable decline of the Wilcox empire.

This decline is suggested by a later passage that overtly alludes to the Wilcox garden scene. Toward the end of the novel, as Leonard Bast makes his way toward Howards End to confess his affair with Helen Schlegel, a speeding car passes by: "In it was another type . . . the Imperial. Healthy, ever in motion, it hopes to inherit the earth. It breeds as quickly as the yeoman, and as soundly; strong is the temptation to acclaim it as a super-yeoman, who carries his country's virtues overseas. But the Imperialist is not what he thinks or seems. He is a destroyer. . . . and though his ambitions may be fulfilled, the earth that he inherits will be grey" (229). The passing car, its quick-breeding driver, and the biblical allusion to inheriting the earth all make clear that Forster's Imperial prototype is Charles Wilcox. Though Charles inadvertently kills Leonard Bast on his arrival at Howards End, both Wilcox males seem to be approaching the end of their reign. For his crime Charles is sentenced to three years in jail, and Henry, already scandalized by the revelation of his past affair with Jacky Bast, gives himself up to the care of Margaret.

By the closing chapter Margaret fully assumes the role of physical and spiritual nursemaid, transforming Howards End itself into a rural convalescent home. Henry is "shut up in the house," and though "not ill" he is "eternally tired." In contrast, following Leonard's traumatic death, Helen admits to her own regained health when she tells Margaret, "I seem cured" (238). Brushing aside Helen's compliments, Margaret still acknowledges her role as caretaker, claiming, "I had two invalids to nurse" (240). Hence her constant sewing throughout the final chapter, which suggests not only Margaret's new matriarchal role but her ability to stitch wounded fragments into a healthy social body. Margaret's success at what Helen calls "pick[ing] up the pieces, and ma[king] us a home" (240) thus emphasizes her ability to stave off the degenerative effects of suburbia's morbid encroachment on Howards End, as indicated by the fact that the sisters are "sitting on the remains of Evie's rockery, where the lawn merged into the field" (238). Margaret's success in seeking to recuperate this former suburban grave site is also suggested by the recurring motifs of harvesting and inheritance. Framed by the image of a farmer cutting hay in the meadow, the closing chapter marks the Schlegels' legal and spiritual inheritance of Howards End: not only does Margaret "feel Howards End peculiarly our own," but Henry has just informed his children that he is leaving the house to his wife "absolutely" and that she will pass it on to Helen and Leonard's son (240, 241).

Despite their apparent victory, Margaret and Helen look over the meadows to discover that "at the end of them was a red rust" (240). As this image of encroaching sprawl suggests, their stay at Howards End can only serve as a temporary respite from the inevitability of suburban invasion. Margaret claims the rust is a sign that "life's going to be melted down, all over the world" (240). For Margaret, then, suburbia is a symptom of global homogenization whose source lies in imperial expansion. As I mentioned in relation to *The War of the Worlds* and its alien red weeds, it is worth recalling here that the color red, signifier of suburbia, was also the color used on maps to designate Britain's colonial possessions. As if combining the Martians' metallic-tasting red weeds, or Masterman's image of the turnip fields at Tooting, with the premature decay of Almayer's folly, Forster's image of red rust offers a final reminder that imperialism abroad leads not to the spread of a healthy civilization, but to the suburban colonization of England itself.

Howard's Beginning

Forster's fictional country house was based on Rooksnest, his family's home near Stevenage, in Hertfordshire, north of London. His title is thought to derive from Rooksnest's longtime owners, the Howards, whom Forster also made relatives of Ruth Wilcox in the novel (146). But in her biography of Forster, Nicola Beauman suggests another possible source for his title. As she points out, an essay by Masterman in a 1904 issue of the *Independent Review* was followed by an article on Ebenezer Howard's proposal for a garden city near Stevenage. Its author's family lived in a large house just north of Rooksnest. Beauman suggests that Ebenezer Howard's name inspired Forster's title (219). Yet it seems unlikely that the novelist wanted his readers to associate Howards End with the garden city inventor, who drew as much from the futuristic utopianism of the American Edward Bellamy and the anarchism of the Russian Peter Kropotkin as he did from English rural tradition.[15] In contrast to Forster's decidedly rural bias, moreover, Howard's goal was to create compact, self-sustaining communities that *united* country and city. If anything, as Lewis Mumford suggests, the garden city was "not a more rural retreat, but a more integrated foundation for an effective urban life" ("Introduction" 35).

Yet as Forster must have known, his novel's title certainly would have resonated in the minds of Edwardian readers with the father of the garden city. An unassuming court stenographer and amateur inventor, Ebenezer Howard would spark a revolution with the publication of *To-morrow: A Peaceful Path to Real Reform* (1898), reissued in 1902 as *Garden Cities of To-morrow.* Howard was not without his detractors: in 1898 the *Fabian News* declared his scheme as practical as "arrangements for protection against visits from Mr. Wells's Martians" (qtd. in Osborn 11). The reviewer had a point, given Howard's objective that garden cities should stave off the suburban sprawl that Wells's Martians represented. But in just over a decade, Howard gained international fame, shedding his image as a naive faddist and crank by lecturing widely on his ideas; garnering disciples, supporters, and financial backers; founding societies to spread his aims; and overseeing construction of the first garden city at Letchworth, in Hertfordshire (Buder 80). His ideas would be instrumental to both the discipline of urban planning that emerged in the Edwardian era and the British New Town movement following World War II. Indeed, the historian Robert Fishman claims that while Howard is now a relatively obscure figure, his influence on modern urban planning may be greater than that of either Frank Lloyd Wright or Le Corbusier (*Urban* 23).[16] Despite his far-reaching influence, however, Howard's ideas were never implemented as he intended. Biographical and historical accounts of Howard and his movement unanimously share a master narrative of radical social ideals diluted by the harsh realities of the marketplace. Although a second garden city was built under Howard's supervision at Welwyn in 1920, financial problems with both communities forced him to compromise his goals of class integration and communal ownership. Likewise, his concept of the garden city, which he intended as an alternative to suburban segregation and sprawl, would in fact breathe new life into suburban development. Howard's followers popularized the more modest garden suburb, which "was not a city unto itself but rather a planned, self-contained extension of a larger urban area" (Meacham 11). Between World Wars I and II, the garden suburb would become the most prolific form of suburbia in Britain.

While this ground has been amply covered by others, I want to underline the garden city movement's imperial context. As both Peter Hall and Robert Home remind us, one of Howard's less acknowledged influences was Edward Gibbon

Wakefield, who had designed a colony for the poor in Adelaide, Australia. In his 1849 book, *The Art of Colonization,* Wakefield argued for establishing foreign colonies along scientifically planned lines, which would serve not simply as receptacles for the refuse of the home society, but as representative communities of its citizens. Indeed, before publishing his garden city plans, Howard was involved in a number of foreign colonization schemes and attempted to establish a "home colony" in England that accorded with Wakefield's principles:[17] "The colonial planning model of the self-contained town is therefore one of the influences upon the garden cities and new towns movement" (Home 32). In turn, improving the health of the empire would remain a consistent motif in the garden city movement's self-fashioning. At the first national conference of the Garden City Association in 1902, the chairman Ralph Neville proclaimed that the question of the garden city's success "is an Imperial question—and it is a question of paramount importance to the Empire, because . . . the ultimate destiny of our Empire depends upon the character and capacity of the citizens of this country" (qtd. in Meacham 66). Howard himself played on the Boer War crisis and its obsession with racial decline: "In the face of physical degeneration," stated his company prospectus for the Letchworth Garden City in 1903, "imperialism abroad and progress at home seem alike an empty mockery" (qtd. in Meacham 96).

Just as the garden city movement emerged from the Boer War crisis over social hygiene and racial degeneracy in Britain, so too were its principles enthusiastically exported in hopes of rejuvenating the British dominion overseas. "We want not only England but all parts of the Empire to be covered with Garden Cities," proclaimed the official journal of the Garden City Association in 1907 (qtd. in King, "Exporting" 203). By 1913 Howard himself looked to one of "the best and brightest chapters" of his movement being written "in the great continent of the Pacific" (qtd. in Freestone 107). It was not only Australia that beckoned: garden city and town planning principles guided the design of new urban centers throughout the British empire in the coming decades. The most influential example, which I discuss in my next chapter, was New Delhi. Led by the celebrated architect of the Hampstead Garden Suburb, Edwin Lutyens, the development of New Delhi inspired garden cities and suburbs in Lusaka, Nairobi, Pretoria, Ottawa, and Kuala Lumpur.[18] To a man, their planners, designers, and architects—including S. D. Adshead, Herbert Baker, and Albert Thompson in Africa; Patrick Geddes, H. V. Lanchester, and Edwin Lutyens in India; and Charles Reade in Malaya—were first- or second-generation disciples of the garden city movement. So enthusiastic were such figures about spreading the garden city idea that some had even begun projects in territories outside the

British empire—though not without the concern of the movement's officials. At the annual meeting of the Garden Cities and Town Planning Association in 1913, Ralph Neville stated: "Glad as I am to see the idea spreading and the efforts made to carry it out in other countries, I must say that with me the Empire stands first, and I should be sorry to find in this respect the Empire lagging behind. It would be rather a sad thing if England, after having saved others, herself should be a castaway" (qtd. in Hardy, *From* 94).

One eminent Edwardian who foresaw the garden city's potential for colonization was George Bernard Shaw. Reportedly tossing aside a review copy of *To-morrow* as unoriginal and impractical, the Fabian Shaw later dubbed Howard "the garden city geyser" (Buder 78; Aalen 39). However, despite his initial skepticism, Shaw was eventually convinced to support Howard's scheme and even contributed financially to it (Holroyd 3: 16).[19] Shaw came to believe that the garden city's greatest innovation lay in its benevolent use by enlightened industrialists (Buder 82), a theme that he would address in *Major Barbara* (1905), in which a munitions magnate runs an idyllic industrial village for his workers. But Shaw's 1904 play *John Bull's Other Island* imagined the garden city's unenlightened misuse for imperial ends.[20] Shaw's protagonist is the Liberal English businessman Thomas Broadbent, who seeks to "develop" Ireland in the wake of the Boer War. "Now that South Africa has been enslaved and destroyed," declares Broadbent, "there is no country left to take an interest in but Ireland" (75). His plan is to build a series of Irish garden cities for an English land development syndicate. Targeting Howard's movement early on, Shaw has Broadbent proselytizing its virtues and handing out copies of *Garden Cities of To-morrow*. But as his Irish partner learns too late, Broadbent's commercial interests are clearly at odds with any desire for social equality. Arriving near Rosscullen, Broadbent claims, "This would be a jolly good place for a hotel and a golf links" (164). Soon afterward Broadbent not only woos the county's only heiress and secures its parliamentary seat but also begins foreclosing on the land's long-standing tenants. Written at Yeats's request for the Abbey Theatre—Yeats rejected it for its mockery of romantic Irish nationalism—*John Bull's Other Island* clearly indicts the garden city's usefulness as a tool of cultural and economic imperialism. Yet the play proved a curious hit with London audiences, who perceived it as celebrating "English imperial guile and efficiency" (Trodd 30).

Emerging amid the crisis over national and imperial decline in the wake of the Boer War, the garden city also partook of Edwardian preoccupations with suburban degeneracy and death. Indeed, Shaw mocks the garden city's promise of a racial resurrection throughout *John Bull's Other Island*. When early in the play Broadbent asks an Irish character, "Have you ever heard of Garden City?"

the broguish reply is "D'ye mane Heavn?" As the play progresses, however, Shaw makes it clear that this is not what *he* means. A later critic of Broadbent's scheme claims, "You have promised me that when I come here . . . you will comfort me with the bustle of a great hotel, and the sight of the little children carrying the golf clubs of your tourists as a preparation for the life to come" (168). In response to Broadbent's claim that by "mak[ing] a Garden city of Rosscullen" he can begin to teach Ireland "efficiency and self-help on sound Liberal principles" (171), one of his critics replies, "And our place of torment shall be as clean and orderly as the cleanest and most orderly place I know in Ireland, which is our poetically named Mountjoy prison" (172). Like Masterman, who saw in Tooting's hygienic asylums and prisons the essential clue to the workings of empire, Shaw imagines the garden city's colonization of Ireland as instituting eternal torment rather than heaven on earth.

Wells and Beyond

Although familiar with Ebenezer Howard, H. G. Wells imagined a heaven on earth quite unlike the self-contained garden city. From the turn of the century, when he began applying himself to social problems, until his death in 1946, Wells devoted himself to the concept of a utopian World State—a "New Republic" whose technocratic rulers would eliminate international and imperial conflicts and provide for the greater good of humanity.[21] My goal is neither to defend nor to critique this concept, but to emphasize its unacknowledged emergence from Wells's thinking about suburban development. As I have already argued, Wells first contemplated the suburb's ambivalent relation to Britain and the empire in *The War of the Worlds*, imagining the unprecedented sprawl of the 1880s and 1890s as an alien and degenerate form of reverse colonization. But as the Edwardian era got under way, his social vision would diverge significantly from Howard's garden city scheme and the Little Englander pastoralism of Masterman and Forster. Wells did not defend a traditional rural England against the omnivorous expansion of tumorous suburbs. Where Forster sought to graft a new social order onto the old, Wells wanted to weed out that old order entirely. A consideration of his 1909 novel *Tono-Bungay* alongside his Edwardian social commentary reveals that he saw suburbia not as a threat to the traditional countryside, but as the decaying outgrowth of the country house system. The dying rural lifestyle that Masterman and Forster wished to resuscitate with progressive ideals was for Wells precisely the cause of suburban degeneracy. Ironically, however, Wells did not seek to contain the suburb's expansive energies, but to tap them more fully and efficiently than newer municipal bodies allowed.

Here Wells's contrast with Howard becomes clear: if the garden city was to decentralize the large metropolitan spaces that divided most Britons from the countryside, Wells sought to centralize older and smaller communities, but along substantially larger regional scales. These new urban regions were Wells's first step toward imagining a form of global governance that would transcend competing imperialisms. "Not for Wells the finite boundaries of a garden city," as Dennis Hardy puts it; "tomorrow the world and then the universe" (*Utopian* 100). As Hardy suggests, Wells's critique of the garden city's limitations, and his belief that suburban expansion required Londoners to think in ever larger geographic scales, played a crucial role in developing his zeal for centralized planning and, ultimately, a single World State that would transcend and obviate the imperial world-system.

Wells's first step in this direction comes toward the end of *The War of the Worlds,* when the narrator claims the Martian invasion has taught humans to strive for a "commonweal of mankind" (162–63). Wells begins to unpack this idea in his monumentally titled *Anticipations of the Reaction of Mechanical and Scientific Progress upon Human Life and Thoughts* (1902). His first work of non-fiction to invoke the idea of global governance (Partington 1), *Anticipations* ends by imagining "the establishment of one world-state at peace within itself" (267). But the book begins with more pedestrian concerns: the social impact of new modes of transport. In his second chapter, "The Probable Diffusion of Great Cities," Wells notes that where limited means of transport kept the traditional city centripetal or inward directed, new technologies have made the modern metropolis centrifugal and expansive. Rather than lamenting this shift, Wells sees it as an opportunity. Based on calculations "that a city of pedestrians is inexorably limited by a radius of about four miles, and that a horse-using city may grow out to seven or eight," Wells claims that "the available area of a city which can offer a cheap suburban journey of thirty miles an hour is a circle with a radius of thirty miles" (52). This meant "that the London citizen of the year 2000 AD may have a choice of nearly all England and Wales south of Nottingham and east of Exeter as his suburb" (52–53). The issue for Wells was whether citizens and officials would embrace the expansive forces of the modern city or continue to constrain them.[22] If citizens were to take advantage of the centrifugal potential of cities, the result would be "a wide and quite unprecedented diversity in the various suburban townships and suburban districts" (62), so much so that the near future would see terms like *town* and *city* become "as obsolete as 'mail coach.'" Thus, Wells suggests a new designation for these emergent spaces: urban districts or regions (67). At the end of his chapter, Wells imagines new urban regions spreading across the earth: "Everywhere, indeed, over the land of the globe between the frozen circles, the railway and the new roads will spread, the network of communication wires and safe and convenient ways" (71). These networks would transform the suburb from what Wells calls "a little private *imperium*" to a truly modern region whose "boundary lines will altogether disappear" (55, 70, original emphasis). The result would be a "new sort of town" and a "new sort of country over which the new sorts of people . . . will be scattered" (71).

Part of Wells's goal in *Anticipations* was to quell the fears of degeneracy that urban expansion typically generated. He would consider how to make his hopeful urban vision a reality in a paper addressing "administrative areas" presented to the Fabian Society and published as an appendix to his 1903 book *Mankind in the Making*. He begins by echoing the initial premise of *Anticipations:* population distribution "is determined almost entirely by the available means of locomotion" (378). But he proceeds to argue that London's capacity for expansion and mobility was hamstrung by municipal bodies whose "areas of activity are impossibly small" (375). Despite the London County Council's effort to unify a congeries of semiautonomous villages, vestries, and parishes, many of the new town councils, borough councils, and district boards continued to resist large-scale regional planning (375). The suburb was a crucial site in this battle between old and new. For Wells it represented "a community of a new sort, the new great modern community." The problem was that it continued "to establish itself in the room of the dwindling, little, highly localized communities of the past" (380). In doing so, the suburbs would, like so many Martians, continue to "suck[ ] the ebbing life from your old communities into the veins of the new" (383). But it was not the passing of these old communities that concerned Wells: new modes of transport rendered them virtually obsolete. What worried him was that suburbs lived on a rotting carcass of traditional administrative bodies. Though in decay, these old bodies continued to vie for control over resources they were ill equipped to manage, obstructing improvements in water supply, sewage, lighting, and lines of transportation and communication—all to the detriment of an efficiently managed England (384). Wells argues that the administration of these services "must be handled in areas of hundreds of square miles to be efficiently done" (387), acknowledging the London County Council as a promising if limited precursor to the kind of urban region he has in mind. Wells claims, "My proposal would be to make a much greater area even than the London County, and try to include in it the whole system of what I might call the London-centered population," which essentially encompassed all of southeast England (389).[23]

These ideas have an obvious bearing on Wells's subsequent fictions like

A Modern Utopia (1905), but they also help to clarify his fictional portrayals of suburbia after *The War of the Worlds*. A particularly telling example occurs in *The New Machiavelli*, when the narrator describes his suburban neighborhood of Bromstead—a thinly veiled reference to Wells's own childhood suburb of Bromley, Kent:

> The outskirts of Bromstead were a maze of exploitation roads that led nowhere, that ended in tarred fences studded with nails . . . and in trespass boards that used vehement language. . . . I suppose one might have persuaded oneself that all this was but the replacement of an ancient tranquility, or at least an ancient balance by a new order. Only to my eyes . . . it was manifestly no order at all. It was a multitude of uncoordinated fresh starts, each more sweeping and destructive than the last, and none of them ever really worked out to a ripe and satisfactory completion. Each left a legacy of products—houses, humanity, or what not— in its wake. It was a sort of progress that had bolted; it was change out of hand, and going at an unprecedented pace nowhere in particular. (37)

Read in light of Wells's social prophecies, this rather conventional-sounding complaint against sprawl reveals a more complex perspective. It is not so much that Wells's narrator decries the construction of new roads and houses, but that such developments "led nowhere." It is not the "fresh starts" that bother him, but their "uncoordinated" character. The culprit is not "progress" per se, but a "progress that had bolted." In other words, what distinguishes this passage from so many other jeremiads against suburban expansion is its emphasis not on what suburbs have done, but on what they have failed to do. Hence the telling reference to developments that never "really worked out to a ripe and satisfactory completion" and that ultimately went "nowhere in particular."

Wells's sense of wasted suburban potential can also correct our view of *Tono-Bungay*, the novel on which a sometimes slapdash Wells lavished his greatest care. *Tono-Bungay* does not directly depict the transformation of the new urban region into a future World State, nor does it champion suburbia as a regenerative force. Rather, the novel seeks to transcend a dying suburban culture and the aristocratic and imperial system that supports it. For many recent critics the commercial empire that Teddy Ponderevo builds around the novel's eponymous sham elixir is an entirely modern enterprise, employing new modes of marketing and financial speculation to destroy a traditional order of landed wealth. This order is represented by Bladesover, the Kent country house where Teddy's nephew George grew up as a servant's son.[24] George describes Bladesover as "a closed and complete social system" (15), recalling Wells's critique of older localities in *Mankind in the Making*—those "complete minor economic systems" that kept urban regions from achieving their full centrifugal potential (376). Rather than a quaint holdover, however, Bladesover is to George "the clue to almost all that is distinctively British." Even forms of national life that are "modern and different" exist merely as "a gloss upon this predominant formula" of Bladesover (21).

When George first visits London from the countryside, his clockwise tour of the suburbs reveals them to be an "unorganised, abundant substance of some tumorous growth-process . . . which indeed bursts all the outlines of the affected carcass and protrudes such masses as ignoble comfortable Croydon, as tragic impoverished West Ham" (108–9). But these suburbs are not some new force to George, and he hardly fears that they will contaminate the countryside. To George London is "a city of Bladesovers, the capital of a kingdom of Bladesovers" (109), and its suburbs strike him as "escaping parts from the seventeenth-century system of Bladesover, of proliferating and overgrowing elements from the Estates" (107). George here echoes *Mankind in the Making,* where Wells compares current administrative areas to "fifteenth-century houses" in which "lath-and-plaster partitions" provide the only form of renovation for modern tenants. Such houses, like modern administrative areas, "have been patched and repaired enormously, but they preserve the essential conceptions of a vanished social organization" (375–76). The same can be said of the suburbs in *Tono-Bungay.*

When George moves to London to join his uncle's business, his existence becomes increasingly suburban, as reflected by the various locales that constitute his world: his student housing (West Brompton); his friend Ewart's lodgings (Highgate Hill); the homes of his fiancé and wife, Marion (Walham Green and Ealing); his paramour Effie's apartment (Orpington); and his uncle's increasingly palatial residences (Beckenham and Chislehurst, and then the Surrey grounds of Lady Grove and Crest Hill). As in other Edwardian accounts of the suburbs, signs of degeneracy and death abound. In his reunion with his boyhood friend Ewart, now a struggling artist at Highgate, George points out that "his neck seemed longer and more stringy" and notes his "knobby countenance, his erratic hair and his general hairy leanness" (115). Ewart admits that his "dissipation" has been caused by his fascination with the "business of sex," and he balks at George's suggestion that desire has some evolutionary role in securing "the continuity of the species" (117). Appropriately, Ewart and George take a long journey around London that returns them to Highgate's famous cemetery. As Ewart motions down upon the breadth of London from Highgate Hill, he takes in "the long slopes about us, tombs and headstones in long perspectives, in limitless rows" (119). Like Forster, Wells here conflates the image of tombs with the endless rows of suburban housing. Interspersed with George's recollections of Ewart are chapters focusing on George's budding relationship with Marion. But if Ewart personifies a kind of excitable degeneracy, Marion and her parents at Walham Green epitomize solemn exhaustion. To George their house is memorable for its "black and amber tapestry carpets and curtains and table-cloths, and the age and irrelevance of its books" (128). Immediately following his wedding ceremony, George notes ironically that it is a neighborhood where "there are no neighbours" because "nobody knows, nobody cares," and that Marion's parents "did not know the names of the people on either side of them" (194). What inspires this comment is the image of Marion's father staring out his window at a neighbor's home, where a funeral took place the day before.

Things do not improve once George moves Marion to their new home in Ealing, whose only signs of life are the fashionable commodities Marion covets, like a spaniel and a new Kodak. As a stereotypical suburban housewife Marion comes to represent degeneracy for George. His descriptions suggest she is deathly by being both dark and pallid: although often referred to as "sombre" (213), she has a "sallow complexion" (200) and "pale face" (204) to match her "faded life" (200). Further reinforcing George's sense of Marion's degeneracy is his view of her shortcomings as pathological "defects" (200), foremost among them her increasing "disgust and dread of maternity" (201). With his marriage a "sombre preoccupation" pervaded by "an air of finality" (206, 201), George see his home life as a kind of residential gravesite. "My married existence became at last like a narrow deep groove in the broad expanse of interests" (200), he claims, and his recurrent references to the cast-iron gate around his yard at Ealing (204, 212) recall his journeys to Highgate Cemetery with Ewart. Not surprisingly, George believes he can resurrect himself from his suburban life-in-death by having an affair with Effie Rink. Though their relationship is short-lived, George's earliest flirtations lead him to believe that "I might be going to some sensuous paradise with Effie" (213).

Significantly, Tono-Bungay gains prominence as a remedy for the nation's increasingly despondent suburban masses. Though he knows it is nothing but "bottles of mitigated water" (167), Ewart sees Tono-Bungay as the perfect placebo for suburban degeneration: "Think of the little clerks and jaded women and overworked people," he implores. "People overstrained with wanting to do, people overstrained with wanting to be. . . . The real trouble is that we *don't* really exist and we want to. That's what this—in the highest sense—muck stands for! The hunger to be—for once—really alive—to the finger-tips!" (168, original emphasis).

In turn Teddy's aspiration to convert Britons to Tono-Bungay takes on the force of a military and missionary conquest. "Section by section we spread it over the whole of the British Isles," George remarks: "first working the middle class London suburbs, then the outer suburbs, then the home counties, then going . . . into Wales." As Teddy puts it in his clipped cockneyisms, "Conquest. Province by province. Like sogers" (161–62). At the head of this conquest is Tono-Bungay itself, the center of a number of domestic conveniences boasting to rejuvenate suburban life and eliminate degeneracy. "We got to make a civilised d'mestic machine out of these relics of barbarism" (231), Teddy tells George. And what goes for the Tono-Bungay enterprise goes for the entire Ponderevo business empire. With "three general trading companies, the London and African Investment Company, the British Traders' Loan Company, and Business Organisations Limited" (238), Teddy's ventures unite modern commerce and colonialism to a greater extent than Henry Wilcox's Imperial and West African Rubber Company. And like Wilcox, who "carved money out of Greece and Africa, and bought forests from the natives for a few bottles of gin" (201), Teddy dupes those he claims to civilize.

Such examples support Benita Parry's claim that *Tono-Bungay* presents "an England internally transformed by imperialism," an England "where domestic space is reconceived on an imperial scale" ("*Tono-Bungay*" 95). Yet while Parry sees this transformation as the result of *modern* capitalist and colonial forces, Wells traces it back to Bladesover. If Teddy's sale of Tono-Bungay reduces degenerate suburbanites to savages, then the increasingly ostentatious homes he builds or buys during the rise of his financial empire—first in the outer suburbs, then further into rural Surrey—are an attempt to mix traditional aristocracy and modern imperialism. The bedrooms of the "big, rather gaunt villa" at Beckenham take their names from Clive, Napoleon, and Caesar, and Teddy lords it over the workmen who install his new amenities, acting "most Napoleonic, on a little Elba of dirt" (251, 252). Recalling Wells's complaints about suburbia in *Anticipations* and *Mankind in the Making,* Teddy seeks to expand within the constraints of an older system. His aspiration is to pass off his new wealth behind a façade of aristocratic privilege. At Chislehurst he determines to "get the hang of etiquette" and lose all signs of "Goochery" (260). He buys his next home, Lady Grove, from a dissipate family of nobles that "sent its blood and treasure . . . upon the most romantic quest in history, to Palestine" (269), and among its clan is a former missionary to China (272). Teddy quickly grows to see Lady Grove as lacking "elbow-room" and "choked with old memories" (290), but his plans for modernizing are a superficial gloss on the old system: "We got to Buck-Up the country," he tells George. "The English country is a going concern still. . . .

Only it wants fresh capital, fresh idees, and fresh methods. Light railways, f'rinstance—scientific use of drainage. Wire fencing—machinery—all that" (274–75). Though Wellsian in his embrace of technology, Teddy unwittingly perpetuates the Bladesover system behind a new façade. George recognizes the irony and, in a wry nod to Wells's social prophecies, recalls reading a "socialist tract" that "says we're all getting delocalised. Beautiful word—delocalised! Why not be the first delocalised peer?" (284). Teddy is not amused.

When he sells Lady Grove, Teddy appears to abandon the aristocratic aura that linked the house to an older era of colonial missionary work in China and Palestine. Appropriately, the construction of his new home, Crest Hill, parallels his proposed scheme for a Palestine Canal. Just as Teddy wants Crest Hill to be "a Mod'un house," "a Twentieth-Century house!" (290, 291), he imagines his canal project inaugurating a new imperial era: "It's a big Progressive On-coming Imperial Time. This Palestine business" (281). Teddy dreams of "Cuttin' canals. . . . Makin' tunnels. . . . New countries. . . . New centres" (282). Crest Hill also develops as a latter-day Bladesover: "At one time," George notes, "he had working in that place—disturbing the economic balance of the whole country-side by their presence—upwards of three thousand men. . . . He moved a quite considerable hill, and nearly sixty mature trees were moved with it to open his prospect eastward" (293). Even more than Teddy's earlier homes, Crest Hill showcases its owner's global aspirations. Built with Canadian marble and New Zealand timber (239), Crest Hill has hanging above its grand entrance a granite "astronomical ball, brass-coopered, that represented the world" (293), a reminder of Bladesover's enormous chandeliers, "each bearing some hundreds of dangling glass lustres" and hanging above "islands and archipelagoes" of furniture (29).

The crowning glory of Crest Hill is "a great wall to hold all his dominions together, free from the invasion of common men" (293–94). But just like the rapidly decaying speculative homes that littered suburbs closer to London, the wall surrounding Crest Hill was "so dishonestly built that it collapsed within a year upon its foundations" (294). Rather than a spectacle of aristocratic and imperial power, Crest Hill not only becomes for George a tribute "as idiotic as the pyramids." With its "forest of scaffold poles" and its "wilderness of broken soil and wheeling tracks" (376), it recalls those spaces colonized but still not settled by European empires. Though the novel's famous quap episode invokes Conrad's *Heart of Darkness,* Crest Hill's incomplete decay recalls the new ruin of Almayer's folly, albeit on a more monumental scale: "For this the armies drilled, for this the Law was administered and the prisons did their duty, for this the millions toiled and perished in suffering, in order that a few of us should build palaces we never finished." The vision comes to George "like a revelation . . . of the abysmal folly of our being" (376).

It seems appropriate that as his uncle's financial empire and colossal home crumble to the ground, George becomes increasingly immersed in scientific work—first taking to the skies in experiments with manned flight, then developing a series of seagoing vessels and destroyers. These ventures, which promise him something more lasting than the ephemera of waste produced by Teddy's business schemes, also recall those Martian invaders who made Wells first confront the effects of suburbia. Indeed, George's experiments near Crest Hill take place in proximity to Woking, site of the first Martian landing (see *Tono-Bungay* 298, 340, 375). But unlike the Martians, who represented a suburban invasion and decimation of the English countryside, George's experiments are an attempt at transcending both the Bladesover system and its suburban outgrowth. In the final chapter of *Tono-Bungay*, George steers his latest destroyer "down the Thames . . . passing all England in review" before heading to the open sea (413). Though he claims journalists have used "turgid degenerate Kiplingese" to describe his destroyer, George confides that it "isn't intended for the empire, or indeed for the hands of any European power" (420). Dubbed "X2," the destroyer represents a desire to obliterate the old English system, a desire that parallels Wells's own attempt to move beyond dying aristocratic traditions and their imperial and suburban legacy.

Because George's closing intimations of scientific autonomy seem naive at best and apocalyptic at worst, readers often find an ironic tension between George and Wells himself. Thus, George seems no more a spokesman for his creator than Stephen Dedalus is for Joyce (Kupinse 70), serving instead as the vehicle through which Wells the novelist questions the utopian longings of Wells the social prophet (Lodge 139). From this perspective George's destroyers perpetuate the devastation wrought by Bladesover, Teddy's business, and the empire as a whole.[25] While I do not want to conflate George Ponderevo with Wells, George's desire to push his experiments beyond the confines of England and the empire parallel Wells's own aims of pushing social organization toward global but nonimperial ends. From his perch behind the destroyer, George surveys "England and the Kingdom" (419), noting that "amidst it all no plan appears, no intention, no comprehensive desire." At just this moment he catches an unexpected sight: three London County Council steamers. Their names—*Caxton, Pepys,* and *Shakespear*—receive the most comment from critics, but I am more interested in their municipal origins. Rather than some imposing authority, or a beneficent reminder of civic good, the steamers appear to George like the toys of an aristocrat: "One wanted to take them out and wipe them and put them back in some English gentleman's library" (418). Still beholden to a dying system like Bladesover, the LCC steamers patrol the outer limits of the municipal planning Wells sought to transcend. Even a modern body like the London County Council proves too small and too antiquated to rein in the destroyer, as it sets its sights on the global unknown of night and the open sea.

PART THREE
Semi-Detachment

6

Ressentiment and Late-Imperial Fiction

In *Growing,* an account of his years as a civil servant in Ceylon, Leonard Woolf—the Bloomsbury affiliate, Hogarth Press publisher, and eminent internationalist—describes imperial society in terms of a typical London suburb: "White society in India and Ceylon, as you can see in Kipling's stories, was always suburban. In Calcutta and Simla, in Colombo and Nuwara Eliya . . . relations between Europeans rested on the same kind of snobbery, pretentiousness, and false pretensions as they did in Putney or Peckham. . . . The flavour or climate of one's life was enormously affected, even though one might not always be aware of it, both by this circumambient air of a tropical suburbia and by the complete social exclusion from our social suburbia of all Sinhalese and Tamils" (17–18). Besides Kipling, Woolf might have also cited his contemporaries George Orwell and Evelyn Waugh or his friend E. M. Forster, whose late-imperial novels similarly exude the "circumambient air of a tropical suburbia."[1] In *A Passage to India* Miss Quested and Mrs. Moore discover that their "romantic voyage" to the subcontinent has led them to "a gridiron of bungalows" (23), where philistine sahibs discourage any contact with the "real" India. Likewise, residents of an English legation in the satirical east Africa of Waugh's *Black Mischief* immerse themselves in gardening, cards, and cheap periodicals, blissfully unaware that rebellion foments around them. And in *Burmese Days* Orwell's liberal protagonist foresees suburbia's wholesale obliteration of Burma's indigenous culture: "Sometimes I think that in two hundred years . . . all this will be gone—forests, villages, monasteries, pagodas all vanished. And instead pink villas fifty yards apart; all over those hills, as far as you can see, villa after villa, with all the gramophones playing the same tune" (42).

Like Woolf, whose autobiography records his gradual disillusionment with imperialism, Forster, Waugh, and Orwell distance themselves from Britain's *mission civilisatrice* by deriding colonial society as inherently and unforgivably suburban. Cataloging the clichés of villadom with particular venom, their portrayals of imperial civil stations and clubs reflect suburbia's long-standing association with the pretentious and second-rate. Indeed, such late-imperial fiction often reads like a diatribe against the shallowness of British middle-class life, evoking a litany of suburban ills that, according to J. B. Priestley, included "miles of semi-detached bungalows, all with their little garages, their wireless sets, their periodicals about film stars, their swimming costumes and tennis rackets" (319–20). In the long weekend between the two world wars, the British suburb's dubious reputation was particularly pronounced. An unprecedented four million new homes sprang up in England and Wales during this period, and the area of Greater London doubled in size, making epithets for suburbia like "bungaloid growth" and "ribbon rash" virtually ubiquitous among the urbane.[2] While such widespread scorn undoubtedly influenced Forster, Waugh, and Orwell, their depictions of suburban colonial society also bespeak the decline in imperial confidence during the 1920s and 1930s, decades that witnessed the founding of the Irish Free State, the rise of Gandhi's civil disobedience movement, and the spread of mass labor strikes across Africa. "Never had a larger area of the globe been under the formal and informal control of Britain than between the two world wars," as Eric Hobsbawm suggests, "but never before had the rulers of Britain felt less confident about maintaining their old imperial supremacy" (*Age of Extremes* 211). Implicit in what follows is the claim that by projecting the pervasive disdain for suburbia on white colonial society, the fiction of Forster, Waugh, and Orwell prepares Britain to divest itself of imperial rule. Equating white colonial communities with mediocre if not despicable suburbs, their novels seek to justify Britain's detachment from its imperial possessions and thereby to facilitate the impending end of empire.

More specifically, I want to show how the suburban subtext of such fiction, particularly *A Passage to India,* intimates imperial dissolution by reflecting a shift in the organization of colonial cities during the early twentieth century, when town planning principles inspired by British suburbs in the Edwardian era were exported across the empire. Such principles, which established or consolidated a regime of spatial divisions between colonizer and colonized, exert themselves on both the content and the form of Forster's novel. Obsessed with replicating middle-class British values, Forster's colonial society appears increasingly incapacitated by the dictates of nostalgia. However, whereas discussions of place often invoke nostalgia as a source of contentment—Gaston Bachelard's poetics of felicitous spaces and the topophilia of Yi-Fu Tuan being classic examples—I wish here to emphasize the discontent of imperialists who fail to sate their longing for home. Nostalgia, so often expressed in ecstatic reminiscence, elegiac melancholy, or swelling pride, comes to occupy a rather different affective register in late-imperial fiction—one dominated by the malice, spite, and impotent outrage of *ressentiment*. A product of the urban planning meant to prolong imperial rule, *ressentiment* became instrumental to Britain's attempted detachment from its colonies.

The Official Suburb

At the 1911 durbar honoring his coronation as British king and emperor of India, George V declared that Delhi would replace Calcutta as capital of the Raj. Over the next three decades Delhi underwent a monumental redevelopment of its layout and architecture that resulted in the creation of a second, new Delhi. Although little more than a district headquarters at the time of George's durbar, Delhi resonated powerfully in the minds of Indians and Britons alike. The city figured prominently in both Hindu and Muslim history, and as a site of rebellion in 1857 it evoked memories of native insurgency—and of Britain's vengeful response. By moving their capital to Delhi, then, the British sought symbolically to resolve centuries of dynastic struggle for control of the subcontinent. Yet relocating to Delhi also revealed the growing instability of the Raj, as the government's departure from Calcutta was a response to increasing civil unrest there after the 1905 partition of Bengal. The move to Delhi was thus a concession to Indian nationalism and a mark of imperial decline. As the architectural historian Thomas Metcalf suggests, Delhi's transformation "went hand in hand with Britain's first defeat in its dealings with India's nationalists. . . . In architecture as in politics, the building of New Delhi was to mark out the beginning of the end of Britain's mastery over India" (211–12).

Initially, representatives of the Raj suggested that the new capital would require a balance of British and Indian design. Secretary of State Lord Crewe proclaimed that while the capital "could not be planned in a manner altogether foreign to Western ideas and Western life . . . it must not be hostile in appearance or in spirit to the Mahomedan ideals of the past" ("New" 9). Likewise, Viceroy Hardinge insisted that new sections of Delhi be integrated with the old, forming a single, unified city (Morris and Winchester 217). Town planning principles derived from Ebenezer Howard's garden city movement would lend coherence and balance to the scheme. Edwin Lutyens, an adherent of Howard's and an architect for the highly praised Hampstead Garden Suburb, was named the capital's principal designer. The head of New Delhi's town planning committee, a former London County Council chair, hoped that "we shall be able to show how those ideas which Mr. Howard put forward . . . can be brought in to assist this first Capital created in our time" (qtd. in King, "Exporting" 203).

But the resulting city, in the words of one urban historian, should have made "the recently dead Ebenezer Howard return to complain" (P. Hall 191). In stark contrast to the garden city objective of social integration, New Delhi was "firmly separated by plan as by manner from the existing city of the indigenes" (Morris and Winchester 219).[3] Located a few miles south of the native town, the capital consisted mainly of government and commercial offices and an exclusive shopping district, all surrounded by expansive low-density suburbs for British residents. By 1920 these "civil lines" housed fewer than ten people per acre, while in the old city, where population density was eighty times greater, half a million people inhabited an area of two and a half square miles (King, *Bungalow* 59). As the capital neared completion, even the *Times* tempered its praise, admitting that New Delhi was not a city in the traditional sense, but rather "an annexe, an official suburb" (qtd. in Evenson 145).

New Delhi offers an apt prototype for Frantz Fanon's dictum that "the colonial world is a world cut in two" (38). In *The Wretched of the Earth,* Fanon distinguishes between the "strongly built," "brightly lit town" of the colonizer and the overcrowded squalor of the native quarter. In the former all is "made of stone and steel," and "garbage cans swallow all the leavings"; in the latter, "a world without spaciousness[,] . . . huts are built one on top of the other" (39).[4] Indeed, New Delhi epitomized, albeit on a grander scale, the urban development and redevelopment taking place not only in the subcontinent but throughout the colonies during the 1920s and 1930s (King, *Colonial* 183), from Nairobi and Lusaka to Canberra and Kuala Lumpur. Although informed by garden city and town planning ideals that originated as antidotes to British suburban sprawl and segregation, New Delhi and its counterparts gave material shape to the "circumambient air of a tropical suburbia" that pervaded colonial society for Leonard Woolf.

In addition to dividing suburb and slum as in the Western metropolis, colonial town planning worked to localize, on an urban level, older and larger geographical mappings, like the spatiotemporal division of British India between the sweltering plains (occupied in winter) and the cooler hills (occupied in summer). Indeed, suburban layout streamlined the mechanisms of racial and social segregation that governed the Raj from its inception. The case of New Delhi is again instructive, for while it embodied "the most advanced ideas on the planning of a colonial capital of its day" (King, *Colonial* 183), its construction also marked the culmination of unofficial policies stretching back to the mid-nineteenth century. Though the maintenance of racial boundaries was a perennial obsession with imperial society, white colonials only began to flee Indian cities for suburban residential enclaves after the so-called Indian Mutiny of 1857.[5] Thus, as much as they promised urban renewal and social improvement, town planning principles that replicated British suburban space evoked the very memory of native insurgency that they tried to suppress.

A Passage from India

The gestation and composition of *A Passage to India* coincided with the development of New Delhi, which was under way by the time Forster first visited the subcontinent in 1912. In a letter home he voiced dismay about the impending changes: "I am thankful to have seen the country before the new capital is built, for . . . there are terrible rumours of tidyings up and conversions" (*Selected* 1: 144). Likewise, Forster's brief return to India in 1921, along with the subsequent publication of *Passage* in 1924, corresponds with the completion of New Delhi's residential scheme by 1925 (King, *Colonial* 251). While the grandiose New Delhi was clearly not the model for his fictional town of Chandrapore— this is usually attributed to Bankipore (Furbank 2: 246–47)—Forster no doubt had the Indian capital in mind when writing *Passage*.[6] Indeed, his attitude toward New Delhi perhaps accounts for the ironic claim, in the novel's opening, that to those viewing Chandrapore from the surrounding hills, it appears to be "a city of gardens" (4). Ostensibly referring to the profuse foliage that veils the squalor of Chandrapore's native quarter—its "mean" streets and "ineffective" temples, its "alleys whose filth deters all but the invited guest" (3)—Forster also invokes the garden city movement itself, reducing it here to an optical illusion that makes foreign terrain easy on imperial eyes. Forster's subsequent description of Chandrapore's layout as a "tropical pleasaunce" (4) reinforces the notion that the town is little more than a visual ruse; referring to that which elicits pleasure, as well as to a private pleasure ground, *pleasaunce* is also synonymous with *pleasantry*, a pleasing trick.[7]

Besides his reference to the garden city movement, Forster overtly associates colonial society with the British suburb. Drawing on a popular discourse stretching back to the nineteenth century, and that I have discussed in relation to Arthur Conan Doyle, Forster derides suburbia as a resting place for retired Anglo-Indians. He notes that the Turtons, the reigning couple of Chandrapore, would soon "retire to some suburban villa, and die exiled from glory" (27), and he later refers to "retired Anglo-Indians in Tunbridge Wells" (291), the suburb in which Forster spent part of his childhood. Though it seems an inauspicious resting ground for colonial rulers, the suburb, Forster also admits, helps to consolidate British rule over the subcontinent. "On twittered the Sunday bells," his narrator remarks at one point, describing the sounds that summon Anglo-India to prayer; "the East had returned to the East via the suburbs of England, and had become ridiculous during the detour" (110). The ridiculous nature of India's suburbanization is not lost on Adela Quested and Mrs. Moore, who bristle at Chandrapore club life. "We hear nothing interesting up at the club," Adela complains. "Only tennis and ridiculous gossip" (79). While her comment speaks to the sensory deprivations imposed by Anglo-India—a theme to which I shall return—it is the club's mental and emotional shallowness that I want to emphasize here. As Forster's narrator remarks, colonial society sees intellectual interest as "bad form" (40), and Mrs. Moore notes that her son, Ronny Heaslop, Chandrapore's hardened young magistrate, has not only given up his viola but enjoys the club's performance of *Cousin Kate,* a comedy he ridiculed in London. Though relatively popular with British audiences, the 1903 play by Hubert Henry Davies signals both the belatedness and the philistinism of colonial culture, recalling the affinity for Gilbert and Sullivan among British colonials in *Black Mischief.* Waugh's novel ends as faceless administrators, who inhabit indistinguishable bungalows and dine punctually each evening on tinned food, play "Three little maids from school are we" over the gramophone. Likewise, Forster's reference to *Cousin Kate* alludes to the popularity of such musical companies in interwar British suburbs (Oliver, Davis, and Bentley 128).

Hyper-Englishness and excess philistinism also saturate imperial society in *Burmese Days* and *Black Mischief,* particularly as these novels emphasize the communal passion for gardening and periodicals. Orwell introduces his imperial community on "English mail day" (19), and Waugh's legation celebrates the same event in a virtual orgy of bourgeois reading material: "Eleven *Punches,* eleven *Graphics,* fifty-nine copies of *The Times,* two *Vogues* and a mixed collection of *New Yorkers, Week End Reviews, St. James's Gazettes,* [and] *Horses and Hounds*" (136). Foreign parcels are also bogged down with resources for gardening: "The bags came out from London laden with bulbs and cuttings," Waugh points out, "and soon there sprang up around the Legation a luxuriant English garden" (67), to which the wife of the envoy extraordinary devotes herself with a care bordering on mania. As cultural historians of empire would suggest, such activities clearly served a colonial agenda. Dane Kennedy and Anthony King have shown, for example, how gardening allowed colonizers to domesticate foreign environments and thereby uphold memories of their homeland (Kennedy 49; King, *Colonial* 142). Similarly, the communities' obsession with domestic periodicals seems in keeping with Benedict Anderson's discussion of the popular press and "print-capitalism" as a means of consolidating imagined communities in the age of empire (33–36). At the same time I want to suggest the distinctly middle-class reputation of gardening and periodicals, which are among the key markers of suburban life between the wars.[8] Rather than passing references, then, these signifiers of English suburbia are central to defining the imperial communities of Orwell, Waugh, and Forster.

But Forster does not deride the suburban character of colonial society merely for its lowbrow taste. Indeed, if he concludes *Passage* by blaming all of India for conspiring to defer true friendship with the British—from the horses ridden by Fielding and Aziz, to the landscape, to the sky itself—then the novel's opening clearly indicts the hermetic nature of British planning for causing interracial tension. After describing Chandrapore's segregated layout, Forster shows us its effects when introducing us to Aziz. Called away from dinner at a friend's home to attend to his superior, Major Callendar, Aziz reluctantly journeys toward the "arid tidiness" of the civil lines (13). Upon arrival Aziz discovers that Callendar is already gone; moreover, the major's wife and another memsahib snub him and take his carriage. This troublesome journey to Chandrapore's civil station is significant not only because it denaturalizes the British residential space, revealing its debilitating effects on the indigenous population; the scene also emphasizes the Britons' absolute ignorance of spaces beyond the compound. Callendar, angered by Aziz's lateness and unaware that he was dining at a friend's home, fails to see his excuse as anything but deception: "He never realized that the educated Indians visited one another constantly, and were weaving, however painfully, a new social fabric" (55).

A stark division between work and home determines the coordinates of Callendar's cognitive map of Chandrapore, rendering Indians utterly incompatible with British private space. It is not so much that urban planning has made Indians invisible to the British, but that the British can only acknowledge Indians on an official level, within the temporal and spatial frame of the workday. As Ronny Heaslop's experience suggests, male members of the imperial community spend their days interacting with natives and in the evenings retreat to their compounds and clubs. Such a schedule relegates Indians to official or public space in the imperial imaginary. "Indians [are] shop" (40), as Forster's narrator points out, and even at the Bridge Party, ostensibly a social gathering, the Collector quietly presses his wife to mingle with Indians by saying, "To work, Mary, to work" (41). Given this association between natives and work for the British, *it does not signify* (as Forster might put it) that Indians have private lives. It is not just that Indians do not matter to the British as social beings—though this is certainly true—but that their social existence does not even register, does not mean anything, in the imperial consciousness: hence Callendar's failure to imagine where Aziz could be during off-hours and Mrs. Callendar's snubbing of him. Aziz suffers a similar snub from Ronny, who angrily disrupts Fielding's garden party and ignores the Indian doctor's attempts at conversation: "Ronny took no notice [of Aziz], but continued to address his remarks to Adela. . . . The only link he could be conscious of with an Indian was the official" (81).

Thus, a rather literal meaning inheres in Fielding's sarcastic suggestion—his first line in the novel—that to experience India one should "try seeing Indians" (25). Indeed, Chandrapore's spatial order makes encountering the indigenous population not simply a social but a perceptual challenge. Adela senses as much when considering how marriage to Ronny and her inevitable transformation into a memsahib would alter her view of India: "Colour would remain—the pageant of birds in the early morning, brown bodies, white turbans, idols whose flesh was scarlet or blue—and movement would remain as long as there were crowds in the bazaar and bathers in the tanks. . . . But the force that lies behind the colour and movement would escape her even more effectually than it did now"(48). Adela's visual transformation of colonial raw materials into a fully modernist perspective is revealing when considered alongside an earlier moment in the imperial encounter. In Conrad's *Lord Jim* Marlow describes a view outside the court in which Jim's trial takes place: "There was, as I walked along, the clear sunshine, a brilliance too passionate to be consoling, the streets full of jumbled bits of colour like a damaged kaleidoscope: yellow, green, blue, dazzling white, the brown nudity of an undraped shoulder, a bullock-cart with a red canopy, a company of native infantry in a drab body with dark heads marching in dusty laced boots, a native policeman in a sombre uniform of scanty cut and belted in patent leather" (158). Considered alongside each other, the passages disclose a telling shift in aesthetic perception from Conrad to Forster, from the moment of high imperialism to that of late imperialism. Like Kim amid the bazaars of Lahore, or Kipling's nocturnal wanderer in "The City of Dreadful Night," Marlow jostles among the colonial urban crowd with unrestricted mobility. As the claustrophobia of Miss Quested and Mrs. Moore suggests throughout *Passage,* however, segregation is more systematically imposed and vigilantly policed during the moment of late imperialism. While gender accounts in part for the women's restriction, I also want to suggest that material changes in the organization of colonial urban space exert themselves on Forster's fiction, necessitating highly regulated interactions (like bridge parties) and quasi-clandestine outings (like the Marabar Cave trip or Mrs. Moore's early mosque visit).

And as the passages above suggest, these differences manifest themselves at the level of style as well as content. Fragmentary and kaleidoscopic, Marlow's

impressions outside the courthouse are noticeably sharper than Adela's, capturing the texture and grain of urban chaos at close range. Where Marlow zooms
in, from colors to the objects that produce them, Adela's perspective moves in
the opposite direction, as specific objects become derealized—smudged and
blurred into a spectacle of abstract "colour and movement." Moreover, if the
proximity of Marlow's crisp but fractured mosaic of colonial urbanity produces
a somewhat discomforting perceptual intensity, "a brilliance too passionate to
be consoling," Adela's distance transforms colonial space into a diffuse swath
of colors and shapes, a "pageant" that recalls Forster's opening description of
Chandrapore as a city of gardens when viewed from the civil lines. The passage
from *Lord Jim* confirms the classic link between modernist aesthetic experimen-
tation and the vicissitudes of urban experience. Forster's description of Adela's
changing consciousness, however, reflects a movement away from the city, and
from contact with the colonized, that has been structured by the boundaries
of Anglo-Indian suburbia. It is with Forster then that we see the markings of
a suburban modernist perception—produced not by urban experience but by
increasing distance from it. As Adela's example suggests, late-imperial suburban segregation affects the Anglo-Indian consciousness not simply by occlud-
ing the view of colonized urban space, but by transforming it into an ocular
pleasaunce.

If suburban segregation makes a picturesque modernist spectacle of India
when viewed from afar, closer interaction can elicit frustration, anger, and anxiety. As Forster's narrator suggests regarding Chandrapore when viewed from
the hills, "New-comers cannot believe it to be as meagre as it is described, and
have to be driven down to acquire disillusionment" (4–5). Likewise, Fielding's
imperative of "seeing Indians"—that is, engaging or simply imagining them in
an unofficial capacity—is one of the surest ways to frustrate veteran members
of colonial society. Callendar's anger with Aziz offers a vivid illustration, as does
Ronny's behavior at the bridge party. His commentary for Adela on the Indian
guests moves rapidly from sarcasm ("What do you think of the Aryan Brother
in a topi and spats?"), to feigned indifference ("The great point to remember is
that no one who's here matters"), to sadistic rancor ("Most of the people you see
are seditious at heart, and the rest 'ld run squealing") (38–39). In the process of
othering these otherwise sophisticated guests, Ronny suggests that the imperial
official must reduce even westernized Indians to stereotypes of native savagery
or cowardice. His comments reflect the extent to which social interaction with
Indians, normally policed by the strict boundaries of the colonial city, troubles
the official consciousness into memories of insurgency.

Nostalgia and *Ressentiment*

With its compulsion to replicate what Forster's narrator calls "life on the home pattern" (66), colonial society reveals symptoms of intense nostalgia. In 1912, the same year that Forster first visited the subcontinent, the *Contemporary Review* published an article entitled "English Society in India," which identifies nostalgia as the core of colonial identity. "Their life and work may be in India," the writer suggests of Anglo-Indians, but "the memories of their youth . . . these are all 'at Home.' *And so it happens that they all, quite unconsciously perhaps, make an effort to forget it and draw together in every way likely to distract one another from dwelling on this idea.* With this object in view, all but the very latest arrivals from England contrive to make their houses as little oriental and as much like an English home as possible" (Ricketts 683, emphasis added). As this writer implies, creating a hermetically sealed and exclusively English residential space requires the imperial community to engage in a process of endless distraction, an attempt to forget its cultural displacement by repressing or ignoring the environment it has colonized. And yet nostalgia—whose literal meaning is homesickness—can never be overcome by such distractions. As one of the club members in Orwell's *Burmese Days* asks, referring to "dear old *Punch, Pink'un*, and *Vie Parisienne*[:] Makes you homesick to read 'em, what?" (20). The question reveals that, rather than satisfying the mania to uphold middle-class life in the colonies, the periodicals—and the suburban life they represent—only intensify feelings of nostalgia. Despite (or because of) this obsessive nostalgia, imperial society must repeatedly confront its failure to make a proper British home in a foreign land, since, as Forster suggests, the attempt to satiate nostalgia only strengthens it. Playing "God Save the Queen" after the performance of *Cousin Kate,* for example, "remind[s] every member of the club that he or she [is] British and in exile" (24). Likewise, though club members strive to maintain a European diet in India, the result is a "food of exiles," "cooked by servants who [do] not understand it": "Julienne soup full of bullety bottled peas, pseudo-cottage bread, fish full of branching bones, pretending to be plaice" (48–49).[9]

By shoring up a reservoir of Englishness, imperial society merely accentuates its own sense of exile and thereby reveals how utterly nostalgic its identity is. Orwell's narrator recognizes this phenomenon with particular insight, claiming, "No Anglo-Indian will ever deny that India is going to the dogs, or ever has denied it—for India, like *Punch,* never was what it was" (29). And yet this recognition by even its most fervent adherents that colonial society is inherently nostalgic does not keep them from reacting against their inability to make a proper British home in the colonies. We see this in the way the community manifests its nostalgia temporally, for nostalgia is a longing not only to return home, but to go back in time. In the communities depicted by Forster and Orwell, there is an obsessive desire to reproduce British culture in a foreign landscape, but also to return to an era when white rule was absolute. As one of the club memsahibs laments in *Burmese Days*, "We seem to have no *authority* over the natives nowadays, with all these dreadful reforms, and the insolence they learn from the newspapers." "In my young days," a male club member chimes in, "when one's butler was disrespectful, one sent him along to the jail with a chit saying 'Please give the bearer fifteen lashes.' . . . Those days are gone forever." To which another sahib replies: "This country'll never be fit to live in again. British Raj is finished if you ask me" (29, original emphasis).

Epitomizing the nostalgia that governs colonial society, such comments also reveal the bitterness and spite prominent among white characters of late-imperial fiction. Most notable are Ronny Heaslop and his more sadistic Orwellian doppelgänger, Ellis, both of whom can barely manage to contain their seething rage and deep-seated longings for vengeance. "Ellis really did hate Orientals," Orwell's narrator remarks, "hated them with a bitter restless loathing" (24). Although slightly more reserved, Heaslop shares this emotion, as revealed in his recurrent disagreements with his mother about the treatment of Indians: "We're not out here for the purpose of behaving pleasantly! . . . We're out here to do justice and keep the peace" (51). As Mrs. Moore notes, her son speaks like "an intelligent and embittered boy" at such moments: "How Ronny revelled in the drawbacks of his situation! How he did rub it in that he was not in India to behave pleasantly, and derived positive satisfaction therefrom!" (52).

Ronny's transformation of bitterness and hatred into a virtue and source of satisfaction—which I take as representative of a larger late-imperial structure of feeling—recalls the Nietzschean revaluation of values produced by *ressentiment*. A corrosive spirit of revenge capable of overturning existing values, *ressentiment* for Nietzsche is at the heart of the most seemingly beneficent morality. In *On the Genealogy of Morals* (1887), Nietzsche excoriates the Victorian assumption that Judeo-Christian morality represents some absolute good or timeless truth. He argues instead that its privileging of weakness (in the guise of humility and selflessness or in practices like abstinence and fasting) stems from the resentment directed toward a previous set of values—namely, the aggressive physicality and possessiveness Nietzsche equates with classical nobility.[10] *Ressentiment* emerged as an affect with social and political force, according to Nietzsche, when the Roman warrior class usurped political power from Jewish rabbis, who saw themselves as the Romans' superiors yet felt unable to retaliate. Rather than acting out their feeling of superiority, the rabbis channeled it into affect, giving rise to what Nietzsche calls slave morality: "The slave revolt in morality begins when *ressentiment* itself becomes creative and ordains values: the *ressentiment* of creatures to whom the real reaction, that of deed, is denied and who find compensation in an imaginary revenge" (22). This imaginary revenge, which replaces authentic action, nonetheless engenders a new value hierarchy—one that Nietzsche deems inherently twisted. Deleuze suggests that rather than vilifying the other due to one's innate sense of worth ("I am good, therefore you are evil"), *ressentiment* functions in reverse, so that one's worth is extrapolated solely from recognizing the other as different ("You are evil, therefore I am good") (119). *Ressentiment* is in this sense "reactive," inferior to "active" forces that require no prior incitement.[11] All morality for Nietzsche follows this reactive logic; all morality is thus perverse and deformed—a negative appreciation of oneself based ironically on an *inability* to act. *Ressentiment* recasts this inability as conscious refusal or self-denial, thereby making failure tantamount to virtue.

Ronny's reveling in his drawbacks follows the lineaments of this logic, exposing *ressentiment* as the venomous underside of the civilizing mission. This is hardly surprising, since the white man's burden has long been recognized as an excuse for the vilest exploitation. Complications arise, however, in reading *ressentiment* as a diagnosis of the imperial ethos, given the political and social superiority of whites enforcing colonial rule. The automatic assumption is to see the imperialist as a Nietzschean master, not a spiteful slave. Yet this assumption can be challenged in a number of ways. For one thing, while *ressentiment* emerges from an imbalance of power, we might also see it as a response to unfavorable or undesirable conditions experienced by the powerful and powerless alike. As Hugh Tomlinson suggests, "The slave does not necessarily stand for someone dominated, by fate or social condition, but also characterises the dominators . . . once the regime of domination comes under the sway of forces which are reactive" (x). For Nietzsche the value system and the forces directing it, rather than the mere condition of power itself, determine whether the powerful are masters or slaves. Moreover, those who ruled abroad often occupied the lower half of the sociocultural ladder in Britain and were frequently reputed as superfluous men who couldn't hack it back home. Max Scheler's 1915 study of *ressentiment* declares the affect most notable among "the petty bourgeoisie and . . . small officials" (66), linking the domestic lower middle class to those who oversaw Europe's colonial outposts. Finally, it should be noted that the ethos reflects a perceived loss of power similar to that felt by the contemporary *homme de ressentiment,* the "angry white male" (Nealon). Perhaps the original angry white men, Anglo-Indian characters, like the Nietzschean slave, constantly begrudge their situation, imagining themselves engaged in a losing battle ("British Raj is finished if you ask me") and implicitly looking on the past with a nostalgia that has turned sour.

Frustrated by its longing to inhabit a time and place beyond its reach, colonial society thus transforms its nostalgia into *ressentiment*—a process confirmed by Albert Memmi in his classic diagnosis of the imperial psyche, *The Colonizer and the Colonized*.[12] Significantly, Memmi dubs this process the colonizer's "exaltation-resentment dialectics" (65). He suggests that while the colonizer no longer feels at home in his native country, he idealizes it from afar, "extolling" and "exaggerating . . . its special traditions" (58). The presence of the colonized subject only exacerbates the colonizer's feeling of displacement. The colonizer "is fed up with his subject, who tortures his conscience and his life. He tries to dismiss him from his mind, to imagine the colony without the colonized" (66). But as Memmi points out, even if the colonizer could "eliminate the colonized . . . it would be impossible for him to do so without eliminating himself" (54): "This intolerable contradiction fills him with a rage, a loathing, always ready to be loosed on the colonized" (66). It is also significant, given the relationship I have been tracing among suburbanization, nostalgia, and *ressentiment,* that Memmi discusses the colonizer's exaltation-resentment dialectics in the context of colonial town planning.[13]

Memmi's exaltation-resentment dialectics are clearly at play in *A Passage to India,* not only in the novel's portrayal of urban space and late-imperial nostalgia but also in its depiction of the vexed interactions between colonizer and colonized. Yet the loathing Memmi identifies as "always ready to be loosed on the colonized" (66) rarely finds an outlet in action in late-imperial fiction. This is especially true of the emotional maelstrom that grips the Anglo-Indian community following Adela's apparent rape in the Marabar Caves. Being driven through the bazaar, the Collector mentally accuses every native he sees of crimes against Adela, saying to himself, "I know what you're like at last; you shall pay for this, you shall squeal" (184). Despite his anger, however, the Collector recognizes his inability to act: "He wanted to flog every native that he saw, but to do nothing that would lead to a riot or to the necessity for military intervention" (202). He is thus in an impossible situation: "There seemed nothing for it but the old weary business of compromise and moderation. He longed for the good old days when an Englishman could satisfy his honour and no questions asked afterwards" (203). The institutions of modern civilization, in whose name the colonizer seeks to justify his presence, restrict him from unleashing the wrath that would give vent to his frustration: "Not only would the Nawab Bahadur and others be angry, but the Government of India itself also watches—and

behind it is that caucus of cranks and cravens, the British Parliament" (203).[14]
Like the memsahib in *Burmese Days* who complains that the British "have no
authority over the natives nowadays, with all these dreadful reforms" (29, original emphasis), the Anglo-Indians of Chandrapore see themselves as hamstrung
by their own government. Indeed, in a Nietzschean sense they position themselves as slaves of the British government, which has forced them to acquiesce in
their relationship with India. The Collector's powerlessness in the face of Adela's
apparent attack affects others in the community as well. McBryde grows "very
bitter" over the prospect of Adela being cross-examined by an Indian, calling it
"the fruits of democracy" (217). The entire Anglo-Indian community "fretted
because they could do nothing for [Ronny] . . . ; they felt so craven sitting on
softness and attending the course of the law" (205).

What characterizes these responses is their reactive quality, their replace-
ment of action with feeling. Deleuze's explication of Nietzsche is especially use-
ful in this regard, demonstrating how excess memory elicits *ressentiment*—or,
more precisely, provides its very content—and thereby subsumes action itself.
"If we ask what the man of *ressentiment* is," Deleuze suggests, "we must not
forget this principle: he does not re-act. And the word *ressentiment* gives a definite clue: *reaction ceases to be acted in order to become something felt (senti)*" (111,
original emphasis). Deleuze here invokes the distinction between active and
reactive forces as they correspond to separate domains of the so-called reactive
apparatus, the Nietzschean analogue, avant la lettre, to Freud's topology of conscious and unconscious. *Ressentiment* occurs when the proper contents of the
conscious and unconscious domains are transposed—or, to be more specific,
when memory, rather than remaining in the unconscious, emerges to interrupt consciousness: "The man of *ressentiment* is characterised by the invasion
of consciousness by mnemonic traces, the ascent of memory into consciousness
itself" (114). Because the trace now occupies the area reserved for excitations,
"reaction itself takes the place of action, reaction prevails over action" (114).
But rather than eliminating action altogether, consciousness must now accommodate both active and reactive forces. Thus, "*ressentiment* is a reaction which
simultaneously becomes perceptible and ceases to be acted" (114).

The Deleuzian diagnosis of *ressentiment* as the product of "prodigious memory" (115)—what Michael André Bernstein calls "reminiscence-as-suffering"
(204)—returns us to the issue of nostalgia, particularly as it manifests itself
among the white communities of late-imperial fiction. Like Memmi, Deleuze
allows us to connect the affective reign of *ressentiment* among members of colonial society to their nostalgia for home. But unlike Memmi, a Deleuzian reading
of *ressentiment* emphasizes the inability to act that we see illustrated by Forster.
And yet, despite the pain it causes the Anglo-Indian consciousness, we also see

ressentiment working to transform Anglo-Indian failure into virtue. After one of Ronny Heaslop's frequent tirades against Indians, his mother claims, "You never used to judge people like this at home." "India isn't home," he snaps back (33). At the most obvious level the response seeks to justify his behavior—a patronizing explanation for the uninitiated. At a deeper level, however, this reply is an admission of failure: Britain's failure to colonize, pacify, and domesticate India. At the same time Ronny makes his proclamation with something like pride, suggesting an attempt on his part to transform Britain's failure to colonize India into a moral victory.[15]

Thus, in its frustrated desire to re-create an excessively British environment abroad, colonial society reveals nostalgia's degeneration into *ressentiment*. This affect is exacerbated by aspects of India that complicate or contradict the colonial community's blinkered perception—a perception shaped by its segregation from the space of the colonized.[16] When challenged by proximity with the colonized, this perception in turn elicits British anxieties of native insurgency. Gathering after Adela's apparent rape by Aziz in the Marabar Caves, the British attempt to replicate domestic society, driving to the club with "the jog-trot of country gentlefolk between green hedgerows." Yet their attempt to maintain a façade of normalcy before the Indians fails: "They exchanged the usual drinks, but everything tasted different," and when they looked at the landscape they "realized that they were thousands of miles from any scenery that they understood" (200). This recognition of their presence within a foreign environment gives way to memories of Indian rebellion: the club, "fuller than usual," takes on "the air of the Residency at Lucknow" (200), and the increasingly conspiratorial rants of its members elicit "the unspeakable limit of cynicism, untouched since 1857" (207). At that point imperial *ressentiment* takes on a kind of communal energy: "the evil was propagating in every direction, it seemed to have an existence of its own, apart from anything that was done or said by individuals" (207–8). In his 1925 anti-imperial treatise *The Other Side of the Medal*, published by the Woolfs' Hogarth Press, Edward Thompson suggests that such communal *ressentiment* had come to dominate general British attitudes about India. Where average Britons once expressed indifference toward the subcontinent, Thompson claims that "to-day indifference is hardening into anger and dislike" (14). "So we are going," Thompson writes, "going bitterly and contemptuously" (10).

Only Disconnect

I have been examining *ressentiment* as the affective sine qua non of colonial society in late-imperial texts like *A Passage to India*—texts, I have argued, in which the suburb plays a crucial material and discursive role. Before concluding, I want to consider the presence and functioning of *ressentiment* within Forster's own aesthetic practice. As Fredric Jameson points out, one of the most striking aspects of the logic of *ressentiment* is "its unavoidably autoreferential structure," by which he means that "the theory of *ressentiment,* wherever it appears, will always itself be the expression and the production of *ressentiment*" (*Political* 202). Or, to paraphrase Jameson's comment on Gissing: Forster clearly resents Anglo-Indians, and what he resents most is their *ressentiment.* To locate traces of *ressentiment* at the heart of Forster's project—even, as I shall suggest, in a weakened form—may seem counterintuitive if not scandalous, given the author's canonical status as a patron saint of liberal humanism.[17] My ultimate goal, however, is not the Nietzschean one of unmasking some impotent hatred that mobilizes either liberalism in general or Forster's work in particular. Rather, I seek to complicate readings of Forster that reduce his politics to a benevolent holdover—"the fag-end of Victorian liberalism" (*Two* 54), as Forster himself put it—that modernity has rendered naively effete. Such generalizations of Forster's ethical position have no doubt become less common; indeed, much recent criticism of *Passage* considers the degree to which Forster's avowed anti-imperialism belies a deeper Orientalism.[18] Yet critics remain caught in a cycle, trying to determine once and for all whether Forster's unwitting espousal of imperialist ideology outweighs his celebrated liberal humanism (or vice versa). Considering *ressentiment* as Jameson wants us to do—as "a form of social praxis . . . a symbolic resolution to a concrete historical situation" (*Political* 117)—offers a way out of this cycle, for it recognizes the contradictory position Forster inhabits.

This impasse functions on a number of levels. First there is the imperial impasse—that is, Britain's inability either to act with the autocratic rule of days gone by or to abandon the subcontinent without tarnishing its reputation as ruler of the world's greatest empire. Second, there is the impasse of segregation and urban conditions that have severely restricted and poisoned whatever social contact might exist between Indians and Britons. This is of course a serious wrench in Forster's narrative machinery, which depends so heavily on personal relationships, intimacy, and the providential. As I have already suggested, Forster must elude these restrictions with all the sophistication he can muster. And this leads us finally to Forster's personal impasse: his inability to engage honestly and intimately with India from a position untainted by imperialism. For what Forster seeks above all is a space in which Indians and Britons can engage one another without the psychosocial baggage that gives the colonizer delusions of grandeur and the colonized an inferiority complex.

Forster attempts to resolve these various tensions in the sequence from *Pas-*

sage that has garnered perhaps the most critical attention: the Marabar Caves. These hermeneutical lacunae have been taken to represent practically anything and everything, from the life-encompassing World Mountain (Stone) to the world-denying philosophy of Jainism (Parry, *Delusions*). Regardless of what they represent, the caves are usually seen as a metonym for India's ultimate opacity, be that a symptom of Forster's Orientalism (as in Suleri) or his self-conscious acknowledgment of the limits of Western consciousness (as in Parry, "Materiality"). But critics have failed to recognize that the caves ironically share some striking similarities with the British civil station. Though distant enough from each other to require a train ride, both civil station and caves mark a geographical movement away from Chandrapore and up into the hills. Yet there is disappointment upon arrival at both places. Like the underwhelming station, whose "sensibly planned" grounds "provoke[ ] no emotion" (5), the caves provide little to either challenge or please, as they are "readily described" (136) and their approach is "tolerably convenient" (162). If the civil station "has nothing hideous in it," though it "charms not" (5), so do the caves undermine a desire for resolution: "Nothing evil had been in the cave, but [Mrs. Moore] had not enjoyed herself" (163); "Nothing was explained, and yet there was no romance" for Adela (155). Yet for all their equivocality, both civil station and caves are stiflingly monotonous. Despite their smooth contours, the caves are as repetitive as the station's "gridiron" layout and its profusion of "right angles" (5, 13, 23). Regardless of how many caves one sees, the same "arrangement occurs again and again," and "the pattern never varies" (136–37). Forster plays up this comparison at one point: Adela's anxiety that "the Marabar caves were notoriously like one another" occurs just as Ronny shuttles her to "a replica of the bungalow she had left" (220–21). The caves' incessant and unchanging echo is "entirely void of distinction" and "utterly dull" (163), recalling Adela's complaint that she "hear[s] nothing interesting up at the club" except "ridiculous gossip" (79). Likewise, when Mrs. Moore "nearly faint[s]" in the "horrid, stuffy" cave, her reaction recalls her flight from the club's stifling heat in the novel's opening (162, 156). Rather than simply representing India's absolute alterity, then, the caves also provide an uncanny echo of the British club and civil station.

But in noting these similarities between the civil station and the caves, I am less concerned with a representational comparison than with how the caves both extend and resolve the segregated spatial logic of the suburban civil station. That is, I am less interested in what the caves *mean* than in how they work—what they *do* for Forster within his own dilemma and at the historical moment of late imperialism. And what they do, I believe, is initiate an imaginary resolution to the real contradiction of Britain's impasse with India. What Forster requires is an event that will allow him to retain both his anti-imperialism and his criticism of India all at once; an event, or more accurately a non-event, that will provide the premise for an irreconcilable split between India and Britain—yet one that ultimately will blame neither side (or will blame both sides equally). The caves fulfill this requirement by allowing Forster, as Jenny Sharpe has shown, to restage the historical after-effects of 1857. And yet, because nothing "happens" in this restaging, or because what happens remains unknown, neither side takes full blame: to the British it seems likely that Aziz attempted to rape Adela; yet this assumption is undermined when Adela withdraws her charge. Significantly, it is the ethereal yet impoverished punkah-wallah—an embodiment of the urban India occluded from Adela's consciousness—who motivates her retraction. The punkah-wallah, who "was of the city . . . [and] would end on its rubbish heaps," makes an impact on this "girl from middle-class England" and forces her to ask herself: "In virtue of what had she collected this roomful of people together? Her particular brand of opinions, and the suburban Jehovah who sanctified them . . . ?" (241–42). While Adela's retraction releases Aziz—and by extension all Indians—from blame, it does nothing to mitigate the rancor between races. The inaction of *ressentiment* thus seems the only proper response. A change in prior conditions is required, but that change merely facilitates Britain's (understandable if ultimately inexplicable) withdrawal from the subcontinent. Thus, after the cave experience Mrs. Moore departs from India, and after the trial she is followed by Adela, then Fielding; we hear little more of Ronny; and Aziz, who claims, "I have decided to have nothing more to do with British India" (280), leaves Chandrapore for the Hindu native state of Mau.

It is notable, however, that before they make their departures, *ressentiment* infects other characters in the novel. Although Heaslop seems increasingly abashed and deferential following the cave incident, and his overt bitterness fades into melancholic befuddlement, his feelings—"half miserable, half arrogant" (276)—recall his earlier *ressentiment*. Likewise, while his apology letter to Fielding proclaims that "life is too short to cherish grievances," Ronny's paranoia and hatred get projected upon a new culprit for the empire's downfall: "My personal opinion is, it's the Jews" (345). More surprising, however, is the *ressentiment* that overtakes Mrs. Moore, who begins to express hatred toward herself and others before she departs and abjures her matronly responsibilities. "A sort of resentment emanate[s] from her," and her former goodwill transforms into "a hardness, a just irritation against the human race" (221). She moves about with an "air of ill-temper" (227), wishing more and more to be left alone. She also comes to recognize evil in herself: "I am not good, no, bad. . . . A bad old woman, bad, bad, detestable" (228).

As well as inspiring Aziz's departure from Chandrapore, the cave incident chills his relations with Fielding, who spends more time with Adela, garners praise from the provincial government, and gains readmission to the club. Augmenting his bitterness is Aziz's suspicion that Fielding has begun to court Adela, having preserved her dowry by convincing Aziz to drop his suit against her. Suspicion of Fielding becomes "a sort of malignant tumour" in Aziz, "a mental malady, that makes him self-conscious and unfriendly" (311). This is so even in their intimate moments, as when Fielding returns to visit Aziz in Mau. Discovering Aziz's assumption that he married Adela, Fielding becomes "more friendly than before, but scathing and scornful" (338). And now, as if Forster is attempting to stage a disagreement between them by divorcing their personal antipathies from imperialist ideology, they become more direct and brash with each other. Their interrupted final embrace on horseback is preceded by disagreements bordering on resentment: "Fielding had 'no further use for politeness,' he said, meaning that the British Empire really can't be abolished because it's rude. Aziz retorted, 'Very well, and we have no use for you,' and glared at him in abstract hate" (360). Fielding mocks Aziz's nationalist sentiment, deriding India's education system, scientific achievement, and unrealistic attempt to end purdah. Aziz suggests that quiet vengefulness will mark India's future relation to Britain: "Clear out, all you Turtons and Burtons. . . . Until England is in difficulties we keep silent, but in the next European war—aha, aha! Then is our time" (360).

When Aziz proposes a conference of Oriental states and proclaims that India will become a nation, Forster's narrator—in a gesture rarely noted by critics—curiously takes over Fielding's accusations: "India a nation! What an apotheosis! Last comer to the drab nineteenth-century sisterhood! Waddling in at this hour of the world to take her seat!" (361).[19] This subtle drop of the internal quotation marks that until now have governed the verbal sparring between Aziz and Fielding suggests that Forster himself has become a surrogate for the latter, allowing his own *ressentiment* both to displace and to double that of Fielding. This is a surprising discovery, one that complicates our received sense of Forster's liberalism. Yet over the course of writing his novel, Forster himself underwent a transition similar to that of his characters. In 1922 Forster wrote tellingly to his close friend Syed Ross Masood, to whom he dedicated *Passage*— and whom he later praised for "w[a]k[ing] me up out of my suburban and academic life" (*Two* 285). "When I began the book," Forster told Masood, with increasing indignation, "I thought of it as a little bridge of sympathy between East and West, but this conception has had to go, my sense of the truth forbids anything so comfortable. I think that most Indians, like most English people, are shits, and I am not interested in whether they sympathize with one another or not" (Furbank 2: 106).

Writhing Impotently

I have been suggesting that if *A Passage to India* represents Forster's abandoned attempt to build a "bridge of sympathy between East and West," then a more fitting objective correlative for the novel's ensuing *ressentiment* can be found in the British colonial suburbs of the early twentieth century. And while we can discern Forster's own *ressentiment* emerging from his liberal humanist critique of a suburbanized Anglo-India, the affect becomes fully operational for subsequent authors of late-imperial fiction in ways I can only gesture toward here. Consider, for example, the bitterness, cynicism, and disgust that saturate novels of empire during the 1930s and 1940s by Orwell, Waugh, Joyce Cary, and Graham Greene. Cary's African fiction—especially *Aissa Saved* (1932) and *The African Witch* (1936)—revels in scenes of retrograde primitivism and gratuitous violence, while Greene's *The Heart of the Matter* (1948) treats British West Africa as an irredeemably seedy locus of self-imposed damnation.[20] For Waugh and Orwell, significantly enough, *ressentiment* continues to be directed at an empire whose suburban qualities are increasingly pervasive. Thus, though Waugh treats most Africans as unmitigated savages in *Black Mischief,* he also clearly abhors the British administrators, whose garden city legation epitomizes their blissful insularity. Consumed by petty affairs, they "potter. . . . in and out of each other's bungalows and kn[ow] the details of each other's housekeeping" (67) yet remain placidly indifferent to events outside their compound. As I mentioned earlier, they are eventually forced to flee Azania, replaced by League of Nations officials who merely prolong the farce ad infinitum—inhabiting identical bungalows, dining on tinned foods, and listening to Gilbert and Sullivan. In addition, Waugh derides the modernizing potential of town planning when taken up by the native elite: in the midst of a national emergency, Seth, the Oxford-educated African leader of Azania, undertakes a regime of modernization that entails a complete reorganization of his capital.[21]

Similarly, Orwell's vague intimations of a post-imperial order are ineluctably bound to suburbia by a *ressentiment* that seeks to disavow any agency for the dissolution of empire. Whereas Waugh's *ressentiment* is mediated through his relentlessly scathing satire of both colonizers and colonized, however, Orwell offers up a more palpable form aimed squarely at the imperialists. In *The Lion and the Unicorn,* Orwell claims that during "the early 'twenties one could see, all over the Empire," officials who were "writhing impotently under the changes that were happening" (*Collected* 2: 73). As I've already demonstrated, *ressentiment* dominates the lives of such figures in *Burmese Days;* but what is striking is that it also now motivates protagonist and author alike. We first see the *ressentiment* of John Flory as he overhears a typically racist exchange between colleagues at his club—in this case condemning the obligatory admittance of a Burmese member: "He must get out of this room quickly, before something happened inside his head and he began to smash the furniture and throw bottles at the pictures. Dull boozing witless porkers! Was it possible that they could go on week after week, year after year, repeating word for word the same evil-minded drivel, like a parody of a fifth-rate story in *Blackwood's*? Would none of them *ever* think of anything new to say?" (33, original emphasis). What hardly needs saying, however, is that "Flory did not say any of this, and he was at some pains not to show it in his face" (33). Internalizing the hatred he feels toward his fellow club members, Flory bottles it up rather than acting on it or speaking its name. "I don't go in for proclaiming from the housetops," he tells his friend and confidant Dr. Veraswami. "I haven't the guts" (43). Consequently, Flory "live[s] inwardly, secretly, in books and secret thoughts that could not be uttered" (70). Watching John Flory stew silently at the club, or listening to him condemn the "Pox Britannica" (41), we see an obvious surrogate for Orwell himself, who distilled from his years as a police officer in Burma an admittedly "simple theory": "that the oppressed are always right and the oppressors are always wrong. . . . At that time failure seemed to me to be the only virtue" (*Road* 138). A textbook study of such empire-born *ressentiment,* Flory anticipates the exemplars of suburban lower-middle-class frustration in Orwell's later fiction: George Comstock, poet manqué of *Keep the Aspidistra Flying,* is consumed by "snubs, failures, insults, all of them unavenged," and "make[s] it his especial purpose *not* to 'succeed'" (77, 45, original emphasis); the insurance salesman George Bowling's narration of *Coming Up for Air* is an extended screed on London's "inner-outer suburbs" (11).[22]

Like these figures Flory is ultimately unable to imagine any workable alternative to suburbia. Thus, he rants at the thought of Burma being overrun by "villa after villa, with all the gramophones playing the same tune" (42). But, since Flory considers Burma "his native country, his home" (71), his only chance of staying on without suffering constant pangs of bad conscience remains wedded to an unmistakably suburban vision of life-after-empire. Hoping to turn a new leaf by marrying a recently arrived Englishwoman, Flory conjures an image of "his home as she would remake it." In an extended reverie of his post-imperial domesticity, he sees "his drawing-room [as] sluttish and bachelor-like no longer, with new furniture from Rangoon, and a bowl of pink balsams like rosebuds on the table, and books and water-colours and a black piano. Above all the piano! His mind lingered upon the piano—symbol, perhaps because he was unmusical, of civilised and settled life" (272).[23] Thus, while Flory seeks to extricate himself from the inanity and racism of Kyauktada's British club, the liberal home he hopes to fashion for himself remains undeniably suburban.[24]

Flory's musings of post-imperial suburban bliss associate him with a figure whom Albert Memmi dubs the colonizer who refuses. While this figure is subject to "fits of verbal furor" against his colleagues, and characterized by "solitude, bewilderment, and ineffectiveness" (Memmi 43), he also longs to remain in the colonies for good: "While he happens to dream of a tomorrow, a brand-new social state in which the colonized cease to be colonized, he certainly does not conceive, on the other hand, of a deep transformation of his own situation and of his own personality. In that new, more harmonious state, he will go on being what he is, with his language intact and his cultural traditions dominating. . . . Without having a clear legal picture, he vaguely hopes to be a part of the future young nation, but he firmly reserves the right to remain a citizen of his native country" (40).

Inhabiting the impossible position of the colonizer who refuses, Flory plays a crucial part in the imperial endgame, merging anti-imperial liberalism with late-imperial *ressentiment*. While he shares the tolerance and sympathy of Forster's Fielding, he expresses these values in the embittered affective register of Ronny Heaslop. Through Flory, then, Orwell seeks to appropriate imperial *ressentiment* on behalf of a critique of empire. However, Flory's resentment only serves to immobilize his agency, foreclosing any further engagement between the British and Burmese. Failing to secure his domestic idyll—his English intended rebuffs him after learning of his long-standing affair with a Burmese concubine—Flory commits suicide. Before doing so, he once again imagines the suburban idyll that might have been: his new wife feeding his dog near their garden, "the pigeons on the drive by the sulphur-yellow phloxes," and inside their home that "impossible, mythical piano—symbol of everything that [his affair] had wrecked!" (278). Turning his revolver on himself, Flory then both submits to and defies the logic of *ressentiment,* taking vengeance with his body on the empire that tortured his soul.

7

George Orwell and the Road to West Bletchley

Flory's suicide did not solve Britain's attempted detachment from its colonial possessions. Nor did it bring an end to Orwell's writing about empire. Perhaps the most surprising place where the subject resurfaces is *The Road to Wigan Pier* (1937), which examines living conditions in English coal country alongside an account of Orwell's evolving political views. The book's second half begins: "The road from Mandalay to Wigan is a long one and the reasons for taking it are not immediately clear" (121). The nod to Kipling—and the unexpected imperial subtext it introduces—suggests the importance of Burma in shaping Orwell's class views. As he tells it in *Wigan Pier*, Orwell chucked his post as an imperial police officer to undergo the regime of self-imposed poverty that led to his first book, *Down and Out in Paris and London* (1933). Somewhere along the way he came to see England's class structure as analogous to colonization, with the working class "playing the same part in England as the Burmese played in Burma. . . . Here in England, down under one's feet, were the submerged working class, suffering miseries which in their different way were as bad as any an oriental ever knows" (*Road* 148–49). Thanks in part to *Wigan Pier*, scholars have long recognized that Orwell's colonial experience framed his view of English poverty and working-class exploitation. As George Woodcock puts it in his classic study *The Crystal Spirit*, Orwell saw England itself as "a colonial world, a world of master race and subject race," with a "great gulf that divided the upper and middle from the lower classes" (56–57). Overlooked is Orwell's increasing sense during the late 1930s that the middle class had devolved from a master race to a subject race.

This chapter thus follows a road less traveled—one leading from Mandalay to West Bletchley, the fictional suburb of Orwell's 1939 novel *Coming Up for Air*. As in *Wigan Pier* the reasons for making this journey may not be obvious. But West Bletchley shares a great deal with the colonized landscape of *Burmese Days*. Flory imagined "forests, villages, monasteries, pagodas all vanished," replaced by "villa after villa, with all the gramophones playing the same tune," the inevitable product of an empire Flory deemed "a kind of up-to-date, hygienic, self-satisfied louse. Creeping round the world building prisons" (42). George Bowling, the narrator of *Coming Up for Air*, lives Flory's nightmare—not in Burma, but "in the inner-outer suburbs" of interwar Britain. A lower-middle-class insurance agent, Bowling describes his street as "a prison with the cells all in a row. A line of semi-detached torture chambers where the poor little five-to-ten-pound-a-weekers quake and shiver, every one of them with the boss twisting his tail and the wife riding him like the nightmare and the kids sucking his blood like leeches" (12). Scholars of suburbia cite Bowling's rant as "a defining illustration of the myths and stereotypes that have arisen around suburban culture" (Webster 1), while for Orwell critics his plight foreshadows the tyrannical world of *Nineteen Eighty-Four*. But Bowling also gives voice to suburban male conformity and enslavement by echoing Orwell's critique of imperialism.[1] The passages above figure suburb and empire in analogous terms: both set down monotonous grids of modern domesticity, imprisoning and torturing their inhabitants and feeding parasitically on their lifeblood. The difference between *Burmese Days* and *Coming Up for Air* is that while Flory is a colonizer, albeit a reluctant one, Bowling speaks from the perspective of the colonized. Flory fears Burma becoming a suburb; Bowling's suburb is already a colony, and its most oppressed subject is the lower-middle-class male.

If suburbia offered a prototype for dystopian future colonies in *Burmese Days*, my argument in this chapter is that Orwell conversely sees England's interwar suburbs imposing a form of domestic colonization on its own men. Read in the context of his scathing critiques of empire, Orwell's suburban males emerge as English avatars of the colonized: exploited, dispossessed of their homes, and plagued by feelings of powerlessness and enslavement. Bowling complains that "in this particular age and this particular country—we don't do the things we want to do" (93) and that "the feeling of not being one's own master overshadow[s] everything" (133). Such statements mark a pivotal shift in the longer history linking suburb and empire. Orwell's suburban male is neither the imperial superman prophesied by Sidney Low nor one of the degenerate and increasingly ineffectual colonizers who form the bulk of this study (Doyle's Major Sholto, Conrad's Almayer, Forster's Henry Wilcox or his parade of Anglo-Indians). Rather, Orwell's suburban male claims to inhabit the subject position of the colonized. Like my previous chapter this one focuses on the historical moment when the explosive growth of England's interwar suburbs coincides with the onset of Britain's imperial decline. But rather than helping Britain disavow its colonial possessions as in *A Passage to India* and *Burmese Days,* here suburbia completely colonizes England's own populace. In the previous chapter suburbia helped the empire go under. In this one suburbia is where the dying empire comes up for air, ensuring that Britain's detachment from its colonies will at best remain partial, incomplete, semi-detached.

Little Men, Little Homes

Imperial decline was not the only problem Britain faced during the interwar period, particularly in the 1930s. Inaugurated by the great slump, the decade did not bode well, as economic depression and mass unemployment gave way to looming clouds of war. A silver lining appeared in the form of improved living standards and decreased living costs. The protection of domestic markets sparked the modest recovery, aided by expanding retail and consumer industries (Hobsbawm, *Industry* chapter 11). Ironically, Britain experienced its greatest housing boom ever, thanks to lower building costs and interest rates and higher investment in the home market (A. Jackson 102). Greater London saw the largest growth, undergoing "the most dramatic phase in the history of [its] physical enlargement" (Whitehand and Carr 37). The residential area of London doubled between the wars and accounted for a third of the population increase in England and Wales (Inwood 722; J. H. Johnson 142).

England thus underwent its greatest suburban growth at a moment of acute economic and political crisis. Alison Light points out that as the nation turned away from "formerly heroic . . . public rhetorics of national destiny," it embraced "an Englishness at once less imperial and more inward-looking, more domestic and more private" (8). The figure that best personified this diminution in national and imperial stature during the 1930s was the suburban little man. Popularized in Sidney Strube's editorial cartoons for the *Daily Express,* this bespectacled and bowler-hatted man of modest means offered a domesticated version of national identity between the wars (Brookes 36). In Strube's cartoons "Britain and its Empire could be caricatured as comprising a vast suburban estate, populated by Little Men and their wives" (Brookes 41–42). Light sees this figure as emblematic of a redemptive, conservative nationalism between the wars, when the English became known as "a private and retiring people, pipe-smoking 'little men' with their quietly competent partners" (211). While fans took him as a symbol of English pluck in the face of adversity, the little man had his share of foes—Orwell among them. In *Keep the Aspidistra Flying,* the novel that precedes *Coming Up for Air,* Orwell's protagonist rails against him as an icon of suburban mediocrity and conformity, "the typical little bowler-hatted sneak—Strube's 'little man'" (48). Many, like Orwell, viewed the suburban little man as symptomatic of Britain's interwar decline. From D. H. Lawrence and poets of the Auden generation to parodists and rural preservationists, suburbia's little man and his little home seemed to mark the end of Britain's national and imperial sovereignty.

Lawrence sets the decade's keynote in his essay "Nottingham and the Mining Country" (1930), rebuking the English as "town-birds" who "don't know how to build a city" (293). His infamous invective—"Away with little homes!"—condemns the "suburban, pseudo-cottagey" structures that "are scrabbling over the face of England . . . like horrid scabs" (294, 293). Not surprisingly, Lawrence reaches a fever pitch imagining the effects of these little homes on national manhood: "The men inside these little red rat-traps get more and more helpless, being more and more humiliated, more and more dissatisfied, like trapped rats" (293). Poets played a similar tune in a different key. In his light "Letter to Lord Byron" (1937), Auden explicitly contrasts "the John Bull of the good old days" with the little man, "the bowler hat who strap-hangs in the tube" and "kicks the tyrant only in his dreams." So internalized is his enslavement that this cartoonish figure reserves his "real implacable resentment" not for the tyrant who enslaves him, but for "those who conceivably might set him free" (51–53). C. Day Lewis likewise sees suburbia and its little men as signs of national weakness. During a brief detour through the suburbs in "The Magnetic Mountain" (1933), he asks, "Where is the bourgeois, the backbone of our race?" His answer: "Bent double with lackeying" (*Collected* 117). Day Lewis underscores this view of suburban enslavement in an analogous prose piece of the same year, where he claims that inhabitants of an invaded countryside have sold their birthright for modern conveniences and shoddy merchandise, "which the town gives them back, as a 'civilised' trader gives savages beads for gold" ("Letter" 40).

Casting the little men as duped savages, Day Lewis melds an older view of suburbia's colonial and racial otherness with a distinctly 1930s concern about national disempowerment. The humorist Charles Duff would write an entire book from the same perspective. His parodic *Anthropological Report on a London Suburb* (1935), credited to the fictitious Professor Vladimir Chernichewski, adapts Bronislaw Malinowski's work on the South Pacific to a suburban setting. Chernichewski claims that "anthropology is not only concerned with the naked savage, but with the man or woman in plus fours or evening dress. To the true man of science it matters little whether he is dealing with suburb or jungle, modern jazz dancing or savage sex orgy, forest magic or the anthropomorphic deism of a suburban greengrocer" (11–12). But as Day Lewis suggests, the suburb itself was a colonized jungle where the Darwinian struggle to survive had led to new forms of institutionalized exploitation. Chernichewski describes suburban life as a series of swindles from cradle to grave, perpetrated by speculative builders, quack doctors, traveling salesmen, and other "innumerable parasites and commercialists" (25). Such an existence transformed average British citizens into powerless victims of economic exploitation.

While Duff's mock ethnography sympathizes with its subjects, other writers would revile the lower middle class in terms that echo Victorian ethnographies of the urban poor. In place of Henry Mayhew's nomadic tribes and General Booth's "Darkest London," writers of the 1930s figure a racialized lower middle class as the new barbarians. Exemplary here is the 1938 collection *Britain and the Beast,* edited by Clough Williams-Ellis in association with National Trust. Condemning suburban growth as an invasion from within that transforms pristine country into slums, its contributors often describe the lower middle class in implicitly racial terms. For Thomas Sharp new suburbs are "hardly more civilized" than the slums that many fled, and though "romantic villas and bungalows" are a "striking contrast to the terrace houses of their old congested quarters," the "contrast is merely between one type of barbarism and another" (144–45).

If lower-middle-class suburbs took the place of urban slums in an interwar discourse of domestic others, these same suburbs also represented an updated form of reverse colonization, revising the invasion-scare stories of the 1890s and the Edwardian era for a brave new world of geopolitical anxiety. J. B. Priestley's 1934 travelogue *English Journey* draws to a melancholy close with a survey of a third, suburban England, a new alien landscape whose "real birthplace" is America: "This is the England of arterial and by-pass roads, of filling stations and factories that look like exhibition buildings, of giant cinemas and dance-halls and cafés" (319). Despite the fact that this Americanized England is "essentially democratic" and "as near to a classless society as we have got yet," Priestley finds its populace shockingly prone to persuasion: too many do "not what they like but what they have been told they would like." In this they recall Day Lewis's duped savages, while anticipating the citizens of Orwell's Airstrip One: "Monotonous but easy work and a liberal supply of cheap luxuries might between them create a set of people entirely without ambition or any real desire to think and act for themselves, the perfect subjects for an iron autocracy" (320–22). It was not only American mass culture that threatened England. In his 1933 essay "Suburban Soviets," G. E. Trevelyan casts middle-class monotony as tantamount to a Communist takeover in England: "Not in their religious persecutions, in their despoiling of churches, in their monkish massacres, have the Soviets done so much" as "this New Communist," the suburban resident, "to negate a deity, as in the willful stamping out of this individual spark in man" (140–41). But the greatest threat of totalitarian invasion came from Nazi Germany. In *The Long Week-End,* their celebrated social history of the interwar era, Robert Graves and Alan Hodge report a popular joke: "if colonies were to be given to Hitler," suburban Hampstead should be first, since it already harbored such a large influx of refugees from Nazi Germany (439).

Seeing suburbia as alien territory, whether invaded by internal "barbarians" or foreigners, no doubt contributed to one of the era's most curious tropes: the prospect of mass extermination. In her 1937 poem "Suburban Classes," Stevie Smith mixes ideas of national decline, class tension, and suburban herd mentality into a modest proposal for mass poisoning. If the suburban classes have degraded England's supremacy, they at least "do as they're told." Their susceptibility provides an easy solution: tell them "'Your King and Your Country need you Dead' / You see the idea? Well, let it spread" (26). But on the eve of another world war, Smith's coy suggestion seemed less likely to end suburban sprawl than did bombing from above.[2] John Betjeman's softly striking summons, "Come, friendly bombs, and fall on Slough," has become the most famous example of an imagined suburban bombing. A close runner-up is cartoonist Osbert Lancaster's "By-Pass Variegated," a rendition of the motley architectural styles packed along England's arterial roads. Since such areas "will inevitably become the slums of the future," Lancaster suggests, one can more readily face "the prospect of aerial bombardment" (68). Betjeman shares the tongue-in-cheek tone of Smith and Lancaster, mocking the little men who frequent "bogus Tudor bars" and their wives who "frizz out peroxide hair." Though comic, Betjeman's insistent rhymes intensify into a disturbing hope that the bombs will "get that man with double chin . . . And smash his desk of polished oak / And smash his hands so used to stroke / And stop his boring dirty joke / And make him yell" (20–21). These can be unsettling images, given the war's legacy of mass extermination, and though I am not suggesting that Smith or Betjeman supported suburban genocide— both had intensely ambiguous relations to the suburbs—their works echo Lawrence's call to do "away with little homes!"[3] Only by imagining suburbia as foreign to an authentic England could writers even facetiously suggest blowing it off the map.

Orwell is not alone, then, in lamenting suburbia's little men and their little homes as emblems of national decline. But unlike writers who imagine blasting these alien suburbs to smithereens, Orwell views the scene from below, in the guise of one of the targets. "Christ! how can the bombers miss us when they come?" George Bowling asks in *Coming Up for Air,* comparing "the houses stretching on and on" to a "great big bull's-eye."[4] This vast tract of identical homes is "a great wilderness with no wild beasts" (24), a tamed and domesticated jungle that recalls "The Magnetic Mountain" and *Anthropological Report on a London Suburb*. Understanding why Orwell chose to inhabit this role in *Coming Up for Air* requires us to consider how his view of suburban enslavement grew from his critique of colonial Burma. Only after Orwell sought to align himself with the colonized and, failing that, the European poor, did he begin to see the lower middle class as England's truly exploited. But to start down the road from Mandalay to West Bletchley, Orwell first had to reject his status as colonial sahib.

From Mandalay to West Bletchley

Orwell's experience of empire shaped his perception of himself as "simultaneously dominator and dominated" (R. Williams, *Orwell* 15). Though raised as a member of the imperial ruling class, he remained stuck in its lower echelons.[5] For all his avowed hatred of imperialism, then, Orwell's colonial writing focuses less on the sufferings of the dominated than on those of the dominator. In a typical passage from *Burmese Days,* Flory fumes over his "ever bitterer hatred of the atmosphere of imperialism." Recognizing that "the Indian Empire is a despotism . . . with theft as its final object," he saves his most heartfelt pity for colonizers like himself, whose "every word and every thought is censored" and whose "opinion on every subject . . . is dictated . . . by the pukka sahibs' code" (68–69). While this passage neither justifies nor whitewashes the exploitation of the colonized, it treats that exploitation as a given so Orwell can focus on his true subject: the colonizer's debasement and stultifying need to conform. Orwell's narrator acknowledges the hypocrisy of this position, asking, "What do you care if the Indian Empire is a despotism, if Indians are bullied and exploited? You only care because the right of free speech is denied you. You are a creature of the despotism, a pukka sahib, tied tighter than a monk or a savage by an unbreakable system" (69). Indicting the hypocrisy of Flory's hatred of despotism, Orwell still suggests that imperialism dominates the colonizer more than the colonized "savage" or Buddhist monk.

This same dynamic is central to "Shooting an Elephant" (1936), which pushes Flory's fictional anguish into the realm of autobiography. Like *Burmese Days* the essay offers Orwell's requisite self-flagellations: imperialism *"oppressed me* with an intolerable sense of guilt" (*Collected* 1: 236, emphasis added). More important, the essay's climactic epiphany reveals the colonizer's ostensible authority as a form of enslavement: "As I stood there with the rifle in my hands . . . I first grasped the hollowness, the futility of the white man's dominion in the East. Here was I, the white man with his gun, standing in front of the unarmed native crowd—seemingly the lead actor of the piece; but in reality I was only an absurd puppet pushed to and fro by the will of those yellow faces behind. I perceived in this moment that when the white man turns tyrant it is his own freedom that he destroys. He becomes a sort of hollow, posing dummy" (*Collected* 1: 239). Rendered powerless by the gaze of an unarmed crowd, Orwell offers a textbook case of what Homi Bhabha calls "the metonymy of presence": "the process by which the look of surveillance returns as the displacing gaze of the disciplined," thereby "menac[ing] the narcissistic demands of colonial authority" (156, 155). It is not merely that imperialism limits the colonizer's agency, but that, in Hegelian terms, the master becomes the slave. Thus, despite recognizing "the British Raj as an unbreakable tyranny, as something clamped down . . . upon the will of prostrate peoples," "Shooting an Elephant," like *Burmese Days,* makes a case for the low-level colonial authority as empire's true victim (*Collected* 1: 236).

Claims of victimization and powerlessness among colonizers are not unique to Orwell. We have already seen them in *A Passage to India,* where *ressentiment* plays an integral part in late-imperial affect by attempting to salvage moral victory from impending political defeat. But Orwell adds to this scenario something that Forster's Anglo-Indians could never countenance: a desire to identify with the colonized in a shared oppression. This desire is especially evident in *The Road to Wigan Pier,* where Orwell claims that his disgust at serving as an agent of colonial tyranny led him to "the simple theory that the oppressed are always right and the oppressors are always wrong." Consequently, he wanted "to get right down among the oppressed, to be one of them and on their side against their tyrants" (148). So while Orwell may seem disingenuous for emphasizing his own lack of freedom in "Shooting an Elephant," doing so also reveals an attempt to disavow his imperial privilege and to gesture—however inadequately—toward a common cause with the colonized.

Others have noted the reversal between colonizer and colonized in "Shooting an Elephant" but see it as anomalous—a view Orwell abandons "once he begins to understand the nature of totalitarian power" (Woodcock 54).[6] In contrast, I suggest that this view undergoes a subtle transformation that will continue to inform Orwell's perspective on English class relations. Much as Orwell wanted to identify with the colonized, such a move was virtually impossible, since he too was one of the tyrants.[7] He attempts to square this circle, if we believe his claims in *Wigan Pier,* by returning to England to live among the poor and working-class, "the symbolic victims of injustice," who "play[ed] the same part in England as the Burmese played in Burma" (148). Seeing class as analogous to colonization, Orwell imagines poverty as capable of giving him a surrogate membership among the colonized—or at least providing some insight into their experience.[8] Orwell seeks such experience in England, where the working class "suffer[ed] miseries which in their different way were as bad as any an oriental ever knows" (*Road* 148–49), as well as in France, where Orwell works as a *plongeur* or dishwasher. Recalling this experience in *Down and Out in Paris and London,* he compares a *plongeur* to "an Indian rickshaw puller." Both provide minor conveniences that "cannot possibly balance the suffering of the men" (117–18). Among Europe's poor Orwell could compensate for and begin to experience—if only indirectly—the abject oppression of the colonized.

But being down and out is not abject enough for Orwell. This is due in part to the solidarity and surprising comfort he finds in poverty, especially in moments when he fears being exposed as an interloper. In *Wigan Pier* he recalls entering an East End lodging house for the first time, expecting a fight. Instead he meets a stevedore's boozy embrace: "'Ave a cup of tea, chum!" (152). In *Down and Out* he helps to right the upset cart of a hawker who responds, "'Thanks mate.' . . . No one had called me mate before in my life" (129). In both passages Orwell's fear of exposure leads to his recognition that the poor don't know he's middle-class—or don't care. Indeed, the tramps seem not ignorant of class origins, but indifferent to them: "From their point of view all that matters is that you, like themselves, are 'on the bum.' . . . Once you are in that world and seemingly *of* it, it hardly matters what you have been in the past" (*Road* 155, original emphasis). Despite its degradations poverty thus conjures feelings of solace, release, and even freedom for Orwell. Early in *Down and Out* he claims that despite the meanness of his Paris dwellings, "things were not a quarter as bad as I had expected." He describes a "great consolation in poverty . . . a feeling of relief, almost of pleasure," in being "genuinely down and out. You have talked so often of going to the dogs—and well, here are the dogs, and you have reached them, and you can stand it. It takes off a lot of anxiety" (20–21).

Orwell does much in the remainder of *Down and Out* to bring home the utter debasement of poverty, so that this early "feeling of relief, almost of pleasure," does not stand as his last word on being poor. But if we believe his claim that he underwent poverty because it offered him a form of oppression unavailable in Burma, then this relief must have helped him expiate his feelings of guilt as a colonizer, uniting him at some level with the colonized. This relief, while self-serving, also creates a new dilemma, since the virtue Orwell associated with being oppressed was antithetical to his embattled persona. As Jeffrey Meyers suggests, Orwell "*liked* having a sense of guilt and needed to prolong it. This inner conviction of his own guilt—of being obscurely to blame—gave him a purpose and inspired his early work" (*Orwell* 78–79, original emphasis).[9] Thus, while poverty provides recompense for Orwell's role as a colonial oppressor, being down and out comforts him in a way that dilutes his masochistic persona.

Orwell moves beyond this impasse by shifting his focus from the poor to the lower middle class. We see this in the progression of his oeuvre, as *Down and Out* gives way to the petit-bourgeois concerns of *A Clergyman's Daughter*, *Keep the Aspidistra Flying*, and *Coming Up for Air*. But the shift also occurs within *Wigan Pier* itself, when its exposé of living conditions in the industrial north unexpectedly becomes an argument that socialism in England depends on the lower middle class. As in the Burmese writing, where colonial exploitation offers a pretext for examining the colonizer's suffering, Orwell's indictment of working-class conditions in *Wigan Pier* turns to the growing disempowerment of "the middle classes, [who] for the first time in their history, are feeling the pinch" and "floundering in a sort of deadly net of frustration" (170). One result of bourgeois disempowerment is that the lower middle class—what Orwell calls "the exploited middle class" (226)—increasingly shares the economic subordination of the proletariat. As such, Orwell feels, the lower middle class must begin to consider itself part of the working class: "It has got to be brought home to the clerk, the engineer, the commercial traveller, the middle-class man who has 'come down in the world,' the village grocer, the lower-grade civil servant and all other doubtful cases that they *are* the proletariat" (227, original emphasis).[10]

At one level Orwell's interest in the lower middle class was politically pragmatic. Since he believed the bourgeoisie would never join the proletariat in common cause, the lower middle class could unite the two sides on the road to socialism. Even more fundamentally, Orwell's interest in the lower middle class reflects his own class origins and psychological profile. Orwell may not have technically belonged to the petite bourgeoisie, being raised in what he calls "the lower-upper-middle class," a group that included "most clergymen and schoolmasters . . . nearly all Anglo-Indian officials, a sprinkling of soldiers and sailors and a fair number of professional men and artists" (*Road* 121, 124). But he suggests economic and affective parallels between these classes. It is not just that "a naval officer and his grocer very likely have the same income," but that his own family's "shabby genteel" lifestyle of "keeping up appearances" replicated that of the traditional lower middle class (*Road* 122, 124). By shifting his attention toward the lower middle class, Orwell gets around the impasse he faced when writing about the poor. Because his own values "are essentially *middle-class*" (*Road* 161, original emphasis), Orwell could identify with this downtrodden subsection of bourgeoisie. Unlike the colonized Burmese, the destitute in *Down and Out,* or the workers in *Wigan Pier,* the lower middle class provided Orwell a debased group to which he already more or less belonged.[11]

And unlike the colonized and the poor, whose victimization was ipso facto virtuous, the lower middle class was hardly above reproach. Rita Felski's account of petit-bourgeois nonidentity helps explain Orwell's interest in this seemingly unredeemable class, particularly its reputation for social submissiveness: "The lower middle class has completely internalized the strictures of authority; it is the ultimate example of psychic self-regulation" (Felski 36). Orwell adheres to this view, even as he seeks to create some sympathy for the lower middle class as England's true victims. Hence his passing comment in *Wigan Pier*—which might be more scandalous were it not so brief—that during his years of destitution he overlooked "the essential fact that 'respectable' poverty is always the worst" (*Road* 149). The reason for this "fact" is presumably the constant anxiety that, for Orwell, was alleviated by true destitution, as well as the petite bourgeoisie's clinging to its paltry status, which he sees as reprehensible. In *Keep the Aspidistra Flying* Gordon Comstock describes his family's fall from grace in the same terms: "It was not poverty but the down-dragging of *respectable* poverty that had done for them. . . . They never had the sense to lash out and just live, money or no money, as the lower classes do. How right the lower classes are! Hats off to the factory lad who with fourpence in the world puts his girl in the family way! At least he's got blood and not money in his veins" (44, original emphasis). Likewise, George Bowling's early cri de coeur in *Coming Up for Air* contrasts suburban enslavement with an exploited yet vital working class: "I'm not so sorry for the proles myself. . . . The prole suffers physically, but he's a free man when he isn't working. But in every one of those little stucco boxes" on George's street, "there's some poor bastard who's *never* free" (12–13, original emphasis).

Thus, while Orwell sees the working class and truly destitute maintaining their individuality, vitality, and freedom—both in their refusal to cow to the social hierarchy and from the virtue and quasi-comfort that come with poverty—these qualities are precisely what the lower middle class lack. True debasement for Orwell exists not in the noble suffering of Europe's economically down and out, but among a lower middle class exploited by a money world to which it remains devoted. So while Orwell's interest in petit-bourgeois powerlessness emerged from Anglo-Indian *ressentiment,* it also brings him closer to inhabiting the position of the colonized than he could achieve either in Burma or among the poor. The little man of the lower middle class becomes the closest Orwell can get to experiencing colonized enslavement.

Aspidistra Jungle

Orwell provides a full-blown account of suburban colonization in *Coming Up for Air,* but he sets the stage for it in *Keep the Aspidistra Flying.* This earlier novel is not overtly set in suburbia but recalls a more bohemian Hampstead where Orwell lived and worked in 1934 and 1935.[12] Yet suburbia pervades the novel and circumscribes Gordon Comstock's life. Raised in Acton, he has a grandfather at Kensal Green, one aunt at Highgate, and another in a Clapham mental house (37, 46, 59, 40). Even his friend Flaxman, exiled by his wife to the same lodging house as Gordon, eventually returns to "aspidistral bliss" in Peckham (209). The inner suburbs thus serve as Gordon's place of origin and the ultimate horizon of his familial and social world. Much as he vows to keep out of that world of respectability and money worship, he fears that he too will end up in "some beastly little semi-detached villa in Putney, with hire-purchase furniture and a portable radio and an aspidistra in the window" (114). The titular aspidistra symbolizes surrender to the dictates of suburban respectability. To keep the aspidistra flying is thus to wave the flag of defeat: "It ought to be on our coat of arms instead of the lion and the unicorn. There will be no revolution in England while there are aspidistras in the windows" (44).

As these passages suggest, Orwell links suburban conformity with a broader decline in English national identity. Gordon's surname, Comstock, represents the nation's common stock, befitting his family's "middle-middle class" status (37). In the past the common stock could make their fortune by combining capitalist and imperial interests, like Gordon's grandfather, who "plundered the proletariat and the foreigner" (37). But Gordon's family dissipates like England as a whole, and Gordon's job at an advertising firm—the New Albion—foreshadows the nation's future. Every employee is a "slave of money," and Gordon abjures "their slavish keep-your-job mentality" (50, 52). He tries to drop out, becoming a bookshop clerk and struggling poet, but is still dogged by the money world he has fled. Perched behind the bookshop counter, Gordon stews at the sights around him, most notably an ad for a vitamin drink: "'Corner Table enjoys his meal with Bovex.' Gordon examined the thing with the intimacy of hatred. The idiotic grinning face, . . . the slick black hair, the silly spectacles." This image of "modern man as his masters want him to be" (15) recurs throughout the novel, a willing victim of the money world that conspires against Gordon's freedom: "That was what it meant to worship the money-god! To settle down, to Make Good, to sell your soul for a villa and an aspidistra!" (48). Indeed, in the paranoid terms of this novel, Gordon comes to see these forces as threatening to colonize not only him but all of Western civilization:

"He had a vision of London, of the western world; he saw a thousand million slaves toiling and grovelling about the throne of money" (150). When Gordon finally gives up his life of poverty for marriage and middle-class conformity, it is treated as a mock-heroic reversal of Caesar: "Vicisti, O aspidistra!" (240).

But the novel ends without adequately resolving its position toward lower-middle-class suburban enslavement. Gordon impregnates his girlfriend, Rosemary, and, having presumably convinced himself he's like "the factory lad who with fourpence in the world puts his girl in the family way," reconciles himself to a respectable life. In fact, he absolutely embraces the prospect, and to some extent Orwell wants us to embrace it too. Having made his decision, Gordon experiences "a peculiar sensation" and asks himself what it is: "Shame, misery, despair? . . . It was relief" (237). Yet for a writer as motivated by guilt and self-punishment as Orwell, such relief is surely a moral defeat, and Orwell wants us to find it disturbing. It is a reversal of the relief-in-poverty described in *Down and Out,* with the goal of showing Gordon's mental submission to be much more troubling than the "comfort" of poverty. Indeed, Gordon's relief is made all the more unsettling by his newfound zeal for respectability: "He would sell his soul so utterly that he would forget it had ever been his" (238), a surrender that anticipates the finale of *Nineteen Eighty-Four,* as Winston Smith wins "the victory over himself" and learns to love Big Brother (245). At the same time Orwell seems to endorse Gordon's volte-face, followed as it is by a puzzling defense of those who fly the aspidistra: "They lived by the money-code . . . and yet they contrived to keep their decency. The money-code as they interpreted it was not merely cynical and hoggish. They had their standards, their inviolable points of honour. . . . Besides, they were *alive.* They were bound up in the bundle of life" (239, original emphasis). The birth references and womb imagery here suggest that Orwell may be rehearsing the claims of his 1940 essay "Inside the Whale," which advocates the artist's retreat from the struggles of modern life: "The whale's belly is simply a womb big enough for an adult" (*Collected* 1: 521). Ultimately, however, Gordon's conversion happens so quickly and so late in the novel that it is unclear whether to take it in earnest or in jest.

All throughout *Aspidistra* Gordon struggles not to be swallowed by the whale, yet he ends up making a home in its belly. In contrast, *Coming Up for Air* features a suburban male who has always lived inside the whale. But rather than succumbing to conformity and quietism, *Coming Up for Air* seeks to politicize its protagonist's situation. As various critics have argued, Bowling represents Orwell's attempt to understand how living inside the whale can yield positive political consequences. Crick, for example, points out that while the novel "satirised lower-middle-class suburban life, it was part of an Orwellian argument that people like Bowling should be the natural leaders, if only they could . . . actively grasp their identity of interest with the workers, as both equally exploited" (251; also see 189).[13] But it is the colonized, not the workers, with whom the lower middle class shares its exploited status in *Coming Up for Air*. The novel's subtle but insistent imperial subtext weaves together anxieties about Britain's decline as a colonial power with a view of England's own populace being enslaved by modern suburban life. Rather than an explicit agenda for revolution, however, *Coming Up for Air* serves as a ground-clearing exercise that seeks to redeem the cultural status of the suburban male. Orwell wants to make Bowling a figure capable of fostering socialism and resisting fascism by investing him with a popular form of English masculinity—one that is cleansed of its associations with war and jingoism because it can identify with the exploitation of the colonized.

Writing on English identity during World War II, Orwell claims, "Myths which are believed in tend to become true, because they set up a type, or 'persona,' which the average person will do his best to resemble" (*Collected* 3: 6). George Bowling is Orwell's attempt to create a new myth of the English suburban male, one who hardly fits the typical lower-middle-class mold. An average sensual man like Leopold Bloom, Bowling, with his good humor, indifference to propriety, and sheer bulk, is a contrast to the Pooterish petite bourgeoisie. Bowling's very name reflects Orwell's desire to create a new myth of suburban masculinity. Sharing a first name with his creator (and with England's patron saint), George Bowling is an Orwell alter ego, the portly Sancho Panza to Orwell's Don Quixote.[14] Reinforcing his status as a Panza figure is Bowling's surname, which evokes his rotund shape and penchant for drink (the *Oxford English Dictionary* defines *bowler* as a late-Victorian term for drunkard). "Bowling" also calls to mind a variety of English games—from skittles to cricket—thereby strengthening his cross-class affiliations. Perhaps most notably, Bowling's surname evokes that ubiquitous signifier of the British bourgeoisie since the mid-nineteenth century, the bowler hat.[15]

But Bowling's surname also bespeaks a decline in imperial power, for Orwell's protagonist is a latter-day Tom Bowling, the legendary personification of the courageous English sailor. Based on a character in Tobias Smollett's 1748 novel, *The Adventures of Roderick Random,* Tom Bowling is the titular subject of the "most celebrated song" by the eighteenth-century composer Charles Dibdin, known for his stirring nautical ballads (Jeffrey Richards 350).[16] Dibdin's song eulogizes Tom Bowling, who dies in a storm, as "the darling of our crew," with a "form . . . of the manliest beauty." Orwell refers to the song when its opening line is quoted at George Bowling's expense. George cannot enter a particular saloon without one customer "prodding me in the ribs and singing out, 'Here a sheer hulk lies poor Tom Bowling!' which is a joke the bloody fools in the bar never get tired of" (20–21). Apart from the obvious contrast between Tom Bowling's "manliest beauty" and George Bowling's rotund shape, the joke jabs at the flaccidity of modern English manhood, transforming the "sheer hulk" of Dibdin's song from a sunken hull to a corpulent body. Yet rather than weighing him down, Bowling's body keeps him coming up for air. Orwell revives Dibdin's legend of Tom Bowling for a less imperialist English identity. In *The Lion and the Unicorn,* Orwell describes England's most famous patriotic songs as "humorous and mock-defeatist," inevitably involving "disasters and retreats" (*Collected* 2: 60–61). While George Bowling reflects the waning imperial power of the suburban male, he also embodies the "humorous and mock-defeatist" attitude Orwell sees as distinctly English—an attitude opposed to the Anglo-Indian *ressentiment* of *Burmese Days* and the embittered persona of Orwell's colonial essays. Bowling thus represents a cultural salvaging of the lower middle class, an attempt to transform it from a despised and seemingly impotent class formation to one at the core of a post-imperial England.

Yet Bowling's suburban world makes such a transformation virtually impossible. He lives in the Hesperides Estate of Ellesmere Road, West Bletchley, a fictional setting Orwell described in a letter as "a suburb which might be Hayes or Southall" (*Collected* 1: 358).[17] Ellesmere Road, presumably named after the picturesque Shropshire market town, suggests a feeble attempt to link modern suburbia with the rural past. Such nostalgia is belied by the imperial connotations of the Hesperides Estate, which takes its name from Greek mythology. A garden on the western edge of the ancient world, Hesperides was the place of the setting sun. Using a classical reference that positions the outermost area of earth in the west, Orwell not only undermines the notion that the "civilized" West is the center of the world but locates Bowling's suburb at the extreme margins of civilization. Moreover, as the place of the setting sun, Hesperides foreshadows the end of an empire on which it was thought the sun would never set. This is reinforced by *West* Bletchley, the western extremity of a western extremity. The name Bletchley is based on *bletch,* an obsolete word meaning to blacken—both literally (as a noun *bletch* is shoe blacking) and figuratively (a verb meaning to stain, sully, or defame). Thus, Orwell's West Bletchley not only suggests suburbia's sullying of England. With its links to the western outpost of the Hesperides, West Bletchley also offers a Conradian caveat that suburbia, too, is a place of darkness.

This darkness is a stark contrast to the era "before the Boer War," when Bowling tells us "it was summer all the year round" (42). Though he immediately discounts this claim as "a delusion" (42), his boyhood recollections, which make up the heart of the novel, are an extended daydream in which "a feeling of security," "a feeing of continuity," is premised on British global supremacy (125). These memories reveal that, as with Gordon Comstock's family, Bowling's adulthood represents a national reversal of fortune reflecting Britain's decline as an imperial power. Thus, his adult feelings of emasculation and enslavement are opposed to "the civilisation which I grew up in and which is now, I suppose, just about at its last kick" (86–87). That civilization depended on Britain's imperial prowess, the signs of which surrounded young George: "the advert for Abdulla cigarettes—the one with the Egyptian soldiers on it" (41–42); the painting of the battle of Tel-el-Kebir that adorns the dining room of the Lower Binfield hotel (219); the barbershop scents of bay rum and Latakia (a Syrian tobacco) (221); and the adventure stories about "Chinese opium dens and Polynesian islands and the forests of Brazil" (102). His favorite serial, *Donovan the Daunt-less,* featured a character who would "fetch incredible things from the various corners of the earth" (104). Even when his father's business fell apart, young George sensed that "you can still keep going. You're still 'your own master'" (118). But the Boer War was the beginning of the end of this civilization, which assumed "that England will never change and that England's the whole world," and in a reversal of Donovan's exploits, Bowling inhabits an England that has become "just a left-over, a tiny corner" (188).

The Hesperides Estate is a microcosm of England's diminished global standing, and the economic swindle it perpetrates on its residents leaves them in a position of colonized subjects. Bowling claims that inhabitants of the Hesperides "all imagine [they]'ve got something to lose," since they are "under the impression that they own their houses." But the Hesperides is "a huge racket" run by a building society—an institution Bowling considers "probably the cleverest racket of modern times" (13). This is not only because the building society is owned by its creditors (who profit from monopolizing on the construction), nor because most inhabitants wrongly presume to own the houses they've paid for ("They're not freehold, only leasehold" [14]). To Bowling "the really subtle swindle" is psychological: "Merely because of the illusion that we own our houses and have what's called 'a stake in the country,' we poor saps in the Hesperides" become the building society's "devoted slaves for ever" (15). Bowling echoes the mock ethnography *Anthropological Report on a London Suburb,* which claims that the majority of residents in a fictional suburb "'own' their houses, that is to say, they are 'buying them on mortgage.' . . . This is euphemistically called 'having a stake in the country' and the 'stakeholders' are from time to time praised in the Press for their robust sense of patriotism" (Duff 17). Ironically, Bowling and his neighbors are exploited, financially as well as mentally, by the idea that a suburban home signifies independence and "a stake in the country"—an idea fostered by seeing suburban expansion in terms of national-imperial power. And Bowling's recurrent descriptions of the estate as a "racket" and a "swindle" echo the very terms Orwell often used to describe imperialism.[18] Yet unlike those who were colonized by the British empire and who gave the lie to its civilizing mission, the "devoted slaves" of the Hesperides believe that suburbia not only civilizes them but frees and empowers them.

Bowling and his male neighbors are not only the housing estate's "devoted slaves." They are also in thrall to their wives and children. In *Wigan Pier* Orwell describes the working-class home as one in which "the man . . . is the master and not, as in a middle-class home, the woman or the baby" (81). Bowling is hardly the master—pointing out, for example, that he is linked to his children by "a ball and fetter" (163). Even more intense is Bowling's subservience to his wife. Daphne Patai claims that with his knowledge of French, Orwell intends *Ellesmere* Road as a portmanteau name for an overabundance of female-maternal power (167). Indeed, Bowling often blames his wife, Hilda, for his own lack of freedom, a view Orwell clearly endorses.[19] As Bowling points out, "*She does everything for negative reasons.* When she makes a cake she's not thinking about the cake, only about how to save butter and eggs. When I'm in bed with her all she thinks about is how not to have a baby" (161, emphasis added). Recalling Pierre Bourdieu's claim that petit-bourgeois disposition manifests itself in "'negative magnitudes' . . . 'savings'—refused expenditures—or birth control" (333), Bowling's examples also confirm that his phrase "negative reasons" is not just a judgment of Hilda's behavior but a diagnosis—one that echoes the Nietzschean notion of *ressentiment.* Raised in a middle-class family where there was "more sense of poverty, more crust-wiping and looking twice at sixpence" than in any farmworker's family, Hilda grew up "with a fixed idea not only that one always *is* hard-up but that it's one's duty to be miserable about it" (160, original emphasis). Like the Anglo-Indians beleaguered by *ressentiment* in *A Passage to India* and *Burmese Days,* Hilda's family transforms its powerlessness into a moral code.

Such behavior should not be surprising, of course, since Hilda's parents are retired Anglo-Indians. Recalling Orwell's own shabby-genteel, ex-colonial upbringing in *Wigan Pier,* Hilda's family is part of the "considerable Anglo-Indian colony" in the London suburb of Ealing. "Do you know these Anglo-Indian families?" Bowling asks. "It's almost impossible, when you get inside these people's houses, to remember that out in the street it's England and the twentieth century. As soon as you set foot inside the front door you're in India in the 'eighties. You know the kind of atmosphere. The carved teak furniture, the brass trays, the dusty tiger-skulls on the wall, the Trichinopoly cigars, the red-hot pickles, the yellow photographs of chaps in sun-helmets, the Hindustani words that you're expected to know the meaning of, the everlasting anecdotes about tiger-shoots and what Smith said to Jones in Poona in '87" (156–57). This passage not only speaks to the suburban ex-colonial as a cultural phenomenon ("You know the kind of atmosphere") but also captures many of the issues I have considered throughout this study: the colonial official who retires to the suburbs, running his new home as if he were still in the subcontinent; the exoticism that lies behind the suburban façade—with the attendant implication of degeneracy that pervades the suburban dwelling; and the blinkered mindset of Anglo-Indians in *A Passage to India* and *Burmese Days*. More than just a kitschy reliquary of dusty artifacts and dated lore, Hilda's girlhood home reproduced the Raj and ignored modern England as stubbornly as Forster's and Orwell's civil stations sought to detach Anglo-Indians from India and Burma. Hilda's home reveals the British suburb breathing new life into a dying imperial culture.

Ressentiment and Fascism

In *Coming Up for Air* Anglo-Indian *ressentiment* transforms into a suburban morality of unceasing angst, Hilda's "feeling that you *ought* to be perpetually working yourself up into a stew about lack of money. Just working up an atmosphere of misery from a sense of duty" (161, original emphasis). Orwell shows how a debilitating late-imperial *ressentiment* becomes a hysterical form of suburban economizing and moral outrage at home. Rather than simply articulating a gendered anxiety, a "male struggle to control the private sphere" from a position of "androcentric ideology" (Patai 200), Orwell sees female dominance over suburbia as a legacy of imperial decline. Misogynistic as they may be, Bowling's complaints about Hilda suggest that suburban slave mentality is a product of broader late-imperial anxieties.[20]

If Hilda's upbringing shows how imperial decline and its resentful affects transform into suburban enslavement, Orwell then suggests that this domesticated structure of feeling can be projected back onto the public sphere for overtly political purposes. We see this most clearly in the Left Book Club lecture Bowling attends on "The Menace of Fascism."[21] By placing this scene immediately after the account of Hilda's family, Orwell implies that imperial and suburban *ressentiment* can coalesce into fascism—the Orwellian irony being that a vehement opposition to German fascism can itself become fascistic. The Left Book Club lecturer is a deranged version of the suburban little man: "A rather mean little man, with a white face and a bald head, standing on a platform, shooting out slogans" and "trying to work up hatred in the audience" (171–72). The speaker not only reminds us of Hilda "working up an atmosphere of misery" at home (161), but he shares her negative motivations ("She does everything for negative reasons"). Contemplating the speaker's strange notoriety—he is introduced as "Mr. So-and-so, the well-known anti-Fascist"—Bowling wonders, "What did he do before Hitler came along?" (172), suggesting the hollowness of one who can only react *against.* Bowling then views the speaker's effects on the crowd. As the lecturer describes Nazis decapitating their victims, a woman knits a baby jumper, her motions keeping time with the speaker's rhythms: "One plain, two purl, drop one and knit two together" (173). In addition to tapping maternal instincts, the speaker channels masculine anxieties. After the lecture Bowling is drawn into a debate, exasperated by a young man who wants to enlist for war. Bowling describes the man as "a bank clerk in a godless suburb, sitting behind the frosted window, entering figures in a ledger, counting piles of notes, bumsucking to the manager. Feels his life rotting away. And all the while, over in Europe, the big stuff's happening" (179). Thanks to the Left Book Club, Orwell suggests, enlisting for war provides a socially sanctioned outlet for avenging male feelings of submission and enslavement that suburbia creates.

This explicit antiwar message works in tandem with an implicit critique of imperialism. Lynette Hunter claims the Left Book Club scene shows how the state channels fear into violence "under the banner of nationalism," a strategy "directly analogous to racism" (212). Indeed, by demonstrating that fear of fascism can be stoked by a process similar to racism, the scene reflects Orwell's counterintuitive belief during the late 1930s that anti-fascism was compatible with, rather than opposed to, imperialism. In his pacifist period between the Spanish Civil War and the beginning of World War II, Orwell saw fascism and capitalist democracy as rival imperialisms. He made this argument in "Spilling the Spanish Beans" and recapitulated it in a letter from September 1937:

> After what I have seen in Spain I have come to the conclusion that it is futile to be "anti-Fascist" while attempting to preserve capitalism. Fascism after all is only a development of capitalism, and the mildest democracy, so-called, is liable to turn into Fascism when the pinch comes. We like to think of England as a democratic country, but our rule in India, for instance, is just as bad as German Fascism, though outwardly it may be less irritating. I do not see how one can oppose Fascism except by working for the overthrow of capitalism, starting, of course, in one's own country. If one collaborates with a capitalist-imperialist government in a

struggle "against Fascism," i.e. against a rival imperialism, one is simply
letting Fascism in by the back door. (*Collected* 1: 284)

As this letter suggests, Orwell aligned imperialism with the potential for fascism
to enter England surreptitiously, transforming its mild if hypocritical democracy into something equally fascistic. If the Left Book Club scene shows how
hatred of fascism can transform meek suburbanites into potential fascists, the
letter above suggests that this dynamic occurs by ignoring class problems at
home and colonial exploitation abroad. Rather than stirring up hatred against
other nations, Orwell implies, the English should put their energy into challenging their own capitalist and imperialist government. While Orwell claims
this conclusion stemmed from his experience in Spain, we might also trace its
source to Morocco, a surprisingly important context for both the Spanish Civil
War and *Coming Up for Air.*

Orwell wrote *Coming Up for Air* in Morocco while nursing a tubercular lung
in the winter of 1938–39. Why he chose Morocco in particular is unclear, and
scholars see its influence on him as negligible.[22] But there is some reason to challenge this view. For one thing, Morocco compensated somewhat for Orwell's
inability to travel to India in 1938, when a Lucknow newspaper invited him to
become an editor. Orwell considered the invitation an opportunity to deepen
his understanding of conditions in colonial India, and he hoped to write a book
on the subject. But poor health forced him to turn down the offer, and after
six months in a Kent sanatorium he left for Morocco. Then divided between
French and Spanish rule, Morocco offered Orwell another look at colonial conditions on the ground. It is not clear that he chose Morocco for this reason,
and the journey's impact certainly paled alongside his profound experiences of
Burma, Paris, and Spain. Still, he kept an extensive diary on Morocco's political climate and economic conditions, and in letters home he regularly weighed
French rule against his experience of the Raj.[23] Instead of the book on India,
Orwell wrote *Coming Up for Air.*

Indeed, the novel highlights two issues central to Orwell's view of Morocco:
the relation between imperialism and the rise of fascism, and the ironic support
of fascism by the colonized.[24] Orwell's belief that defeating fascism was impossible without ending imperialism stemmed from Morocco's role in the Spanish
Civil War. Franco was the military commander of Spanish Morocco, launching
his uprising there with the support of Moroccan troops. In *Homage to Catalonia* Orwell points out that "Franco was trying to set up an infamous dictatorship, and the Moors actually preferred him to the Popular Front Government!"
(69). Asking how this could have been, Orwell concludes that "no attempt was

made to foment a rising [against Franco] in Morocco" (69). Orwell blames Franco's coup on continued Spanish colonization of Morocco. In his thinking independence would have ensured Moroccan support of the Popular Front against Franco. But it also would have angered the French and British empires. By refusing to liberate Morocco, Orwell argues, Spain's government undermined the Civil War's broader revolutionary potential. With the Spanish Left in the pocket of imperial powers, "the best strategic opportunity of the war was flung away in the vain hope of placating French and British capitalism" (70).[25] Orwell's journey to Morocco reinforced his view of the colony's importance to the rise of European fascism. In French Morocco, where he spent nearly all his time, he found little anticolonial presence and feared a reprise of the Spanish Civil War: "The Arabs will be easy game for the Fascists. French opinion here is predominantly pro-Franco, and I should not be greatly surprised to see Morocco become the jumping-off place for some French version of Franco in the years to come" (*Complete* 11: 239).

Upon returning from Morocco, Orwell wrote two essays that, in different ways, synthesize his thoughts on the Left's indifference to colonial exploitation and failure of nerve against fascism. "Marrakech," his only published work devoted to Morocco, offers the personal perspective of "Shooting an Elephant" without the latter's power and pointed moral. Nevertheless, left-wing blindness to colonial abuse is its central motif, and Orwell ends the essay viewing French commanders lead a column of Senegalese troops. He suggests such a sight raises questions for "every white man," socialists included: "How much longer can we go on kidding these people? How long before they turn their guns in the other direction?" (*Collected* 1: 393). In the context of Orwell's view that Moroccan independence would have prevented Franco's rise to power, the implication here is that freeing the colonized would keep them from turning their weapons on Europeans. Conversely, prolonging colonialism can only undermine European peace, whether by directly provoking anticolonial insurgency or by indirectly encouraging the colonized to support fascism.

The second piece, provocatively titled "Not Counting Niggers," more explicitly links the rise of fascism with European blindness to colonialism. Orwell's title refers to an unspoken assumption he attributes to left-wing proposals that would unite democratic nations against fascism while continuing to ignore their own colonial regimes. How can Britain battle Hitler, Orwell asks, "except by bolstering up a far vaster injustice," namely imperialism? "For of course it *is* vaster. What we always forget is that the overwhelming bulk of the British proletariat does not live in Britain, but in Asia and Africa" (*Collected* 1: 397, original emphasis). On the eve of World War II, Orwell's only hope is for "a real mass party whose first pledges are to refuse war and to right imperial injustice" (*Collected* 1: 398). More vehemently than "Marrakech," "Not Counting Niggers" proclaims Orwell's hope that by making colonial exploitation visible, Western democracies will see defeating fascism as impossible without ending imperialism.

With its links to Franco's rise to power and its evidence that even the colonized could be won over by fascism, Morocco exhibited issues Orwell contemplated—albeit from a distinctly English point of view—in *Coming Up for Air*. We can now return to West Bletchley with a better sense of Orwell's reason for depicting Bowling as colonized by suburbia. It is not to lament the decline of empire, but to reveal the threat of the lower middle class responding to their powerlessness in ways that can be transformed into fascism. For Orwell fascism entered Spain's back door not only because the Moroccans did not strike at Franco from behind (*Homage* 69), but because their continued colonization by the Republic made them Franco's shock troops, without whom Franco could not have taken power in Spain. Orwell seeks to avoid the same situation in England, where a "struggle 'against Fascism,' i.e. against a rival imperialism," will mean "simply letting in Fascism by the back door" (*Collected* 1: 284)—especially when those bringing it in are England's own colonized, the suburbanites being roused to a frenzy at the Left Book Club. Despite the obvious differences between the lower middle class and the truly colonized, Orwell suggests they both may become fascistic in compensating for their feelings of powerlessness. Recognizing their shared exploitation, Orwell implies, would unite the colonized with Britain's "exploited middle class" (*Road* 226), the suburban petite bourgeoisie. But recognizing this exploitation would also require avoiding a resentment whose consequence—capitalist-imperialist war—runs counter to their shared interest in freedom.

Bombs Away

To escape the suburban milieu that culminates in the Left Book Club—and risks transforming anti-fascist resentment into fascism—Bowling plans a clandestine trip to his boyhood village of Lower Binfield. Often read as an homage to Wells's *History of Mr. Polly*, the sequence is also a darkly comic tribute to *Heart of Darkness,* with Bowling's return to his enchanted fishing hole standing in for Marlow's journey up the Congo. The parallel between Bowling and Marlow may appear to obviate the link between the lower middle class and the colonized. But the expedition ultimately confirms Bowling's enslaved status, proving the suburban colonization of England is a greater threat to national identity than even a Nazi invasion. Just as Marlow's journey to the heart of darkness begins and ends in London, so Bowling discovers that the road to his former village begins and ends in West Bletchley.

Like Marlow, who as a boy "dream[ed] gloriously over" African maps and their "blank space[s] of delightful mystery" (12), Bowling hopes the Binfield trip will rejuvenate his childhood feelings of freedom and enchantment. In fleeing the suburbs, he seeks to escape the forces that dominate his every waking moment—a "huge army" of "soul-savers" that wants to "rule [his] destiny." It is a military and missionary force tantamount to imperialism itself, and Bowling sees it coming at him with "wheeling prams and mowing-machines and concrete garden-rollers" (205). But like Marlow, who discovers an Africa invaded by the industrial and bureaucratic machinery he sought to escape, Bowling learns in his flight from suburbia that his rustic village is becoming what he thought he fled. Atop a hill overlooking Binfield, he sees wider roads, fewer trees, and "a whole lot of fake-picturesque houses" that are "dotted about in a kind of colony" (210). Like his youthful hero Donovan the Dauntless, who recovered "buried Inca treasures from the lost cities of Peru" (104), Bowling discovers that Binfield too is "swallowed up and buried like the lost cities of Peru" (214). But what has buried Binfield is a savage civilization, a "jungle of red houses" (233), like that "wilderness with no wild beasts" that is West Bletchley (24). Capping it all is a "stream of clerky-looking chaps . . . hurrying along . . . as if this had been a London suburb" (232–33).

Bowling is disenchanted that Binfield has become just like "these new towns that have suddenly swelled up like balloons in the last few years, Hayes, Slough, Dagenham" (215). But his true horror comes upon returning to his most sacred childhood space, the pool at Binfield House. His memories of his fishing hole are reminiscent of Conrad's nostalgia for secret enclaves that have evaded modernity, and Bowling holds out hope that the pool would still be "hidden in the woods" where "no one had discovered it existed" (250). He hopes in vain. Approaching foliage once as thick as a "tropical jungle," Bowling finds "houses, houses, houses" arranged in "sham-Tudor colonies," lamenting that he "might as well have been in the outer suburbs" (252–53). Trying to fathom the pool's destruction, Bowling sees an "oldish chap with a bald head" (253). Initially suggesting the "impressively bald" Kurtz (49), the old man turns out to be more like Kurtz's court jester—the Russian harlequin with the "beardless boyish face" and "little blue eyes that were perfectly round" (53–54). Bowling describes him as "one of those old men who've never grown up" and whose "blue eyes . . . kind of twinkled at you" (253). And like the Russian the old man serves as Bowling's eyewitness to a variety of local Kurtz figures. Among them is the architect Edgar

Watkins ("You've heard of him, of course," the old man says, reminiscent of the rumors that swirl around Kurtz). Rather than looting ivory, Watkins has made his name by pillaging English architecture, "finding genuine Elizabethan beams in old farmhouses and buying them at ridiculous prices" (254). Another Kurtz figure is Professor Woad, the "psychic research worker" who "goes wandering out into the woods" so that his "family can't find him at mealtimes" (255). Recalling Kurtz's tendency to "disappear for weeks" while he "wandered alone far in the depths of the forest" (55–56), Woad claims "he's walking among the fairies" (255). Indeed, Binfield is rife with Kurtzes. All of its residents are what the old man calls "very exceptional people," "enlightened people" who are "determined to enrich the countryside instead of defiling it" (254). At the same time Binfield's inhabitants are also savages, and the old man admits that "our life up here is in some ways primitive," his reference to the community's "simple life" (256) recalling the Russian's reference to Kurtz's African followers as "simple people" (53).

More than even in Kurtz's inner station, then, madness reigns throughout Binfield. Not only is the village manor now a mental asylum, but home owners have gone off the deep end with "faked-up Tudor houses" and "rock gardens with concrete bird-baths and those red plaster elves you can buy at the florists'. . . . Even the pavements were crazy" (255). As these descriptions suggest, Binfield's suburban faux-heritage is a local form of going native, mixing ersatz English nostalgia with all the trappings of leftist faddishness that Orwell despised.[26] In the heart of darkness that is modern Binfield, vegetarians are the new cannibals, nudist parties replace tribal ceremonies, garden gnomes are the latest fetish, and the grove of death is called "Pixy Glen" (257). But Bowling's greatest horror comes as he realizes why his beloved fishing hole has been drained. His dawning recognition that "they've turned the pool into a rubbish-dump" (256) parallels Marlow's growing realizations regarding Kurtz's exploits. In Binfield what had once "been field" is not just a "loony-bin" (251) but a "dustbin" (257).

With their penchant for vegetarianism, nudism, and fairy worship, Binfield's citizens hardly seem fodder for the kind of proto-fascist inculcation evident at the Left Book Club. And that is precisely Orwell's point. "Scratch the average pacifist," he claims in *Wigan Pier,* "and you find a jingo" (163). It seems fitting, then, that while the heart of Binfield is a leftist suburban sanctuary, its industrial outskirts house a munitions factory and an aerodrome. These settings account for the group of schoolchildren Bowling sees "marching down the street in columns of fours," carrying a banner that reads "BRITONS PREPARE." This miniature air raid patrol is led by "a grim-looking woman marching alongside of them like a sergeant-major" (233). In their rigid subservience the children are both a younger generation and a fuller realization of Binfield's "stream of clerky-looking chaps." Scratch the average clerk, Orwell suggests, and you might find a warmonger.

Binfield's burgeoning military-industrial complex provides the climax to Bowling's trip: an accidental bombing near the high street by an RAF plane. Critics often deride this finale as heavy-handed and contrived. But in demonstrating that preparations for war are as dangerous to British identity as the Nazis themselves, the bombing shatters once and for all any nostalgic aura Binfield may have had.[27] In contrast to Lawrence's "Away with little homes!" or Betjeman's "Come, friendly bombs," the accident does not destroy the suburbs. Quite the opposite. It wipes out a greengrocer's, one of the last vestiges of old Binfield, and kills the owner, a Mr. Polly figure named Perrott. The bombing is thus a final exclamation point to the suburbanization that has buried Binfield. At the same time the bombing wreaks havoc on the citizens: besides Perrott two die, one loses a leg, and another bites off her own tongue. But the bombing's deepest impact is psychological, ensuring that like the rest of the nation, Binfield's suburban citizens will remain in thrall to the war effort that upholds the empire.

Brave New Towns, Brave New Worlds

When the bombs really began to fall on Britain, the largest house-building boom in the nation's history came to an almost immediate end (Whitehand and Carr 37). Before private building could resume, legislators ensured that the unchecked, ad hoc sprawl of the interwar period would not continue. A parliamentary act of 1946 called for the creation of eleven "New Towns" throughout England, most designated for outer London. Influenced by the same garden city and town planning principles that created the sprawling interwar garden suburbs, New Towns were intended not as suburbs, but as economically self-sustaining areas to be built anew by government-appointed corporations. Another act in 1952 sought to extend existing towns according to more disciplined planning principles. Like the outskirts of Binfield many of these new or extended towns were part of so-called slum clearance programs, meant to receive working-class residents from inner-city areas like London's East End. Though such programs began in the 1930s, they continued with the public sector housing that reached its highest levels Britain in the decades following World War II. And while private suburban development would resume with the lifting of austerity measures in the 1950s, it would never reach the same extent as in prior decades.[28] Even though these new and extended towns were not technically suburbs, they were a target of postwar disdain for "subtopia," the architecture critic Ian Nairn's catch-all term for "the chaotic landscape of the urban fringe and beyond" (Gold and Gold 164).

This new subtopian landscape continued to be seen in terms similar to the Binfield bombed by Britain's own military. In "The Challenge of Our Time," a 1946 talk for the BBC, E. M. Forster reported learning that the first New Town would be built in Stevenage, near his boyhood home of Rooksnest, the model for Howards End. Discovering that farmland in Stevenage had been "commandeered" by the Ministry of Town and Country Planning ("Commandeered for what? Had not the war ended?"), Forster went on to describe the consequences for the area's rural population in terms that mix Wells's Martian invasion and Orwell's bombing of Binfield. Ministry officials declared "a satellite town for sixty thousand people is to be built. The people now living and working there are doomed. . . . The satellite town has finished them off as completely as it will obliterate the ancient and delicate scenery. Meteorite town would be a better name. It has fallen out of a blue sky" (*Two* 56–57). Unlike Forster's talk Orwell's nonfiction considered how moving to suburban council estates affected the migrants themselves. In *The Lion and the Unicorn,* he calls attention to "the spread of middle-class ideas and habits among the working class" (*Collected* 2: 76), so that the traditional proletariat grows ever more suburban in attitude and taste. Indeed, suburban housing provides Orwell with his key bit of evidence in proving proletarian assimilation to bourgeois values. Two people may be born of working-class parents, Orwell suggests, but the one "who has grown up in a council housing estate is likely to be—indeed, visibly is—more middle-class in outlook than a person who has grown up in a slum" (*Collected* 2: 77).

If Forster and Orwell ultimately moved beyond the colonial terms that informed so much of their earlier writing on the suburbs, others took up their project of linking the nation's waning global power to its widespread suburbanization. One of the suburb's few defenders in the postwar era was the architectural critic and editor J. M. Richards. Like Orwell, who wrote *Coming Up for Air* in Morocco, Richards wrote his 1946 book *The Castles on the Ground* while stationed in Cairo for the wartime Ministry of Information.[29] Reading *Castles* alongside *Coming Up for Air* reveals striking differences in response to their shared late-imperial milieu. Where Orwell links this context to suburban conformity and enslavement, Richards turns that view on its head, celebrating suburbia as nurturing forms of individuality and freedom that usher in an incipient form of postcolonialism. Written just as the first wave of colonial independence was about to begin, *The Castles on the Ground* fuses late-imperial melancholy with claims for indigenous rights on behalf of suburbanites.

Richards implies that the escapism and isolation associated with suburbia may stem from Britain's shifting political fortunes. Such escapism, he admits, is not an "enterprise appropriate to a mind that looks outward at an expanding world with confidence in its own relation to it." Rather, it reflects a desire for "a world where an illusion of security can be obtained" (39). Richards thus concedes that suburbia reflects and compensates for England's lack of agency in a post-imperial world. At the same time he imagines the average suburban male as a Crusoe figure, "at the mercy of elements which he cannot in the least control," yet seeking "to contrive for himself an environment . . . in which he is master" (35–36). Like the island under Crusoe's resourceful eye, the suburban home provides "a kind of oasis in which every tree and every brick can be accounted for," the better "to exclude the unpredictable as far as possible from everyday life" (36).

But alongside this colonial desire for order and control, Richards develops a complementary sense of suburbia as a benignly primitive if "well-stocked jungle." Richards applies his jungle rhetoric to suburbia's architecture and layout ("this intricate jungle of red peaked gables and evergreen hedges, multicoloured chimneys and winding, tree-shaded avenues" [19]), but also to its social relations ("this jungle . . . keeps itself to itself and seldom receives visitors from worlds outside" [33]). Inhabiting such a jungle involves the "discovery of an unspoilt world" where "no foot from any other world seems ever to have trodden" (21). Consequently, "the groves of the suburban jungle must be kept sacred to the suburban ritual" (84). In this environment Richards's latter-day Crusoes become more like primitive Fridays, noble savages whose habitat nurtures a vital way of life threatened by imperious planners and designers. Richards's bête noire is thus the newer "planned suburb," the architecturally and socially sterile product of local town councils. The planned suburb "not only imposes . . . a regular and inflexible pattern" on inhabitants. It also enforces a planner's "alien" taste, which seeks to "govern" suburban residents. Yet "the most successful suburbs," Richards implores, are those in which taste "is not governed at all" (9).

Suburbs for Richards should thus be enclaves of local autonomy in taste and style, indigenous communities that protect native rights and preserve a form of aesthetic home rule: "To inculcate restraint and refinement . . . in the depth of the suburban jungle is only to put a brake on the creative instinct" of suburban natives (66). These people are "willing slave[s]" (55), "from whom the suburban jungle draws much of its vitality and for whose creative instincts it caters" (67). Their untutored impulses are "the local colour the inhabitants gather round themselves in accordance with their particular instincts. . . . If you take this colour away by teaching them that there are other tastes they ought to prefer, or by means of other improvements imposed from without, you take away suburbia itself" (67). Richards's suburb is a primitive, premodern space that no planner or architect working on behalf of a higher civilization should seek to improve. Even so, Richards ends his defense of the suburban jungle with the hope that "these elusive territories—now the heart of England . . . will no longer be a strange unknown country" (96).

Nicholas Taylor's 1973 book *The Village in the City* shows that Richards's primitivist defense of suburbia did not take. Like Richards, Taylor views suburban ascendance in a wider global history. He notes in English architects since the mid-1950s "a quite remarkable and unreasonable loss of confidence," a decline that is "perhaps partly because of unrelated psychological problems connected with the decline of Britain's imperial power in the world" (11). And like Richards, Taylor defends suburbs as places where "the majority of our citizens not only live but prefer to live" (27), places that provide residents with "freedom, diversity and individuality" (28). Moreover, Taylor echoes Richards's critique of planned suburbs, and he sees the liberties of council tenants undermined when they have "no control over the environment in which the architect-planners put them" (19). Taylor found such situations rife in the New Towns, where a "managerial diktat" (imploring children not to play on the grass or teens not to congregate in communal areas) works in tandem with a "visual diktat" of rectilinear uniformity, a "dogmatically" enforced "aesthetic dictatorship" (108, 109, 111). The result is nothing short of what Taylor calls "municipal fascism, with its embattled 'laager mentality'" (100). This striking description conflates anti-totalitarian and anti-colonial rhetoric (*laager* being an Afrikaans term for defensive encampments that came to connote the entrenched insularity of the apartheid state). Against such rigid lifestyles Taylor wants to maintain the freedoms inherent in the "ordinary red-brick suburbs" of "present-day Mr. Pooters," the detached and semi-detached suburbs that Taylor dates from the 1880s to the 1930s (198). The problem Taylor sees in maintaining these areas, however, is their increasing distance from political decision making. The 1963 Greater London Act replaced the London County Council with a larger local authority, and the 1972 Local Government Act proposed similarly expanded councils throughout Britain. Taylor writes that when it comes to the "bread-and-butter problems of local government . . . the pattern of representation imposed" by these two acts "seems to bear no more relation, in terms of boundaries and responsibilities, to the people it is supposed to serve than do those arbitrary lines on the map of Africa, slicing across tribes, which the colonial conquerors left behind them as fixed national boundaries" (199). Under this new dispensation, Taylor fears, suburban citizens in Greater London and across the British Isles would be no better off than the formerly colonized.

Many working-class "migrants" to the new suburbs described their plight in similar terms. When it came to the London County Council's relocation schemes, a man testifying for a Royal Commission in 1938 called the LCC "a colonizing power . . . pouring out the treasure and labour of her citizens in order to make new homes for them in foreign lands" (qtd. in Richardson 262). Such statements are central to sociological studies detailing the relocation of East Enders to suburban housing estates and New Towns, most notably in the work of Michael Young and Peter Willmott. In *Family and Kinship in East London* (1957), the authors examine migrants from Bethnal Green who speak of their new suburban housing project as if in exile. "You're English, but you feel like a foreigner here," says one. "It's like a strange land in your own country," says another (121, 127). In Willmott's subsequent work on Dagenham, the largest residential estate in the world, an inhabitant complains of the constant displacements caused by the relocation schemes: "Where [residents] go . . . in the next generation, God knows. We can only assume they'll put them on rafts and set them adrift" (Willmott 38). A young man leaving the East End for the New Town of Milton Keynes recalled his mum weeping at his departure: "I think she thought we were going to the other side of the world" (Clapson, *Invincible* 83). An association for relocated Londoners perhaps summed up the situation best in a 1955 letter to the *Times:* "We are in opposition to the view that people are simply units to be moved about the face of the earth in line with the impersonal schemes of some 'Big Brother'" (qtd. in Young and Willmott 139). The letter indicates how much the anxieties of new suburbanites resonated not just with the dystopian tyranny that was synonymous with Orwell, but with the postcolonial emigrants who had set sail for Britain.

Epilogue

"In the Blood and Not on the Skin"

As white working-class migrants continued to make the trek from inner cities to suburban estates and New Towns, another era of migration was getting under way—one that resulted in today's "multiracial" Britain. In 1948 colonial subjects of color were granted right of entry to the country under the British Nationality Act, and in some cases the government positively encouraged their immigration to make up for postwar labor shortages. The docking of the SS *Empire Windrush* later that year brought the first members of the so-called New Commonwealth to British shores, and their presence has changed the face of Britain, particularly its urban areas. Labor shortages in the steel and textile industries brought immigrants to cities and towns with depopulating core areas, especially London. They arrived just in time to occupy the urban centers that many white working-class resident had fled—or been forced to leave—for suburban estates and New Towns. In their account of the *Windrush* generation, Mike Phillips and Trevor Phillips point out that while "the tendency to suburbanisation" led England's former city dwellers "out to the borders" of the metropolis, the New Commonwealth immigrants played a major part in transforming "huge swathes of the inner city" for themselves (383).

The results of this process are fairly well-known. On the one hand, Commonwealth immigrants to London and other cities faced poverty, lack of opportunity, and racism that led to riots, most notably in the London neighborhoods of Notting Hill and Brixton. Paul Gilroy has shown how thoroughly "contemporary definitions of 'race'" in postwar Britain have been intertwined with "the supposed primitivism and violence of black residents in inner-city areas," so that the very idea of race itself has "come to connote the urban crisis as a whole" and to "embody racial problems even where they are not overtly acknowledged or defined" (228–29). To this extent their placement in the city has marked subjects of color, quite literally, as a race apart from the nation proper. On the other hand, as Phillips and Phillips suggest, members of the *Windrush* generation and their descendents also embraced urban life because it allowed them "to engage with the broad currents of modernity" while at the same time "remodelling and modernising British cities" for themselves (383). In a nation where they confronted inequality, prejudice, and segregation, many immigrants saw London and other cities as places that could "equalise choices," "level out differences," and "put people together. . . . The consequence has been to radicalise public discussion about the identity of the nation" (387). Not surprisingly, urban settings dominate postcolonial immigrant literature. From Sam Selvon and George Lamming to Buchi Emecheta, Salman Rushdie, and Monica Ali, London—and particularly the "inner city"—has for better or worse been the primary backdrop of the postcolonial experience in Britain.

But in recent years, as James Procter points out, suburbia has also become "one of the most significant settings of black and Asian cultural production" (125). This is a surprising turn of events, since non-whites were long kept out of the suburbs—by estate agents who discouraged them from moving and by home owners who refused to sell to them. Those who attempted to make the move to the suburbs likely did so without large numbers of fellow immigrants (Clapson, *Suburban* 85–87). Yet certain inner suburbs were not without a minority presence. Saskia Sassen locates London's non-white residential concentration in two main areas: the "inner city" boroughs with a high African and Caribbean population and the "outer city" or inner suburban boroughs with high numbers of South Asians (like Brent, Ealing, Hounslow, and Waltham Forest) (271). In contrast to the experience of West Indians and Africans, suburbanization has been relatively common among Hindus, Sikhs, and to a lesser extent Muslims (Clapson, *Suburban* 117).[1]

Suburbia's recent prominence as a site of multiracial British culture is due in large part to the filmmaker and fiction writer Hanif Kureishi. Though Kureishi was not the first postcolonial artist to set his work in a suburb—that claim probably belongs to V. S. Naipaul's *The Mimic Men* (1967)—his 1990 novel *The Buddha of Suburbia* has done more than any recent work to naturalize mixed-race suburbans within the national imaginary by demonstrating their physical, cultural, and emotional connectedness to suburbia.[2] Kureishi is central to the generation of writers and artists whom Stuart Hall describes in terms of British "new ethnicities." What characterizes this post-negritude moment of racial relations for Hall is a "recognition of the extraordinary diversity of subjective positions, social experiences and cultural identities which compose the category 'black'" (443). This means not only "that 'black' is essentially a politically and culturally *constructed* category" but also that "the black subject cannot be represented without reference to the dimensions of class, gender, sexuality, and ethnicity" (443, 444, original emphasis).

By placing his novel squarely in suburbia, Kureishi seemed to confirm Hall's account, provocatively declaring the emergence of a new generation of British citizens. Complicating the typical postcolonial paradigm in which the author addresses the imperial "center" from the colonial "margins," Kureishi occupies the suburban margins that have also, during the time period covered by my study, come to occupy the nation's center. Yet, if this study has done nothing else, it has, I hope, shown why the apparent novelty and irony of Kureishi's setting are at the same time absolutely fitting.

Since *The Buddha of Suburbia* the mixed-race suburb has become a relatively common setting in British cultural products that have attracted international attention. Most notable here is Zadie Smith's widely feted novel *White Teeth* (2000), set in Willesden, but so too are Meera Syal's earlier *Anita and Me* (1996) and Diana Evans's more recent *26A* (2005). The popular 2002 film *Bend It like Beckham* takes place in the suburbs near Heathrow Airport, while the BBC hit series *The Kumars at Number 42* (costarring the *Anita and Me* author Syal) features a British-Indian family who converts their Wembley home into a TV studio for their talk-show-host son. Though of indeterminate ethnic origins, even Ali G, a comic persona of Sacha Baron Cohen (and the star of HBO's *Da Ali G Show*), admits in Jamaican patois that he lives with his nan in Staines. To the extent that these works and artists use suburbia as their characters' place of origin, suburbia itself might be seen as a central setting for Hall's new ethnicities.

Appropriate to Hall's account of new ethnicities, *The Buddha of Suburbia* is widely held to challenge essentialisms of all stripes—sexual, gender, class, racial, and ethnic. Thanks in part to Kureishi's interest in acting and fashion, the novel encourages a view of identity as inherently provisional and fluid. Karim Amir, the novel's mixed-race, middle-class, bisexual narrator, thus emerges from critical accounts as a paradigmatic postmodern *bricoleur* who fashions his identity as he goes—all the while subverting any notion of an essential self. Karim "refut[es] any vestigial belief in transcendental racial or cultural categories" (Yousaf 44); "signals the move away from unitary subject positions" (Childs 100); and "eludes definition by any one, all-purpose, determinant" (Lee, qtd. in Moore-Gilbert, *Hanif* 201). Indeed, Moore-Gilbert elevates Kureishi's view of the "terminally polymorphous and unstable nature of selfhood" to the level of "an ethical principle" (*Hanif* 130). Yet such readings of Karim's identity—and Kureishi's identity politics—often ignore a crucial aspect of the novel: Karim's suburban upbringing exerts subtle but profound effects that linger long after he has fled South London. If Karim recognizes his identity as largely contingent and constructed, his suburban origins continue to structure his affective response and bodily disposition with an intensity and persistence unequaled by any other part of his subjectivity. Indeed, while Karim eludes racial essentialism in his flight from the suburbs, his suburban background not only remains the ineluctable foundation of his subjectivity, but it gets reinforced as a racial identity in its own right. Just as the other authors featured in this study have found themselves and the nation colonized by suburbs that in various ways they attempt to resist, so too does Karim remain bound to the suburban identity he so desperately seeks to escape. From this perspective Kureishi's novel is less a celebration of some newfound suburban hybridity than it is an object lesson in the inescapable constraints of suburban background—even for those who seemingly transcend it.

Many readings of *Buddha* tacitly accept Sukhdev Sandhu's claim that "suburbia's only function" in the novel "is to serve as 'a leaving place'" (136) or John Clement Ball's suggestion that Karim's departure from suburbia "is a one-way journey, a permanent relocation in a new and stimulating urban space" (231). Both critics, moreover, read Karim's flight from suburbia as a domesticated form of postcolonial migration. For Sandhu "Karim flees to London with all the desperation and relief of the political refugee" (135). For Ball "Karim's move from the suburbs to 'London proper' becomes a local, miniaturized version of postcolonial migrancy and culture shock—the move from ex-colony (country) to metropolis (city)" (232). Ironically, such views foreclose what most postcolonial scholars take as axiomatic: that migration to a metropolitan center neither guarantees migrants a metropolitan identity nor dissolves their ties to their places of origin. A properly postcolonial reading of *Buddha,* then, should begin by recognizing Karim's ties to his own peripheral homeland—in this case suburbia.

Karim's suburban origins qualify any sense of relief or independence he feels upon arriving in the metropolis. His escape to London is overdetermined by his peripheral status both as a newcomer to the city and as the dark-skinned son of an Indian immigrant. In response Karim initially fashions subject positions for himself that are opposed to his newcomer/immigrant status: urban flaneur and English colonizer. For Baudelaire's flaneur, the "passionate spectator" of city life, "it is an immense joy to set up house in the heart of the multitude . . . to be away from home and yet to feel . . . everywhere at home" (9). Likewise, Karim seeks to get "lost in the crowd," viewing London as "a house with five thousand rooms, all different; the kick was to work out how they connected" (126). Ironically, however, Karim's flanerie emerges in tandem with an imperial will-to-mastery. Karim describes the streets of Kensington as his "new possession" and fine-tunes a scopic gaze that registers those marginalized by England's colonial authority: IRA bombers, Australian travel agents, Bengali shopkeepers (126–27). But Karim's pose as flaneur and imperialist is soon disrupted. Comparing his own clothes to the fashion on display outside a London club, Karim admits he "could have been from Bombay" (128). Once inside the club Karim tries to maintain proper ethnographic distance while witnessing his first punk performance, but the primitive rituals of what he calls this "alien race" only leave him doubting his attempted metropolitan persona: "Maybe I was just a provincial," he tells himself (129).

Foiled in his attempts to master the foreign city as colonizer and flaneur, Karim is thus forced into the two roles he came to London to escape: immigrant and provincial. This dual identity is reinforced, appropriately enough, at the party Eva throws to celebrate their flight from suburbia. In language that invokes the tragedies of postcolonial migration, Karim's friend Changez, himself a recent arrival from India, begs Karim to remember his suburban roots, imploring, "Don't leave your own people behind" (136). Eva, on the other hand, angry that Karim and his father did not avail themselves of the actors, directors, musicians, and writers at her party, snipes afterward, "You two behaved as if we were still in the sticks" (138). Even as he revels in the novelty of London, then, Karim cannot easily escape his suburban status as immigrant and provincial.

But neither is Karim always trying to elude the suburbs, as suggested by his feelings of displacement and longing for home while in London. Learning that he will have to wear "shit-brown cream" (146) and speak with an Indian accent in his starring role in a production of *The Jungle Book,* Karim claims, "I wanted to run out of the room, back to South London, where I belonged, out of which I had wrongly and arrogantly stepped" (148). Even more telling than this affirmation of his suburban identity is Karim's later discomfort with an acting exercise that involves narrating his life story to fellow members of his troupe. Considering himself "the English sort to be embarrassed by such a Californian display of self" (169), Karim implicitly codes his sensibilities as suburban when describing Tracey, a fellow actor, who is "respectable in the best suburban way. . . . She seemed shy and ill at ease in the world, doing her best to disappear from a room without actually walking out" (179). Ironically, Tracey is also the daughter of a Jamaican housekeeper and, besides Karim, the only "black" actor in the company. Though memorable for her criticism of the immigrant character Karim develops for a performance—a scene often recounted by critics—Tracey, like Karim himself, confounds racial essentialism, even as her bodily comportment betrays her suburban upbringing.

Given Karim's discomfort with self-display, the passages above cast performance as a complication of identity formation rather than simply a solution to it. Karim initially recognizes this problem after viewing his first punk concert with Charlie. The scene demonstrates that, despite their shared desire to refashion themselves in London, Karim and Charlie employ entirely different means of doing so. Karim chafes at Charlie's suggestion that "suburban boys like us" can identify with punks. "It would be artificial," he replies. "We're not like them. We don't hate the way they do. We've got no reason to" (132). Dick Hebdige's claim that punk shares a "deep structural" connection to "black British subcultures" (29) is apposite here, for if punk is "a white 'translation' of black 'ethnicity'" (64), Karim's refusal to identify with it anticipates his later refusal to identify with the strategic essentialism of black British identity. What confirms behavioral and affective authenticity for Karim is its correspondence to his suburban origins. Charlie, however, seeks to liberate himself from the stale and inauthentic emotions rooted in his past. Charlie sheds this past by ripping off his shirt and leaping into a carload of punks. Significantly, it is *Karim's* borrowed shirt that Charlie tears off, a gesture apparently meant to symbolize the revelation of his true self by discarding a borrowed, transitory identity—an artificial skin—that constrains him. Yet this scene problematizes the notion that suburban identity can be so easily shed. Charlie's symbolic gesture may suggest a liberating lack of essence—he *can* reinvent himself anew, as his acceptance by the punks confirms. But Karim's claim that he and Charlie don't legitimately share the punks' rage renders Charlie something of blank slate onto which any new environment or persona can inscribe itself. Rather than revealing a true self, Karim would have us view Charlie's act as leaving him exposed.

That Charlie's flaying of his suburban skin remains an inadequate solution to the constraints of his identity is reinforced soon after, at Eva's first London party. Watching Eva chat up her urbane guests—the same ones she castigated Karim and his father for avoiding—Karim claims: "I saw she wanted to scour that suburban stigma right off her body. She didn't realize it was in the blood and not on the skin" (134). This is a complex and counterintuitive statement, especially given Kureishi's apparent emphasis on the performative self. The claim seems to reject a suburban identity imagined in racial terms, only to confirm that racialized suburban identity at a deeper level. Perhaps it is more accurate to say that Karim's formulation racializes suburban identity as an invisible element "in the blood," not a chromatic register "on the skin." One critic has read Karim's comment as "a deliberately outrageous appropriation of race-politics language to describe a bored suburbanite's makeover" (Ball 232), and at some level this reading is appropriate. At the same time I want to take seriously

Karim's diagnosis of suburban identity as something that inheres below the surface, not in the outer bodily forms of the physiognomy, but in the physiological function of organs, like the circulation of blood. Karim suggests that, as with Charlie's symbolic tearing of his suburban skin, Eva's desire to "scour that suburban stigma right off her body" overlooks that stigma's deeper somatic origins. Thus, as Karim seeks to dispense with essentialized racial categories, he racializes suburban identity—though as something less apparent than the color of one's skin.

Curious as Karim's diagnosis of Eva's suburban stigma may be, however, he fails to see that it also applies to himself, as evident in moments when others call attention to traces of Karim's suburban self. He is utterly abashed, for example, when his white upper-class girlfriend Eleanor mentions his accent: "You're from South London—so that's how you speak. It's like cockney, only not so raw. . . . It's different to my voice, of course" (178). Significantly, this revelation occurs as Karim laments the suburban inability to talk about art and culture with the ease of Eleanor's set: "For us it could only ever be a second language, consciously acquired" (178). With Karim speaking a language marked by its difference from the metropolitan center, Kureishi again translates Karim's suburban origins into racial terms.

There is a similar suggestion that Karim has little control repressing traces of his suburban identity when he develops a character for one of Pyke's theatrical productions. Karim plays "an immigrant fresh from a small Indian town," coordinating an outfit of "high white platform boots, wide cherry flares that stuck to my arse like sweetpaper . . . and a spotted shirt with a wide 'Concorde' collar" (220). While the immediate inspiration for Karim's character is Changez, the costume echoes Karim's own clothing at the novel's outset. Consciously choosing "the right clothes" for a party, Karim emerges in "turquoise flared trousers, a . . . flower-patterned see-through shirt, [and] blue suede boots with Cuban heels" (6). Karim apparently fails to recognize the sartorial affinities between his slightly younger self and the immigrant character he plays. This lends added force to Changez's comments on Karim's performance. Though Karim fears Changez will be angry with his send-up, Changez tells him, "I am glad in your part that you kept it fundamentally autobiographical and didn't try the leap of invention into my character" (231). Karim inserts this line without comment—as a comic exclamation point at the expense of a deluded Changez—but Karim's shortsighted costume choice suggests that Changez is correct. Indeed, the director Pyke allows Karim to play the part because of the similarity Pyke sees between Karim and his immigrant character: like Karim, then dating the sophisticated and moneyed Eleanor, his immigrant character is out of place "among the upper classes" due to his relationship with an English woman he meets (189). Karim's feelings of suburban inadequacy in his relationship with Eleanor thus inform his portrayal of the immigrant character—more so than the costume choice and comic minstrelsy, which, thanks to Changez, we see right through.[3]

I have been suggesting that despite the novel's apparent celebration of a performative or improvisational self, Karim's suburban origins resist his conscious attempts at styling a new persona. At the same time Karim develops a mode of performance that does justice to his imperative of linking his suburban origins to his behavioral, affective, and bodily disposition. Indeed, Charlie's and Karim's divergent responses to the punk concert anticipate the opposed performative personae they eventually develop in their respective avatars as rock star and actor. The director Pyke instructs Karim that, as an actor, "you are trying to convince people that you're someone else, that this is not-me. The way to do it is . . . to be yourself. To make your not-self real you have to steal from your authentic self"; in other words, "to be someone else successfully you must be yourself." (219–20). While Karim the actor receives this advice as nothing short of an epiphany, Karim's everyday suburban self has been performing this way all along. Karim's failed attempt to fashion an urban identity as flaneur or colonizer, and his refusal to mimic the punks, are the twin sides of Pyke's lesson that performing as another requires acting like yourself. And while the immigrant character based on Changez suggests that Karim may not fully control the meaning of his performances, the role he accepts at the end of the novel corresponds to his own life experiences. Playing "the rebellious student son of an Indian shopkeeper" on a television soap opera (259), Karim has his own past to draw on, as well as Jamila's.

To appreciate the positive valence of Karim's performative persona, we need only compare it with Charlie's toward the end of the novel. Visiting Charlie in New York, Karim finds that his friend's stardom depends on "selling Englishness," a working-class variety to which Charlie can lay no legitimate claim (247). Once a suburban schoolboy mocked for "talking so posh," Charlie now cultivates a cockney accent and drops rhyming slang, which to Karim "didn't seem of [Charlie's] essence, but a temporary, borrowed persona" (247, 246). At the same time Karim appears to realize that, as with Charlie's exposure before the punks, the "borrowed persona" is precisely of Charlie's essence. Invited to watch Charlie have sex with a dominatrix, Karim recalls his own brief sexual encounter with Charlie in the novel's opening: "he wanted me—he let me touch him—but refused to acknowledge it, as if he could remove himself from the act while remaining there" (253). If Charlie distances himself from even the most intimate acts, Karim ultimately seeks to perform in ways that correspond to his origins. Recalling Karim's claim that suburban origins reside in the blood and not on the skin, Charlie and Eva try to scrape away the detritus of their identity, whereas Karim comes to see this as impossible, since suburban identity inheres within the self rather than adhering to it externally.

Toward the end of the novel, Karim's father, Haroon, claims, "I have lived in the West for most of my life, and I will die here, yet I remain to all intents and purposes an Indian man" (263). To a great extent this statement also crystallizes Karim's relation to suburbia. For like his father, inhabiting a divided position between India and England, Karim inhabits a space between London, where he appears intent on staying at the novel's end, and suburbia, which indelibly grounds his affective and behavioral dispositions. At the same time, however, Haroon's claim that he remains Indian while living in England is less like Karim's performative persona—being yourself to be someone else—than that of Charlie, who removes himself from the acts in which he engages. In contrast to both Charlie and Haroon, who distance themselves from their immediate surroundings, Karim develops a persona whose performative aspects are conditioned by—indeed, dependent upon—his lived experience in the South London suburbs. While this optimistic reading of Karim's persona may be more in line with critical accounts of the novel's anti-essentialism, it should not allow us to underestimate the tenacity of Karim's suburban origins. In a claim that captures the dynamics of semi-detachment, James Procter rightly notes that Karim "remains profoundly attached to the suburbs he has sought to leave behind" (149). Yet I disagree with Procter's conclusion that "Karim is a chameleon" who "reinvents and repositions himself as black or white, Asian or cockney as the situation suits him," "shuttl[ing] between identities, positions and politics without ever firmly committing or attaching himself to any" (153–54). Where Procter sees Karim's "unstable, hybrid identity" as a product of his suburban "*locality*" (153, original emphasis), I have argued that suburbia is not a locale from which Karim can detach himself.

Like the imperial attempt to detach from suburban colonies in *A Passage to India,* or the suburban attempt to detach from imperial *ressentiment* in *Coming Up for Air,* Karim will remain, at best, in a state of semi-detachment. As we have seen, Karim's inability to distance himself completely from his suburban origins keeps him from creating a free-floating identity. More significantly, even as Kureishi's novel goes about contesting and subverting various forms of essentialism, Karim's suburban identity is repeatedly racialized—in his speech, in his dress, in his bodily comportment—even though it lies "in the blood and not on the skin." In an era when racial, gender, ethnic, and sexual differences have profoundly challenged the façade of a unified British subjectivity, suburbia remains at the foundation of Karim's identity. If, as I have argued throughout this study, semi-detachment defines the relationship between suburbia and empire, that same dynamic shows why Karim's plight has a great deal to tell us not only about mixed-race suburbanites. While I would not wish to detach *The Buddha of Suburbia* from Kureishi's overt concern with Britain's formerly colonized subjects or their descendents, I hope this study has also shown why Karim's plight is one with which a broad range of suburban subjects could identify.

NOTES

1. SEMI-DETACHED EMPIRE

1. I use *modern* here to distinguish nineteenth- and twentieth-century suburbs from their medieval and early modern predecessors, which often housed a town's greatest poverty and "most noxious trades" (F. M. L. Thompson 2). On medieval and early modern suburbs, also see Dyos, *Victorian* 34; Inwood 127–31, 183–94.

2. On growth rates see Porter 234; Dyos, *Victorian* 20; Inwood 572; F. M. L. Thompson 5–7. On suburban Birmingham, Manchester, and Leeds, see Gunn 38–39. For a detailed examination of Leeds, see Treen. On Irish suburbs see E. Jones and also MacLaran 30, 40–44. On Scottish suburbs see Adams 187–201; Gordon; and Robb.

3. The most prominent readings of imperialism's impact on Britain's domestic sphere include Said's discussion of *Mansfield Park* in *Culture and Imperialism* 80–97; Spivak's reading of *Jane Eyre* in "Three Women's Texts"; Jameson's "Modernism and Imperialism"; and McClintock. On the exporting of British domestic ideals, see Baucom; George; Grewal; and Pecora. For a more detailed overview of this scholarship, see David.

4. See the collections by Burton; Cooper and Stoler; and Driver and Gilbert (*Imperial Cities*); as well as the studies by Crinson; Jacobs; and Schneer. The major exception to these claims is the work of the architectural historian Anthony King.

5. Architectural scholars view the semi-detached home as an aesthetic and economic compromise between the detached country estate or villa and the urban terrace or town house, providing the largest residence that the middle classes could afford and individualize for themselves: see Burnett 102–3; Edwards 32–35; A. Jackson 133–34; Oliver, Davis, and Bentley 115–17, 157. Semi-detached houses were first used in the early eighteenth century as laborers' cottages in Cambridgeshire, Norfolk, and later Dorset and were introduced to London in the 1780s (Edwards 33; Girouard 276–77). Alan Jackson, however, dates their appearance in London to the late seventeenth century (133). In any case, the first residential development to use semi-detached homes for "gentlefolk" was in the 1790s at Eyre Estate, St. John's Wood, now considered one of the first consciously built suburban areas.

6. As this formulation suggests, my thinking on semi-detachment is indebted to a range of scholarship across the humanities—especially in literary studies, anthropology, and history—that treats home and empire as articulated categories. Semi-detachment shares with Edward Said's notion of contrapuntal reading a desire "to think through and interpret together experiences that are discrepant, each with its particular agenda and pace of development" (32). Likewise, it partakes of the dialectic between "the domestication of the colonies and the racializing of the metropolis" examined by Anne McClintock (43), as well as Frederick Cooper and Ann

Laura Stoler's argument that "Europe was made by its imperial projects, as much as colonial encounters were shaped by conflicts within Europe itself" (1). Their work builds on that of the anthropologist Nicholas Dirks, who claims that "colonialism was less a process that began in the European metropole and expanded outward than it was a moment when new encounters within the world facilitated the formation of categories of metropole and colony in the first place" (6).

7. *Imperialism* entered British political discourse in the 1870s and was taken up by journalists during the 1890s (Hobsbawm, *Age of Empire* 60). According to J. A. Hobson, the word was "on everybody's lips" when his study *Imperialism* appeared in 1902 (xvii). *Suburbia* is first cited by the *Oxford English Dictionary* in 1895, the year Edwin Pugh published his story collection *A Street in Suburbia*. But as a "collective gibe," the word may have been used as early as the 1880s (Dyos and Reeder 363).

8. Until recently, criticism on the suburbs has been sparse, limited to articles or parts of book chapters: see Carey 46–70; Creese, "Imagination"; V. Cunningham 256–60; Dentith, "Thirties"; Flint; Keating, *Haunted* 319–27; Ruddick; and Trotter 128–32. Lynne Hapgood's recent *Margins of Desire* is the first study to focus solely on British suburban literature. The collections edited by Silverstone and by Webster are a gauge of recent interest in the suburbs, as are the articles by Elfenbein; Hammerton; Whelan; and E. Williams. One of the best examples of this recent work is Sharon Marcus's fascinating chapter on middle-class housing conditions and London ghost tales in *Apartment Stories* 83–132. Recent criticism on the literature of the American suburb includes insightful work by Jurca and also Plotz.

9. As Eliot shows, suburbia is often treated with disdain in works of high modernism. *The Waste Land* casts suburbia as a Dantean netherworld of constant if unfulfilled activity: with their "trams and dusty trees," Highbury, Richmond, and Kew are the undignified backdrop for a Thames daughter's undoing, while death undoes the faceless "crowd" of commuters that "flowed over London Bridge" (*Complete* 70, 62). In *The Rock* suburbia likewise requires residents to abandon all hope: "We toil for six days, on the seventh we must motor / To Hindhead, or Maidenhead" (*Complete* 147). And in *Burnt Norton* all of human existence is reduced to the "metalled ways" of an underground train belching passengers to "the gloomy hills" of London's inner suburbs: "Hampstead and Clerkenwell, Campden and Putney, Highgate [and] Primrose" (*Complete* 174). Regarding Virginia Woolf, Andrew Thacker claims that "the southern suburbs of London float through [her] work as . . . non-places that can never enter into literary representation but which are gestured to as dismal destinations for certain lower-middle-class characters" (156). For a survey of modernist antipathy toward suburbia, see Carey 46–70.

10. Esty's own explanation of this situation—that England did not nurture a cosmopolitan, metacultural modernism because its national identity at the height of empire was "already universalist and metacultural" (35)—begs the question of why other nations with extensive empires (like Germany and France) developed more potent modernisms.

11. See Alison Light as well as the collections edited by DiBattista and McDiarmid; by Hapgood and Paxton; and by Kaplan and Simpson.

12. Within this continuum Mark Clapson usefully identifies three types of suburbs. These are "the residential, middle-class, owner-occupied suburbs of large detached houses"; "the less prestigious but still sought-after middle-class estates of small detached and semi-detached houses"; and working-class local council estates of a kind "largely absent from the American suburbs" (*Suburban* 4). For a helpful introduction to different forms of British suburbs in their historical contexts, see Wilson 103–12.

13. "The fact of the suburb influenced the environment of the slum; the threat of the slum entered the consciousness of the suburb." However, "there was no simple polarity. There were degrees of slumminess just as there were degrees of suburban exclusiveness, and there were many irregularities in the declension between them" (Dyos and Reeder 360, 363).

14. In his preface Mayhew introduces himself as a "traveller in the undiscovered country of the poor," a population less understood than "the most distant tribes of the earth" (1: xv), and his opening chapter divides all humanity into two "races," "the nomadic and the civilized tribes." The poor, Mayhew claims, are the "wanderers" within the "civilized" or "settled tribe" (1: 1).

15. For overviews of the Victorian writers, see Burgan; Keating, *Into* 13–32; and Nord. On Sims and Greenwood see Keating, *Working* 38–40; and also Bivona and Henke. On Munby see McClintock 132–80. On Charles Booth see Walkowitz 30–38 and also P. K. Gilbert 188–95. On images of the "urban jungle" in Harkness, Doyle, General Booth, Jack London, Conrad, and Eliot, see McLaughlin.

16. Gilbert and Preston point out that "despite the existence of substantial areas of suburban development around Cardiff, Edinburgh, Glasgow and Belfast, the suburb has been primarily associated with Englishness" (190). Whitehand and Carr suggest that England "is today the archetypal country of suburbs" because "relative to city size," the impact of suburbs on streets, building form, and land use "is probably greater in England than in any other country" (6). The suburb's nation of origin has been subject to debate among historians. For English claims to primacy see Robert Fishman ("American") and the response by Kenneth T. Jackson. For Australia see Davison.

17. Before 1760 almost no Europeans lived in the villages outside Madras. In 1780 there were "upwards of two hundred suburban houses," and by 1800 "at least four hundred suburban residences had been built by Europeans," who bought up nearly half the cultivable land near Madras from village proprietors (or mirasdars). Both the indigenous and colonial elite facilitated the process: while the mirasdars found that selling their land could earn them more than farming it, the East India Company discovered a new source of tax revenue (Neild 243, 225–26). In the case of Patna Rebecca Brown suggests that in the early nineteenth century the term *suburb* was used to designate areas distinct from either the indigenous town or the European settlements. In Patna the suburb was "an in-between, liminal, transitional space, undefined in terms of population" (163).

18. Nash's development of Regent's Park roughly coincided with his design of the famous Mughal-inspired Royal Pavilion at Brighton. Nash built the pavilion between 1815 and 1823, but his architecture showed Eastern influences as early as 1800 (T. Davis 38, 43). One of his first clients was a solicitor for Warren Hastings, the impeached governor-general of India (Summerson 37). Nash had been a pupil of Robert Taylor, whose commissions came primarily from East India Company officials and West Indian merchants (Harris and Baker 975). Nash's fellow pupil under Taylor was Samuel Pepys Cockerell, a surveyor for the East India Company and an architect of Hindu-influenced country houses, including Sezincote, which in turn inspired Nash's partner, the landscape gardener Humphry Repton, to redesign the Brighton Pavilion (T. Davis 84; Meadows 364–65). Though Nash's professional relationship with Repton ended long before work began at Brighton, Nash's design was based in part on Repton's (Daniels 501; Tyack 216).

19. For more on Bayswater's popularity among colonials, see Reeder 263. On the exotic reputation of Westbourne Grove and Whiteley's, see Rappaport 16–25.

20. Harvey comes closest to addressing the British context when he describes suburbaniza-tion "on both sides of the Atlantic" as a result of the "acute threats of civil strife . . . associated with the marked concentration of the working class and the unemployed in space." Harvey attributes these perceived threats to "the revolutions of 1848 across Europe, the Paris Commune of 1871, the urban violence that accompanied the great railroad strikes of 1877 in the United States and the Haymarket incident of 1886 in Chicago" (*Urbanization* 28–29).

21. On suburban building cycles see Dyos, "Speculative" 659–60; on patterns of foreign investment see Edelstein 174–76; and on relations between the two see Dyos, *Victorian* 80–81, and King, *Global* 78–80.

22. Conversely, in *Rural England* (1902) H. Rider Haggard claims that the "result of this desertion of the countryside and of the crowding of its denizens into cities" will be "nothing less than the progressive deterioration of the race" and "may in the end mean the ruin of the race" (qtd. in Keating, *Into* 217–18).

23. One LCC staff member, Lionel Curtis, left to serve in the Boer War and stayed in South Africa, where he helped to organize the municipality of Johannesburg—and the government's apartheid policy (Pennybacker 20, 70). It was a former LCC employee who, as governor of Madras, brought town planning principles to India and another LCC chair who resigned his position to lead the planning committee for New Delhi (Home 48–49). I discuss the planning of New Delhi in relation to Forster's *A Passage to India* in chapter 6.

24. For a sketch of Rosebery's imperial views, see Faber 68–71.

25. On the exhibition also see Walthew. For a reading of Woolf's *Mrs. Dalloway* in relation to the exhibition, see Cohen.

26. In his social history of London, Roy Porter lists a number of street names reflecting the city's imperial identity in the late nineteenth century, but the areas he identifies were primarily suburban (326–27). On street names also see King, *Spaces* 101, 220.

27. Like his forecast of Britain's continued suburban development, Low's remarks on Aus-tralia were especially prescient. By the beginning of the twentieth century, the unusually low density of Australian cities like Sydney, Melbourne, and Adelaide made them "predominantly suburban in character"; their national dominance, in turn, made Australia "the most suburban-ized nation on earth" (Davison 60, 63). Davison argues that Australia's suburban phenomenon was "deeply rooted" in the continent's "colonial experience" (42). Moreover, since a high num-ber of its immigrants came from England, particularly the Home Counties, Davison suggests that Australia was in a way "the farthest suburb of urban Britain" (52). Indeed, Australia's suburbs offered a much lower cost of living than their British equivalents (54)—and much more room.

28. Hapgood elsewhere cites Low's article as an instance of such representations ("Lit-erature" 308; "'New'" 41–42) and points to fiction that adheres to her description. In the first installment of John Galsworthy's Forsyte saga, *The Man of Property* (1906), the titular protagonist Soames Forsyte builds a mansion near Epsom and fancies himself "the pioneer-leader of the great Forsyte army advancing to the civilization of this wilderness" (Galsworthy qtd. in Hapgood, "Unwritten" 171). In another article Hapgood quotes from William Pett Ridge's 1899 collection *Outside the Radius,* in which suburban males leave their homes daily at 8:20 "in search of gold"; in the evening "the detachment which went off in the morning to attack the City and to loot it" returns home for its dinner (Pett Ridge qtd. in Hapgood, "Literature" 297).

29. Echoing Dickens's "suburban Sahara" is Mrs. Humphry (Mary) Ward's 1888 novel

Robert Elsmere, part of which takes place in a Surrey landscape that is "a strange mixture of suburbanism and the desert" (151).

30. In *The Suburban Gardener and Villa Companion* (1838), an architectural and horticultural guide for building a quasi-aristocratic estate on a middle-class budget, Loudon writes: "The respect, or the good opinion, of his friends and neighbours, or of the inhabitants of the parish in which he resides, are, to the citizens retired to the suburbs, of as great value as the respect of the inhabitant of a district, or of the whole nation, is to the wealthy landholder or senator" (9). In an 1877 article on London's suburbs for the American magazine *Galaxy,* Henry James writes that the term *suburban* has always had "a peculiarly English meaning" for him, conjuring "ivy-covered brick walls . . . riverside holiday-making . . . old royal seats at an easy drive . . . [and] little open-windowed inns, where the charm of rural seclusion seems to merge itself in that of proximity to the city market" ("Suburbs" 778).

31. Ruskin's relation to the suburbs was more complex than this suggests. As Dinah Birch points out, Ruskin grew up in the prosperous suburb of Herne Hill, which provided a "fertile and secure background" that "Ruskin came to see . . . as a lost paradise" with London's encroachment (242). Thus, "a catastrophic fall from grace in the suburbs that produced him . . . becomes a controlling image" in his later critical texts (234).

32. Hapgood cites this passage for the "unequivocal pleasure" with which Low describes the new suburbs ("'New'" 42). In contrast, I have been attempting to underline the touches of ambivalence—if not outright disdain and fear—that occur in Low's article. My point is that such anxieties about suburbia reflect precisely the popular mindset of Low's general audience, a mindset that Low ultimately sought to overcome. As such, these anxieties should not be bracketed from the wider discursive field to which Low's writing belongs.

2. Reverse Colonization in *The War of the Worlds*

1. For parallels between the novel and Wells's early articles, especially "Through a Microscope" and "Luminous Plants," see Hughes and Philmus 107–9. In a 1920 article for the *Strand,* Wells said of his conversation with Frank: "Perhaps we had been talking of the discovery of Tasmania by the Europeans—a very frightful disaster for the native Tasmanians! I forget" (qtd. in Bergonzi 124).

2. John Hammond and also Wakeford discuss Woking's role in the novel, but not in terms of suburban development. Other critics mention the novel's suburban setting, but not its specific locale. See Bergonzi 130; Hughes and Geduld 1; and Parrinder, *Shadows* 86–87. Gail Cunningham makes the most direct link between Wells's Martians and suburbia (429–32).

3. Also see Markley 121–27; Fitting 140; Simpson 143; and Bergonzi 134.

4. Virginia Woolf famously attacks Wells (along with Galsworthy and Bennett) in "Mr. Bennett and Mrs. Brown" (*Collected* 1: 319–37). James's criticism of Wells has a more complex history, reflected in the documents in Edel and Ray's *Henry James and H. G. Wells.*

5. I look at some of the narrator's own misperceptions shortly but simply note here his repeated complaints regarding the information newspapers disseminate (or fail to disseminate) regarding the Martians. Of the accounts of the Martian advance wired to Sunday papers by correspondents, for instance, the narrator claims: "None of the telegrams could have been written by an eyewitness" (74; for other examples see 32–33, 34, 72, 73, and 124). Parrinder reads such corrections as an index of Wells's adherence to realist convention ("From" 70; "H. G. Wells" 57). But such a claim is undermined by the narrator's constant reminders that his own account is lacking. At one point the narrator laments those who have never seen the Martians and their

technology firsthand and who "have only the ill-imagined efforts of artists or the imperfect descriptions of such eyewitnesses as myself to go upon" (124). Moreover, the narrator regularly punctures the authoritative tone of his own hypotheses about the heat ray, poison smoke, and Martian deaths by reinforcing the provisional status of his theories (27, 87–88, 178).

6. It is perhaps worth noting another late-Victorian text that invokes suburban development from the vantage of an imagined future. William Morris's *News from Nowhere* offers a dialectical counterpoint to *The War of the Worlds,* insofar as it seeks to historicize an increasingly suburban present in more optimistic terms than Wells. But this is not, as some critics suggest, because Morris provides a "utopian vision of a suburbanised future" in "human-scale communities on the margins of the city" (Hapgood, *Margins* 29, 18; also see G. Cunningham 425). Morris's narrator, William Guest, happily exchanges his life in "the shabby London suburb" of Hammersmith for a rural utopian future in which the former "suburbs . . . melted away into the general country" (54, 116). Guest looks favorably on these rural environs, often contrasting them with his own memories of ever-increasing suburban development, including "the philistines" who sought to "landscapegarden" over Epping Forest and the "cockney villas" whose "hideous vulgarity" once "marred the beauty of the bough-hung banks" of the Thames (67, 186; also see 198, 202, 216). Morris's rendering is thus more optimistic than Wells's because it imagines the present from the vantage of a future in which suburbs have completely disappeared. If utopia in *News from Nowhere* was not suburban, however, Morris's Arts and Crafts ideals would nonetheless influence a range of suburban architects and planners (see Bolus-Reichert and also Dentith, "From").

7. The historian Frederic Harrison, a contemporary of Wells, would depict late-Victorian suburban growth in similar terms, even as it spreads further toward the Home Counties: "The Bricks pour down in irregular heaps, almost as if, in some cataclysm or tornado, it were raining bricks out of the heaven on the earth below. The huge pall of smoke gets denser and more sulphurous, stretching out, they say, some thirty miles into the country, til Berkshire, Bucks, Herts, and Kent are beginning to be polluted by its cloud" (413).

8. In an earlier draft of *The War of the Worlds,* the narrator clearly projects his marital dissatisfactions on the curate (Huntington 143–44).

9. In *Abinger Harvest* E. M. Forster notes that "most of us see our first mosque at Woking," when "a small bulbous building appears among the fir trees" and "someone in the railway carriage says 'That's Oriental'" (274). On Leitner and the Shah Jehan Mosque, also see Whiteman and Whiteman 49–52.

3. SHERLOCK HOLMES AND THE CASE OF THE ANGLO-INDIAN

1. Unless otherwise noted, all Doyle quotations are from *The Complete Sherlock Holmes.* Doyle variously referred to his second novel by its original title, *The Sign of the Four,* and by the shorter title (without the second definite article); for simplicity I retain the shorter title.

2. South London was notorious for its dearth of culture. Walter Besant describes it as lacking in tradition, communal identity, and local memory: "It is a city without a municipality, without a centre, without a civic history; it has no newspapers, magazines or journals; it has no university . . . it has no intellectual, artistic, scientific, musical, literary center" (320).

3. On Holmes's aestheticism and penchant for collecting, see Barolsky and also Langbauer.

4. Admiral Hay Denver served in Bomarsund, Alexandria, Zanzibar, East India, and Halifax. His son invests shares in New Zealand and other colonies. The outspoken Mrs. Westmacott

has just returned from studying natives in the South Pacific, and she argues with the admiral that the English should play a part in deciding imperial policy. The parents of her nephew were killed in the so-called Indian Mutiny of 1857.

5. Likewise, McLaughlin writes: "While *The Sign of Four* is the uneasy sign of a future that includes a more widespread colonial presence, in the final analysis, the Holmes plots are not meant to scare but to reassure" audiences, by "rechannel[ing] paranoid protectionary fears about invasion into stimulating optimism about new kinds of expansionist consumer consumption and reassurances about Britain's continual imperial mastery" (72–73).

6. In this chapter, as throughout this study, I use *Anglo-Indian* in its older form, to designate Britons living in India (rather than Eurasians, to whom it now usually refers).

7. Since the tales are geographically wide-ranging, it is difficult to tie any particular story to a single setting. By my count, however, suburban areas are the crime scene in ten tales: "The Beryl Coronet," "The Blue Carbuncle," "Charles Augustus Milverton," "The Greek Interpreter," "The Illustrious Client," "The Norwood Builder," "The Retired Colourman," *The Sign of Four,* "The Six Napoleons," and *A Study in Scarlet.* Only the setting of "The Blue Carbuncle" is predominantly urban. Another ten tales make suburban areas a primary site of investigation: "The Bruce-Partington Plans," "The Cardboard Box," "The Dying Detective," "The Disappearance of Lady Frances Carfax," "The Man with the Twisted Lip," "The Naval Treaty," "A Scandal in Bohemia," "The Three Gables," "The Veiled Lodger," and "The Yellow Face." Four other tales use rural settings for areas that were undergoing suburban development: "The Abbey Grange," "The Reigate Puzzle," "The Solitary Cyclist," and "The Wisteria Lodge." Central London settings dominate in "A Case of Identity," "The Empty House," "The Mazarin Stone," "The Noble Bachelor," "The Red Circle," "The Red-Headed League," "The Resident Patient," and "The Second Stain."

8. On Holmes's anti-rural sensibility see Poston. Stephen Knight argues that Doyle's representation of the countryside "omits that more real criminal pressure from dispossessed, outcast London in a period of economic depression" and thereby "demonstrates how far Doyle is from presenting a realistic account of the sources and patterns of real crime in late nineteenth-century England" (94–95). Moretti makes a similar point based on Doyle's London settings (*Atlas* 134–37).

9. The Three Randalls, a gang from Lewisham, are the initial suspects in "The Abbey Grange"; both the Spencer John Gang and the Barney Stockdale Gang prowl Harrow in "The Three Gables."

10. Villas are the primary domestic scene in "The Bruce-Partington Plans," "The Crooked Man," "The Man with the Twisted Lip," "The Norwood Builder," "A Scandal in Bohemia," "The Six Napoleons," "The Three Gables," and "The Yellow Face." In "A Scandal in Bohemia" Briony Lodge is called a "*bijou* villa" (168), and the eponymous home in "Wisteria Lodge" is also referred to as a villa (873). In contrast are the manors featured in "The Dancing Men" (Riding Thorpe Manor), "The Musgrave Ritual" (Hurlstone Manor), "Thor Bridge," and *The Valley of Fear* (Birlstone Manor). Halls are featured in "The Blanched Soldier" (Tuxbury Old Hall), *The Hound of the Baskervilles* (Baskerville Hall), and "The Priory School" (Holdernesse Hall). *Place* is another name for a large rural home (as in the eponymous "Shoscombe Old Place" and Yoxley Old Place in "The Golden Pince-Nez").

11. Laura Otis claims that the yellow face "suggests anger in a jaundiced and choleric sense, and it resonates with the yellow fever of which [Effie's] black husband conveniently died. It also links the black child to England's Asian colonial subjects." In this sense the yellow face is

"a condensation of all of England's colonials, their diseases, and their anger" (117). Jinny Huh reads "The Yellow Face" alongside Doyle's writing about Africa and his memories of meeting an African American man, arguing that "the emergence of detective fiction . . . is in direct response to the anxieties produced by a failed racial detection" (554).

12. These are "Charles Augustus Milverton" (in Hampstead), "The Illustrious Client" (in Kingston), "Lady Frances Carfax" (in Brixton), and "The Retired Colourman" (in Lewisham). "The Bruce-Partington Plans" is set mostly in a suburban part of Woolwich, but Holmes robs a residence in Kensington.

13. Huh notes that Norbury both signifies and represses Holmes's failure to read racial difference, projecting that failure on the (racially unspecific) place name (566). But as I hope to have suggested, the name *Norbury* accommodates racial hybridity and suburban identity under a single heading.

14. Ex-colonials abound in the Holmes canon, often as villains. In addition to the examples below, see "The Adventure of the Speckled Band," "The Adventure of the Empty House," and "The Adventure of the Devil's Foot."

15. Doyle was not the first to present exotic suburban criminals. In Wilkie Collins's *The Woman in White* (1859–60), the sinister Italian spy Count Fosco resides in St. John's Wood, and in *The Moonstone* (1868), the thief of the titular jewel is an Anglo-Indian who lives in Hampstead. Count Dracula also hopes to settle in Hampstead, and the less famous if no less fascinating title character of Richard Marsh's *The Beetle* (1897)—a giant, shape-shifting Egyptian scarab—lives in a detached villa near Walham Green. Nor would Doyle be the last. The climax of John Buchan's spy thriller *The Thirty-Nine Steps* (1915) has the protagonist Richard Hannay tracking a group of foreign anarchists plotting pan-European war to a holiday home in Kent. Their ruse, which nearly works, is to disguise themselves as "three ordinary, game-playing, suburban Englishmen" (105).

16. King claims that since the bungalow first appeared in Britain as part of a booming leisure resort industry, it retained connotations of sanitary and health ideals when it moved to the airier fringes of the congested city. See "Excavating" and *Bungalow* chapters 2 and 3.

17. French colonizers gallicized the Tamil fishing village Puducherri ("new village") to Pondichéry in 1674, after which it was occupied alternately by British and French forces. In 1817 France regained sovereignty over Pondicherry, but the city's French residents "were not allowed to erect any fortifications or maintain any more troops than were required for police duties" (Chopra 118).

18. Like Holmes's encyclopedia the 1887 *Whitaker's Almanack* describes the Andamans as "inhabited by a diminutive race of savages" (386). For a detailed comparison of Holmes's encyclopedia entry on the Andamans with that of the 1881 *Imperial Gazetteer of India,* see McBratney 154–56.

19. But neither is Sholto completely innocent. As Ronald Thomas points out, Doyle evacuates the Mutiny backdrop of its political implications: "Despite the elaborate historical and political framework that is set up here—corrupt army officers, colonial rebellion, military looting, blackmail and secrecy among thieving military prison guards—there is no political motive offered for this crime. There is no sense of outrage over conquest or plunder, only the natural action bred by the 'instincts' of a 'savage' criminal body, the traces of which are easily discernible to [Holmes's] scientific eye." For Thomas both Small and Holmes "suppress the political character of this crime" (233).

20. For details on Bayswater's reputation as "Asia Minor," see Buettner, *Empire* 211–16; Rappaport 21–26.

21. On his move to South Norwood, see Doyle, *Memories and Adventures* 97. On Bungalow Road and Captain Bamford, see King, *Bungalow* 69. Doyle does not mention Bungalow Road, but maps from the late nineteenth century show that it existed at the time.

22. Arata claims that the Anglo-Indian was the prototype of a "new, reinvigorated Briton" in the late nineteenth century (158). Yet most critics, like Moore-Gilbert, note that the Anglo-Indian's "distinct identity" made him "obscure and puzzling to the wider metropolitan population" (*Kipling* 6); "the sense of alienation which so often accompanied the Anglo-Indian on his return to Britain" offered a "particularly pathetic index of the dislocations caused by exile" (*Kipling* 42). Likewise, Benita Parry suggests that although "an aristocracy in India, the Anglo-Indians often felt themselves regarded as redundant men and quaint outsiders when they returned Home" (*Delusions* 35). For excellent historical accounts of the returned Anglo-Indian, see Buettner.

23. Auckland's entry in "The Song of the Cities" reads: "Last, loneliest, loveliest, exquisite, apart— / On us, on us the unswerving season smiles, / Who wonder 'mid our fern why men depart / To seek the Happy Isles!" (Kipling 176).

24. In *Degeneration* Max Nordau sees "the present rage for collecting" and "the piling up, in dwellings, of aimless bric-a-brac" as "an irresistible desire among the degenerate" (27). Benjamin claims that "perhaps the most deeply hidden motive of the person who collects can be described this way: he takes up the struggle against dispersion" (*Arcades* 211). Langbauer, quoting Haraway, notes that critics view collecting as "a practice to produce permanence, to arrest decay" (102).

25. Published in a literary magazine, the article anticipates Doyle's later forays into science fiction. It begins by describing blood circulation from the perspective of a man who can shrink himself to microscopic size and "convey himself through the coats of a living artery" ("Life" 178). A disease-fighting white blood cell would appear as "a polyp of gigantic proportions and formidable aspect": "gelatinous in consistence, and irregular in shape, capable of pushing out long prehensile tentacles with which to envelope its food" ("Life" 178). Doyle then provides a brief history of vaccination, reaching a climax with Louis Pasteur. By rendering smallpox microbes innocuous, Pasteur made his "great discovery: *If a few drops of this innocuous material be introduced into an animal's system, it is protected for ever afterwards against the original disease*" ("Life" 180, original emphasis). Doyle sees using vaccines to immunize animals as merely a prelude to their potential benefits for humans, and he concludes by looking toward a future free of diseases: "Given that a single disease . . . can be effectually and certainly stamped out, why should not all diseases depending upon similar causes be also done away with?" ("Life" 180).

26. Though infant vaccination against smallpox became mandatory in England and Wales in 1853, it remained subject to heated debate throughout the late nineteenth century. Disputes involved the question of whether the benefits of vaccination outweighed the risks. And as one of the few statutory measures imposed by the state, vaccination came to be seen as a threat to individual liberty (Barrow).

27. See Canon Harris; Childers; Keep and Randall; McLaughlin.

28. Laura Otis argues that Holmes acts as an imperial "immune system" (6, 90), but she does not consider inoculation as a means of immunity. In his discussion of foreign dirt and filth, Joseph W. Childers sees the Holmes tales working in terms similar to vaccination:

"Englishness is most formidable after being 'touched' and potentially contaminated by the other; only against the face of foreignness can it show its true mettle" (205; also see 211). But Childers associates this power with Holmes alone: his "dalliances with exotic drugs work as vaccines, allowing him to push the limits of Englishness, to move about the London cesspool with relative immunity" (217).

4. Outposts of Progress

1. Of Conrad's brief time in Borneo, biographer Zdzisław Najder writes, "To no other period of his life has so much time and inventiveness, and so many hundreds of pages of scholarly analysis and speculation, been devoted" (*Chronicle* 98). The pioneering work, by Allen and also Sherry (*Eastern*), has been followed by Gavin Young's *In Search of Conrad* (1991), as well as a study in Polish, another in German, and a French documentary (Knowles and Moore 44). According to Ian Watt, Conrad "had been ashore much too briefly to have anything but the most superficial understanding of Malay life" (44). Though Allen estimates that "Conrad spent more than three weeks altogether in Berau" (190), the settlement on which he based the setting of *Almayer's Folly* and *An Outcast of the Islands,* Sherry claims that Conrad's stay lasted "some twelve days only" (*Eastern* 139). Najder thinks these are both overestimates (*Chronicle* 520).

2. Early in 1880 Conrad lived at Tollington Park, near Finsbury Park station, then an important suburban railway junction (Weinreb and Hibbert 845). A few months later he moved to Dynevor Road in Stoke Newington, which remained his London base until 1886 (van Marle 257). In estimating Conrad's time spent in London, I have depended on Knowles.

3. On London building cycles see Dyos, "Speculative" 659–60; on the lower-middle-class influx see F. M. L. Thompson 17 and Porter 234; on transportation see Waller 159; on the term *suburbia* see Dyos and Reeder 363; and on the fiction of suburbia see Flint 70.

4. Ian Watt claims that the title's "literal reference [to Almayer's home] is largely peripheral to the action of the novel itself" (65). Thus, critics have attributed the title's significance to Almayer's racism, sham marriage, political blundering, inflated ego, dependence on others, dreams of retiring a wealthy gentleman, and even outright madness (GoGwilt 82; Watt 65–66; Watts 122–23). Daniel Schwarz reads *Almayer's Folly* as a projection of Conrad's own domestic dilemmas—particularly his emigration to England (4–5). As in *The Secret Agent* and a number of short stories, the domestic sphere in *Almayer's Folly* is a site of tension, dread, and danger. Thus, Rosemary Marangoly George reads the novel as the antithesis of Victorian domestic values, claiming that "Conrad's fiction examines the foreign, but only to make the most disturbing assessment of domestic culture" (65).

5. Derived from Lukács, the condition of transcendental homelessness is described by Torgovnick as "secular but yearning for the sacred, ironic but yearning for the absolute, individualistic but yearning for the wholeness of community" (188).

6. On Conrad's subversion of adventure tale and imperial romance motifs see White and also Dryden; on the "modernist intelligence" of *Almayer's Folly* see Lane, "Almayer's" 408–9.

7. In *The Mirror of the Sea,* Conrad provides an extended passage on "a stretch of the Thames from London Bridge to the Albert Docks," which "recalls a jungle by the confused, varied, and impenetrable aspect of the buildings that line the shore" (107–8).

8. For similar readings of colonial fiction, see McClintock and also Pecora.

9. Anthony King provides an excellent primer on both of these historical processes in *Urbanism, Colonialism, and the World-Economy.* On colonial cities in particular see Ross and Telkamp, who argue that colonialism "demanded many unequivocally urban functions":

colonial cities were needed to serve as ports, military towns, financial and governmental centers, and even industrial establishments. In this sense cities "were the very essence of colonial life" (Ross and Telkamp 1–2). On colonial cities in Conrad see Berthoud, "Modernization," and also Stape.

10. For the latter reading see Chrisman, "Tale"; Moses; and J. Williams. John Kucich has recently emphasized Conrad's "class-coded endorsement of imperialism" (235), noting that "readers eager to celebrate Conrad's selective critiques of imperialism often miss their class-bound character" (227). Rather than criticizing imperialism tout court, "Conrad remained an unforgiving critic of class ideologies that he believed degraded the imperial project" (235).

11. Kurtz may be the exception that proves the rule: though a "universal genius" in art, music, politics, and writing, he "wasn't rich enough" to gain the approval of the Intended's family, and he gave Marlow "some reason to infer that it was his impatience of comparative poverty that drove him" to Africa (71, 74). Critics have described Conrad's colonialists, and Almayer specifically, as petit bourgeois, but such references are made in passing: see Berthoud, "Introduction" xxxi; Fleishman 124; Kucich 227; Watt 52. Conrad himself described Camille Delcommune, the manager of the Société Anonyme Belge pour le Commerce du Haut-Congo and the model for the Manager in *Heart of Darkness,* as "a kind of African shop-keeper" (*Collected* 1: 62).

12. Conrad's handwritten manuscript emphasizes the folly's decay from the outset. In the published novel, Conrad excised from its opening paragraph a reference to Almayer seeking "the solitude of his new, half-built house. So new and so decayed!" The original first paragraph went on to describe the "unfinished verandah" in greater detail, with Almayer "standing carefully in the middle of the plank lest it should tilt over and precipitate him amongst the rubbish of many years, accumulated underneath" (qtd. in Eddleman and Higdon 201).

13. According to Ford, Conrad expressed enthusiasm for the sensation novelists Mrs. Henry Wood and Mary Elizabeth Braddon, as well as gratitude to "the *Family Herald*—a compilation of monthly novelettes"—for teaching him English (*Joseph Conrad* 96–97). On Conrad's supposed submission to *Tit-Bits,* see Najder, *Chronicle* 114, 339. Conrad's reading of *Punch* is mentioned in Tutein xii and also in Knowles and Moore 306.

14. Moreover, Conrad recalls reading "one of Trollope's political novels" on the eve of starting *Almayer's Folly* (*Personal* 122). This was likely *Phineas Finn,* among the works Conrad claims he was "considerably impressed with . . . in the early eighties" (qtd. in Karl 68). But he also may have known Trollope's *Three Clerks* (1858) or *Marian Fay* (1882), part of which is set in the fictional Paradise Row of Holloway, north London.

15. Lingard, as the head of the trading post Almayer ostensibly oversees, might even be seen as a backwater avatar of those "gentlemanly capitalists" who infused aristocratic values among "the lower levels of service capitalism inhabited by the likes of Pooter" (Cain and Hopkins 123). As Kucich points out, Lingard is equally "a successful tradesman and a would-be gentleman" (226).

16. Pooter's drinking causes him minor embarrassments, especially in the presence of his maid. He purchases a new suit of "green with bright yellow-coloured stripes" (228), and his brief foray into speculation costs him eighteen pounds, thanks to a bad stock tip from his son.

17. Eliot's "young man carbuncular" is a "small house agent's clerk" (*Complete* 231). Before enlisting in the Great War, Septimus Smith works under the "managing clerk at Sibleys and Arrowsmths, auctioneers, valuers, land and estate agents" (*Mrs. Dalloway* 85). Robert Crawford claims that one of Eliot's sources for *The Waste Land* was Kipling's "Finest Story in the World,"

in which a north London clerk unwittingly recalls earlier incarnations as a Greek galley slave and a Viking; Conrad twice noted his admiration for this story in the 1890s (see *Collected* 2: 108–9, 216). *The Diary of a Nobody* drew admirers from a later generation of writers, including John Betjeman, Osbert Lancaster, and J. B. Priestley. Evelyn Waugh considered it "the funniest book in the world," studying its structure and adapting its rhythms to his own work (Morton).

18. The author's note to *Almayer's Folly* makes overtures similar to the epigraph, declaring sympathy "with common mortals, no matter where they live, in houses or in huts, in the streets under a fog, or in the forests," since "their hearts—like ours—must endure . . . the curse of facts and the blessing of illusions, the bitterness of our wisdom and the deceptive consolation of our folly" (lxii).

19. "The lower middle class often feels itself to be culturally superior to the working class . . . while lacking the cultural capital and the earning power of the professional-managerial class" (Felski 35). Also see Bédarida, for whom *The Diary of a Nobody* best exemplifies the lower-middle-class "feeling of being superior to the proletariat [and] inferior to the established middle class" (208).

20. "There is not a single work of [Conrad's] . . . in which the typical, gratuitously malevolent bearer of this diseased passion does not lie in wait for the innocent and unsuspecting" (*Political* 268). Thus, Jameson sees *ressentiment* as one of Conrad's characteristic containment strategies: "We will assume . . . that the theory and vision of *ressentiment* will necessarily form the outer limit of any political or historical reflection conceived by Conrad" (*Political* 271).

21. According to the *Oxford English Dictionary,* the prefix *jury* is equivalent to *jerry,* indicating a makeshift contrivance, particularly on ships (as in *jury-mast, jury-rudder,* and *jury-tiller*).

22. Conversely, for Masterman profits from imperial expansion led directly to speculative building. Masterman describes a scenario in which a speculative builder buys land, and "borrowed money is advanced . . . from South African millionaires impatient for high interest and quick returns; and the Belle Vue or Fair Light estate is in the process of development" (*From* 42). The result is immediate decay that replicates Almayer's folly: "Ceilings bulge in; walls bulge out; paint peels off; windows break and remain unmended; water-supply and sanitary apparatus fall permanently out of repair. . . , Contemplate Belle Vue or Fair Light estate some two or three years after completion. . . . The grotesque newness of the houses, the remains of the painted lines of mortar, the pretentious pillared porticoes and iron work in the front garden yield . . . a kind of half humorous, half pathetic touch to the prevailing decay. Curtains have disappeared from the front windows; the open doors disclose passages with blackened walls and staircases gaping with holes . . . rubbish and waste paper line the gutters" (*From* 45–46).

23. See Watt 36; Najder, *Chronicle* 166; White, *Joseph Conrad* 113.

24. Of course, *A Personal Record* evokes record keeping in its title, and at significant points in his fiction Conrad uses the terms *record* and *account* with reference to narrative, documentation, payment, and confession. Marlow is especially sensitive to the richness of these terms. He repeatedly tries "to account to myself for—for—Mr. Kurtz" (*Heart* 50), no doubt recalling the fastidious bookkeeping of the accountant he so admired. And after securing Jim a safe position in Patusan, he prepares to return home, a journey that is "like going to render an account." Mixing storytelling with payment, Marlow claims that in going home "you must touch your reward with clean hands, lest it turn to dead leaves" (*Lord Jim* 206).

25. The 1854 *Fraser's* article claims the carriage ride from Batavia to Buitenzorg took "three

hours and fifty minutes" ("Excursion" 112). In the 1890s the American travel writer Eliza Ruhamah Scidmore claims the rail trip from Batavia to Buitenzorg took an "hour-and-a-half's ride" (52).

26. In concluding with some other references to colonial suburbs in Conrad, I do not want to overlook his mention of metropolitan suburbs. His later work refers to female-dominated households of dubious morality and marital tension in Leytonstone ("The Black Mate"), Norwood ("The Partner"), and an unnamed north London suburb ("Typhoon"). Suburbs also harbor male violence, misanthropy, and anarchy. In *The Mirror of the Sea*, a gun smuggler and "guileless specimen of an outcast" grew up "in a well-to-do London suburb" (158). Heyst's seclusion in *Victory* recalls that of his father, a philosopher who wrote Nietzschean tracts in "a quiet London suburb" (91). And in *The Secret Agent* the Professor's Islington home provides sanctuary for developing his perfect detonator.

5. BEYOND THE ABYSS

1. In *Efficiency and Empire* (1901) and articles for the *Weekly Sun*, Arnold White cited reports by the inspector general of recruiting that three of five army applicants in Manchester were physically unfit. Seebohm Rowntree later claimed that this ratio also applied to York, Sheffield, and Leeds. Following the war, Major General Frederick Maurice lent credibility to these claims, inspiring a panic over the status of national health. On responses to the public health scandal, see Davin; Greenslade 182–90; Searle; and Soloway.

2. Since it sought to check suburban expansion rather than reorganize existing towns, the 1909 act has been criticized as limited in scope. But it also gave impetus to further reform and inspired a town planning movement throughout Britain and the empire. As a comprehensive scheme for organizing the urban environment, which arose partly in response to "social concerns generated by the Boer War" (Sutcliffe 290), town planning would pave the way for the British New Town developments following World War II. And as I show later in this chapter and in the next, it would also transform the shape of cities and suburbs in India, Africa, and Australasia.

3. For biographical information on Masterman see Boulton as well as L. Masterman. Hynes reads Masterman as epitomizing the failure of the Edwardian liberal imagination (58).

4. Hereafter I capitalize *Suburban* to distinguish C. F. G. Masterman's version of the type.

5. Masterman reinforces this idea in his chapter on the Suburbans: "It is not from the [nouveaux riches and aristocratic] 'Conquerors' but from a rather harassed and limited Middle Class that the 'Empire builders' are now drawn," whether "by love of adventure or absence of opportunity at home" (*Condition* 62).

6. Such literary invocations are typical of Masterman's style. Boulton notes his "habit of paraphrasing passages from other writers and—one suspects—of quoting from memory with consequent errors" (viii). Boulton attributes the "extraordinarily wide range of literary reference and allusion" in Masterman's writing "to his experience as a reviewer" (xxvi).

7. The narrator of *From the Abyss* continues in this vein: "The Abyss has budded. And the bud detached from the parent stalk has fallen into the midst of a matrix of suburbs. . . . That tiny bud is destined to prove a canker which will eat out the heart of the peaceful township" (*From* 43–44). Or, in a different metaphoric register: "So in a kind of irresistible muddy wave the Abyss rolls sullenly onward. . . . In a few years the active and populous region now resisting our advance will have disappeared beneath the onward flood . . . [and] the whole line of the

suburbs will have vanished" (*From* 47–48). Yet as Bivona and Henke rightly point out, this passage suggests that "the poor of East London do not threaten the middle classes from afar but rather threaten to become them as they expand their empire geographically" (173).

8. Based on the belief that dead bodies effused toxic fluids and gases, the campaign against urban burial gained support from Chadwick's 1842 *Report on the Sanitary Condition of the Labouring Classes of Great Britain,* as well as from medical and architectural journals. Even John Claudius Loudon, the author of *The Suburban Gardener and Villa Companion,* advocated suburban burial in a later book, *On the Laying Out, Planting, and Managing of Cemeteries; and on the Improvement of Churchyards* (Brooks 32–33). Sharon Marcus shows that as reformers relegated cemeteries to the suburbs, grave sites were invested with precisely those qualities—individuality, comfort, eternal peace—said to be lacking in middle-class dwellings. Thus, "London's new suburban burial grounds had finally provided the city with a site that realized the domestic ideal so often contradicted by its houses" (128): "The ability to own a family plot meant that the one place where the London paterfamilias could realize the national and domestic implications of the phrase 'the Englishman's home is his castle' was the grave" (131).

9. Masterman's description of the cemetery at Tooting might have been penned by Foucault: "In the old English town the houses gathered comfortably by the churchyard in a kind of sanitary reformer's nightmare. For in former days it was desired that the dead should be unforgotten, and death should be much in the minds of the living. But in the modern city . . . nothing is less desired than the evidence of the end of it all. . . . So it came to pass that the dead were hurriedly shovelled into the ground at Upper Tooting" (*Peril* 155–56).

10. May suggests that Masterman could have provided Forster a model for transforming liberalism into a version of pragmatism (29–32), while Sillars points to echoes of Masterman's phraseology in *Howards End* (54–57).

11. Daniel Born uses Masterman's account of the Town type to emphasize "how carefully Forster relies on contemporary understandings of the abyss to draw his portrait of Bast" ("Private" 149). Yet Forster's narrator makes clear that Leonard "was not in the abyss, but he could see it" (35). Both Jon Hegglund and Andrew Thacker show that Bast's residences place him in lower-middle-class suburbia. Though the site of the Bast residence depicted in chapter 6 of *Howards End* is fictional, Hegglund puts it "in the south London inner suburbs" (410); Thacker, more specifically, suggests Brixton or Stockwell (55). Leonard later moves to Tulse Hill, a real neighborhood in lower Lambeth, south London, which lost its exclusive character in the 1870s when a new suburban rail line sparked a population boom (Weinreb and Hibbert 894). Hegglund sees Leonard as "reduced to the qualities and appearances of 'suburbia'" (413); Thacker emphasizes Forster's inability "to connect the novel's textual space to Bast's suburban class" (57).

12. Until recently, Jameson's essay has garnered surprisingly little comment. Among the first responses were Booth and Rigby 5–7; Parry, "Materiality" 174–75; and Stewart. Esty pursues the implications of Jameson's argument for late modernism. Chrisman offers the first substantial critique of Jameson's argument in "Imperial Space, Imperial Place." A number of contributors to the more recent collection by Begam and Moses provide further critical engagement.

13. Forster's passage recalls a number of images from Masterman's sketch "June in England," which examines the quiet countryside near a Kent train station. Masterman describes a passenger viewing "habitations" of "little red houses" as another train passes in the opposite direction, hurling "all the traffic of Empire" toward places like "Brindisi and Singapore" (*Peril* 147). Masterman's "white roads which lead to the end of the world" seem a conscious

acknowledgment of Jameson's imperial infinite, and "the wealth of South Africa [that] pours as through a funnel into the countryside" has an affect similar to that of Henry Wilcox's changes to Howards End, which I discuss below (*Peril* 149).

14. As David Bradshaw notes, rubber was the most important new commodity—and given King Leopold's methods for extracting it from the Belgian Congo, the most morally tainted—at the time Forster was writing (164).

15. However, see Kalliney for a reading of *Howards End* in relation to the garden city movement. See P. Hall for an overview of the diverse influences on Ebenezer Howard.

16. On the disciples of the garden city movement, also see Creese, *Search;* MacFadyen; Meacham.

17. On Howard's affiliation with colonization schemes at home and abroad during the 1890s, see Buder, especially chapter 5. The influence on Howard of the industrial villages built by William Lever (Port Sunlight, near Liverpool) and George Cadbury (Bourneville, near Birmingham) is worth noting here, since both their companies made products derived from colonial raw materials (Home 214).

18. A less famous example was the oil town of Abadan, Iran. See Crinson, *Modern* 66–71.

19. "Shaw challenged the initial premise of the garden city movement, that a non-capitalist utopia could be built upon money market borrowings . . . held under a trust deed. The garden city's need to compete for private capital and offer competitive terms would preclude attempts to appropriate the benefits of rising land values for a self-governing garden city community" (Hebbert 167).

20. For a fuller account of *John Bull's Other Island* and *Major Barbara* in relation to the garden city movement, see Grene 138–41.

21. Dennis Hardy claims that Wells once served as vice president of the Garden City Association (*Utopian* 98). As the biographer David Smith points out, Wells wrote a series of articles on utopian cities for the *Daily Mail* in 1905, the first of which was an attack on Howard's garden city (186). For an overview of Wells's thinking on the World State, see Partington, especially chapters 3 and 4. For a fascinating meditation on the links among Wellsian globalism, interdisciplinarity, and contemporary cultural studies, see Fluet, "H. G. Wells."

22. Wells contrasts the advantages of centrifugal and centripetal lifestyles: the first offers a healthy environment with access to nature and a greater potential for residential privacy, while the second provides convenience for communication and shopping, access to schools and doctors, and proximity to crowds and fashions. Part of his prophecy—that the city center will become a "great gallery of shops and places of concourse and rendezvous," with moving sidewalks and weatherproof enclosures (*Anticipations* 62)—would become fodder for the Saturday matinees. But in ways we can recognize today, he also foresaw that improvements in transport and communication would gradually loosen the strictures that bind citizens to the urban center. There would be less need to keep businesses and trades tethered to cities, while telephone and parcel services would replace crucial errands like visiting the shops.

23. For contemporary reactions to Wells's scheme, see Young and Garside 107–12.

24. Brantlinger reads Teddy Ponderevo's dubious speculative gains "in contrast to the pastoral calm and prosperity of Bladesover" (*Fictions* 209). Parry claims that "finance has displaced the fixed scheme of place, rank and precedence sustained by rent" (*"Tono-Bungay"* 99). T. Richards reads Bladesover as "a fossil embedded in the capitalist world economy" (90). In perhaps the most insightful recent analysis of *Tono-Bungay,* William Kupinse sees waste purely as a product of multinational capitalism. Daniel Born is correct that *Tono-Bungay* "disavow[s]

any hopes that England's future lies in a revitalized country aristocracy," but as my reading of the novel suggests, I disagree with Born that Wells "promptly demolishe[s]" the power of the country estate in *Tono-Bungay*, "blowing the whole house down" and "sweep[ing] the stage clear at the outset" (*Birth* 150).

25. On the links between George's experiments and Teddy's business, see Born, *Birth* 155; Kupinse 60; and Parry, "*Tono-Bungay*" 101. T. Richards sees George's experiments as "a new and better Bladesover system ruled by science" (103). Cheyette sees George's scientific work as an extension of both Tono-Bungay and Bladesover (xl), and he reads the novel's closing as "an extravagant parody of Britain's colonial pretensions," with George "implicated in the worst aspects of Britain's Imperial plutocracy" (xli).

6. *Ressentiment* and Late-Imperial Fiction

1. An early literary confidant of Forster, Woolf motivated him to complete *Passage* when his enthusiasm was waning (Furbank 2: 106). "When writing the *Passage* I thought it a failure," Forster later claimed, "and it was only owing to Leonard that I was encouraged to finish it" (*Selected* 2: 152).

2. On anti-suburban sentiment between the two world wars, see V. Cunningham 256–60; Dentith, "Thirties"; and Oliver, Davis, and Bentley.

3. As Narayani Gupta suggests, "The first serious attempt at long-term town-planning for Delhi's urban area" grew out of "the combined fear of the old town encroaching on and spoiling the symmetry of the new, and of the 'Indian town' (a term now used for Delhi city, with a patently racialist overtone) polluting the imperial one" (181).

4. Until recently, scholarship on colonial cities tended to echo Fanon's dichotomy of white town and native town. However, urbanists and architectural historians including Rebecca Brown, Swati Chattopadhyay, William J. Glover, and Jyoti Hosagrahar have begun to challenge this model, arguing that more fluid and permeable boundaries existed between Anglo and indigenous quarters in cities like Patna, Calcutta, Lahore, and Delhi. Indeed, Hosagrahar demonstrates that a residential development for Indians was planned outside Delhi in the late 1880s to relieve the city's congestion and encourage business growth: "Unlike in the city, people of different castes, occupational groups, or religious persuasion could be neighbors in the new suburban development" (125). However, financial problems plagued the development, which fell by the wayside once New Delhi was begun. I would like to thank Anthony King for directing me to these sources.

5. On urban segregation and suburban development after 1857, also see Wolpert 244–45. King writes that "though spatially segregated," Indians and Britons "lived as neighbours in adjoining neighbourhoods" of pre-1857 Delhi (*Colonial* 208). This seems more measured than Home's claim that "before the Mutiny British officials and Indian citizens had often lived and worked side by side" (123).

6. Before 1857 Bankipore (or Bankipur) served as Patna's residential area for employees of the East India Company. Rebecca Brown argues that in this period "Bankipur's categorization lies in a nebulous space somewhere between a separate town and a distant suburb" (162).

7. British communities in India were often planned this way, "not out of sight of the 'native town' but with sufficient distance between to ensure that . . . it should appear only as a distant element in a 'view'" (King, *Colonial* 153). Like Forster, Waugh scoffs at the pleasaunce afforded by garden city principles, but for him their effects are less cosmetic than impractical.

His English legation, "a miniature garden city in a stockaded compound," is cut off from the capital by a road "encumbered with boulders, landslides, and fallen trees" (*Black* 65). The passage recalls Waugh's 1931 African travelogue, *Remote People,* in which he describes the British legation outside Addis Ababa as "a little garden city . . . of pretty thatched bungalows," whose distance from the town is doubly ineffective, providing neither protection from nor interaction with the indigenes (31). As in England, where otherwise progressive planning often resulted in segregated suburbs, Forster and Waugh suggest that the nominal advocacy of such schemes in the colonies exacerbates cultural differences and undermines social integration.

8. Despite encouragements for the Victorian working classes to take up gardening, it remained an activity of the urban and rural elite until the house-building boom of the 1920s and 1930s. Indeed, most of the four million new homes constructed in England and Wales during this time came with attached private gardens (Constantine 395). A reduction in working hours and a rise in wages and vacation time also contributed to the popularity of gardening, but it was only "with the spread of owner-occupied suburbia in the 1920s [that] a garden became an inalienable right, and gardening a national occupation" (Ottewill 139).

Perhaps the most substantial interwar jeremiad against the deterioration of national reading taste is Q. D. Leavis's *Fiction and the Reading Public,* which lambastes magazines and newspapers for suggesting to "the ordinary uncritical man" that "it is pleasanter to be one of the herd, i.e. less wear and tear is involved in conforming than in standing out against mass sentiment; righteousness and goodwill are accordingly arrogated to the man who behaves like his fellows, the lowbrow, who accepts uncritically the restrictions imposed by the herd" (194). The comment speaks not only to the effects of popular periodicals on the suburban middle class, Leavis's ostensible target, but also to their impact on highly insular groups like the imperial elite. Indeed, Forster refers to Chandrapore's club as a place where the "herd-instinct" flourishes (65), and his comments on *Punch* in "Notes on the English Character" ("There is neither wit, laughter, nor satire in our national jester—only the snigger of a suburban householder who can understand nothing that does not resemble himself" [*Abinger* 9]) clearly compare with the attitude of the British clubs of late-imperial fiction.

9. Such moments of failed excess recall Homi Bhabha's description of Englishness in a colonial setting. "What is 'English,'" writes Bhabha, "cannot be represented as a plenitudinous presence; it is determined by its belatedness. . . . Paradoxically, however, such an image [of Englishness] can neither be 'original'—by virtue of the act of repetition that constructs it—nor 'identical'—by virtue of the difference that defines it. Consequently, the colonial presence is always ambivalent, split between its appearance as original and authoritative and its articulation as repetition and difference" (107). As Bhabha suggests, the "plenitudinous presence" of Englishness in imperial society masks neither its "belatedness" (as figured in the Forster passage above by the profusion of bygone cultural relics like dated newspapers and passé plays) nor its difference from an original Englishness (as suggested by the national anthem or the European food).

10. "The knightly-aristocratic value-judgments presuppose a powerful physicality, a rich, burgeoning, even overflowing health, as well as all those things which help to preserve it—war, adventure, hunting, dancing, competitive games, and everything which involves strong, free, high-spirited activity" (Nietzsche 19).

11. "The aristocratic mode of evaluation acts and grows spontaneously," according to Nietzsche; by contrast, slave morality "from the outset always needs an opposing, outer world . . .

its action is fundamentally reaction" (22). It is perhaps worth contrasting Hegel with Nietz-sche vis-à-vis the role of action in master-slave relations. For Hegel action allows the slave to overcome the master: while the former labors, exercising praxis and gaining consciousness, the latter remains static, losing possession of the world. For Nietzsche the slave remains inactive—or to be more precise, reactive—but overcomes the master all the same, transforming his values rather than the world itself.

12. Though I draw on Memmi here, Ranajit Guha's psychoanalytic model, which considers imperial isolation in terms of anxiety and the uncanny, is also pertinent. Guha argues that while British isolation was integral to maintaining "dominance without hegemony" (or autocracy without consent), such insularity made the colonizer's inevitable interaction with indigenous society all the more unsettling: "What made [the isolation] worse and difficult to forget was the absurdity of Britain's claim to have fitted the roundness of colonial autocracy to the squareness of metropolitan liberalism. A sore that refused to heal, it went on festering by being compul-sively touched" (485).

13. Rather than emphasizing the colonizer's attempt to create a nostalgic simulacrum of home, however, Memmi emphasizes the colonizer's indifference to the living space of the colo-nized: "Why does [the colonizer] do nothing about town planning . . . ? When he complains about the presence of bacterially infected lakes at the gates of the city, of overflowing sewers or poorly functioning utilities, he seems to forget that he holds the power in the government and should assume the blame. Why does he not direct his efforts in a disinterested manner, or is he unable to? . . . The true reason, the principal reason for most deficiencies is that the colonial-ist never planned to transform the colony into the image of his homeland, nor to remake the colonized in his own image!" (68–69).

14. Curiously, however, the Collector later projects his repressed hatred of Indians onto Adela. He admits to himself: "'I don't hate [Indians], I don't know why,' and he didn't hate them; for if he did, he would have to condemn his own career as a bad investment. He retained a contemptuous affection for the pawns he had moved about for so many years, they must be worth his pains. 'After all, it's our women who make everything more difficult out here,' was his inmost thought . . . and beneath his chivalry to Miss Quested resentment lurked, waiting its day—perhaps there is a grain of resentment in all chivalry" (237).

15. Unlike the Nietzschean master, who in no way requires an other to confirm his identity or spur his action, the colonizer depends on the colonized to give his existence meaning—an axiom postcolonial critique has appropriated from Hegelian dialectics and structuralism. Thus, whatever satisfaction Ronny derives from his work is because "it prove[s] that the British [are] necessary to India" (103). This mentality brings with it the presumption that the work of empire entails serving some higher power—civilization, justice—at the expense of personal comfort. It is fitting, then, that Ronny Heaslop should be a magistrate: as Nietzsche suggests, the man of *ressentiment* "attempts to sanctify *revenge* under the name of *justice*" (54, original emphasis). Indeed, while Ronny imagines that his quest for justice lessens his imperial burden, it is clear that *ressentiment* provides his true solace: "Every day [Ronny] worked hard in the court trying to decide which of two untrue accounts was the less untrue, trying to dispense jus-tice fearlessly. . . . He expected no gratitude, no recognition for this. . . . It was his duty" (52). The Anglo-Indian work ethic to which Ronny so thoroughly subscribes is not action in the Nietzschean sense, however, but reaction: a sublimated suffering for the greater good of empire that finds an outlet in dispensing "justice." Nietzsche unmasks the apparent disinterestedness of such "justice" as a deep-seated longing for vengeance, a longing continually reinforced by a

job that suggests Ronny can do nothing effectual. As magistrate of Chandrapore, Ronny enacts on its Indian populace the bitterness of the entire imperial community.

16. On the contrary, Fielding, whose defense against *ressentiment* is that he "travel[s] light" (131, 303), does not carry with him to India the same baggage for re-creating home by denying or ignoring the East. He can act as he wants because he has nothing to lose. Sitting on a train next to two Anglo-Indian males—a newcomer and a seasoned veteran—Fielding realizes: "A gulf divided him from either; he had seen too many cities and men to be the first or to become the second. New impressions crowded on him, but they were not the orthodox new impressions; the past conditioned them" (64). Fielding evades the reign of *ressentiment* because he is able to keep the past in harmony with the present, without one overtaking the other.

17. Christopher Lane also alludes to moments of what might be described as *ressentiment*—although he does not refer to the affect as such—in Forster's aesthetic practice. Of *Passage* Lane writes that "the gap between Forster's liberal vision and his narrative's faltering practice underscores a caesura between what he represents as the novel's ideal (harmony, union) and what he demonstrates inadvertently is part of its colonial practice (acrimony, division)" ("Volatile" 194). Likewise, Lane claims that in "The Life to Come" and "The Other Boat," there is a "substitution of hostility for desire [that] again seems to resolve an otherwise insoluble drama" ("Volatile" 208). For Lane such instances reveal "that liberalism is both inattentive to historical antagonisms, and that it displaces unconscious hostility, suspicion, and aversion toward the 'other'" ("Volatile" 199).

18. See JanMohamed, "Economy"; Parry, "Materiality"; Said; and Suleri.

19. Indeed, some read the narrator here as Fielding himself: see McClure 128–29.

20. JanMohamed attributes the bitterness of Cary, who served as a district officer in Nigeria, to his isolation: feeling betrayed and exploited by the colonial government, Cary also experienced "a paranoid fear of [African] unpredictability" and "the consequent assumption of savagery" (*Manichean* 23).

21. Seth is based loosely on the Ethiopian ruler Ras Tafari, whose 1930 coronation Waugh covered for the *Times,* the *Daily Express,* and the *Graphic.* Among other schemes, including Soviet-style economic planning, mandatory birth control, and the widespread use of Esperanto, Seth busies himself in meticulous urban planning, "orient[ing] all the roads . . . by the points of the compass. I cannot upset my arrangements" (169). Later, Waugh has Seth "moodily pouring [*sic*] over the map of the new city" amid strikes and evacuations, complaining that a cathedral has not yet been demolished for his new road: "You see it is right in the way of the great Northern thoroughfare. Look at it on the plan—so straight" (241). Such mockery is aimed at modern town planning methods as well as the geometric Corbusien architecture that Waugh despised.

22. As Terry Eagleton points out (75, 77–78), Flory's entrance recalls another representative of lower-middle-class resentment: Flory's initial thoughts upon looking at the Burmese town of Kyauktada—"Bloody, bloody hole!" (18)—invoke the opening curse of Wells's dyspeptic protagonist in *The History of Mr. Polly.* On Orwell's fiction and lower-middle-class identity, see Eagleton; Felski.

23. Alan Jackson claims that the piano was a crucial signifier of gentility among even the lowliest of suburbans, as reflected by the phrase "Pride, Poverty and a Piano" (48).

24. A curious footnote: reviewing Greene's *The Heart of the Matter,* Orwell complained that the novel was so removed from its African setting that "the whole thing might as well be happening in a London suburb" (*Collected* 4: 440).

7. GEORGE ORWELL AND THE ROAD TO WEST BLETCHLEY

1. On links between *Coming Up for Air* and *Nineteen Eighty-Four,* see J. R. Hammond 147; J. Hunter 44; L. Hunter 211; Meyers, "Apocalypse" 71, 76; Patai 184; Van Dellen 65; and Woodcock 128, 142. Critics have overlooked the subtle if sustained imperial subtext of *Coming Up for Air,* despite recent works by Kristin Bluemel, Christopher Hitchens, and John Newsinger that emphasize Orwell's vocal and long-standing engagement with imperialism—not simply in his colonial writing, but as part of his wider political outlook until his death.

2. In 1932 Stanley Baldwin proclaimed in Parliament that it was important "for the man in the street to realize that there is no power on earth that can prevent him from being bombed" (qtd. in Graves and Hodge 326). Rod Brookes points out that Baldwin presented himself as a version of the little man (32).

3. Of Smith's "Suburban Classes" Kristin Bluemel writes: "The poem's humor keeps readers from totally identifying Smith's attitude toward her subject with the contempt of its speaker, although the poem's satire also distances Smith from the inhabitants of Palmers Green," the suburb that was her lifelong home (63). Simon Dentith points out that "Betjeman's assault on the horrors of suburban England" in "Slough" "merely comes from someone who inhabits an older and more established suburb" ("Thirties" 113).

4. The threat of England being bombed is a recurrent motif in *Coming Up for Air* and *Keep the Aspidistra Flying;* it also concludes *Homage to Catalonia* (1938) and opens *The Lion and the Unicorn* (1941).

5. Brought up in England, Orwell was born Eric Blair in India, where his father worked as an opium agent for the Raj. Blair's mother grew up in a family of teak merchants in Burma, where he served as a police officer from 1922 to 1927 and where his maternal grandmother remained until his return. In addition, his paternal great-grandfather ran a Jamaican plantation and owned slaves (Crick 6, 97). It was precisely this imperial connection that placed his family in the "lower-upper-middle class," the type of family "struggling to live genteel lives on what are virtually working-class incomes" (*Road* 122, 124). Ingle claims that imperialism influenced Orwell's account of his public school days, "Such, Such Were the Joys," in which he portrays his young self "not as exploiter but as exploited" (12).

6. Also see Patai 49; Shelden 106; Stansky 229–34; and Woodcock 61.

7. Nor should we overlook Orwell's violently mixed feelings toward the Burmese. In "Shooting an Elephant" he acknowledges both his "rage against the evil-spirited little beasts who tried to make my job impossible" in Burma and his feeling while there that "the greatest joy in the world would be to drive a bayonet into a Buddhist priest's guts" (*Collected* 1: 236).

8. Crick claims that Orwell "backdates" his view of poverty as a form of colonization (108). Hammond likewise suggests that Orwell retroactively justified his poverty to align with his anti-imperialism: *Wigan Pier* implies Orwell's "smooth transition" from British colonizer to English tramp, with no "mention [of] his five years in the literary wilderness, nor the interval he spent living in Paris" (126).

9. Guilt is key to Meyers's Orwell, framing his biography from its opening sentence ("George Orwell was burdened from birth by colonial guilt") and casting a shadow over Orwell's youth ("He felt guilty about his colonial heritage, his bourgeois background, his inbred snobbery, and his elite education") (*Orwell* 3, 15).

10. In his conclusion to *Wigan Pier,* Orwell refers again to this "sinking middle class—the private schoolmaster, the half-starved free-lance journalist, the colonel's spinster daughter with

£75 a year, the jobless Cambridge graduate, the ship's officer without a ship, the clerks, the civil servants, the commercial travellers and thrice bankrupt drapers in the country towns" (232).

11. Rai summarizes Orwell's embrace of socialism in similar terms: "Identifying with 'victims,' Orwell becomes a socialist: yet being a 'victim' (his own, for he is also the 'victimiser'), Orwell must cling to his own cultural characteristics" (76–77).

12. Crick gives Hampstead locations for some of the novel's fictional addresses: "Willowbed Road [where Gordon lodges] for Willouhby Road and Coleridge Grove [an acquaintance's home] for Keats Grove" (162).

13. Reading *Coming Up* in relation to "Inside the Whale," Robert J. Van Dellen argues that the novel suggests the individual can survive modern technocracy "only if he passively submits to it" (63). But rather than defeat, this submission "not only means endurance, it means the ultimate victory of man's basic humanity" (66). Annette Federico examines *Coming Up* via Michel de Certeau's tactics of quotidian subversion, arguing that the novel's "liberatory potential . . . is derived less from a position of overt rebellion against the existing order than from a position of faith in the existence of the ordinary as a repository of meaning in a technocratic, politically unstable, and almost entirely secular society" (51). David Kubal claims: "Not only is Bowling the 'crystal spirit' which Orwell counted on to endure totalitarianism, but also . . . he embodies all the basic elements of Orwell's socialism: He is middle class, yet deeply part of the common culture; furthermore, Bowling is something of an intellectual, widely read and knowledgeable" (119). In a feminist reading that attacks Bowling's (and Orwell's) misogyny, Patai calls this "a bizarre socialism, if true" (195).

14. On Orwell's image as Don Quixote, see Rodden 121–34.

15. In his cultural history of the bowler, Fred Miller Robinson examines a range of the hat's semantic associations: "sport, leisure, urbanity, suburbanity, finance, respectability, conformity, democracy, aspiration, comedy, capitalism, republicanism, Jews" (7). Though these associations are broadly middle-class, Robinson emphasizes the bowler's distinctly lower-middle-class identity (32–57).

16. E. D. Mackerness points out that in the late eighteenth century the English government paid ballad writers to "awaken a sense of national pride. The outstanding example of this is Charles Dibdin" (135). *Tom Bowling* is also the title of an 1841 novel by Frederick Chamier, whose work is modeled on the sea tales of Captain Frederick Marryat (Brantlinger, *Rule* 49).

17. Between 1932 and 1933 Orwell was a schoolmaster in Hayes, "one of the most godforsaken places I have ever struck" (*Collected* 1: 81).

18. Orwell refers to "the empire-racket" in *Wigan Pier* (159) and claims in an autobiographical note that his years in Burma led him to see imperialism "as very largely a racket" (*Collected* 2: 23). In a letter composed while writing *Coming Up for Air* in French Morocco, Orwell notes that the colony lacks the "white man's burden atmosphere" of British colonies. "But economically it is just the usual swindle for which empires exist" (*Complete* 11: 239).

19. Orwell has been faulted on this count not only by feminists like Patai. Woodcock, for example, notes his recurrent use of female characters who (sometimes unwittingly) tempt men into conformity, whether via marriage or the Thought Police (102–4, 142).

20. In *Aspidistra* women serve as less concentrated signifiers of colonial authority. Gordon's girlfriend, Rosemary, has brothers who "were farming in Canada, on tea-plantations in Ceylon, in obscure regiments of the Indian Army" (111)—obvious contrasts to Gordon's rebellious anti-heroism. A female customer whom Gordon attends to in the bookshop is "middle-aged,

tough and curried—India, presumably," with "the voice of a drill-sergeant. She was no doubt a colonel's wife, or widow" (17).

21. Tom Jeffery notes that Left Book Club groups reflected the surprising upswing in lower-middle-class radicalism during the 1930s: "More than 2,000 groups, Aid Committees, Food-ships Committees, Basque Children's Committees . . . notably strong in the suburbs, adopted every conceivable means of raising relief for Spain. In 1937 and 1938 the London suburbs hummed with the activity of these groups" (87).

22. Crick claims there is no evidence why he chose Morocco (249); Shelden attributes the choice to Orwell's doctors (296). In a letter Orwell writes that he originally planned on southern France, but "they [doctors?] now say I ought to spend the winter in Africa, so as far as we have any definite plan we are arranging to go to Morocco" (*Complete* 11: 188). For Woodcock Morocco's influence in *Coming Up for Air* "was probably its complete difference from the England which was once again the subject of his novel. I suspect that distance from the subject had a great deal to do with the high color and great vitality of *Coming Up for Air* in comparison with his two previous books" (122). Crick claims that while Orwell "contrived to work knowledgeable references to North Africa into reviews and minor wartime writings, the experience did not affect him in any other obvious way" (249).

23. Orwell's avowed boredom in Morocco may have resulted from his inability to forge local ties. In one letter he describes the trip as "something quite new to me, because for the first time I am in the position of a tourist. The result is that it is quite impossible . . . to make any contact with the Arabs, whereas if I were here, say, on a gun-running expedition, I should immediately have the entrée to all kinds of interesting society" (*Collected* 1: 353). In another letter he writes: "I don't know how it would compare with the poorer parts of India, but Burma would seem like a paradise compared to it, so far as standard of living goes. The French are evidently squeezing the country pretty ruthlessly. . . . On the surface their administration looks better than ours and certainly rouses less animosity in the subject race, because they have very little colour-prejudice. But I think underneath it is much the same" (*Complete* 11: 237).

24. Among the few commentators to link Orwell's anti-imperialism to the role of Morocco in the Spanish Civil War are Hitchens 21–22 and Newsinger 12.

25. The logic of this argument is debatable. The historian Sebastian Balfour claims that while the Spanish government's refusal to grant independence did help Franco recruit Moroccans, many signed on to support their families after a period of drought and bad harvests (273–74): "The fundamental motive . . . for the successful recruitment of thousands of Moroccans into the ranks of the rebel army was economic" (273). Religion also played a role, as many Muslims believed themselves to be supporting a crusade against the godless Spanish Republic (Balfour 273; Esenwein 154). Moreover, by collaborating with Spain, some Moroccans could gain an upper hand in long-standing intertribal disputes (Balfour 193). It is unclear whether Moroccan independence would have trumped these factors. Nevertheless, Balfour implicitly agrees with Orwell's claim that Morocco secured Franco's victory: "It is unquestionable that the Nationalists would have been defeated had they risen without the participation of the Army of Africa" (312).

26. In *The Road to Wigan Pier,* for example, Orwell blames socialism's inability to take hold in England on the eccentrics it typically attracts: "One sometimes gets the impression that the mere words 'Socialism' and 'Communism' draw towards them with magnetic force every fruit-juice drinker, nudist, sandal-wearer, sex-maniac, Quaker, 'Nature Cure' quack, pacifist and feminist in England" (174). For similar catalogs see *Road* 182, 216, 222.

27. In this sense I disagree with Michael Levenson's otherwise excellent recent overview of Orwell's 1930s novels, in which he describes Orwell's "open nostalgia" in *Coming Up* as "unembarrassedly affirmative" and "frankly sentimental" (72–73).

28. For an overview of postwar residential development, see Clapson, *Invincible*.

29. Richards served in the position from 1943 to 1946 and claims he wrote *Castles* "during spare moments in the Middle East" (*Memoirs* 188). His suburban memories were based on his childhood years in Carshalton, Surrey (*Memoirs* 27). (Thanks to Rebecca Preston for pointing me to Richards's memoir.) Elizabeth Wilson claims that writing in Cairo accentuated Richards's "romantic re-creation of [his] own past as well as of a distant, almost dreamlike place" (106). Richards would have been sensitive to the relation between architecture and empire, having not only served in Egypt but written on the problem of projecting an imperial identity in architecture (Crinson, *Modern* 91, 120).

Epilogue

1. During the 1970s most Caribbeans of African descent remained in inner London, while half of the Indian population moved to the suburbs (Sassen 270). For a more nuanced mapping of South Asian settlement in London, see Eade, Fremeaux, and Garbin: "Indian and Pakistani settlement overlapped across three main areas—(a) the western and north-western belt running from Finchley round to Wembley and down to Hounslow, (b) the northeast between Newham and Waltham Forest, and (c) the southern concentration of Totting." Bangladeshis tended to congregate more closely to the urban center (161).

2. In contrast, suburbia is a site of displacement for Naipaul's Ralph Singh, an exiled government minister from a fictional Commonwealth country. Singh notes that while "so many of my fellow exiles . . . live in a suburban semi-detached house," he "could not pretend even to myself to be part of a community," writing his memoirs in a "far-out suburban hotel" (13–14). For more on postcolonial and multiracial writing about suburbia, see Childs and also Procter 125–59.

3. I would like to thank the students in my spring 2005 postcolonial literature course at Western Michigan University for shaping my reading of this scene.

BIBLIOGRAPHY

Aalen, Frederick H. A. "English Origins." In S. V. Ward, 28–51.

Abeyasekere, Susan. *Jakarta: A History.* Singapore: Oxford UP, 1987.

Ackroyd, Peter. *T. S. Eliot: A Life.* New York: Simon and Schuster, 1984.

Adams, Ian H. *The Making of Urban Scotland.* London: Croom Helm, 1978.

Allen, Jerry. *The Sea Years of Joseph Conrad.* Garden City, NY: Doubleday, 1965.

Almond, Hely Hutchinson. "The Breed of Man." *Nineteenth Century* 48 (October 1900): 668.

Anderson, Benedict. *Imagined Communities: Reflections on the Origin and Spread of Nationalism.* Rev. ed. London: Verso, 1991.

Anderson, G. L. "The Social Economy of Late-Victorian Clerks." In Crossick, 113–33.

"Anglo-Indian's and English Opinions." Letter. *Times* 25 September 1891: 7.

"An Anglo-Indian's Complaint." Letter. *Times* 25 September 1891: 6.

Arata, Stephen. *Fictions of Loss in the Victorian Fin de Siècle.* Cambridge: Cambridge UP, 1996.

Archer, John. *Architecture and Suburbia: From English Villa to American Dream House, 1690–2000.* Minneapolis: U of Minnesota P, 2005.

———. "Colonial Suburbs in South Asia, 1700–1850, and the Spaces of Modernity." In Silverstone, 26–54.

Auden, W. H. *Collected Longer Poems.* 1969. New York: Random House, 2002.

Bachelard, Gaston. *The Poetics of Space.* 1964. Trans. Maria Jolas. Boston: Beacon, 1994.

Balfour, Sebastian. *Deadly Embrace: Morocco and the Road to the Spanish Civil War.* Oxford: Oxford UP, 2002.

Ball, John Clement. *Imagining London: Postcolonial Fiction and the Transnational Metropolis.* Toronto: U of Toronto P, 2004.

Barolsky, Paul. "The Case of the Domesticated Aesthete." *Critical Essays on Sir Arthur Conan Doyle.* Ed. Harold Orel. New York: G. K. Hall, 1992. 92–102.

Barrow, Logie. "Clashing Knowledge-Claims in Nineteenth-Century English Vaccination." *Cultural Approaches to the History of Medicine: Mediating Medicine in Early Modern and Modern Europe.* Ed. Willem de Blécourt and Cornelie Usborne. Hampshire, UK: Palgrave, 2004. 171–91.

Baucom, Ian. *Out of Place: Englishness, Empire, and the Locations of Identity.* Princeton: Princeton UP, 1999.

Baudelaire, Charles. *"The Painter of Modern Life" and Other Essays.* London: Phaidon, 1964.

Beauman, Nicola. *Morgan: A Biography of E. M. Forster.* London: Hodder and Stoughton, 1993.

Bebbington, Gillian. *London Street Names.* London: Batsford, 1972.

Bédarida, François. *A Social History of England 1851–1990.* 2nd ed. Trans. A. S. Forster and Jeffrey Hodkinson. London: Routledge, 1991.

Begam, Richard, and Michael Valdez Moses, eds. *Modernism and Colonialism: British and Irish Literature, 1899–1939.* Durham: Duke UP, 2007.

Benjamin, Walter. *The Arcades Project.* Trans. Howard Eiland and Kevin McLaughlin. Cambridge, MA: Harvard UP, 1999.

———. *Illuminations.* Trans. Harry Zohn. New York: Schocken, 1968.

Bergonzi, Bernard. *The Early H. G. Wells: A Study of the Scientific Romances.* Manchester: Manchester UP, 1961.

Bernstein, Michael André. "The Poetics of *Ressentiment.*" *Rethinking Bakhtin: Extensions and Challenges.* Ed. Gary Saul Morson and Caryl Emerson. Evanston, IL: Northwestern UP, 1989. 197–223.

Berthoud, Jacques. "Introduction: Conrad's Realism." Conrad, *Almayer's Folly* xi–xxxviii.

———. "The Modernization of Sulaco." In Moore, 139–57.

Besant, Walter. *London, South of the Thames.* London: Adam and Charles Black, 1912.

Betjeman, John. *Collected Poems.* New York: Farrar, 2006.

Bhabha, Homi K. *The Location of Culture.* London: Routledge, 1994.

Birch, Dinah. "A Life in Writing: Ruskin and the Uses of Suburbia." *Writing and Victorianism.* Ed. J. B. Bullen. London: Longman, 1997. 234–49.

Bivona, Dan, and Roger B. Henke. *The Imagination of Class: Masculinity and the Victorian Urban Poor.* Columbus: The Ohio State UP, 2006.

Bluemel, Kristin. *George Orwell and the Radical Eccentrics: Intermodernism in Literary London.* New York: Palgrave, 2004.

Bolsterli, Margaret Jones. *The Early Community at Bedford Park: "Corporate Happiness" in the First Garden Suburb.* Athens: Ohio UP, 1977.

Bolus-Reichert, Christine. "Everyday Eclecticism: William Morris and the Suburban Picturesque." *Nineteenth-Century Prose* 29.2 (2002): 162–96.

Bongie, Chris. *Exotic Memories: Literature, Colonialism, and the Fin de Siècle.* Stanford: Stanford UP, 1991.

———. "Exotic Nostalgia: Conrad and the New Imperialism." *Macropolitics of Nineteenth-Century Literature: Nationalism, Exoticism, Imperialism.* Ed. Jonathan Arac and Harriet Ritvo. Philadelphia: U of Pennsylvania P, 1991. 268–85.

Booth, Charles. *Life and Labour of the People in London.* 17 vols. London: Macmillan, 1902–3.

Booth, Howard, and Nigel Rigby, eds. *Modernism and Empire: Writing and British Coloniality, 1890–1940.* Manchester: Manchester UP, 2000.

Booth, William. *In Darkest England and the Way Out.* 1890. New York: Funk and Wagnalls, 1891.

Born, Daniel. *The Birth of Liberal Guilt in the English Novel: Charles Dickens to H. G. Wells.* Chapel Hill: U of North Carolina P, 1995.

———. "Private Gardens, Public Swamps: *Howards End* and the Revaluation of Liberal Guilt." *Novel* 25.2 (1992): 141–59.

Boulton, J. T. "Editor's Introduction." *The Condition of England.* By C.F.G. Masterman. London: Methuen, 1960. ix–xxix.

Bourdieu, Pierre. *Distinction: A Social Critique of the Judgement of Taste.* Trans. Richard Nice. Cambridge, MA: Harvard UP, 1984.

Bradshaw, David. "*Howards End.*" *The Cambridge Companion to E. M. Forster.* Ed. David Bradshaw. Cambridge: Cambridge UP, 2007. 151–72.

Brantlinger, Patrick. *Fictions of State: Culture and Credit in Britain, 1694–1994.* Ithaca: Cornell UP, 1996.

———. *Rule of Darkness: British Literature and Imperialism, 1830–1914.* Ithaca: Cornell UP, 1988.

Briggs, Asa. *Victorian Cities.* 1963. New York: Harper, 1970.

Briggs, R. A. *Bungalows and Country Residences: A Series of Designs and Examples of Recently Executed Works.* London: Batsford, 1891.

Brookes, Rod. "'Everything in the Garden Is Lovely': The Representation of National Identity in Sidney Strube's *Daily Express* Cartoons in the 1930s." *Oxford Art Journal* 13.2 (1990): 31–43.

Brooks, Chris. *Mortal Remains: The History and Present State of the Victorian and Edwardian Cemetery.* Exeter: Wheaton, 1989.

Brown, Rebecca M. "The Cemeteries and the Suburbs: Patna's Challenges to the Colonial City in South Asia." *Journal of Urban History* 29.2 (2003): 151–72.

Buchan, John. *The Thirty-Nine Steps.* 1915. Ware: Wordsworth, 1993.

Buder, Stanley. *Visionaries and Planners: The Garden City Movement and the Modern Community.* New York: Oxford UP, 1990.

Buettner, Elizabeth. *Empire Families: Britons and Late Imperial India.* New York: Oxford UP, 2004.

———. "From Somebodies to Nobodies: Britons Returning Home From India." *Meanings of Modernity: Britain from the Late-Victorian Era to World War II.* Ed. Martin Daunton and Bernhard Rieger. Oxford: Berg, 2001. 221–40.

"Buitenzorg." *The Encyclopedia Britannica.* 11th ed. 1911.

Bullock, Shan. *Robert Thorne: The Story of a London Clerk.* London: T. Werner Laurie, 1907.

Burgan, Mary. "Mapping Contagion in Victorian London: Disease in the East End." *Victorian Urban Settings: Essays on the Nineteenth-Century City and Its Contexts.* Ed. Debra N. Mancoff and D. J. Trela. New York: Garland, 1996. 43–56.

Burke, Andrew. "Life and Death in Suburbia." *Culture of Cities . . . Under Construction.* Ed. Paul Moore and Meredith Risk. Oakville, ON: Mosaic, 2001. 147–55.

Burnett, John. *A Social History of Housing: 1815–1970.* Newton Abbot: David and Charles, 1978.

Burton, Antoinette, ed. *After the Imperial Turn: Thinking with and through the Nation.* Durham: Duke UP, 2003.

Cain, P. J., and A. G. Hopkins. *British Imperialism: Innovation and Expansion 1688–1914.* London: Longman, 1993.

Cannon Harris, Susan. "Pathological Possibilities: Contagion and Empire in Doyle's Sherlock Holmes Stories." *Victorian Literature and Culture* 31.2 (2003): 447–66.

Cantlie, James. *Degeneration amongst Londoners.* 1885. New York: Garland, 1985.

Carey, John. *The Intellectuals and the Masses: Pride and Prejudice among the Literary Intelligentsia, 1880–1939.* London: Faber, 1992.

Carrick, Hartley. "The Song of the Six Suburbs." *Punch* 16 January 1907: 54.

Chattopadhyay, Swati. *Representing Calcutta: Modernity, Nationalism, and the Colonial Uncanny.* London: Routledge, 2005.

Cheyette, Bryan. "Introduction." Wells, *Tono-Bungay* xii–xli.

Childers, Joseph W. "Foreign Matter: Imperial Filth." *Filth: Dirt, Disgust, and Modern Life.* Ed. William A. Cohen and Ryan Johnson. Minneapolis: U of Minnesota P, 2005. 201–21.

Childs, Peter. "Suburban Values and Ethni-Cities in Indo-Anglian Writing." In Webster, 90–107.

Chopra, Preeti. "Pondicherry: A French Enclave in India." *Forms of Dominance: On the Architecture and Urbanism of the Colonial Enterprise.* Ed. Nezar AlSayyad. Aldershot: Avebury, 1992. 107–37.

Chrisman, Laura. "Imperial Space, Imperial Place: Theories of Empire and Culture in Fredric Jameson, Edward Said and Gayatri Spivak." *New Formations* 34 (July 1998): 53–69.

———. "Tale of the City: The Imperial Metropolis in *Heart of Darkness.*" *Postcolonial Contraventions: Cultural Readings of Race, Imperialism, and Transnationalism.* New York: Palgrave, 2003. 21–38.

Clapson, Mark. *Invincible Green Suburbs, Brave New Towns: Social Change and Urban Dispersal in Postwar England.* Manchester: Manchester UP, 1998.

———. *Suburban Century: Social Change and Urban Growth in England and the United States.* Oxford: Berg, 2003.

Clarke, W. S. *The Suburban Homes of London.* London: Chatto and Windus, 1881.

Cohen, Scott. "The Empire from the Street: Virginia Woolf, Wembley, and Imperial Monuments." *Modern Fiction Studies* 50.1 (2004): 85–109.

Collins, Wilkie. *Basil.* 1852. Oxford: Oxford UP, 2000.

———. *Hide and Seek.* 1854. New York: Dover, 1981.

Colmer, John. *E. M. Forster: The Personal Voice.* London: Routledge, 1975.

"Commons Round London." *Westminster Review* 85 (April 1866): 216–24.

Conrad, Joseph. *Almayer's Folly: A Story of an Eastern River.* 1895. Oxford: Oxford UP, 1992.

———. *The Collected Letters of Joseph Conrad.* 9 vols. to date. Ed. Frederick R. Karl and Laurence Davies. Cambridge: Cambridge UP, 1983–.

———. "The End of the Tether." 1902. *Youth, Heart of Darkness, The End of the Tether.* Oxford: Oxford UP, 1984. 163–339.

———. *Heart of Darkness.* 1899. New York: Norton, 1988.

———. *Last Essays.* Freeport, NY: Books for Libraries P, 1923.

———. *Lord Jim.* 1900. London: Penguin, 1989.

———. *The Mirror of the Sea.* 1906. Garden City, NY: Doubleday, 1925.

———. *Notes on Life and Letters.* 1921. Garden City, NY: Doubleday, 1925.

———. *An Outcast of the Islands.* 1896. Oxford: Oxford UP, 1992.

———. "An Outpost of Progress." 1897. *The Collected Stories of Joseph Conrad.* Ed. Samuel Hynes. Hopewell, NJ: Ecco, 1991. 38–61.

———. *A Personal Record.* 1912. Marlboro, VT: Marlboro P, 1982.

———. *The Shadow-Line: A Confession.* 1917. Oxford: Oxford UP, 1992.

———. *Victory.* 1915. Oxford: Oxford UP, 1986.

Constantine, Stephen. "Amateur Gardening and Popular Recreation in the 19th and 20th Centuries." *Journal of Social History* 14.3 (1981): 387–406.

Cooper, Frederick, and Ann Laura Stoler, eds. *Tensions of Empire: Colonial Cultures in a Bourgeois World.* Berkeley: U of California P, 1997.

Crawford, Robert. "Rudyard Kipling in *The Waste Land.*" *Essays in Criticism* 36.1 (January 1986): 32–46.

Creese, Walter. "Imagination in the Suburb." *Nature and the Victorian Imagination.* Ed. U. C. Knoepflmacher and G. B. Tennyson. Berkeley: U of California P, 1977. 49–67.

———. *The Search for Environment: The Garden City, Before and After.* New Haven: Yale UP, 1966.

Crick, Bernard. *George Orwell: A Life.* Boston: Little, 1980.

Crinson, Mark. *Empire Building: Orientalism and Victorian Architecture.* London: Routledge, 1996.

———. *Modern Architecture and the End of Empire.* Burlington, VT: Ashgate, 2002.

Crosland, T. W. H. *The Suburbans.* London: John Long, 1905.

Crossick, Geoffrey, ed. *The Lower Middle Class in Britain 1870–1914.* New York: St. Martin's, 1977.

Cunningham, Gail. "Houses in Between: Navigating Suburbia in Late Victorian Writing." *Victorian Literature and Culture* 32.2 (2004): 421–34.

Cunningham, Valentine. *British Writers of the Thirties.* Oxford: Oxford UP, 1988.

Daniels, Stephen. "Humphry Repton." Matthew and Harrison 498–502.

Darras, Jacques. *Joseph Conrad and the West: Signs of Empire.* Trans. Anne Luyat and Jacques Darras. Totowa, NJ: Barnes and Noble, 1982.

David, Deirdre. "Imperial Chintz: Domesticity and Empire." *Victorian Literature and Culture* 27.2 (1999): 569–77.

Davin, Anna. "Imperialism and Motherhood." Cooper and Stoler 87–151.

Davis, John. *Reforming London: The London Government Problem, 1855–1900.* Oxford: Oxford UP, 1988.

Davis, Terence. *John Nash: The Prince Regent's Architect.* South Brunswick, NJ: Barnes, 1967.

Davison, Graeme. "Australia: The First Suburban Nation?" *Journal of Urban History* 22.1 (1995): 40–74.

Day Lewis, C. *Collected Poems.* London: Jonathan Cape, 1954.

———. "Letter to a Young Revolutionary." *New Country: Prose and Poetry by the Authors of New Signatures.* Ed. Michael Roberts. London: Hogarth, 1933. 25–42.

Deleuze, Gilles. *Nietzsche and Philosophy.* Trans. Hugh Tomlinson. New York: Columbia UP, 1983.

Dennis, Richard. "Modern London." *The Cambridge Urban History of Britain.* Ed. Martin Daunton. Vol. 3. Cambridge: Cambridge UP, 2000. 3: 95–131.

Dentith, Simon. "From William Morris to the Morris Minor: An Alternative Suburban History." In Webster, 15–30.

———. "Thirties Poetry and the Landscape of Suburbia." K. Williams and Matthews 108–23.

DiBattista, Maria, and Lucy McDiarmid, eds. *High and Low Moderns: Literature and Culture, 1889–1939.* New York: Oxford UP, 1996.

Dickens, Charles. *Dombey and Son.* 1846–48. London: Penguin, 1970.

———. *Great Expectations.* 1860–61. London: Penguin, 1985.

———. *Our Mutual Friend.* 1864–65. Oxford: Oxford UP, 1989.

Dilke, Charles Wentworth. *Greater Britain: A Record of Travel in English-Speaking Countries during 1866 and 1867.* 1868. New York: Harper, 1869.

Dirks, Nicholas, ed. *Colonialism and Culture.* Ann Arbor: U of Michigan P, 1992.

Dossal, Mariam. *Imperial Designs and Indian Realities: The Planning of Bombay City, 1845–1875.* Bombay: Oxford UP, 1991.

Doyle, Arthur Conan. *Beyond the City: The Idyll of a Suburb.* 1892. Bloomington, IN: Gaslight, 1982.

———. *The Complete Sherlock Holmes.* New York: Doubleday, 1906.

———. "Life and Death in the Blood." *Good Words* 24 (1883): 178–81.

———. *Memories and Adventures.* 1924. London: Greenhill, 1988.

Driver, Felix, and David Gilbert. "Heart of Empire? Landscape, Space and Performance in Imperial London." *Environment and Planning D: Society and Space* 16 (1998): 11–28.

———, eds. *Imperial Cities: Landscape, Display, and Identity.* Manchester: Manchester UP, 1999.

Dryden, Linda. *Joseph Conrad and the Imperial Romance.* New York: St. Martin's, 2000.

Duff, Charles. *Anthropological Report on a London Suburb.* London: Grayson, 1935.

Dyos, H. J. "A Castle for Everyman." *London Journal* 1.1 (1975): 118–34.

———. "The Speculative Builders and Developers of Victorian London." *Victorian Studies* 11 (Summer 1968): 641–90.

———. *Victorian Suburb: A Study of the Growth of Camberwell.* Leicester: Leicester UP, 1961.

Dyos, H. J., and D. A. Reeder. "Slums and Suburbs." *The Victorian City: Images and Realities.* 2 vols. Vol. 1. Ed. H. J. Dyos and Michael Wolff. London: Routledge, 1973. 359–86.

Eade, John, Isabelle Fremeaux, and David Garbin. "The Political Construction of Diasporic Communities in the Global City." *Imagined Londons.* Ed. Pamela K. Gilbert. Albany: SUNY P, 2002. 159–75.

Eagleton, Terry. *Exiles and Émigrés: Studies in Modern Literature.* London: Chatto, 1970.

Eddleman, Floyd Eugene, and David Leon Higdon, eds. *Almayer's Folly: A Story of an Eastern River.* By Joseph Conrad. 1895. Cambridge: Cambridge UP, 1994.

Edel, Leon, and Gordon N. Ray, eds. *Henry James and H. G. Wells: A Record of Their Friendship, Their Debate on the Art of Fiction, and Their Quarrel.* Urbana: U of Illinois P, 1958.

Edelstein, Michael. "Foreign Investment and Accumulation, 1860–1914." *The Economic History of Britain since 1700.* Ed. Roderick Floud and Donald McCloskey. 2nd ed. Vol. 2. Cambridge: Cambridge UP, 1994. 173–96.

Edwards, Arthur M. *The Design of Suburbia: A Critical Study in Environmental History.* London: Pembridge, 1981.

Elfenbein, Andrew. "Stricken Deer: Secrecy, Homophobia, and the Rise of the Suburban Man." *Genders* 27 (1998): 57 pars.

Eliot, T. S. "Books of the Quarter." *Criterion* 8 (1929): 552–56.

———. *The Complete Poems and Plays, 1909–1950.* New York: Harcourt, 1971.

Engels, Friedrich. *The Condition of the Working-Class in England in 1844. With Preface Written in 1892.* Trans. Florence Kelley Wischnewetzky. London: Swan Sonnenschein, 1892.

Esenwein, George R. *The Spanish Civil War: A Modern Tragedy.* New York: Routledge, 2005.

Esty, Jed. *A Shrinking Island: Modernism and National Culture in England.* Princeton: Princeton UP, 2004.

Evenson, Norma. *The Indian Metropolis: A View toward the West.* New Haven: Yale UP, 1989.

"An Excursion to Buitenzorg, in the Interior of Java." *Fraser's Magazine for Town and Country* 50 (July 1854): 111–20.

Faber, Richard. *The Vision and the Need: Late Victorian Imperialist Aims.* London: Faber, 1966.

Fanon, Frantz. *The Wretched of the Earth.* 1961. Trans. Constance Farrington. New York: Grove, 1977.

Federico, Annette. "Making Do: George Orwell's *Coming Up for Air.*" *Studies in the Novel* 37.1 (2005): 50–63.

Felski, Rita. "Nothing to Declare: Identity, Shame, and the Lower Middle Class." *PMLA* 115.1 (2000): 33–45.

Fishman, Robert. "American Suburbs/English Suburbs: A Transatlantic Comparison." *Journal of Urban History* 13.3 (1987): 237–51.

———. *Bourgeois Utopias: The Rise and Fall of Suburbia.* New York: Basic, 1987.

———. *Urban Utopias in the Twentieth Century: Ebenezer Howard, Frank Lloyd Wright, and Le Corbusier.* New York: Basic, 1977.

Fitting, Peter. "Estranged Invaders: *The War of the Worlds.*" *Learning from Other Worlds: Estrangement, Cognition, and the Politics of Science Fiction and Utopia.* Ed. Patrick Parrinder. Durham: Duke UP, 2001. 127–45.

Fitzgerald, Percy. *London City Suburbs as They Are To-day.* London: Leadenhall, 1893.

Fleishman, Avrom. *Conrad's Politics: Community and Anarchy in the Fiction of Joseph Conrad.* Baltimore: Johns Hopkins UP, 1967.

Flint, Kate. "Fictional Suburbia." *Literature and History* 8.1 (1982): 67–81.

Fluet, Lisa J. "'Distinct Vocations' and the Anglo-Indian in Sherlock Holmes' England." *Victorian Review* 24.2 (1998): 130–62.

———. "H. G. Wells, Disciplinarity and Cultural Studies." *Critical Matrix: The Princeton Journal of Women, Gender and Culture* (Summer 2004): 31–59.

Ford, Ford Madox. *Joseph Conrad: A Personal Remembrance.* 1924. Boston: Little, 1925.

———. *The Soul of London: A Survey of a Modern City.* 1905. London: J. M. Dent, 1995.

———. *Thus to Revisit: Some Reminiscences.* 1921. New York: Octagon, 1966.

"The Formation of London Suburbs." *Times* 25 June 1904: 8.

Forster, E. M. *Abinger Harvest.* 1936. San Diego: Harcourt, 1964.

———. *Howards End.* 1910. New York: Norton, 1998.

———. *A Passage to India.* 1924. San Diego: Harcourt, 1984.

———. *Selected Letters of E. M. Forster.* 2 vols. Ed. Mary Lago and P. N. Furbank. Cambridge, MA: Harvard UP, 1983–85.

———. *Two Cheers for Democracy.* 1951. *The Abinger Edition of E. M. Forster.* Vol. 11. Ed. Oliver Stallybrass. London: Arnold, 1972.

Foucault, Michel. "Of Other Spaces." *Diacritics* 16.1 (1986): 22–27.

Freestone, Robert. "The Australian Garden City." In S. V. Ward, 107–26.

Fried, Michael. "Almayer's Face: On 'Impressionism' in Conrad, Crane, and Norris." *Critical Inquiry* 17 (Autumn 1990): 193–236.

Furbank, P. N. *E. M. Forster: A Life.* 2 vols. London: Secker, 1977–78.

Gardner, Philip, ed. *E. M. Forster: The Critical Heritage.* London: Routledge, 1973.

Gaskell, S. Martin. "Housing and the Lower Middle Class, 1870–1914." In Crossick, 159–83.

George, Rosemary Marangoly. *The Politics of Home: Postcolonial Relocations and Twentieth-Century Fiction.* Berkeley: U of California P, 1996.

Gilbert, Bentley B. "Introduction." C. F. G. Masterman, *Heart* xi–xxxiv.

Gilbert, David, and Rebecca Preston. "'Stop Being So English': Suburban Modernity and National Identity in the Twentieth Century." *Geographies of British Modernity: Space and Society in the Twentieth Century.* Ed. David Gilbert, David Matless, and Brian Short. Oxford: Blackwell, 2003. 187–203.

Gilbert, Pamela K. *Mapping the Victorian Social Body.* Albany: SUNY P, 2004.

Gilroy, Paul. *"There Ain't No Black in the Union Jack": The Cultural Politics of Race and Nation.* 1987. Chicago: U of Chicago P, 1991.

Ginzburg, Carlo. "Morelli, Freud, and Sherlock Holmes: Clues and Scientific Method." *The Sign of Three: Dupin, Holmes, Peirce.* Ed. Umberto Eco and Thomas A. Sebeok. Bloomington: Indiana UP, 1988. 81–118.

Girouard, Mark. *Cities and People: A Social and Architectural History.* New Haven: Yale UP, 1985.

Gissing, George. "The House of Cobwebs." *The House of Cobwebs and Other Stories.* New York: E. P. Dutton, 1906. 1–27.

———. *In the Year of Jubilee.* 1894. London: Everyman, 1994.

———. *The Nether World.* 1889. Brighton, UK: Harvester, 1974.

Gloag, John. *Victorian Comfort: A Social History of Design from 1830–1900.* London: A. and C. Black, 1961.

Glover, William J. *Making Lahore Modern: Constructing and Imagining a Colonial City.* Minneapolis: U of Minnesota P, 2008.

GoGwilt, Christopher. *The Invention of the West: Joseph Conrad and the Double Mapping of Europe and Empire.* Stanford: Stanford UP, 1995.

Gold, John R., and Margaret M. Gold. "*Outrage* and Righteous Indignation: Ideology and Imagery of Suburbia." *The Behavioural Environment: Essays in Reflection, Application, and Re-evaluation.* Ed. Frederick W. Boal and David N. Livingstone. London: Routledge, 1989. 163–81.

Gordon, George. "The Status Area of Edinburgh in 1914." Gordon and Dicks 168–96.

Gordon, George, and Brian Dicks, eds. *Scottish Urban History.* Aberdeen: Aberdeen UP, 1983.

Graves, Robert, and Alan Hodge. *The Long Week-End: A Social History of Great Britain, 1918–1939.* 1940. New York: Norton, 1963.

Green, Oliver, ed. *Metro-land.* 1924 ed. London: Southbank, 2004.

Green, Roger Lancelyn. *Kipling: The Critical Heritage.* London: Routledge, 1971.

Greenslade, William. *Degeneration, Culture and the Novel 1880–1940.* Cambridge: Cambridge UP, 1994.

Grene, Nicholas. "The Edwardian Shaw, or the Modernist That Never Was." DiBattista and McDiarmid 135–47.

Grewal, Inderpal. *Home and Harem: Nation, Gender, Empire, and the Cultures of Travel.* Durham: Duke UP, 1996.

Grossmith, George, and Weedon Grossmith. *The Diary of a Nobody.* 1892. London: J. M. Dent, 1982.

Guha, Ranajit. "Not at Home in Empire." *Critical Inquiry* 23 (Spring 1997): 482–93.

Gunn, Simon. *The Public Culture of the Victorian Middle Class: Ritual and Authority in the English Industrial City, 1840–1914.* Manchester: Manchester UP, 2000.

Gupta, Narayani. *Delhi between Two Empires, 1803–1931: Society, Government and Urban Growth.* Delhi: Oxford UP, 1981.

Haggard, H. Rider. *Allan Quatermain.* 1887. Oxford: Oxford UP, 1995.

Hall, Peter. *Cities of Tomorrow: An Intellectual History of Urban Planning and Design in the Twentieth Century.* Oxford: Blackwell, 1996.

Hall, Stuart. *Critical Dialogues in Cultural Studies.* Ed. David Morley and Kuan-Hsing Chen. London: Routledge, 1996.

Hammerton, A. James. "The Perils of Mrs. Pooter: Satire, Modernity and Motherhood in the Lower Middle Class in England, 1870–1920." *Women's History Review* 8.2 (1999): 261–76.

———. "Pooterism or Partnership? Marriage and Masculine Identity in the Lower Middle Class, 1870–1920." *Journal of British Studies* 38.3 (1999): 291–321.

Hammond, John. "Wells and Woking." *Foundation* 77 (Autumn 1999): 3–7.

Hammond, J. R. *A George Orwell Companion: A Guide to the Novels, Documentaries and Essays.* New York: St. Martin's, 1982.

Hapgood, Lynne. "The Literature of the Suburbs: Versions of Repression in the Novels of George Gissing, Arthur Conan Doyle and William Pett Ridge, 1890–1899." *Journal of Victorian Culture* 5.2 (2000): 287–310.

———. *Margins of Desire: The Suburbs in Fiction and Culture 1880–1925.* Manchester: Manchester UP, 2005.

———. "'The New Suburbanites' and Contested Class Identities in the London Suburbs, 1880–1900." In Webster, 31–49.

———. "The Unwritten Suburb: Defining Spaces in John Galsworthy's *The Man of Property.*" Hapgood and Paxton 162–79.

Hapgood, Lynne, and Nancy L. Paxton, eds. *Outside Modernism: In Pursuit of the English Novel, 1900–30.* New York: Palgrave, 2000.

Hardy, Dennis. *From Garden Cities to New Towns: Campaigning for Town and Country Planning, 1899–1946.* London: Spon, 1991.

———. *Utopian England: Community Experiments, 1900–1045.* London: Spon, 2000.

Harris, John, and Malcolm Baker. "Sir Robert Taylor." Matthew and Harrison 974–76.

Harris, José. *Private Lives, Public Spirit: A Social History of Britain 1870–1914.* Oxford: Oxford UP, 1993.

Harrison, Frederic. *The Meaning of History.* London: Macmillan, 1894.

Harrison, Michael. *In the Footsteps of Sherlock Holmes.* London: David and Charles, 1971.

Harvey, David. *Spaces of Hope.* Berkeley: U of California P, 2000.

———. *The Urbanization of Capital: Studies in the History and Theory of Capitalist Urbanization.* Baltimore: Johns Hopkins UP, 1985.

Hassam, Andrew. "Portable Iron Structures and Uncertain Colonial Spaces at the Sydenham Crystal Palace." Driver and Gilbert, *Imperial Cities* 174–93.

Hebbert, Michael. "The British Garden City: Metamorphosis." In S. V. Ward, 165–86.

Hebdige, Dick. *Subculture: The Meaning of Style.* London: Methuen, 1979.

Hegglund, Jon. "Defending the Realm: Domestic Space and Mass Cultural Contamination in *Howards End* and *An Englishman's Home.*" *English Literature in Transition (1880–1920)* 40.4 (1997): 398–423.

Hewlett, Geoffrey, et al. *A History of Wembley.* London: Kingfisher, 1979.

Higdon, David Leon. "Conrad and Mark Twain: A Newly Discovered Essay." *Journal of Modern Literature* 12.2 (1985): 354–61.

Hitchens, Christopher. *Why Orwell Matters.* New York: Basic, 2002.

Hobhouse, Hermione. *Thomas Cubitt: Master Builder.* London: Macmillan, 1971.

Hobhouse, L. T. *Democracy and Reaction.* 1904. Ed. P. F. Clarke. Brighton, UK: Harvester, 1972.

Hobsbawm, Eric. *The Age of Empire: 1875–1914.* New York: Vintage, 1989.

———. *The Age of Extremes: A History of the World, 1914–1991.* New York: Vintage, 1994.

———. *Industry and Empire: From 1750 to the Present Day.* Harmondsworth: Penguin, 1969.

Hobson, J. A. *Imperialism: A Study.* 1902. Ann Arbor: U of Michigan P, 1965.

Holroyd, Michael. *Bernard Shaw.* 3 vols. New York: Random House, 1988–91.

Home, Robert. *Of Planting and Planning: The Making of British Colonial Cities.* London: Spon, 1996.

Hosagrahar, Jyoti. *Indigenous Modernities: Negotiating Architecture and Urbanism.* London: Routledge, 2005.

Howard, Ebenezer. *Garden Cities of To-morrow.* 1902. London: Faber, 1945.

Howard, Keble. *The Smiths of Surbiton: A Comedy without a Plot.* 1906. London: T. Fisher Unwin, 1925.

Hughes, David, and Harry M. Geduld. "Introduction." *A Critical Edition of* The War of the Worlds. Bloomington: Indiana UP, 1993. 1–40.

Hughes, David, and Robert M. Philmus. "The Early Science Journalism of H. G. Wells: A Chronological Survey." *Science-Fiction Studies* 1.2 (1973): 98–114.

Huh, Jinny. "Whispers of Norbury: Sir Arthur Conan Doyle and the Modernist Crisis of Racial (Un)Detection." *Modern Fiction Studies* 49.3 (2003): 550–80.

Hunter, Jefferson. "Orwell, Wells, and *Coming Up for Air.*" *Modern Philology* 78.1 (1980): 38–47.

Hunter, Lynette. "Blood and Marmalade: Negotiations between the State and the Domestic in George Orwell's Early Novels." K. Williams and Matthews 202–16.

Huntington, John. "Problems of an Amorous Utopian." *Critical Essays on H. G. Wells.* Ed. John Huntington. Boston: G. K. Hall, 1991. 136–47.

Hutchins, Francis G. *The Illusion of Permanence: British Imperialism in India.* Princeton: Princeton UP, 1967.

Hynes, Samuel. *The Edwardian Turn of Mind.* Princeton: Princeton UP, 1968.

Ingle, Stephen. *George Orwell: A Political Life.* Manchester: Manchester UP, 1993.

Inwood, Stephen. *A History of London.* London: Macmillan, 1998.

Jackson, Alan A. *Semi-Detached London: Suburban Development, Life, and Transport, 1900–1939.* London: Allen and Unwin, 1973.

Jackson, Kenneth T. "Suburbanization in England and North America: A Response to 'A Transatlantic Comparison.'" *Journal of Urban History* 13 (1987): 302–6.

Jacobs, Jane M. *Edge of Empire: Postcolonialism and the City.* London: Routledge, 1996.

Jaffe, Audrey. "Detecting the Beggar: Arthur Conan Doyle, Henry Mayhew, and 'The Man with the Twisted Lip.'" *Representations* 31 (1990): 96–117.

James, Henry. *English Hours.* 1905. New York: Orion, 1960.

———. "The Suburbs of London." *Galaxy* 24 (December 1877): 778–87.

James, Robert Rhodes. *Rosebery: A Biography of Archibald Philip, Fifth Earl of Rosebery.* London: Weidenfeld and Nicholson, 1963.

Jameson, Fredric. *Archaeologies of the Future: The Desire Called Utopia and Other Science Fictions.* London: Verso, 2005.

———. "Modernism and Imperialism." *Nationalism, Colonialism, and Literature.* By Terry Eagleton, Fredric Jameson, and Edward Said. Minneapolis: U of Minnesota P, 1990. 43–66.

———. *The Political Unconscious: Narrative as a Socially Symbolic Act.* Ithaca: Cornell UP, 1981.

JanMohamed, Abdul R. "The Economy of Manichean Allegory: The Function of Racial Difference in Colonialist Literature." *Critical Inquiry* 12 (Autumn 1985): 59–87.

———. *Manichean Aesthetics: The Politics of Literature in Colonial Africa.* Amherst: U of Massachusetts P, 1983.

Jann, Rosemary. *The Adventures of Sherlock Holmes: Detecting Social Order.* New York: Twayne, 1995.

Jeffery, Tom. "A Place in the Nation: The Lower Middle Class in England." *Splintered Classes: Politics and the Lower Middle Class in Interwar Europe.* Ed. Rudy Koshar. New York: Holmes and Meier, 1990. 70–96.

Johnson, Bruce. "Conrad's Impressionism and Watt's 'Delayed Decoding.'" Conrad, *Heart of Darkness* 345–57.

Johnson, James H. "The Suburban Expansion of Housing in London 1918–1939." *Greater London.* Ed. J. T. Coppock and Hugh C. Prince. London: Faber, 1964. 142–66.

Jones, Emrys. "Late Victorian Belfast: 1850–1900." *Belfast: The Origin and Growth of an Industrial City.* Ed. J. C. Beckett and R. E. Glasscock. London: BBC, 1967. 109–19.

Jones, Gareth Stedman. *Outcast London: A Study in the Relationship between Classes in Victorian Society.* Oxford: Oxford UP, 1971.

Jurca, Catherine. *White Diaspora: The Suburb and the Twentieth Century American Novel.* Princeton: Princeton UP, 2001.

Kalliney, Peter J. *Cities of Affluence and Anger: A Literary Geography of Modern Englishness.* Charlottesville: U of Virginia P, 2007.

Kaplan, Carola M., and Anne B. Simpson, eds. *Seeing Double: Revisioning Edwardian and Modernist Literature.* New York: St. Martin's, 1996.

Karl, Frederick R. *Joseph Conrad: The Three Lives.* New York: Farrar, 1979.

Keating, Peter. *The Haunted Study: A Social History of the English Novel 1887–1914.* London: Secker and Warburg, 1989.

———, ed. *Into Unknown England, 1866–1913: Selections from the Social Explorers.* Manchester: Manchester UP, 1976.

———. *The Working Classes in Victorian Fiction.* London: Routledge, 1971.

Keep, Christopher, and Don Randall. "Addiction, Empire, and Narrative in Arthur Conan Doyle's *The Sign of the Four.*" *Novel* 32.2 (1999): 207–21.

Kennedy, Dane. *The Magic Mountains: Hill Stations and the British Raj.* Berkeley: U of California P, 1996.

King, Anthony D. *The Bungalow: The Production of a Global Culture.* New York: Oxford UP, 1995.

———. *Colonial Urban Development: Culture, Social Power and Environment.* London: Routledge, 1976.

———. "Excavating the Multicultural Suburb: Hidden Histories of the Bungalow." In Silverstone, 55–85.

———. "Exporting Planning: The Colonial and Neo-Colonial Experience." *Shaping an Urban World.* Ed. Gordon E. Cherry. New York: St. Martin's, 1980. 203–26.

———. *Global Cities: Post-Imperialism and the Internationalization of London.* London: Routledge, 1990.

———. *Spaces of Global Cultures: Architecture, Urbanism, Identity.* London: Routledge, 2004.

———. *Urbanism, Colonialism, and the World-Economy: Cultural and Spatial Foundations of the World Urban System.* London: Routledge, 1990.

Kipling, Rudyard. *Rudyard Kipling's Verse.* Definitive ed. New York: Doubleday, 1940.

Knight, Stephen. *Form and Ideology in Crime Fiction.* Bloomington: Indiana UP, 1980.

Knowles, Owen. *A Conrad Chronology.* Boston: G. K. Hall, 1990.

Knowles, Owen, and Gene M. Moore. *Oxford Reader's Companion to Conrad.* Oxford: Oxford UP, 2000.

Krebs, Paula. *Gender, Race, and the Writing of Empire: Public Discourse and the Boer War.* Cambridge: Cambridge UP, 1999.

Kubal, David. *Outside the Whale: George Orwell's Art and Politics.* Notre Dame: U of Notre Dame P, 1972.

Kucich, John. *Imperial Masochism: British Fiction, Fantasy, and Social Class.* Princeton: Princeton UP, 2006.

Kupinse, William. "Wasted Value: The Serial Logic of H. G. Wells's *Tono-Bungay.*" *Novel* 33.1 (1999): 51–72.

Kureishi, Hanif. *The Buddha of Suburbia.* New York: Penguin, 1990.

Lancaster, Osbert. *Pillar to Post: English Architecture without Tears.* New York: Scribner's, 1939.

Lane, Christopher. "Almayer's Defeat: The Trauma of Colonialism in Conrad's Early Work." *Novel* 32.3 (1999): 401–28.

———. "Volatile Desire: Ambivalence and Distress in Forster's Colonial Narratives." *Writing India 1757–1990: The Literature of British India.* Ed. Bart Moore-Gilbert. Manchester: Manchester UP, 1996. 188–212.

Langbauer, Laurie. "The City, the Everyday, and Boredom: The Case of Sherlock Holmes." *Differences* 5.3 (1993): 80–120.

Lawrence, D. H. *Late Essays and Articles.* Ed. James T. Boulton. Cambridge: Cambridge UP, 2004.

Lawrence, F. W. "The Housing Problem." C. F. G. Masterman, *Heart* 53–110.

Leaf, Michael. "The Suburbanisation of Jakarta." *Third World Planning Review* 16.4 (1994): 341–56.

Leavis, Q. D. *Fiction and the Reading Public.* London: Chatto, 1939.

Levenson, Michael. "The Fictional Realist: Novels of the 1930s." *The Cambridge Companion to George Orwell.* Ed. John Rodden. Cambridge: Cambridge UP, 2007. 59–75.

Lewis, Wyndham, ed. *BLAST* 1. 1914. Santa Rosa, CA: Black Sparrow, 1992.

Light, Alison. *Forever England: Femininity, Literature, and Conservatism between the Wars.* London: Routledge, 1991.

Lockwood, David. *The Blackcoated Worker: A Study in Class Consciousness.* 2nd ed. Oxford: Clarendon, 1989.

Lodge, David. "*Tono-Bungay* and the Condition of England." *H. G. Wells: A Collection of Critical Essays.* Ed. Bernard Bergonzi. Englewood Cliffs, NJ: Prentice-Hall, 1976. 110–39.

Loudon, John Claudius. *The Suburban Gardener and Villa Companion.* London: Longman, 1838.

Low, Sidney J. "The Rise of the Suburbs." *Contemporary Review* 60 (1891): 545–58.

———. *A Vision of India as Seen during the Tour of the Prince and Princess of Wales.* London: Smith, 1906.

MacFadyen, Dugald. *Sir Ebenezer Howard and the Town Planning Movement.* Cambridge, MA: MIT P, 1970.

Mackerness, E. D. *A Social History of English Music.* London: Routledge, 1964.

MacLaran, Andrew. *Dublin: The Shaping of a Capital.* London: Belhaven, 1993.

Marcus, Sharon. *Apartment Stories: City and Home in Nineteenth Century Paris and London.* Berkeley: U of California P, 1999.

Markley, Robert. *Dying Planet: Mars in Science and the Imagination.* Durham: Duke UP, 2005.

Marshall, Howard. "The Rake's Progress." In Williams-Ellis, 164–75.

Masterman, C. F. G. *The Condition of England.* London: Methuen, 1909.

———. "The English City." *England: A Nation. Being the Papers of the Patriots' Club.* Ed. Lucian Oldershaw. London: R. Brimley Johnson, 1904. 44–94.

———. *From the Abyss: Of Its Inhabitants, by One of Them.* 1902. London: Garland, 1980.

———, ed. *The Heart of the Empire: Discussions of Problems of Modern City Life in England.* 1901. Brighton, UK: Harvester, 1973.

———. *In Peril of Change: Essays Written in Time of Tranquility.* New York: Huebsch, 1905.

———. "Realities at Home." C. F. G. Masterman, *Heart* 2–52.

Masterman, Lucy. *C. F. G. Masterman: A Biography.* 1939. New York: Kelley, 1968.

Matthew, H. C. G., and Brian Harrison, eds. *Oxford Dictionary of National Biography.* Oxford: Oxford UP, 2004.

May, Brian. *The Modernist as Pragmatist: E. M. Forster and the Fate of Liberalism.* Columbia: U of Missouri P, 1997.

Mayhew, Henry. *London Labour and the London Poor.* 1861–62. 4 vols. New York: Dover, 1968.

McBratney, John. "Racial and Criminal Types: Indian Ethnography and Sir Arthur Conan Doyle's *The Sign of Four.*" *Victorian Literature and Culture* 33.1 (2005): 149–67.

McClintock, Anne. *Imperial Leather: Race, Gender, and Sexuality in the Colonial Contest.* New York: Routledge, 1995.

McClure, John A. "Late Imperial Romance." *Raritan* 10.4 (1991): 111–30.

McLaughlin, Joseph. *Writing the Urban Jungle: Reading Empire in London from Doyle to Eliot.* Charlottesville: U of Virginia P, 2000.

Meacham, Standish. *Regaining Paradise: Englishness and the Early Garden City Movement.* New Haven: Yale UP, 1998.

Meadows, Peter. "Samuel Pepys Cockerell." Matthew and Harrison 364–65.

Mehta, Jaya. "English Romance: Indian Violence." *Centennial Review* 34.3 (1995): 537–58.

Memmi, Albert. *The Colonizer and the Colonized.* 1957. Trans. Howard Greenfeld. Boston: Beacon, 1991.

Metcalf, Thomas R. *An Imperial Vision: Indian Architecture and Britain's Raj.* Berkeley: U of California P, 1989.

Meyers, Jeffrey. *Orwell: Wintry Conscience of a Generation.* New York: Norton, 2000.

———. "Orwell's Apocalypse: *Coming Up for Air.*" *Modern Fiction Studies* 21.1 (1975): 69–80.

Miles, William F. S. *Imperial Burdens: Countercolonialism in Former French India.* Boulder: Lynne Rienner, 1995.

Moore, Gene M., ed. *Conrad's Cities: Essays for Hans van Marle.* Amsterdam: Rodopi, 1992.

Moore-Gilbert, Bart. *Hanif Kureishi.* Manchester: Manchester UP, 2001.

———. *Kipling and "Orientalism."* New York: St. Martin's, 1986.

Moretti, Franco. *Atlas of the European Novel 1800–1900.* London: Verso, 1998.

———. *Graphs, Maps, Trees: Abstract Models for a Literary History.* London: Verso, 2005.

Morris, Jan. *Farewell the Trumpets: An Imperial Retreat.* New York: Harcourt, 1978.

Morris, Jan, and Simon Winchester. *Stones of Empire: The Buildings of the Raj.* Oxford: Oxford UP, 1983.

Morris, William. *News from Nowhere.* 1890. Ed. Stephen Arata. Peterborough, ON: Broadview, 2003.

Morton, Peter. "'The Funniest Book in the World': Waugh and *The Diary of a Nobody.*" *Evelyn Waugh Newsletter and Studies* 36.1 (2005): 1–5.

Moses, Michael Valdez. *The Novel and the Globalization of Culture.* New York: Oxford UP, 1995.

Mumford, Lewis. *The Culture of Cities.* New York: Harcourt, 1938.

———. "Introduction." E. Howard 29–40.

Naipaul, V. S. *The Mimic Men.* 1967. New York: Vintage, 2001.

Najder, Zdzisław. *Conrad's Polish Background: Letters to and from Polish Friends.* Trans. Halina Carroll. London: Oxford UP, 1964.

———. *Joseph Conrad: A Chronicle.* New Brunswick, NJ: Rutgers UP, 1983.

Naylor, Simon, and James R. Ryan. "The Mosque in the Suburbs: Negotiating Religion and Ethnicity in South London." *Social and Cultural Geography* 3.1 (2002): 39–59.

Nealon, Jeffrey T. "Performing Resentment: White Male Anger; or, 'Lack' and Nietzschean Political Theory." *Why Nietzsche Still? Reflections on Drama, Culture, and Politics.* Ed. Alan D. Schrift. Berkeley: U of California P, 2000. 274–92.

Neild, Susan M. "Colonial Urbanism: The Development of Madras City in the Eighteenth and Nineteenth Centuries." *Modern Asian Studies* 13.2 (1979): 217–46.

"The New Capital of India: Lord Crewe on Town Planning." *Times* 5 August 1912: 9.

Newsinger, John. *Orwell's Politics.* Basingstoke: Macmillan, 1999.

Nietzsche, Friedrich. *On the Genealogy of Morals.* 1887. Trans. Douglas Smith. Oxford: Oxford UP, 1996.

Nord, Deborah Epstein. "The Social Explorer as Anthropologist: Victorian Travelers among the Urban Poor." *Visions of the Modern City: Essays in History, Art, and Literature.* Ed. William Sharpe and Leonard Wallock. New York: Proceedings of the Heyman Center for the Humanities, Columbia University, 1983. 118–30.

Nordau, Max. *Degeneration.* New York: Appleton, 1895.

Norgate, G. Le G. "Thomas Pell Platt." Matthew and Harrison 542.

Nurse, Bernard. "Planning a London Suburban Estate: Dulwich 1882–1920." *London Journal* 19.1 (1994): 54–70.

Oliver, Paul, Ian Davis, and Ian Bentley. *Dunroamin: The Suburban Semi and Its Enemies.* London: Barrie and Jenkins, 1981.

Olsen, Donald J. *The Growth of Victorian London.* New York: Holmes, 1976.

Orwell, George. *Burmese Days.* 1934. San Diego: Harcourt, 1962.

———. *The Collected Essays, Journalism, and Letters of George Orwell.* 4 vols. Ed. Sonia Orwell and Ian Angus. Boston: Nonpareil, 2000.

———. *Coming Up for Air.* 1939. San Diego: Harcourt, 1950.

———. *The Complete Works of George Orwell.* 20 vols. Ed. Peter Davison. London: Secker and Warburg, 1998.

———. *Down and Out in Paris and London.* 1933. San Diego: Harcourt, 1961.

———. *Homage to Catalonia.* 1938. Boston: Beacon, 1967.

———. *Keep the Aspidistra Flying.* 1936. San Diego: Harcourt, 1956.

———. *Nineteen Eighty-Four.* 1949. New York: Signet, 1981.

———. *The Road to Wigan Pier.* 1937. San Diego: Harcourt, 1958.

Osborn, F. J. "Preface." E. Howard 9–28.

Otis, Laura. *Membranes: Metaphors of Invasion in Nineteenth-Century Literature, Science, and Politics.* Baltimore: Johns Hopkins UP, 1999.

Ottewill, David. *The Edwardian Garden.* New Haven: Yale UP, 1989.

Pain, Barry. *Robinson Crusoe's Return.* 1906. *Humorous Stories.* London: Laurie, 1930. 503–65.

Panton, J. E. *Suburban Residences and How to Circumvent Them.* London: Ward and Downey, 1896.

Parker, Eric. *Highways and Byways in Surrey.* London: Macmillan, 1908.

Parrinder, Patrick. "From Mary Shelley to *The War of the Worlds:* The Thames Valley Catastrophe." *Anticipations: Essays on Early Science Fiction and Its Precursors.* Ed. David Seed. Liverpool: Liverpool UP, 1995. 58–74.

———. "H. G. Wells and the Fiction of Catastrophe." *Renaissance and Modern Studies* 28 (1984): 40–58.

———. *Shadows of the Future: H. G. Wells, Science Fiction, and Prophecy.* Syracuse: Syracuse UP, 1995.

Parry, Benita. *Conrad and Imperialism: Ideological Boundaries and Visionary Frontiers.* London: Macmillan, 1983.

———. *Delusions and Discoveries: Studies on India in the British Imagination, 1880–1930.* 1972. London: Verso, 1998.

———. "Materiality and Mystification in *A Passage to India.*" *Novel* 31.2 (1998): 174–94.

———. "*Tono-Bungay:* Modernisation, Modernity, Modernism and Imperialism, or the Failed Electrification of the Empire of Light." *New Formations* 34 (July 1998): 91–108.

Partington, John S. *Building Cosmopolis: The Political Thought of H. G. Wells.* Aldershot: Ashgate, 2003.

Patai, Daphne. *The Orwell Mystique: A Study in Male Ideology.* Amherst: U of Massachusetts P, 1984.

Pecora, Vincent P. *Households of the Soul.* Baltimore: Johns Hopkins UP, 1997.

Peel, C. S. *The New Home: Treating of the Arrangement, Decorating and Furnishing of a House of Medium Size to Be Maintained by a Moderate Income.* London: Constable, 1898.

Pennybacker, Susan D. *A Vision for London 1889–1914: Labour, Everyday Life and the LCC Experiment.* London: Routledge, 1995.

Perkin, Harold. *The Rise of Professional Society: England since 1880.* 1989. London: Routledge, 2002.

Phillips, Mike, and Trevor Phillips. *Windrush: The Irresistible Rise of Multi-Racial Britain.* London: HarperCollins, 1998.

Pick, Daniel. *Faces of Degeneration: A European Disorder, c. 1848–c. 1918.* New York: Cambridge UP, 1989.

Platts, Beryl. *A History of Greenwich.* Newton Abbot: David and Charles, 1973.

Plotz, John. "Virtually Being There: Edmund Wilson's Suburbs." *Southwest Review* 87.1 (2002): 10–28.

Porter, Roy. *London: A Social History.* Cambridge, MA: Harvard UP, 1995.

Poston, Lawrence. "City versus Country: A Holmesian Variation on an Old Theme." *Etudes Anglaises* 33 (1980): 156–70.

Power, Arthur. *Conversations with James Joyce.* 1974. Dublin: Lilliput, 1999.

Preston, Rebecca. "'The Scenery of the Torrid Zone': Imagined Travels and the Culture of Exotics in Nineteenth-Century British Gardens." Driver and Gilbert, *Imperial Cities* 194–211.

Price, Richard N. "Society, Status, and Jingoism: The Social Roots of Lower Middle Class Patriotism, 1870–1900." In Crossick, 89–112.

Priestley, J. B. *English Journey.* New York: Harper, 1934.

Procter, James. *Dwelling Places: Postwar Black British Writing.* Manchester: Manchester UP, 2003.

Rai, Alok. *Orwell and the Politics of Despair: A Critical Study of the Writings of George Orwell.* Cambridge: Cambridge UP, 1988.

Rappaport, Erika Diane. *Shopping for Pleasure: Women in the Making of London's West End.* Princeton: Princeton UP, 2000.

Rawcliffe, J. M. "Bromley: Kentish Market Town to London Suburb, 1841–81." F. M. L. Thompson 28–91.

Redmond, Donald A. *Sherlock Holmes, A Study in Sources.* Kingston, ON: McGill-Queen's UP, 1982.

Reed, Robert R. "Remarks on the Colonial Genesis of the Hill Station in Southeast Asia with Particular Reference to the Cities of Buitenzorg (Bogor) and Baguio." *Asian Profile* 4.6 (1976): 545–91.

Reeder, D. A. "A Theatre of Suburbs: Some Patterns of Development in West London, 1801–1911." *The Study of Urban History.* Ed. H. J. Dyos. London: Arnold, 1968. 253–71.

Richards, Jeffrey. *Imperialism and Music: Britain 1876–1953.* Manchester: Manchester UP: 2001.

Richards, J. M. *The Castles on the Ground: The Anatomy of Suburbia.* 1946. London: John Murray, 1973.

———. *Memoirs of an Unjust Fella.* London: Weidenfeld and Nicolson, 1980.

Richards, Thomas. *The Imperial Archive: Knowledge and the Fantasy of Empire.* London: Verso, 1993.

Richardson, John. *London and Its People: A Social History from Medieval Times to the Present Day.* London: Barrie and Jenkins, 1995.

Ricketts, L. C. "English Society in India." *Contemporary Review* 101 (1912): 681–88.

Robb, J. G. "Suburb and Slum in Gorbals: Social and Residential Change, 1800–1900." Gordon and Dicks 130–67.

Robinson, Fred Miller. *The Man in the Bowler Hat: His History and Iconography.* Chapel Hill: U of North Carolina P, 1993.

Rodden, John. *George Orwell: The Politics of Literary Reputation.* New Brunswick, NJ: Transaction, 2002.

Rodin, Alvin E., and Jack D. Key. *Medical Casebook of Doctor Arthur Conan Doyle: From Practitioner to Sherlock Holmes and Beyond.* Malabar, FL: Robert E. Krieger, 1984.

Rosebery, Archibald Philip Primrose, Earl of. *Miscellanies: Literary and Historical.* 2 vols. London: Hodder and Stoughton, 1921.

Ross, Robert J., and Gerald J. Telkamp. *Colonial Cities: Essays on Urbanism in a Colonial Context.* Dordrecht, the Netherlands: Martinus Nijhoff, 1985.

Rothfield, Lawrence. *Vital Signs: Medical Realism in Nineteenth-Century Fiction.* Princeton: Princeton UP, 1992.

Ruddick, William. "The Suburban Villa in Literature: 1880–1940." *Charles Lamb Bulletin* 87 (July 1994): 95–97.

Rush, James R., ed. *Java: A Traveller's Anthology.* Kuala Lumpur: Oxford UP, 1996.

Ruskin, John. *The Complete Works.* 39 vols. Ed. E. T. Cook and Alexander Wedderburn. London: Allen, 1903–12.

Ryan, Deborah S. "Staging the Imperial City: The Pageant of London, 1911." Driver and Gilbert, *Imperial Cities* 117–35.

Said, Edward. *Culture and Imperialism.* New York: Knopf, 1993.

Saint, Andrew. *London Suburbs.* London: Merrell, 1999.

———. "'Spread the People': The LCC's Dispersal Policy, 1889–1965." *Politics and the People of London: The London County Council 1889–1965.* Ed. Andrew Saint. London: Hambledon, 1989. 215–35.

Sala, George. "The Great Invasion." *Household Words* 10 April 1852: 69–73.

Sandhu, Sukhdev. "Pop Goes the Centre: Hanif Kureishi's London." *Postcolonial Theory and Criticism.* Ed. Laura Chrisman and Benita Parry. Cambridge: Brewer, 1999. 133–54.

Sassen, Saskia. *The Global City: New York, London, Tokyo.* Princeton: Princeton UP, 1991.

Scheler, Max. *Ressentiment.* 1915. Trans. William W. Holdheim. New York: Schocken, 1972.

Schneer, Jonathan. *London, 1900: The Imperial Metropolis.* New Haven: Yale UP, 1999.

Schwarz, Daniel R. *Conrad:* Almayer's Folly *to* Under Western Eyes. Ithaca: Cornell UP, 1980.

Scidmore, Eliza Ruhamah. *Java: The Garden of the East.* New York: Century, 1897.

Searle, G. R. *The Quest for National Efficiency: A Study in British Politics and Political Thought, 1899–1914.* Oxford: Blackwell, 1971.

Seeley, J. R. *The Expansion of England: Two Courses of Lectures.* London: Macmillan, 1883.

Sharp, Thomas. "The North-East—Hills and Hells." In Williams-Ellis, 141–59.

Sharpe, Jenny. "The Unspeakable Limits of Rape: Colonial Violence and Counter-Insurgency." *Gender* 10 (Spring 1991): 25–46.

Shaw, Bernard. John Bull's Other Island, *with* How He Lied to Her Husband *and* Major Barbara. London: Constable, 1960.

Shelden, Michael. *Orwell: The Authorized Biography.* New York: Harper, 1991.

Sherry, Norman, ed. *Conrad: The Critical Heritage.* Boston: Routledge, 1973.

———. *Conrad's Eastern World.* London: Cambridge UP, 1966.

Sillars, Stuart. *Structure and Dissolution in English Writing, 1910–1920.* London: Macmillan, 1999.

Silverstone, Roger, ed. *Visions of Suburbia.* London: Routledge, 1997.

Simpson, Ann B. "The 'Tangible Antagonist': H. G. Wells and the Discourse of Otherness." *Extrapolation* 31.2 (1990): 134–47.

Smith, David C. *H. G. Wells: Desperately Mortal.* New Haven: Yale UP, 1986.

Smith, Stevie. *The Collected Poems of Stevie Smith.* 1975. Ed. James MacGibbon. New York: New Directions, 1983.

Soloway, Richard. "Counting the Degenerates: The Statistics of Race Deterioration in Edwardian England." *Journal of Contemporary History* 17 (1982): 136–64.

Spangenberg, Bradford. "The Problem of Recruitment for the Indian Civil Service during the Late Nineteenth Century." *Journal of Asian Studies* 30.2 (1971): 341–60.

Spivak, Gayatri. "Three Women's Texts and a Critique of Imperialism." *Critical Inquiry* 12 (Autumn 1985): 243–61.

Stansky, Peter. *From William Morris to Sergeant Pepper: Studies in the Radical Domestic.* Palo Alto: Society for the Promotion of Science and Scholarship, 1999.

Stape, J. H. "Conrad's 'Unreal City': Singapore in 'The End of the Tether.'" In Moore, 85–96.

Stewart, Garrett. "The Foreign Offices of British Fiction." *MLQ* 61.1 (2000): 181–206.

Stoll, Rae Harris. "The Unthinkable Poor in Edwardian Writing." *Mosaic* 15.4 (1982): 23–45.

Stone, Wilfred. *The Cave and the Mountain: A Study of E. M. Forster.* Stanford: Stanford UP, 1966.

"Suburban Depredators." Letter. *Times* 3 September 1870: 7.

"Suburban Dwellings." *Times* 24 September 1880: 4.

"Suburbanity." *Spectator* 12 April 1884: 482–83.

"Suburban Miseries." *All the Year Round* 11 February 1888: 130–32.

"Suburban Quiet." Letter. *Times* 23 October 1874: 9.

"Suburban Safety." *Punch* 19 January 1878: 16.

Suleri, Sara. "The Geography of *A Passage to India*." *E. M. Forster.* Ed. Harold Bloom. New York: Chelsea, 1987. 169–75.

Summerson, John. *The Life and Work of John Nash, Architect.* Cambridge: MIT P, 1980.

Sutcliffe, Anthony. "Britain's First Town Planning Act: A Review of the 1909 Achievement." *Town Planning Review* 59.3 (1989): 289–303.

Swettenham, Frank. *British Malaya.* 1906. 4th ed. London: John Lane, 1920.

Tarn, John Nelson. "Housing Reform and the Emergence of Town Planning in Britain before 1914." *The Rise of Modern Urban Planning: 1800–1914.* Ed. Anthony Sutcliffe. New York: St. Martin's, 1977. 71–97.

Taylor, Jean Gelman. *The Social World of Batavia: European and Eurasian in Dutch Asia.* Madison: U of Wisconsin P, 1983.

Taylor, Nicholas. *The Village in the City.* London: Temple Smith, 1973.

Thacker, Andrew. *Moving through Modernity: Space and Geography in Modernism.* Manchester: Manchester UP, 2003.

Thomas, Ronald R. *Detective Fiction and the Rise of Forensic Science.* Cambridge: Cambridge UP, 1999.

Thomas, Sir William Beach. "The Home Counties." In Williams-Ellis, 200–211.

Thompson, Edward. *The Other Side of the Medal.* London: Hogarth, 1925.

Thompson, F. M. L. *The Rise of Suburbia.* London: Leicester UP, 1982.

Thompson, Jon. *Fiction, Crime, and Empire: Clues to Modernity and Postmodernism.* Urbana: U of Illinois P, 1993.

Thorne, James. *Handbook to the Environs of London.* 1876. Bath: Adams and Dart, 1970.

Tilby, A. Wyatt. "A Century of Suburbanization." *Edinburgh Review* 245 (January 1927): 92–107.

Tomlinson, Hugh. "Preface to the English Translation." Deleuze ix–xiv.

Torgovnick, Marianna. *Gone Primitive: Savage Intellects, Modern Lives.* Chicago: U of Chicago P, 1990.

Tosh, John. "What Should Historians Do with Masculinity?" *History Workshop Journal* 38 (1994): 179–202.

Treen, C. "The Process of Suburban Development in North Leeds, 1870–1914." F. M. L. Thompson 158–209.

Trevelyan, G. E. "Suburban Soviets." *Red Rags: Essays of Hate from Oxford.* Ed. Richard Comyns Carr. London: Chapman and Hall, 1933. 135–50.

Trevelyan, G. O. *The Competition Wallah.* 1866. New York: AMS, 1977.

Trilling, Lionel. *E. M. Forster.* 1943. New York: New Directions, 1964.

Trodd, Anthea. *A Reader's Guide to Edwardian Literature.* London: Harvester Wheatsheaf, 1991.

Trotter, David. *The English Novel in History, 1895–1920.* London: Routledge, 1993.

Tuan, Yi-Fu. *Topophilia: A Study of Environmental Perception, Attitudes, and Values.* Englewood Cliffs, NJ: Prentice Hall, 1974.

Tutein, David W. *Joseph Conrad's Reading: An Annotated Bibliography.* West Cornwall, CT: Locust Hill, 1990.

Tyack, Geoffrey. "John Nash." Matthew and Harrison 213–20.

Van Dellen, Robert J. "George Orwell's *Coming Up for Air:* The Politics of Powerlessness." *Modern Fiction Studies* 21.1 (1975): 57–68.

van Marle, Hans. "Conrad's English Lodgings, 1880–1896." *Conradiana* 8 (1976): 257–58.

Visser, Ron. "An Out-Of-The-Way Place Called Berau." *Conradian* 18.1 (1993): 37–47.

Wakeford, Iain. "Wells, Woking and *The War of the Worlds.*" *Wellsian* 14 (Summer 1991): 18–29.

Walkowitz, Judith R. *City of Dreadful Delight: Narratives of Sexual Danger in Late-Victorian London.* Chicago: U of Chicago P, 1992.

Waller, P. J. *Town, City, and Nation: England 1850–1914.* Oxford: Oxford UP, 1983.

Walthew, Kenneth. "The British Empire Exhibition of 1924." *History Today* 31 (August 1981): 34–39.

Ward, Mrs. Humphry. *Robert Elsmere.* 1888. Lincoln: U of Nebraska P, 1967.

Ward, Stephen V., ed. *The Garden City: Past, Present, and Future.* London: Spon, 1992.

Watt, Ian. *Conrad in the Nineteenth Century.* Berkeley: U of California P, 1979.

Watts, Cedric. *A Preface to Conrad.* 2nd ed. London: Longman, 1982.

Waugh, Evelyn. *Black Mischief.* 1932. Boston: Little, 1977.

———. *Remote People.* 1931. New York: Penguin, 1985.

———. *Vile Bodies.* 1930. Boston: Little, 1977.

Webster, Roger, ed. *Expanding Suburbia: Reviewing Suburban Narratives.* New York: Berghahn, 2000.

Weinreb, Ben, and Christopher Hibbert, eds. *The London Encyclopedia.* London: Macmillan, 1983.

Wells, H. G. *Ann Veronica.* 1909. London: Everyman, 1995.

———. *Anticipations of the Reaction of Mechanical and Scientific Progress upon Human Life and Thoughts.* New York: Harper and Brothers, 1902.

———. *The Complete Short Stories of H. G. Wells.* London: Ernest Benn, 1966.

———. "The Degeneration of the Ravensbourne: A Memory of Bromley, Kent." Unsigned. *Pall Mall Gazette* 12 July 1894: 3.

———. *Experiment in Autobiography.* New York: Macmillan, 1934.

———. *Mankind in the Making.* 1903. New York: Scribner's, 1904.

———. *The New Machiavelli.* 1911. Harmondsworth: Penguin, 1946.

———. *Tono-Bungay.* 1909. New York: Oxford UP, 1997.

———. *The War in the Air.* 1908. London: Penguin, 1967.

———. *The War of the Worlds.* 1898. New York: Modern Library, 2002.

West, Rebecca. *The Return of the Soldier.* 1918. New York: Penguin, 1998.

Whelan, Lara Baker. "Between Worlds: Class Identity and Suburban Ghost Stories, 1850 to 1880." *Mosaic* 35.1 (2002): 133–48.

———. "Lines in the Sand: A Defense of Suburban Turf in Later Victorian Literature." *genre* 18 (1997): 125–47.

Whitaker, Joseph. *Almanack for the Year of Our Lord 1887.* London: 12 Warwick Lane, 1887.

White, Andrea. "Conrad and Imperialism." *The Cambridge Companion to Joseph Conrad.* Ed. J. H. Stape. Cambridge: Cambridge UP, 1996. 179–202.

———. *Joseph Conrad and the Adventure Tradition: Constructing and Deconstructing the Imperial Subject.* Cambridge: Cambridge UP, 1993.

Whitehand, J. W. R., and C. M. H. Carr. *Twentieth-Century Suburbs: A Morphological Approach.* London: Routledge, 2001.

Whiteman, J. R., and S. E. Whiteman. *Victorian Woking: An Account of the Development of the Town and Parish in the Victorian Era.* Old Woking: Gresham, 1970.

"Who and Where are the Unemployed?" *Blackwood's* 177 (April 1905): 449–65.

Wiener, Martin J. *English Culture and the Decline of the Industrial Spirit, 1850–1980.* Cambridge: Cambridge UP, 1981.

Williams, Erin. "Female Celibacy in the Fiction of Gissing and Dixon: The Silent Strike of the Suburbanites." *English Literature in Transition (1880–1920)* 45.3 (2002): 259–79.

Williams, Jeffrey. "Conrad and Professionalism." *Approaches to Teaching Conrad's "Heart of Darkness" and "The Secret Sharer."* Ed. Hunt Hawkins and Brian W. Shaffer. New York: MLA, 2002. 48–53.

Williams, Keith, and Steven Matthews, eds. *Rewriting the Thirties: Modernism and After.* London: Longman, 1997.

Williams, Raymond. *The Country and the City.* New York: Oxford UP, 1973.

———. *George Orwell.* New York: Viking, 1971.

———. *The Politics of Modernism: Against the New Conformists.* London: Verso, 1989.

Williams-Ellis, Clough, ed. *Britain and the Beast.* London: J. M. Dent, 1938.

Willmott, Peter. *The Evolution of a Community: A Study of Dagenham after Forty Years.* London: Routledge, 1963.

Willy, Todd G. "*Almayer's Folly* and the Imperatives of Conradian Atavism." *Conradiana* 24.1 (1992): 3–20.

Wilson, Elizabeth. *The Contradictions of Culture: Cities, Culture, Women.* London: Sage, 2001.

"The Woes of Mrs. Caractacus Brown." *Cassell's Family Magazine* 1892.

Wolpert, Stanley. *A New History of India.* 4th ed. New York: Oxford UP, 1993.

Woodcock, George. *The Crystal Spirit: A Study of George Orwell.* 1966. Montreal: Black Rose, 2005.

Woolf, Leonard. *Growing: An Autobiography of the Years 1904 to 1911.* London: Hogarth, 1961.

Woolf, Virginia. *Collected Essays.* 4 vols. London: Hogarth, 1967.

———. *Mrs. Dalloway.* 1925. San Diego: Harcourt, 1981.

Yeats, William Butler. *Explorations.* London: Macmillan, 1962.

Young, Gavin. *In Search of Conrad.* London: Hutchinson, 1991.

Young, Ken, and Patricia L. Garside. *Metropolitan London: Politics and Urban Change 1837–1981.* New York: Holmes and Meier, 1982.

Young, Michael, and Peter Willmott. *Family and Kinship in East London.* 1957. London: Routledge, 1986.

Yousaf, Nahem. *Hanif Kureishi's The Buddha of Suburbia: A Reader's Guide.* New York: Continuum, 2002.

INDEX